# BLOSSOMS IN THE WIND

# BLOSSOMS IN THE WIND

## HUMAN LEGACIES of the KAMIKAZE

· · · · ·

### M.G. SHEFTALL

NAL Caliber
Published by New American Library, a division of
Penguin Group (USA) Inc., 375 Hudson Street,
New York, New York 10014, USA
Penguin Group (Canada), 10 Alcorn Avenue, Toronto,
Ontario M4V 3B2, Canada (a division of Pearson Penguin Canada Inc.)
Penguin Books Ltd., 80 Strand, London WC2R 0RL, England
Penguin Ireland, 25 St. Stephen's Green, Dublin 2,
Ireland (a division of Penguin Books Ltd.)
Penguin Group (Australia), 250 Camberwell Road, Camberwell, Victoria 3124,
Australia (a division of Pearson Australia Group Pty. Ltd.)
Penguin Books India Pvt. Ltd., 11 Community Centre, Panchsheel Park,
New Delhi - 110 017, India
Penguin Group (NZ), cnr Airborne and Rosedale Roads, Albany,
Auckland 1310, New Zealand (a division of Pearson New Zealand Ltd.)
Penguin Books (South Africa) (Pty.) Ltd., 24 Sturdee Avenue,
Rosebank, Johannesburg 2196, South Africa

Penguin Books Ltd., Registered Offices:
80 Strand, London WC2R 0RL, England

First published by NAL Caliber, an imprint of New American Library,
a division of Penguin Group (USA) Inc.

First Printing, July 2005
10   9   8   7   6   5   4   3   2   1

LIBRARY OF CONGRESS CATALOGING-IN-PUBLICATION DATA:
Sheftall, Mordecai G.
  Blossoms in wind : human legacies of the kamikaze / Mordecai Sheftall.
    p.   cm.
  ISBN 0-451-21487-0 (trade hardcover : alk. paper)
  1. World War, 1939–1945—Aerial operations, Japanese.   2. Kamikaze airplanes.   3. Kamikaze pilots.
4. Suicide—Japan—Psychological aspects.   5. World War, 1939–1945—Campaigns—Pacific Ocean.   6.
Japan. Kaigun. Kamikaze Tokubetsu Kōgekitai.   7. Japan—History, Military.   I. Title.
D792.J3S43 2005
940.54'26—dc22          2004027356

Set in Fairfield
Designed by Ginger Legato

Printed in the United States of America

For my sons,
that they may know a world without war

# CONTENTS

## PART THREE: THE ULTIMATE SMART BOMB

## PART FOUR: A SOLDIER'S SCRAPBOOK

## PART FIVE: NADESHIKO

## PART SIX: BRIDE DOLL

## PART SEVEN: DOCTOR HIROSHIMA

## PART EIGHT: TORPEDOMEN IN TWILIGHT

You and I, blossoms of the same cherry tree
That bloomed at the naval academy.
Blossoms know they must blow in the wind someday
Blossoms in the wind, fallen for their country.

—From "Dōki no Sakura,"
the Japanese naval aviators' hymn

A mother, at least with the face she wore in public,
was obliged to appear happy and grateful
to the emperor and country
for giving her son such a fine way to die.

—Hideo Suzuki, former Japanese naval aviator

# PART ONE

# A TIME FOR HEROES

# *ST. LO* OVERTURE

I t is 1050 hours on October 25, 1944, the fifth day of the American invasion of the Philippines. The scene is the bridge of the escort carrier *Fanshaw Bay* (CVE-70), Rear Admiral Clifton A. F. Sprague's flagship in Task Unit 77.4.3, a force of five small escort carriers, three destroyers, and four destroyer escorts now steaming off the coast of Samar Island in the Philippine Sea on a heading of 135 degrees. TU 77.4.3, or "Taffy 3," is one of three similarly sized escort carrier forces of the U.S. Seventh Fleet charged with providing air support for the Leyte Gulf area of operations. At present, Taffy 3's five escort carriers are recovering planes from the morning's close air-support missions against targets inland of the beachhead.

Not even a year old, the *Fannie Bee,* as she is affectionately referred to by her crew, is an escort or "jeep" carrier of the type most other American sailors refer to with dissimilar sentiment as "Kaiser coffins," after the name of their manufacturer and for their alleged tendency to explode, disintegrate into their prefabricated sections, and sink within minutes when taken under hostile fire. The *Fannie Bee* is the product of a shipyard in Vancouver, Washington, one of several on the West Coast owned by Henry J. Kaiser, an enterprising industrialist who will go on to short-lived postwar automotive-industry notoriety building a series of eccentrically styled, poorly selling cars.

Kaiser is an equal opportunity employer, and the underpaid women and minorities he hires are kicking in and doing their part for Uncle Sam despite the discrimination they suffer outside the shipyard gates, setting spectacular new production records for merchant marine Liberty Ships and U.S. Navy vessels month after month. Kaiser's workers are so industrious and hardworking that they have been featured in war bond advertising. Slapped together death traps or not, the "jeep carriers" they build are playing an enormous role in the war effort.

At the moment, Admiral Sprague is perched in his air boss chair on the bridge of the *Fanshaw Bay.* He is a jowly man, rawboned and put together a little awkwardly. He does not really look the part of a flag officer. It is much easier to imagine him as the somewhat self-important mayor of an insignificant little Southern town, or a damp-collared, seersuckered Mississippi lawyer with a glib gift of the gab, a penchant for cheap cigars, and a passing resemblance to Huey Long. He could even be a Laurel and Hardy foil, destined to end up covered head to toe in house paint or baking flour at some point during the second reel. To look at him, you would never guess that, behind the spare tire and the double chin, he is all guts and backbone.

About three and a half hours ago, from this very chair, the admiral looked through powerful Bausch & Lomb binoculars and could gradually make out something horrible and unthinkable taking shape in the mist, miragelike in the humidity, distance, and heat. Still hull-down in the defilade of the curvature of the earth's surface but just poking up over the horizon were the unmistakable giant pagodalike masts of Japanese battleships barreling straight for Taffy 3 at flank speed. Seconds later, fourteen- and eighteen-inch colored-dye marker shells bracketed Sprague's ships with towering red, yellow, green, and purple geysers as the Japanese ranged for their first salvos. What had started as another workaday morning of routine antisub patrols and air support missions had suddenly become a sailor's worst nightmare.

Over the next two and a half hours, Sprague directed a touch-and-go running sea battle that cost him one of his carriers, *Gambier Bay,* and three of his screening destroyers and destroyer escorts, *Johnston, Hoel,* and *Samuel B. Roberts.* The losses were steep, but now that the smoke has cleared, it is becoming increasingly clear that with frenzied Wildcat and Avenger sorties, superhumanly courageous fighting by her destroyer screen, and a lot of smoke, bluff, and divine providence, Taffy 3 has just fought off the main force of Vice Admiral Takeo Kurita's battleship flotilla and saved the American invasion fleet at Leyte Gulf from certain disaster in one of the most dramatic upsets in naval history.

The *Fannie Bee* stood down from general quarters about fifty minutes ago. Crew members are taking catnaps or coffee breaks, trying to talk themselves down from the battle rush. Others smoke Camels and Lucky Strikes and stare off at the flat gray horizon in silence, wondering why they are still alive and if their hands will ever stop shaking. They have just endured two hours of the twentieth-century naval equivalent of hand-to-hand combat with fists and clubs, but they have prevailed, and the *Fannie Bee* came through like a trouper. She took four eight-inch shells from the cruiser *Chikuma* but is still making speed. Not too shabby for a "Kaiser coffin."

The year-old CVE-63—a year and two days old, to be exact—is another jeep from Kaiser's Vancouver yards. Christened *Midway* in 1943, she was renamed *St. Lo* just two weeks ago in order to clear her original moniker for a larger carrier. The decision has not sat well with her 889-man crew,[1] for in addition to having to bear the unwelcome onus of a name in honor of some goddamned army victory, it has to be the absolute worst kind of luck to have your ship's name changed right before going into combat like this.

Ever since the shooting started this morning, however, it seems that *St. Lo* is the luckiest jeep in Taffy 3. She did not suffer as much as a scratch while mixing it up with Kurita's ships, and a sizable number of her crew even had the exceedingly sublime experience of watching one of their own planes, an Avenger piloted by Lieutenant Leonard E. "Tex" Waldrop, successfully strafe and explode a torpedo from one of Kurita's cruisers that had been heading straight for their sister ship, *Kalinin Bay*.* A few

---

*McKenna, Francis J., "Report of Action Against Japanese Enemy, October 25, 1944" (posted on www.stlomidway6365.org). During the Battle of the Philippine Sea, a Japanese pilot, Naval Aviator Sakio Komatsu, pulled off an unusual "torpedo interception" of his own after discovering a wake speeding toward his ship, the carrier *Taiho*, shortly after takeoff. In Komatsu's case, however, instead of strafing the torpedo with machine-gun fire, he opted to crash his plane into it, exploding both the offending item of American ordnance and himself in the process. The reader is free—and encouraged—to contemplate the different cultural values at work behind his and Lieutenant Waldrop's acts of selfless heroism.

seconds after that close call, another of the deadly "Long Lance" Type 93 Japanese torpedoes missed *St. Lo*'s bow by only a couple of yards.

Radar Technician Third Class Evan "Holly" Crawforth of McGill, Nevada, is on duty in the radar plot room just below *St. Lo*'s flight deck. While he was unable to see Lieutenant Waldrop's heroics and other events of this morning's fight with the naked eye, his spot in the plot room nevertheless gave him a unique vantage point on the action.

At 0650 this morning, he and the other crewmen in the room were about to secure from their customary early morning general quarters alert* when an unsettling report from one of *St. Lo*'s patrol pilots came in over the radio.

"Heads up," the pilot had said. "It looks like you've got the whole Jap fleet behind you."

Crawforth immediately looked at his screen and saw that it was filled with flickering green spikes—each one representing an enemy warship barreling down hard on Taffy 3. The larger spikes—and there were four distinct ones—meant battleships, and one of these was so big it could mean only one thing—the superbattleship *Yamato*, which could take out the unarmored *St. Lo* or any other ship in Taffy 3 with a single round from her main battery of eighteen-inch guns. Realizing how badly Taffy 3 was outnumbered and outgunned, Crawforth and his mates in the plot room also realized that their own prospects for survival were minimal at best. Just as they were entertaining these happy thoughts, the first deafening Japanese salvo began landing around the *St. Lo*.

Some two hours and fifty minutes of thunder and fury later, the men in the plot room were completely mystified when the range between Kurita's force and Taffy 3 began opening up. The Japanese—having sent *Gambier Bay* to the bottom and fairly well decimated the American destroyer escort—had victory firmly within their grasp. Then, for some inexplicable reason, they appeared to be turning around. When a *St. Lo* pilot radioed in visual confirmation of this development, the radarmen in the plot room broke out in cheers. They were going to live after all!

---

*U.S. ships in combat areas were always on general quarters at dawn and dusk, the most likely times for enemy air attack because of the favorable cloaking characteristics of low-light conditions at these times of day. See Lott (1964).

Now going on an hour and ten minutes after their deliverance from near-certain death, Crawforth and his shipmates are still upbeat. But their jubilation will be short-lived. The man on the air search radar—who already has a screenful of friendly blips from the Taffy planes overhead coming in for landings from the morning's missions—is reporting unidentified contacts on his screen. The plot room springs into action again as the men begin hurriedly checking IFF (Identification Friend or Foe) on the bogeys. Suddenly the busy dialogue in the room is ripped in half by the general quarters gong, followed a beat or two later by the ship's antiaircraft batteries opening up.

"My God," Crawforth mutters. "They're coming back. . . ."

Back on the bridge of the *Fannie Bee,* a loud chorus of *Ohh*'s and *Oh, my God*'s rings out on the bridge, followed by an explosive *whap* a few seconds later—more wallop of air than sound—that rattles the portholes on the bulkheads of the bridge and the big plate glass windows in front of the air boss chair.

"It's *Kitkun Bay!*" someone shouts.

Admiral Sprague instinctively snaps a look due south just in time to see a cascade of flaming aviation fuel and debris pouring off *Kitkun Bay*'s flight deck and into a large geyser of water on the port side of the stricken ship.

Before anyone has time for an emotional reaction, black smudges of exploding antiaircraft rounds are darkening the sky between *Kitkun Bay* and the *Fannie Bee,* and lookouts are frantically calling out Japanese Zero fighters as they see them.

*Whap, whap.* Two Zeros have just slammed into *Kalinin Bay,* which is already walking wounded from this morning's battle with Kurita. There's no way she can survive a pounding like this.

A lookout is calling out a Zero due south, headed for *White Plains.*

*Whap. White Plains* is sprouting an orange-and-soot fireball near her fantail as big as an office building.

Admiral Sprague is frozen for a moment, watching in stunned silence as his heroic little task force appears to be in the process of being decimated before his eyes. But he quickly throws off his initial shock and begins shouting orders. In another few seconds, reports start coming in over the radio from the other jeeps. The damage is bad, but not as bad as it had looked from the bridge of the *Fannie Bee*.

When all hell begins breaking loose at 1052, *St. Lo* has a flight deck full of glossy dark blue planes that have just landed from the morning's missions. There are more being loaded out and gassed up for new sorties forward of the crash gate and down below on the hangar deck. *St. Lo* has been lucky this morning—incredibly lucky—and now, two minutes into the Japanese fire-and-brimstone show over the rest of Task Unit 77.4.3, it seems that she has also been rendered invisible. "Suiciders" are hitting every other flattop in the force but her.

But it is too soon to feel safe. Something is wrong. Past the aft end of the crowded flight deck, black AA blossoms appear around a green plane about five hundred yards out coming in low, almost as if it's lining up for a landing. There are orange flashes on its wings, pieces falling off of it as it gets too big way too fast. A bomb is seen falling from under its fuselage as the plane inverts in a slow roll. The bomb penetrates the wood planking of the *St. Lo*'s flight deck a split second before the plane itself plows into the ship, smashing men and machine alike, spraying everything in its path with flaming aviation fuel.

The impact of this crash is the loudest sound Holly Crawforth has ever heard, and for a second or two of sheer terror, he expects that it will be the last. But as he shakes off the shock, the receding echoes of the initial explosion are slowly replaced with a sound that is even worse—the screams of mangled *St. Lo* crewmen being burned to death. Smoke is billowing everywhere, some of it a sickly yellowish color, but mostly a sooty, impenetrable black.

*St. Lo* is a brave ship, veteran of the Marianas Turkey Shoot and Molotai air strikes. Her sailors pray that she can pull through this, and swear that the bad guys cannot be allowed to do her in. Not like this. Perhaps there is still hope. Burning planes can be pushed off into the sea, the fires can be stopped through well-coordinated teamwork, ordnance can be secured, and that gaping hole in the flight deck can be patched over in an hour or two. In the meantime, the dead, dying, and wounded can be tended to as best as possible.

But all of these hopes are put on hold when a sudden, sickening lurch from the first round of secondary explosions rocks the ship. Orange flames and smoke pour through and out from under the flight deck, which has been lifted up and knocked crooked by the force of the blast. In addition to the mangled, flaming Wildcats and Avengers on the flight deck, fires have reached more planes being gassed up underneath on the hangar deck.

A few seconds later, an even more violent explosion pulverizes the section of flight deck aft of the initial impact. Yet another blast seconds after this tears a chunk out of the forward section in a shower of wood planking and metal railings. Then, to the incredulity of all who witness the scene, another blast blows the entire forward elevator out of its shaft like a rocket, high into the air on a column of smoke and flames.

Now the explosions come with heartbreaking regularity as ordnance and fuel are set off by flames reaching ever deeper into the bowels of the ship, fingering and worming toward the aviation fuel tanks and the main bomb magazine. Firefighting efforts will be meaningless. One of Henry J. Kaiser's cost-cutting measures was to use cast iron instead of steel for the *St. Lo*'s fire mains. When the "suicider" hit, the impact shattered these pipes like so many terra-cotta flowerpots. Now there is no water for fighting the spreading fires.[2] Despite the best efforts of her crew, her fire hoses are limp and useless. The fate of the *St. Lo* is sealed.

Seven minutes after the initial hit, Captain Francis J. McKenna gives the painful but necessary order to abandon ship. Explosions are blowing off structural, load-bearing sections of the ship by now, shaking her like a child's bathtub toy as officers and men go over the sides, some clambering down lines with wounded shipmates over their shoulders, others jumping into the water to save themselves. At 1115, after a quick, final sweep of the ship with Lieutenant Commander Richard L. Centner and Buglemaster Stuart A. Neale to look for survivors, the captain is the last living man over the side.

At 1120, the bomb magazine goes for the eighth and fatal explosion. Five minutes after that, what remains of *St. Lo* slips beneath the waves, still rumbling with underwater secondaries as she takes 114 Americans with her.[3]

Back on *Fanshaw Bay,* the panic and confusion of the last half hour has subsided into a painful reality of grieving losses, cleaning up the wreckage, and trying to come to rational and emotional terms with the horror the suiciders have wrought. There are no doubts in the minds of the men still standing that they are at war with the most determined and fanatical foe the nation has ever faced—the marines on Tarawa a year earlier could have told them that much—but what they have no way of knowing as the reeking smoke of the suicide attack still lingers in the air, and the groans of the dying and wounded still echo in their ears, is that what they have just witnessed is only a prelude to the horrors the United States Navy will have to endure over the next ten months.

Holly Crawforth was one of the 775 *St. Lo* crewmen rescued by Taffy 3's remaining destroyers and destroyer escorts. Fifty-nine years after that terrible day, I ask him to recall his feelings at the time toward the men who almost killed him: "I think there was some hatred of the Japanese," he writes, "but with time, most of us felt there was a job to do and we wanted to get it finished and go home. . . . After we were sunk (and rescued) . . . I think we were so happy to be alive, we didn't think of hating anybody.

"The kamikaze tactics were obviously a desperation move," he continues. "But we always felt that if the invasion of Japan had occurred, the kamikazes would have done terrible damage, as demonstrated at Okinawa and Iwo Jima. Even though many of my friends and shipmates were killed by the action of Yukio Seki [commander of the kamikaze flight that attacked Taffy 3], I feel that he was doing what his country asked him to do—right or wrong. I also feel that the war was a terrible waste of human lives and resources. I'm proud of my part in it and think, given the same set of circumstances, I would do it again."[4]

Reading the thoughts and sentiments of a man who experienced the receiving end of a kamikaze attack prompts questions about the nature of the men on the other side, the ones who flew the planes Holly Crawforth and his comrades faced. What kind of society, education, and culture could have sanctioned such tactics and produced the fighting men needed to carry them out? Was their conduct due to a uniquely Japanese context, or are there identifiable universals that can shed light on our modern-day era, when the hijacked airliner is the deadliest nonnuclear guided missile ever devised? When the suicide bomber is the preferred weapon of resistance throughout much of the developing world?

My search for answers to these questions began in January 2002. I thought it only appropriate that my first step be taken at the spiritual center of the kamikaze legacy—the great Shinto shrine of Yasukuni in downtown Tokyo.

## two

# YASUKUNI

I n winter, air masses from Siberia sit over Tokyo, pushing out the cloud cover and humidity that make the megalopolis feel like a giant shower stall the rest of the year. Brisk westerly winds smelling of dry foliage and faraway soil keep a crisp snap in the breeze, pumping in frigid air faster than car exhaust and BTU-hemorrhaging buildings can heat it up, blowing the normally lethal smog away before it can stain the sunny blue skies. Native residents, with their higher tolerance for heat and muggy air, usually complain about the cold temperatures and short daylight hours of this season, but for most anyone else born and raised in a temperate zone, this is one of the few times of the year when the weather here can be called pleasant.

One weekday afternoon in January 2002, I am enjoying some of this rare vintage "champagne weather" as I walk the tree-lined, flagstone-paved promenade of Yasukuni, the sanctum sanctorum of extinct Japanese martial machismo. Modern Shinto tradition holds that the souls of some 2.5 million Japanese servicemen who died in the service of Meiji, his son, Emperor Taishō, and grandson, Emperor Shōwa (Hirohito), lie in peaceful repose here. A variation of this traditional belief popular with old veterans is that the spirits of these fallen soldiers, sailors, and airmen gather in this placid Valhalla to mingle amidst the branches of the carefully pruned cherry arbors, drinking heavenly sake poured by nubile *ten'nyo* angels in flowing silk robes, reunited with their old comrades in wholesome masculine companionship for eternity.

Less romantic interpretations of Yasukuni's raison d'être—especially prevalent in Asian countries victimized by Japan in the Second World War—tend to see the shrine as an unrepentant, in-your-face manifestation of poisonous nostalgia for Japanese militarism. These criticisms were only exacerbated when the souls of Class A war criminals hanged by the Allies after the Tokyo Tribunals were welcomed to the shrine in a formal Shinto ceremony in 1978.* Prime Minister Yasuhiro Nakasone then pulled the issue out of the frying pan and tossed it into the fire with an official (and possibly illegal) prayer visit in 1985, and international controversy has surrounded the institution ever since.

But I am not here this morning to pass judgment on the moral implications of Yasukuni's existence. I am here to observe and record, and to visit the shrine's library. I have arrived before the library opens, so I decide to pass the time with a little exploration of these hallowed premises. Perhaps the walk will help me focus my thoughts, despite the feeling I cannot quite seem to shake that something—or someone—in the cherry branches is watching my every move here.

The first thing that strikes one about the shrine is the sheer size of the land it occupies, which would be exceptional in any other world-class city, but is downright mind-boggling to behold in the center of the capital of this space-starved nation. Yasukuni sits on about ten acres of astronomically expensive real estate in Kudan, Tokyo, located on a gently rising slope that faces the northern border of the giant moat surrounding the Imperial Palace grounds (an even more astounding piece of land— worth more than the combined public and private real estate value of the entire state of California during the heady days of Japan's bubble economy in the late eighties). The shrine was originally built on the orders of Emperor Meiji to honor imperial troops fallen in the restoration campaign that wrested political sovereignty from the Tokugawa shogunate, but it is currently maintained by funding from the Tokyo metropolitan government, generous private donations, and collections from a large tithing box in front of Yasukuni's altar that is kept filled with coins and cash by daily throngs of worshipers and tourists.

---

*Contrary to the common Western belief, there are no actual physical remains—cremated or not—interred at Yasukuni. The shrine is in function a memorial and an institutionalized political statement, not a cemetery.

If you can look past the lines of tour buses, souvenir stands, and the uniformed rent-a-cop next to the altar, there is an almost Gothic air of masculine dignity about this place—a Japanese West Point or Notre Dame with white-robed Shinto attendants flitting about all the macho masonry and elegant woodwork. It seems a worthy final resting place for the souls of modern-era samurai, as well as a neat architectural metaphor for Japan's Jekyll-and-Hyde cultural identity in the first half of the twentieth century—all bamboo flutes and battleships, tea ceremonies and around-the-clock assembly lines, brush calligraphy and long-range bombers. Although the aged tone of the wood used in the main ceremonial buildings makes them appear to be centuries old, they are actually of recent construction, and represent only the latest of several reincarnations of the shrine. Nevertheless, their breathtaking carpentry and decorative carvings, however, firmly places the aesthetic at work here in ancient Japanese tradition.

A quick look around at the rest of the facilities suggests that most of the place dates from the 1930s, built in the handsome stone-and-copper Frank Lloyd Wright–influenced Asian Art Deco style that was used in official Japanese buildings before the postwar stucco-slathered steel-reinforced concrete look took over as the de rigueur architectural style for the nation's public infrastructure. The thirty-meter-high steel *tori'i* gate at the main entrance of the grounds accentuates the exotic early-twentieth-century atmosphere of industrialized military might crossed with "traditional" Japanese culture. Passing under this gate, the promenade continues around and past a columned statue of topknot-coiffed and kimono-clad Masujirō Ōmura, founding father of the imperial army, who was assassinated by counterrevolutionaries in 1869. Perhaps a hundred meters past this imposing piece of statuary, the entrance to the inner sanctum compound is guarded by ten-meter-high glass-paneled limestone snow lanterns. The lanterns rest on stout pedestals with wraparound bronze bas-relief friezes depicting heroic scenes from the Russo-Japanese War and Chinese campaigns, naval scenes on the right-side pedestal, army scenes on the left.

After visitors walk past these and under a smaller bronze *tori'i*, they are now considered to be on hallowed ground. Before proceeding farther into the compound, I must undertake a Shinto purification ritual at a large granite water-filled trough that looks almost like an Egyptian sarcophagus. It must weigh several tons. I walk under a copper roof resting on dark wood posts that covers the holy trough, and read a kanji sign written only in Japanese that gives a step-by-step explanation of what I am to perform here. I follow the instructions, dipping a wood-handled tin ladle into the water, splashing it over my hands, ridding myself of the uncleanliness of the outside world. I dart glances at the Japanese people around me to make sure that I'm doing everything correctly. I watch a bespectacled corporate type in his early thirties take water into his mouth from his cupped left hand, swish the water around a bit, and spit it out in the stone gutter below the trough. Another glance at the sign confirms that this is what I'm supposed to do, so I mimic what I've just observed. There is a faint aftertaste of copper in the water.

Following the general flow of my fellow pilgrims, I walk through a handsome wooden gate about as tall as a three-story house. The hinged doors look almost battering-ram-proofed, like they could have been built for an old samurai castle, and are at least a hand span thick. They are emblazoned with large gold *kikunomon*, the sixteen-petal chrysanthemum device that has been the heraldic crest of the imperial family since medieval times.

A souvenir photo hawker who has set up shop next to the gate is also conducting a ritual of sorts, tossing chunks of bread that are snatched up in midair by half-tame starlings swooping down from the gate eaves. A small cluster of uniformed junior high school girls here on a class trip has stopped to watch the show. The girls squeal with delight each time a starling makes a successful bread catch. *"Sugoi! Moikkai!"* "Wow! Do it again!"

I stop directly in front of the main altar and bow in the direction of the inner sanctum, which is half-hidden behind purple-and-white *kikunomon*-patterned curtains. As I approach the altar, the rent-a-cop eyes me warily, perhaps weighing tactical options in the event that I'm some gaijin* weirdo with a protest banner smuggled in my coat lining or a volley of red paintballs stashed in my attaché case. I smile at him and climb three steps to the altar, bow, and clap my hands to get the attention of the resident spirits (as if they aren't already eyeballing me as intently

---

*A common Japanese term for *foreigner* often interpreted as pejorative by receivers of the moniker.

as the security guy is). I toss my coin into the tithing box, bow once more, and move on to get out of the way of the people behind me.

I walk by some smaller memorials tucked amongst the trees on the northern edge of the main promenade. One of them is done with an interesting sunken grotto effect—a covered reflecting pool surrounded with stepped layers like a miniature Greek amphitheater—but it has a neutered sixties prefab energy out of place here, almost as if the architect had been too timid to incorporate more recognizably Japanese elements into the designs when work crews were still cleaning up B-29 raid rubble in the suburbs and the Socialist Party still made decent showings in elections. While this monument may have looked cutting-edge when it was put up, it now looks like a soot-streaked, mold-mottled Omaha Beach gun emplacement designed by some failed Le Corbusier pupil— a sad reminder of how unflattering the humid Japanese climate is for steel-reinforced concrete, and how ungracefully the International Style has aged.

I walk back out onto the promenade and past a column of camera-toting old men led by a pennant-waving young female tour bus guide in a navy-blue Jackie O ensemble, replete with pillbox hat and sensible pumps. Suddenly, bugle notes begin to echo throughout the compound. I'm not sure whether the music is coming from Yasukuni's sound system or one of the right-wing militant groups' loudspeaker trucks lined up in the parking lot, but the effect is goose bump inducing nonetheless. The notes temporarily drown out the buzz of the soft-drink vending machines and the giggling gaggles of schoolgirls taking a shortcut through the shrine to get to the subway stop across the street. For a moment I can almost hear ghostly parade-ground commands wafting through the trees, somber minor-key army hymns in a pentatonic scale, the rhythmic crunch of ethereal army boots passing in review. The imagery is a tad spooky—both supernaturally and politically—but there are echoes of melancholy old glory in it as well, like those horns in the opening scenes of *Patton*.

The men in the tour group stir with smiles of recognition and approving sighs. A comment from one of them confirms my guess that what we are hearing is the old Japanese army version of taps, and I find myself wondering how many of these fellows used to drift off to sleep to these same bugle notes sixty-odd years ago. Is nostalgia for fading memories and the glory of past youth at least some small part of what has brought these men to Yasukuni this afternoon—what brings millions of others like them here year in and year out? As the last note of the haunting bugles echoes off of the office buildings ringing Yasukuni, I cannot help but feel that yes, just as Japan's neighbors suspect, a certain degree of nostalgia is at work here. However, the overwhelming emotional dynamic I see in the faces of these old men—evident in the faces of almost every visitor I have seen today—is neither misplaced nostalgia nor healing grief, but rather a melancholy lost-cause desperation that hangs in the very air of this place like a smoky layer of funerary incense. It is the desperate hope that some lasting value can be found in the deaths of millions of young men in a crushing defeat, and an equally desperate denial of the intolerable, unspeakable, and unthinkable possibility that friends and loved ones—that the best of an entire generation—may have died in vain.

This notion makes me feel a little self-conscious, suddenly aware of myself as a red-nosed six-foot-four gaijin galumphing about this hope-hallowed ground in size thirteen Bass Weejuns with a camera dangling from my red neck, wondering how many of these old folks look at me and hear air raid sirens in their heads.

I check my watch and slowly head for the library building, which is about a hundred meters from the main altar. On the way, I pass a rest area occupied by another group of old men, many wearing matching baseball caps, who are sitting on benches covered with faded red vinyl patched in places with red duct tape. Most of the men huddle in tight, smoky powwows around ashtray stands. Gales of rattling coughs notwithstanding, the overall mood is mirth and camaraderie: I catch a funny anecdote and some laughter from a nearby group, then a complaint followed by a snarled retort somewhere else that brings on another round of hard laughs. In a quieter group, someone's recent surgery is described in detail I'm sure everybody but the raconteur could do without, but the story is punctuated at appropriate intervals by rounds of sympathetic hemming and hawing echoed by the white pigeons clucking and fussing over birdseed and bread crumbs in the gravel underfoot.

I am still a bit early when I arrive at the library, but the door is open and I walk in. I am welcomed by the library curator, Shinsuke Daitō. He has a mild, hospitable manner—a Japanese Mister Rogers comes to mind as a possible destiny in an alternate universe—and I would imagine that most people are surprised to learn that he is a retired professional soldier. A member of the first graduating class (1953) of the National Defense Academy (combined postwar incarnation of the old imperial military and naval service academies), Daitō-san retired from the Japan Ground Self-Defense Forces as a major general in 1992. For him, working at Yasukuni is not simply something to do in his retirement. It is a great honor, and he performs every task here with equal devotion, whether it is running the daily operations of this library and archiving its records, or helping the young Shinto acolytes with their morning duties, sweeping up around the main altar area and raking gravel in the atrium rock garden.

Daitō-san shows me to a table where I can have some privacy, then goes off into the stacks to retrieve some material he thinks will give me a good starting point for my research. He returns with an armload of yellowing newspaper clippings, attack rosters, and thick Japanese tomes. The selection makes me realize just how much I will have to read, learn, and record during this project. Opening an age-browned tome, I get a pungent, meditative whiff of old-book smell, and so with the turn of a page begins my journey into the soul of the kamikaze.

## three

## THE ROAD TO MABALACAT

*October 17, 1944—Eight Days Before the St. Lo Is Sunk*

Wood-paneled radios are tuned throughout Japan early on this crisp October morning. Pilot trainees line up outside their barracks at Akeno Army Airfield near Nagoya. Midshipmen stand at rigid attention in a mess hall at the Naval Academy in Hiroshima. A Tokyo banker in a neatly pressed Mao suit skims the morning paper for business news at his elegant dining room table, only half listening to—and even less interested in—the radio his plump wife has switched on in the living room. Sendai homemakers in baggy work pajamas meet in front of their neighborhood block watch leader's house to hear the broadcast. Buddhist monks sit in quiet repose in the anterooms of an ancient Kyoto temple.

In Shizuoka, a forty-five-year-old woman lights an incense stick for her son, killed a year and a half ago at Guadalcanal. She has four other sons in uniform, flung to the far reaches of the empire. If they are near radios right now, they are listening, too, linked with their mother and the rest of their countrymen in an electromagnetic telepathy relayed through the concrete canyons of Ginza, over slag heaps and terraced rice paddies, through crematorium smoke and shimmering bamboo groves to reach wood-and-paper houses packed wall-to-wall on every level patch of land in the archipelago; beamed by army and navy stations, the signal crosses staggering expanses of Asian landmass and thousands of leagues of ocean from the Siberian frontier to the jungles of Borneo to reach His Imperial Majesty's resolute young soldiers and sailors.

The somber yet stirring open notes of the patriotic dirge "Umi Yu-kaba" crackle from speakers across the empire. Millions join in with the radio chorus for the song's only verse:

> *Though you lead me*
> *To a watery grave,*
> *Or to molder in the grass*
> *Of mountain dales*
> *I will die for you, my lord,*
> *With no regrets.*

As the song fades out on a heroic note of brass and rumbling timpani, a theatrically virile voice cues in, fairly bursting with pride and barely contained excitement. There is thrilling news to report from the waters off Taiwan:

> The name of Vice Admiral Mitscher . . . together with the name Saipan, is indelibly stamped in the hearts of us, the one hundred million people of Japan, as a name to be remembered for vengeance. He was one of the planners of the Doolittle raid . . . participated in the Battle of Midway . . . was made air force commander in the Solomons. His ability was recognized, and he became commander of the jewel of the Pacific Fleet, Task Force 58, and invaded Saipan. The pitiful end of Task Force 58 must have been vividly witnessed by him from his watery grave.[1]

The broadcast ends, but most listeners remain tuned for the daily radio calisthenics program. The war can wait at least long enough for jumping jacks and back stretches before another day of maximum effort in fields, on factory floors, in office buildings. Exercise maintains fighting spirit, the people are told every morning. And only the morally degenerate complain about deep knee bends. After all, just think of what the boys at the front are going through.

That evening, day-shift munitions plant workers file out past the night shift punching in. Office workers and schoolchildren hurry home before sunset and the nightly blackout. A reasonably well-to-do family is lucky to be having a dinner of barley rice and burdock root tonight, and truly blessed to have a slice or two of pickled radish and a few flakes of fish meat to go with it. The less fortunate scrounge—sponging from relatives or, in the saddest cases, rifling through garbage. Others, still few but increasing daily, steal what they need for themselves and their families, regardless of the humiliation they face if caught.

Weary from yet another day of life during wartime, parents tuck small children into their futon bedding, lighting mosquito coils and whispering promises to keep the nightmares away. Before turning in themselves, they check the door latch and the status of the rice jar in the kitchen, perhaps wondering where tomorrow's meals will come from and how fast an American incendiary bomb can burn through a tight row of wooden houses. They try to get some rest before the next eighteen-hour sleepwalk through the grind of their daily routines, pretending to be brave and cheerful for their neighbors and coworkers and loved ones. But bonetired or not, they find that sleep does not come easily when they are beginning to doubt what they hear on the radio and read in the papers. And if they suspect that their harsh lives are about to get even worse, they are right, for the three-year-long Battle of the Pacific is now over, and the ten-month-long Battle of Japan is about to begin.

*Manila, Occupied Philippines, the Greater East Asian*
*Co-prosperity Sphere*
*October 19, 1944*

The CO's sleek black Packard limousine pulled out of the First Air Fleet HQ compound with an urgent hiss of driveway gravel, a vice admiral's pennant on the front fender bright yellow in the late-afternoon sun, snapping smartly despite the humid Manila air. The sentry saluting the limo through the gates could not have been blamed for thinking how ordinary the passenger in the backseat looked. A different breed altogether from the stream of Brahmin brass who regularly passed through these gates, the kind who might have been politicians or bankers or intellectual types back in Japan. No, the new CO of the First Air Fleet was not one of those fancy fellows, and did not look the part of an admiral at all. In fact, he did not even look like an officer. With his course facial features, buzz cut, short, stocky build, and overall scruffy appearance, he could have easily passed for a capable if somewhat boozy NCO. A craftsman type, perhaps, with a quick temper, a sharp Osaka tongue, and sure hands who fixed aircraft engines or rewired radio equipment or performed some other skilled but nonetheless dirty-fingernailed job, biding his time and waiting for the war to end so he could go home to his stonemasonry or furniture-reupholstering business.

It was only when you got close enough to see the fire in his eyes that you knew you were in the presence of a man who was anything but ordinary. Many saw in those eyes the stern, far-seeing gaze of a visionary genius and paragon of samurai virtue—just the type of decisive leader the nation was sorely in need of at the moment, not afraid of rattling a few cages to get results. More saw the eyes of a self-aggrandizing bully—a geisha-slapping pub crawler, tantrum thrower, and compulsive gambler[2] who could do serious damage to the nation's war efforts if given free rein to act on his dangerously unconventional ideas. But whatever the veracity of various critiques upon his character, nobody ever accused Vice Admiral Takijirō Ōnishi of being ordinary.

Patience was not one of his virtues, either. True to character, he felt fidgety riding in the backseat of the limo, as he always did when his range of physical movement was limited and he found himself in a situation in which he was forced to wait for something he wanted. In this case, he found himself stuck in the backseat of some long-skedaddled American big shot's Packard and he wanted to get to Mabalacat Naval Air Station in the Clark Field complex northwest of Manila as soon as possible, preferably before sundown. They would be cutting it close, but by his calculations, which were almost always flawless, the fifty-mile drive could be covered in about two hours. That would be just enough time to get them there before dark.

Sitting in his office just a few minutes before, he had watched the sun getting low, felt one of his hunches, and suddenly decided that he could not wait for Captain Sakae Yamamoto to come down to Manila for their prearranged meeting. Instead, Ōnishi would make the trip to Mabalacat himself to meet with the 201st Air Group CO. It would be better than sitting in his office, twiddling his thumbs and waiting for his tardy subordinate. Besides, the long drive would give him some quality thinking time away from the many distractions in the HQ office. He needed this time to mull over how he was going to say what had to be said when he got to Mabalacat. And given the nature of what he was going to lay on the table, it was looking like a hard sell was going to be the way to go. He was not going up to the 201st tonight to make speeches. He was ordering men to their deaths. The speeches could come later, for the send-offs. And the eulogies.

Security considerations warranted an armed escort for the trip, but he had passed on the suggestion. There was no time to put an escort together. And even if there had been, it would only have slowed them down and made a more tempting target from the air, where American Hellcats, Corsairs, Avengers, and Helldivers from Admiral William Halsey's Task Force 38 and Admiral Thomas Kinkaid's Seventh Fleet escort carriers were now ranging over the entire Philippine archipelago with increasing impunity, utterly disdainful of Japanese antiaircraft capability (what little was left), chewing up anything that moved. There were reports of American pilots waving to people on the ground as they pulled out of their attack runs, flying so low you could see them through the cockpit Plexiglas, chewing gum and grinning as they bombed and strafed.

A night drive would give the admiral's entourage protection from these prowling American cowboys, but the downside was that it would also leave them vulnerable to ambush by resistance fighters, who could be lurking behind any patch of tall grass or copse of banyan trees or bend in the road after dark, watering at the mouth for the chance to bag a choice target like a Japanese flag officer. Guerrillas from the American-supported resistance groups as well as the communist Hukbalahap independence movement infested the region, growing bolder by the day as the Allied forces made their presence felt.

Ōnishi preferred to take his chances with impudent American naval aviators than with Huk guerrillas. He had not clawed and blazed his way up and out of the boondocks of Hyōgo Prefecture, graduated from the Imperial Naval Academy at Etajima, and risen to flag rank just to be shot through the window of his limousine by some savage in chopped Goodyear-tire sandals with a Spanish-American War muzzle-loader. With all due apologies to his Filipino brothers of the Greater East Asian

Co-prosperity Sphere, there would be no honor in such a fate for Taki-jirō Ōnishi. He was a hero—a man who had helped build Japanese naval aviation from a collection of rickety canvas-skinned seaplanes into what had until recently been the most powerful carrier navy in the world[3]; he was a courageous bomber of Chinese cities, tactical mastermind of the sinking of the British battleships *Prince of Wales* and *Repulse* off Malaya, and the genius behind the shallow-run torpedoes used at Pearl Harbor. Such a man was destined to die as a samurai, when and where he chose, with honor.

The Americans were quite generous in providing chances for such honorable deaths of late. It was fast becoming a trend in the imperial navy. And there would be even more opportunities for noble self-sacrifice in the very near future. In fact, Ōnishi himself was hand-delivering some choice ones fresh from First Air Fleet headquarters at this very moment.

As the limo made the turn onto the Lingayen Road, the national highway that would take them to Mabalacat, the admiral broke the heavy silence in the car with a long, worn-out sigh recognizable as *Why me?* in any language. Adjutant Yoshinori Moji and the enlisted driver stirred a bit in the front seat, then settled back into their road trance when it was evident that there would be no follow-up comment. The atmosphere in the car resumed its reflection of the CO's determined, silent, somber mood.

The admiral stared out of a side window in the rear of the Packard, watching the wet green and yellow monsoon-season landscape whip by while the men in the front seat stared straight ahead, motionless except for the driver's occasional wheel adjustments, the only sound in the car the hypnotic throbbing of the painstakingly maintained Detroit horsepower under the hood and the hum of the tires grabbing kilometer after kilometer of highway, click-clacking over divider lines in the macadam.

Ōnishi was only two days in-country but he was already exhausted. He had hardly warmed the wicker executive chair under the lazy ceiling fans of his Manila command post and he was already on "Ōnishi time," out running around with the troops, pushing himself like a twenty-three-year-old ensign in a fifty-three-year-old body. In yet another variation upon a theme in the lifelong seesaw struggle for possession of his soul, the rational strategist side of his character urged that he could keep this up for only so long, while the samurai poet-warrior in him was desperate to believe otherwise, militant in a cherished faith that what was right in the great scheme of the universe was stronger than what was real. He wanted to believe that, in the fatherland's hour of need, his *yamato damashi** ("fighting Japanese spirit") would push on, mind over matter, and he would perform his duties as his nation required. There were six million other Japanese men in uniform ready to do exactly the same thing. Ready to go all the way.

But then, the vast majority of them were not fifty-three.

Physical manifestations of the whining demands of mortal flesh were becoming urgent of late. He had started passing blood in his urine, but had yet to tell any of the corpsmen in headquarters about it. More worrisome still, at least from a quality-of-life viewpoint, was his nervous stomach, which had afflicted him since the Battle of the Philippine Sea and the fall of Saipan four months earlier. But that miserable fact, too, was kept to himself. A warrior suffered in silence, shunning sympathy and succor from others; a commander who had to keep an anxious eye peeled for the nearest latrine or suitable clump of bushes everywhere he went did not exactly instill confidence in his men. How could he be expected to keep control of an organization of thousands of men and complicated machinery under the stress of combat if he could not even control his elimination urges?

Tied in with the gut problem, and of considerably more serious health consequences, was an absolute, utter loss of appetite that he had also taken great care to conceal from his men, especially his orderlies. Proffered meals could usually be evaded with something gruff (and painfully ironic) like, "Who can think of his stomach at a time like this?" but there were times when this would not do. Dining with fellow flag officers and Tokyo political types, he would have to rally every ounce of physical courage and willpower in his body to go through the motions of

---

*This was a national identity concept institutionalized in Meiji-era political dogma and prose-lytized to subsequent generations of Japanese until the end of World War II through Ministry of Education policies. Although the phrase can be found in eighteenth-century Japanese *koku-gaku* nationalistic poetry, its modern permutation was influenced in form and function by nineteenth-century German Romanticism, encapsulating a theory that innate archetypal qualities in the character of the Japanese afforded the race unique spiritual attributes beyond those of other walks of life. It was easily extrapolated in a "manifest destiny" vein for the legitimization of expansionist policies in Asia.

pleasurable dining—raising his chopsticks to his mouth, shoveling the food in, chewing it, and, worst of all, having to swallow the stuff down, which always brought on instantaneous and hair-raising howls of protest from his digestive tract. At such times it was difficult to even comment on the food in front of him without a commensurate lurch in his guts. Sometimes he went days without partaking of any more sustenance than a few forced bowls of rice gruel washed down with weak green tea.

How he had pushed himself this far at his age without succumbing to a more serious illness was, he liked to think, a testament to his tough Japanese constitution and warrior's capacity for hardship. But his nagging conscience was right. This could go on for only so long. Combined with the chronic insomnia that had plagued him for the last three years, the eventuality of malnutrition and stress laying him out on a hospital cot sooner or later was a foregone conclusion. The goal would be to keep this inevitability at bay long enough to carry out his mission. For the time being, he could stay fueled and operational on adrenaline, nerves, and green tea alone. Ailments and physical fears could be subsumed by willpower. This was not the time for weakness. He had to be a rock. He was Vice Admiral Takijirō Ōnishi, dispatched to the Philippines to pull another miracle out of his hat. That was a direct order from Imperial General Headquarters. He was to provide air support for Operation Sho, the last-ditch Japanese naval plan for the "decisive battle" that would save the Philippines and stop the Allied advance in its tracks, or, in the most conservatively optimistic scenario, at least bloody the Americans badly enough to bring them to the peace table with favorable terms, Roosevelt's "unconditional surrender" declaration at Casablanca be damned.

This would be the most crucial naval engagement for Japan since Admiral Heihachirō Tōgō stopped the Russians in the Tsushima Strait in 1905,[4] and like that fateful sea clash thirty-nine years earlier, failure to achieve the assigned strategic objectives would spell doom for the Japanese empire. Of course, Admiral Jisaburō Ozawa had used this line when addressing his fleet before the Battle of the Philippine Sea the previous June, repeating Tōgō's famous command verbatim. Twenty-four hours later three of his carriers were at the bottom of the Pacific, along with irreplaceable veteran aircrews and over three hundred aircraft. But there was no need for burdening the rank and file or the folks back home with such depressing figures, and one had to admit that Tōgō's words made for great motivational speeches. Four decades of Japanese schoolboys had learned them by heart, and they would no doubt be brought out, brushed off, and used again to send thousands more off to their deaths before the war was finally and irretrievably lost.

Uplifting speeches aside, Ōnishi's mission was clear: Turn the flight decks of the American escort carriers in Leyte Gulf into matchsticks by any means available, clearing the way for Vice Admiral Takeo Kurita's and Vice Admiral Shōji Nishimura's battleship squadrons to sweep in and wreak havoc on the Allied fleet unharried by American airpower. Turn back the invasion and send MacArthur and Halsey skulking back to their lairs in New Guinea and Ulithi with their tails between their legs. With five hundred planes and veteran aviators to fly them, yes, maybe it could be pulled off. But even Ōnishi, inveterate optimist though he was, had to face the fact that he did not have five hundred planes to put in the air. He had only thirty Zero and Shidenkai fighters and a smattering of operational bombers, transports, and recon planes with which to stop the greatest carrier armada the world had ever seen. And though he was a Japanese warrior—a spiritual (if not biological) descendant of samurai with supernatural, superhuman fighting spirit—he was not omnipotent. He could not bring back to life all of the veteran pilots lost in the Marianas and during the disastrous air battles off Taiwan in early October; even if he had the luxury of a thousand of the world's best fighter planes at his disposal, there was nobody left to fly them. The Americans had shot all but a handful of the emperor's finest Sea Falcons out of the sky in flames, never to return.

In the meantime, flying corps entrance requirements back in Japan had been drastically relaxed and flight school curricula had been slashed in desperate attempts to meet the navy's aerial combat needs. Although the army had been doing this for years—and never had anything near the navy's demanding standards for its air cadets even in the best of times— the fact that naval aviation now had to stoop to this level invited only the grimmest sense of foreboding.

Salient in Ōnishi's long list of concerns, however, was something that would literally change history—something that, at present, he and a handful of officers at First Air Fleet HQ were the only people in the entire Philippine archipelago privileged to know. Tokyo had given him carte blanche to employ any tactical expedient he deemed necessary to ensure the success of his mission, and he was personally convinced that nothing less than supreme sacrifice from all concerned could turn the tide of the war they had been losing for the last two years. During change-of-command orientation sessions in Manila two days earlier, his predecessor, Vice Admiral Kimpei Teraoka, had agreed. *Tokubetsukōgeki* ("special attack") or *tokkō*, in the abbreviation rapidly gaining widespread usage, was going to be the way to go. Interservice dialogue with Lieutenant General Kyōji Tominaga and the army people confirmed that the Fourth Air Army covering the Philippines was leaning in this direction, too, although they were typically stingy with operational details.*

Army or navy, no one with gold on their shoulders back in Japan seemed to have any better ideas, either, and the *taiatari seishin* ("body-crashing spirit") central to *tokkō* was already attaining servicewide recognition at the field- and company-grade officer level in both branches. *Taiatari* was being promoted by right-wing firebrands such as Captain Ei'ichirō Jō in the navy and Colonel Masanobu Tsuji in the army not only as a legitimate tactical expedient for desperate times, but also as an exciting new philosophical development in the Japanese warrior ethic that would make fundamental and heroic changes in the psychological landscape of the Japanese national character as a whole. Prime Minister Hideki Tōjō had agreed with this concept in principle as early as March 1944, issuing a top-secret memorandum to both services that "informal" studies should be made as soon as possible, so that procedures would be ready if and when the tactics became necessary.

*Taiatari* had a fine "no guts, no glory" feel to it that went over well with middle-aged career men sitting around conference tables and gambling with other people's lives. Although there was no Japanese historical precedent for organized "suicide" tactics, per se, the idea *seemed* like something that warriors of old might have done, and it could be sold along those lines; invent some convincing traditions, their origins shrouded in mystery, playing up the usual *yamato damashi* angle. If it was done well,

---

*The army formed its own *tokkō* air unit independently of the navy (but no doubt motivated by a sense of competition with same as rumors began flying) when the Banda Unit, flying twin-engined *Ki*-48 bombers rigged with 800 kg bombs, was formed at the Hokota Flight Training Center in Ibaragi Prefecture on October 20. See Warner (1982), p. 115n.

the public would drink it up. Of course, it remained to be seen what the young men who flew the planes would do when the actual orders were cut, but their courage and fine sense of self-sacrifice had never come into question before. There was no reason to fear any wavering on their part now. They knew what had to be done, and did not need balding armchair warriors to tell them why. Just when, where, and how.

Ozawa's Marianas debacle—what the Western press was still trumpeting as the "Marianas Turkey Shoot"[5]—had proven once and for all, at least for the duration of the current conflict, that the once-invincible Imperial Japanese Navy could no longer dare to stand toe-to-toe with the Allies like the good old days, when they could still win using conventional weapons and tactics. No, those snapshots were already yellowing and curling at the edges. The current situation called for unconventional ideas from unconventional men, and Takijirō Ōnishi was the man of the hour. Should his efforts come to naught, he knew he would most likely be vilified by generations of his countrymen to come. As painful as this was to acknowledge for an egotist of Ōnishi's magnitude, he knew that the distance of time would someday ensure that he would be remembered for his loyalty, dedication, and sacrifice. It might take centuries, but a grateful nation would someday honor him as he wanted to be remembered: as a patriot.

His eyes still fixed on the yellow rice paddies and jade mountains rolling by the window, a landscape vaguely reminiscent of his home village in late summer, the admiral noted mean black clouds menacing the horizon behind Mount Arayat, inviting comparison both with his own mood and with the relentless dark armada closing in from across Leyte Gulf. How many more of Japan's finest young men would die trying to stop this American storm of steel? All of them? Was that the catch? Was that the burnt offering required this time? It was possible that an entire generation would have to be sacrificed to save the empire. Failing that, these young heroes would be in the vanguard for the national death leap—the *ichioku gyokusai* "honorable death of the 100 million," as the papers would soon be calling it—painting a wide-brushed, bloodred swath of Japanese pride, honor, and virility on the pages of history in indelible glory. It would be a fitting epitaph for the proudest race the world had yet known. The entire nation would go down in flames, standing on its feet, with its gene pool intact, its women pure, and its civilization unsullied. It would die unconquered and unbowed, steadfast in its resistance to the white man's juggernaut of world domination and soulless rationalism.[6] Perhaps other non-Anglo-Saxon nations would take up the struggle in the future, and Japan's historical example could inspire other races of color to fight on. It would be a good death.

Educated Japanese males of Ōnishi's generation who had spent time living and studying in the West—especially America—tended to harbor extreme feelings at both ends of a love-hate continuum toward their former hosts and teachers, ranging from unabashed schoolboy hero worship to utter repulsion fueled by a desperate need to believe in their own racial and cultural superiority. The emotional packages of most comprised a tortuous Freudian mélange of admiration and inferiority complex: a healthy respect for the Westerners' technological prowess, material abundance, and sheer physical size; disdain for their shameless materialism, their smug, easy pride, their maddeningly nonchalant tolerance of disorder, their racist immigration legislation and the woeful history of the American Negro. Not to mention poisonous, half-buried memories of patronizing cocktail party slights ("Oh, your English is excellent. Were you taught by missionaries?"), sneering hotel clerks, withering locker room anxiety, and the impotent rage of coming home to see giggling Japanese girls on the arms of strapping white men in the streets of the larger port cities. Just as everyone tapping pointers on maps in the war rooms of Tokyo and cutting orders for young men to die at the front carried his own personal portfolio of similar psychological baggage regarding Westerners, none of them had ever really expected the nation to win its duel to the death with the West—win, that is, in the sense of Japanese troops marching up Pennsylvania Avenue and pitching their tents on the White House lawn.[7] Nor did they see the war as being pursued primarily for the practical strategic objectives of securing vital industrial resources and fuel. Seeing things in such simple terms was to confuse means with ends.

The goal, really, had always been, first and foremost, to humble the West—to daub the teacher's face with mud—by kicking the white man out of Asia and bringing about the end, once and for all, win or lose, of what former Prime Minister Konoe had so aptly termed Anglo-Saxon global hegemony.[8] The Caucasian bogeyman—and the unspeakable fear that he might really be the superior being he seemed to think himself—had whispered in the ear and haunted the nightmares of the Japanese psyche for the last ninety years, since Commodore Matthew C. Perry's Black Ships first fouled the waters of Uraga Bay, humiliating the nation by forcing it to accommodate the Americans and their insulting demands. Whipping Russia had been a promising start toward righting old wrongs, but holy war with the United States—inevitable, really, since that dark day at Uraga in 1853—had given Japan the chance to silence the unsettling murmurs in the nation's troubled conscience and the mocking laughter of that blue-eyed blight once and for all. The white man had been swallowing cultures and civilizations for too long. Now it was time for him to choke on one.

If inconceivable carnage was what was called for to achieve this, then so be it. Ōnishi had the will to both give and follow the appropriate orders, and the courage to face the consequences of his actions after his duty had been performed. He was comforted by the knowledge that the worst possible personal consequence—his own death—was something he had resigned himself to years ago. Now, as his country faced almost certain defeat, it was a fate he welcomed. Whether his mission was successful or not, he would die either in combat or by his own hand when his death would cause the least worry for his superiors, and only after a suitable replacement had been found to relieve him of his command duties. In a neat, twentieth-century populist turn on the traditional Japanese warrior ethic, this time it would be the lord following his loyal retainers in death rather than vice versa.

In coming months, the Japanese public at large would be called upon to make unimaginable sacrifices while maintaining the will to fight to the end—literally to the last man, woman, and child, fighting off the white barbarians at the landing beaches with bamboo staves if it came to that.[9] Sooner or later the Imperial War Council would have to begin planning how to sell this idea, and what the admiral had in the works right now was just the kind of PR needed for such a campaign. And mission gloriously accomplished or nobly failed, a conscious act of atonement on his part—something dramatic yet elegant—would be the perfect final touch. The nation would be that much stronger knowing that its leaders were as committed to making supreme sacrifices as they were to ordering them.

Ōnishi continued to stare at the smothering black clouds on the horizon, which now seemed so close they could have been images in an imported brass stereoscope he had once marveled at as a child in Hyōgo.

"I'm off to form a suicide squad," he muttered aloud to no one in particular, still staring off at Mount Arayat.[10] These words were the first and last spoken until the limo reached Mabalacat nearly an hour later.

## four

### ŌNISHI'S GAMBLE

Startled-looking sentries were still fumbling to straighten their caps and button their jackets when the yellow-flagged limo sped by on its way to Mabalacat airfield. The car drove up to the base flight ops shack, a rough canvas tent with an open flap under which officers, some in fatigues, others in flight suits, could be seen sitting around a folding table. A tattered wind sock next to the tent hung limply from its pole, dyed a pale salmon pink in the setting sun.

"Stop here," Ōnishi ordered the driver in his second and last intelligible comment of the journey. He was already out of the limo giving his khakis a peremptory straightening and walking toward the tent before the driver could come around to open the door for him. The group of officers around the table, jolted out of their sunset lull by this unexpected visitation from on high, nearly knocked over their chairs as they scrambled to attention. Ōnishi returned a road-weary salute and motioned for the men to sit back down. He joined them in a chair vacated by a quick-thinking clerical type, darting assessing glances over maps for upcoming operations spread on the table with a few nods of his head as he sat down, still without a word of greeting or explanation for his visit. Of course, as a vice admiral, he was under no obligation to explain anything to anyone present, or, for that matter, to say anything at all if he did not wish to. And no one else would speak until he did. This was basic *bushidō* senior/subordinate protocol.

The admiral rubbed his eyes with his stubby stonemason's fingers and turned his attention to the activities on the airfield. Maintenance crews casting long shadows on the muddy ground bustled around parked aircraft, performing last-minute repairs in the dying light, preparing the planes for the next day's missions and towing them to their camouflaged revetments to hide them from the marauding Americans, covering anything and everything else with bundles of tree branches and mats of high grass sod ripped up from the ground. Other groups cleaned up debris from damage the base had suffered from the morning's Hellcat sweep, a courtesy call from Rear Admiral John McCain's Task Group 38.1.[1] Several men with long poles poked through the smoldering, twisted skeletons of a row of Zeros that had been caught in the open in the raid. Nothing would be salvaged from these forlorn wrecks.

A seasoned military eye could tell in a single glance that this was a fighting force that, at least physically and logistically, was on its last legs. Running on fumes. Even the functional aircraft looked like scrap-heap material, weathered and battle-worn, many of the planes with nearly half of their paint finish scoured off by heat, prop wash, runway gravel, and combat, rectangles of fresh hunter-green paint betraying patched-over shell and shrapnel damage. Their engines sounded rough, belching intermittent puffs of sooty black smoke, suffering from the crappy turpentine- and alcohol-spiked low-octane fuel the navy was now forced to use. With the surface fleet unable to safeguard the sea-lanes from the major oil sources in Borneo and the Dutch East Indies in the wake of the Marianas and Taiwan disasters, Allied subs and bombers had virtually free rein to litter the seabed with hundreds of thousands of tons of Japanese oil tanker and merchant marine shipping each month.[2] Loss of the Philippines would completely shut off the fuel spigot. The nation would have to go on what little reserves it had in domestic tank farms, and conservative estimates gave them no more than a few months' worth at current consumption rates. After that, the choice would be simple: capitulation to the Allies, or national suicide.

Even if a tenuous hold on the southwest oil routes could somehow be maintained, it was clear that the fuel situation was only going to get worse from here on in. Reports were endemic of aircraft engines in all commands breaking down due to the new fuel mix, which both naval aviators and army pilots were referring to as "Marianas gas." If engine failure occurred in the midst of combat—which was now happening with alarming frequency—at least veteran pilots had a fighting chance of surviving such a calamity. Provided, of course, that they could survive the numberless swarms of expertly piloted Hellcats and Corsairs. But rookies—who now made up the greater portion of the fliers in both services—had little or no training for such contingencies, and were usually made quick work of by the Americans.

Quality control on the manufacturing end was suffering, too, both in engines and airframes. But with the best of the nation's mechanics and skilled labor now being squandered in combat duties, stranded on remote island outposts behind enemy lines, or already dead, and strategic matériel quickly running out, it was unreasonable to expect anything better than what they were getting. The industry was doing the best it could with what it had on hand, and doing a commendable job of it, at that, given the circumstances. Monthly production numbers were now at record levels.

But now, even women and children were being pressed into service. The nation's aircraft plants largely relied on mobilized teenage schoolgirls to toil away on the assembly lines, working brutally long hours with no pay. Dressed in dowdy gray padded pajamas with Rising Sun headbands over their uniformly pigtailed black hair, they left their little wooden geta clogs in neat rows on the factory floor and scurried barefoot over the airplanes that would carry their young war gods into battle, the wings of Zero fighters as sacred for them as the inner sanctum of a Shinto shrine. Riveting airframes with undying love, devotion, and hope, they cheered electrifying reports from the front ("American forces in full retreat on all fronts! Our forces victorious!") and sang along with strident military marches played around the clock over tinny loudspeaker systems as they worked. Mechanics in frontline units told of often finding brightly colored origami cranes tucked away into recesses of the airframes for good luck, and exhortations to "Fight to the end!" or "Exterminate the white swine for us" grease-penciled in a childish, feminine hand on the insides of inspection access hatches or landing-gear wells. The girls were the best the Japanese race had ever produced, enduring atrocious conditions and great physical danger without complaint, ever cheerful, with hearts as pure and brave as that of any fabled samurai. They were resourceful under duress, beautiful in adversity, proud and undefeated in body and mind.

The admiral shifted his gaze to the ground crews. They looked as rough and ramshackle as the planes they were servicing. Their uniforms were threadbare and patched, some bleached off-white from years of wear and tropical sunlight. Their faces showed the strain of months of sleep deprivation, combat fatigue, and their miserable diet of mashed taro roots and green bananas. You could count the ribs of the men working bare-chested. And yet there was a spring in their sinewy frames as they performed their tasks. There were smiles on their haggard faces. Their voices were hoarse but cheerful, their speech peppered with laughter and encouragements, still full of fight. Like the girls in the aircraft plants, they would work and fight until they dropped. They, too, were undefeated.

A lifetime of indoctrination and thirty years as an officer of His Majesty's Imperial Navy told the admiral that with such spirit, anything was possible. Military history showed that with the right combination of motivation and courage, even the direst circumstances could be overcome. Miracles could occur. Everyone knew that the Americans were spiritually weak—that one Japanese soldier had the guts and willpower of ten of the cursed Yankees. Perhaps a miracle could happen here, too. A divine wind could blow again, like the fabled *kami kaze* that swept away a Mongol armada menacing Japan some seven centuries past. The odds were daunting, but not impossible. It was worth a try.

After nearly ten minutes of silence, the admiral cleared his throat to speak.

"I have come here to discuss with you something of great importance. May we go to your headquarters?"[3]

The men around the table gathered their maps and gear and prepared to shut down the shack for the night. The admiral was joined in the backseat of his limo by Commander Rikihei Inoguchi,* a pleasant, self-effacing staff officer from First Air Fleet sent down to assess the situation at the 201st Air Group some days before, and Commander Asaichi Tamai, the bull-necked but mild-mannered XO of the 201st standing in for the

---

*Inoguchi's older brother Toshihira was commander of the superbattleship *Musashi*, at this point steaming toward the Philippines from Lingga Roads with Kurita's main force. He would go down with his ship five days later in the Sibuyan Sea in the opening phase of the Battle of Leyte Gulf.

absent unit CO, Captain Sakae Yamamoto. The other officers got in a truck and led the way for the entourage to the HQ compound, located in the town of Mabalacat in an old plantation-style house requisitioned from a Filipino fruit company, which had once used it as an executive residence.

The house, which also served as the air group's officer billets, was a tile-roofed two-story structure with warm cream-colored stucco walls and green trim on the windows and doorways. There were half-rotted wicker chairs on the veranda and makeshift laundry lines in the backyard hung with uniforms, flying suits, long mustard-brown gaiter strips, and off-white *fundoshi* loincloth underwear. A rusty fifty-five-gallon drum was placed at one corner of the house to collect rainwater from the roof gutters. A low stone fence wall enclosing the compound gave it a distinctively Western appearance incongruous with the landscape—a decaying Californian land baron's mansion plunked down on the outskirts of this dingy old Filipino banana town, slowly succumbing to undergrowth, overrun by chirping lizards and cigar-sized cockroaches.

Inside, with the exception of the CQ desk in the foyer and an orderly room in an old butler's pantry, most of the space was devoted to billeting. The main living room smelled like sour flying boots and wet canvas, its wide expanse of teak parquet floor filled nearly wall-to-wall with steel-framed folding cots strewn with gear and uniforms, map cases, rabbit fur–lined flying helmets, and the occasional comatose aviator sleeping off the day's combat.

Commander Tamai led the group to the back of the room, where he switched on a naked lightbulb over a small conference table. The officers spread out their operations maps and took seats.

The overhead light gave the men around the table a sallow, unhealthy color, deepening shadows under intense eyes looking down at the table or gazing off at some distant, imaginary horizon rather than directly at the senior officer present. Ōnishi looked at the drawn faces one by one, measuring the men behind them, timing the impact of what he was about to say for maximum effect.

"I don't think anyone at this table needs any big lecture about the war situation right now," the admiral started. "That's not what I came up here for."

"Everyone is aware, of course, of the official commencement of Operation Sho,"* Ōnishi continued. "Needless to say, failure of this operation will result in the worst possible consequences. The mission of the First Air Fleet will be to provide air support for the main thrust of the operation, which will be made by Admiral Kurita's battleship squadron sweeping down into Leyte Gulf, catching and destroying the invasion fleet at anchor before the Americans can secure a beachhead on the main island. To accomplish this, we must render the American escort carriers' flight decks unusable for at least one week."

Ōnishi paused here not only for emphasis, but to prepare himself for what he had to say next. The words would change history. Once uttered, there would be no retracting them. He would be signing a death warrant not only for thousands of young men, but for himself as well.

"The only practical way I see of our accomplishing our mission will be to use special attack techniques, strapping two-hundred-and-fifty-kilogram bombs to Zeros and crashing them into the carriers. It's the only method I can come up with that can ensure hits. Now I'd like to hear your thoughts on this."[4]

Ōnishi, veteran of thousands upon thousands of hours of naval staff meetings, was not particularly surprised when nobody uttered a peep. A Japanese officer did not go to the mat with a superior over a difference in opinion unless he was absolutely sure that he was right and that what he had to say was going to save an operation from certain disaster. Given the premium placed on respect and loyalty in the Japanese warrior tradition, it was not a move to be taken lightly. In the good old days of topknots

---

*Formally speaking, this was Operation Sho #1; four potential Sho "decisive surface battle" scenarios had been planned months earlier in the wake of the fall of Saipan, dealing with contingencies for Allied invasion moves against the Philippines, Taiwan, the Ryūkyūs (Okinawa, etc.), or the home islands (Kyūshū, Honshū, etc.) themselves, respectively. In striking at the Philippines, the Americans put Sho #1 into motion. Halsey's massive air raids with Task Force 38 against Taiwan a week earlier had very nearly caused the combined fleet to be fully committed to a Sho #2 deployment in Taiwan, but this was averted at the last moment when Halsey's force left the area to move on to bigger and better things, a development that gave the Japanese the mistaken impression that they had just successfully turned back a massive American invasion force: This error gave rise to widespread—and extremely short-lived—celebrations throughout the empire, including bases in the Philippines. In fact, Ōnishi had arrived at 1AF HQ in Manila just as the heady bubble was being burst by reports of a gargantuan American armada spotted at the mouth of Leyte Gulf.

and samurai swords, a faulty or less than tactfully presented argument often ended up with the subordinate hosting a somber sake party, writing a farewell haiku, and plunging a dagger into his guts. Dissent toward a superior officer required the conviction only thorough mental preparation could provide, but the bombshell the admiral had just dropped on the table pretty much blew away any chance for counterargument, leaving only this stunned silence instead. These twentieth-century samurai were well trained in the art of keeping their feelings to themselves.

Of course, from the admiral's point of view, the silence was not entirely unwelcome. He had not come to Mabalacat to make a proposal. He had come to give an order—the kind of order a man of honor can only give another man face-to-face. And now that order—albeit ostensibly in the form of a discussion topic—had been given.

The "bad news" now safely out of the way, Ōnishi wanted to get the ball rolling and turn the discussion to maps, names, and numbers as soon as possible. But first he had to take care of the responsibility issues so critical in Japanese decision making before there would be any moving on to operational details. Commander Tamai would no doubt come up with the counterargument that no orders for the formation of a suicide squad could be issued while Captain Yamamoto was away.

If Ōnishi had been in Tamai's shoes, he probably would have made the same move. It was a natural and understandable reaction in this situation, but seeing the second senior ranking officer at the table pull this administrative trump card successfully, the other officers were sure to fall into line right behind him. Ōnishi could not allow this to happen.

Chain-of-command protocol was far more rigid in the Japanese military than in the armed forces of its Western counterparts, but in many ways it was also far more egalitarian; just as there was no "jumping the chain" by subordinates to make requests of superiors above the level of one's immediate commander, the reverse was also true. The rules were nearly as strict for orders moving down the chain as well. No one could be left out of the loop, especially under circumstances requiring the issuing of orders as unprecedented as sending men off on suicide missions. The responsibility in this case was simply too onerous for anything to be put into motion without the entire chain in accordance, right down to the men who would crash the American flight decks.

The admiral knew that nothing could be done until this organizational impediment was squared away, but his hand was weak and the clock was ticking. Unsure of his next move, all he could do was wait for Tamai to move first. Ōnishi stared a hole in him as he waited for a response. The attention of the other officers at the table gradually focused on the XO.

"Begging the admiral's pardon," Tamai said, blinking behind his round horn-rimmed glasses, his craggy ex-judo wrestler's face beginning to gleam with a film of sweat. "But I am only the executive officer. Under the circumstances, I cannot assume authority to issue such orders for the 201st Air Group. I believe we must hear the opinion of Captain Yamamoto in this matter before any decision can be made."

Earlier in his career, right around the time of the highly publicized "geisha slapping" incident that had almost ended it, Ōnishi had entered and won the all-Tokyo mah-jongg championships under an assumed name, going all the way to the national championships, only to lose in the final round. Anyone who had had the singularly humbling experience of gambling with him knew that he was a master of the bluff, possessing a poker face that could turn the wiliest opponent's nerves to jelly.

If there was ever a time for the admiral's fabled gambling acumen, it was now. He decided to try a bluff. It would be the most important one of his career.

"I've already spoken with Captain Yamamoto in Manila," Ōnishi lied,* not missing a beat, drilling Tamai with the sternest gaze in his repertoire. "And he told me to consider your opinion as his own. He has complete trust in your judgment, and leaves the decision in this matter up to you."

Trumped by a virtuoso, Tamai was out of maneuvering room. Placing his hands palm down on the tabletop, he bowed from the shoulders.

"With the admiral's permission," he said, "I will assume responsibility for the formation and deployment of the 201st Air Group's Special Attack Unit."

---

*Crossed signals (and impatient personalities) had caused Yamamoto to miss his scheduled meeting with Ōnishi. At this moment, he was nursing a sprained ankle in a hospital in the suburbs of Manila after crash-landing his liaison plane (a borrowed A6M5 Zero) in a rice paddy. Cause of the crash was engine failure, most likely attributable to "Marianas gas."

"Carry on," Ōnishi replied, clearly relieved but, at the same time, with a somewhat pained facial expression. He excused himself from the table and was shown to a small room with a single bunk on the second floor. He dismissed the orderly with a request to be roused as soon as the planning group downstairs had something to report, whatever hour of the night that might be.

He removed his boots and stretched out on the thin rack, determined to get a few hours of shut-eye but resigning himself to the probability that he faced yet another night of being, in the age-old warrior's lament, too tired to sleep. The success or failure of the crucial Operation Sho weighed heavily on his shoulders. Ōnishi's First Air Fleet was a key element in a battle plan that called for swift, complicated maneuvering with pinpoint timing by a disparate collection of slapped-together air units and the last remnants of Japan's surface fleet (some of these "remnants," admittedly, were pretty awesome; the surface attack force included the legendary superbattleships *Yamato* and *Musashi*). The operation also relied, to an extent, on cooperation with army units whose commanders harbored only slightly less hostility toward their counterparts in the navy than they did toward the Allies, and who saw Leyte as nothing more than a delaying action for the defense of Luzon and the capital of Manila, a strategic picture completely at odds with the navy's plans.

Interservice rivalries and questionable priorities aside, the plan looked doable on the war-gaming tables, but the tiniest foul-up in movement or coordination would invite catastrophe, triggering a snowballing chaotic chain of events that would bring the whole complex, unwieldy system crashing down. The damage could very well be even more catastrophic than the Marianas. They were staking everything on this.

Shock—defined here in the military sense of the application of overwhelming force on a concentrated area upon an unprepared enemy—was a key principle in the plan, and Kurita's top-heavy battleship armada was to be the prime instrument in its application. If all went according to plan, he would catch the American invasion fleet off guard in a pincer maneuver from the north and south ends of Leyte Gulf. To facilitate the pincer, his force was divided into two battleship squadrons, each with its own supporting force of cruisers and destroyers. Kurita's flagship, the heavy cruiser *Atago,** would be in the northern or "strong" half of the force along with *Yamato* and *Musashi,* the battleships *Nagato, Kongō,* and *Haruna,* thirteen cruisers, and fifteen destroyers. The southern half of the force, led by Vice Admiral Shōji Nishimura, consisted of the venerable old battlewagons *Yamashiro* and *Fusō,* the heavy cruiser *Mogami,* and four destroyers. Sallying from Lingga Roads near Singapore after topping its tanks with precious fuel oil, Kurita's formidable flotilla would divide into its "northern" and "southern" elements off the southwestern tip of the island of Palawan to enter the Philippine archipelago from the west. The northern group would cut through the Sibuyan Sea, snaking through the San Bernardino Strait out into the Pacific, skirting the island of Samar and penetrating Leyte Gulf from the north, and Nishimura's squadron would come in through the back door in a dash across the Mindanao Sea to slip through the Surigao Strait and out into the gulf from the other end to close the pincer on the Americans from the south. A third supporting force under Vice Admiral Kiyohide Shima with three cruisers and seven destroyers would sortie south from Hashirajima anchorage in Japan and follow Nishimura through the Surigao Strait to exploit the situation in the event of a breakthrough, lure American battleships in the area away from the main striking force, or, in the worst-case scenario, try to rescue survivors in the event of a disaster.

Success or failure hinged on taking as much American airpower out of the equation as possible, with the fire-breathing dragon in this case being Halsey's unbeatable Third Fleet and its ferocious fast carrier Task Force 38 under Vice Admiral Marc Mitscher. They would have to be dealt with first for anything to work, but not even the most optimistic planners in Combined Fleet HQ had any hope that this could be accomplished through conventional air tactics alone—the Americans were simply too good and too many.

Vice Admiral Shigeru Fukudome was due in from Taiwan in a few days with the remnants of his land-based Second Air Fleet, still a formidable

---

*En route to the Philippines for Operation Sho, *Atago* had the misfortune of crossing the path of the USS *Darter,* an American submarine patrolling the Palawan Passage with its partner, the USS *Dace.* After making the command decision not to go down with his ship, Admiral Kurita had to endure the ignominy of having to swim to be rescued by one of his own picket destroyers. The admiral's flag moved to *Yamato,* where it remained for the rest of the Battle of Leyte Gulf. See "USS Darter": http://www.csp.navy.mil/ww2boats/darter.htm.

force in its own right with nearly two hundred planes left, including a sizable number of the outstanding new Shidenkai fighters. They were slated to provide straight air cover for Kurita and strikes on targets of opportunity.* But this force—provided it arrived from Taiwan relatively intact—was still too small to take on all of Task Force 38, even with *tokkō* assistance. Instead, Admiral Seomu Toyoda and his staff had devised a clever but risky ruse to deal with the huge American force of six fast new battleships, fourteen fleet carriers, and over a thousand planes: Vice Admiral Jisaburō Ozawa, in a personnel choice that was tantamount to an honorable sword to fall on for the loss of the Marianas, would be put in command of a decoy/sacrifice force consisting of the carriers *Zuikaku*,[†] *Zuiho, Chiyoda*, and *Chitose*, hybrid heavy battle cruiser/aircraft carriers *Ise* and *Hyūga*, three light cruisers, and eight destroyers. Sallying down from Hashirajima with less than half of their standard aircraft complement and pretty much the last of Japan's carrier-qualified aviators, their role would be to twitch tantalizing tail feathers under Halsey's nose, get him to commit Task Force 38 to go after the bait and leave the invasion fleet in Leyte wide open with Kurita's battleship squadrons barreling down on them from opposite directions. There would be nothing but Kinkaid's aging shore bombardment battleships[‡] (most likely carrying minimal stores of armor piercing rounds for ship-to-ship combat, in light of their primary ground support mission) and thin-hulled escort carriers to protect them.

If Ōnishi's *tokkō* boys could then take out the escort carriers' flight decks, effectively grounding Kinkaid's dedicated air cover, Kurita could concentrate on the Seventh Fleet's old battle line, which might very well be

---

*At this point, Fukudome was still not convinced of the wisdom of *tokkō* tactics. Ōnishi would eventually win him around by the morning of the twenty-sixth, but this was too late to change Japanese fortunes at Leyte Gulf.

†The last surviving carrier from the Pearl Harbor raid; her sister *Shokaku* was sunk by the U.S. submarine *Cavalla* at the Battle of the Philippine Sea. The other four Pearl Harbor veterans—*Akagi, Kaga, Soryū* and *Hiryū*—had all been sunk within hours of each other at Midway on June 4, 1942. See "First Patrol" http://www.carvalla.org/firstpat.html.

‡The Seventh Fleet shore bombardment battle line consisted of six World War I–era battleships, *California, Tennessee, West Virginia, Pennsylvania, Maryland*, and *Mississippi*, all but the last of which were severely damaged in the Pearl Harbor raid, subsequently repaired/refitted, and returned to duty. *California* and *West Virginia* were actually sunk at their moorings in the raid, salvaged, and, along with *Tennessee*, so extensively refitted as to almost qualify as completely new ships. The new Mark 8 gunnery radar fitted to the latter three vessels was to play an enormous role in the night engagement in Surigao Strait six days later.

tricked into going after only one prong of the pincer instead of both at once, leaving its other flank wide open. If all of this worked, and Halsey and Mitscher were off chasing ghost carriers, too far out of range to double back and help when calamity struck, then there would be nothing between at least one of Kurita's battleship squadrons and a gulf full of defenseless troop ships and cargo vessels except a weak screen of destroyers, any of which could be sunk with a single well-placed main battery round.

If everything worked according to plan, this time it would be the Japanese navy that enjoyed a "turkey shoot." There were nearly a hundred thousand GIs on the beachhead, and the cargo ships, loaded to the gunwales with ammo and fuel, would send up pillars of fire and smoke that would turn the sky red for a hundred kilometers. It would be a beautiful sight, indeed. Maybe even MacArthur himself could be caught in the snare— Admiral Yamamoto avenged at last!

The arrogant, overconfident Americans had sailed into a potential death trap—which could very well turn out to be the greatest naval debacle since Actium.

At least according to official doctrine, Ōnishi and his fellow flag officers were supposed to be chomping at the bit now that the *kaijō-kessen,* or "decisive surface engagement," with the Allied fleet the Imperial Japanese Navy had sought for so long was at hand. This spirit was implicit in the use of the kanji character *sho* as the code name for the operation, a gesture of inspired eloquence and wishful thinking in equal measure that demothballed a simple yet elegant old Chinese ideogram no longer in colloquial Japanese usage by the 1940s. Implying in a martial context the blink-of-an-eye speed of a master swordsman's killing blow, the character captured the very essence of Japanese tactical doctrine since time immemorial. You could trace an evolutionary line with it from the craftsmanship of the swordsmith and *yoroi* armorer right through to the spirit and principles behind Operation Sho: fight light, tactics taking precedence over logistical concerns; strike quickly, staying always on the offensive; let your opponent worry about defense. It was the same line of thinking that had banished the shield from the samurai warrior's panoply,[5] that had designed a mainstay naval fighter plane, the fabled Zero, with superlative range, maneuverability, and hitting power but no diving speed, protective armor, or self-sealing fuel tanks,[6] that had sent the nation into war against an enemy with almost double the population, ten times the industrial capacity, and hundreds of times the arable landmass on the pretext that spiritual strength could overcome material might.

This spirit had been adequate for pitched medieval battles fought with swords and longbows, but where had it gotten the Japanese warrior now? To a situation so hopeless the whole Sho operation was keyed on young men making suicidal crash dives into enemy ships.

To use Ōnishi's own words, directed at Ei'ichirō Jō in a heated debate at Imperial General Headquarters less than a year before, *tokkō* was "heresy, coming from the mouth of a professional officer"*—insanity that no officer with any kind of respectability had any business tolerating in his command.

It was also, he now found himself admitting, the Imperial Japanese Navy's only hope.

The navy had been working on worst-case-scenario prototypes for weird weapons—manned torpedoes, piloted rocket bombs, and the like—since Tōjō's original rubber-stamping in March, and support for *tokkō* had been voiced up and down the ranks as early as 1943, when the nation's military fortunes took an alarming turn after the Guadalcanal defeat. Momentum for a decision on actual combat use was reached only after Rear Admiral Masabumi Arima (INA'14) established the necessary precedent on October 15 by trying to crash a Mitsubishi G4M2 Isshiki Rikkō bomber into the side of the fleet carrier *Franklin* during the height of the Taiwan air battles.[7] But Arima had crashed into the sea too far from the *Franklin* to do any damage, and rumor had it that the act itself was motivated more by the man's fragile nervous condition cracking under the stress of command in a losing battle than by any conspicuous bravery on his part. However, as was so often the case in wartime reportage, once the propaganda people in Imperial GHQ got hold of the story, it was transformed into a media campaign, and Taiwan was described as a potentially war-winning rout of the Americans. The emperor was delighted—told that his forces had sunk as many as eleven enemy carriers and turned back a

---

*Even though probably concocted on the spot, the phrase Ōnishi actually used, *tōsotsu no gedō*, has the Zen-like ring of a time-honored Buddhist parable. It is untranslatable into an English phrase as concise, eloquent, and devastatingly direct as the original Japanese.

massive Allied invasion fleet, he issued a special imperial rescript calling for mass public celebrations of the great victory at Taiwan. A wave of "victory fever" reminiscent of the post–Pearl Harbor raid euphoria swept over Japan, transforming the mood of the nation virtually overnight from one of patient dread to heady (if short-lived) optimism. Arima was elevated to national hero status; schoolchildren knew his name within days of the event. Even more significantly, the words *taiatari* and *tokubetsukōgeki*, splashed across headlines and shrieked from radio speakers, were now firmly ensconced in the national vernacular. The *tokkō* cat was out of the bag, and Tokyo had determined that this was all going to be immensely beneficial for home-front morale. It was now green lights all the way for suicide dives.

With Arima having already broken the ice, selling the rest of the *tokkō* concept to the public would be a simple enough matter of convincing it that the powers that be had determined that this was the best course of action for the nation to take at this particular time—that despite these seemingly extreme measures, everything was under control because the military authorities could read the Americans' next moves like cablegrams, and that their heroic young war gods would carry the day before long. If the people's psychological needs were taken care of properly, with the ultimate reassurance being that everything was being undertaken in the emperor's name and with his seal of approval, then the sale was already made. Post–Meiji Restoration compulsory education and two decades of high-intensity Shōwa-era agitprop had done a magnificent job of laying the psychological groundwork for mass sacrifice on the part of the civilian population.

The motivational package for the *tokkō* fliers themselves did not have to be so consciously concerned with romanticized ideals like bravery and loyalty, dying for emperor and fatherland. Those boys had long since been indoctrinated with such values, and moreover, they had spent the last two years since Midway watching their older brothers die and their nation's armed forces getting steadily trounced westward across the Pacific by the seemingly unstoppable Americans. In their case, the desire to avenge losses and the lure of empowerment were the right psychological buttons to push. These motivational factors could be enhanced through regalia and ceremony—speeches could be written and, as always, appropriate "traditions" could be invented as needed.

For a smooth-cheeked eighteen-year-old just out of flight school, there would be an undeniably seductive power in the notion that he could tie on a headband, sit behind the controls of an aircraft, and change the course of history single-handedly. This excitement would have a trickle-down effect on the military establishment as a whole, spreading from there to the entire nation, playing on the great hope inherent in the idea that when you were losing a game playing by rules favoring your opponent, you always had the option of changing those rules. As a fearless militant engaged in what later generations would call asymmetrical warfare, you could confound your foe's logic, play on his worst nightmares, and, in the process, destroy his will to continue fighting. This was the power—and the beauty—of the *tokkō* concept; it was Poe's "imp of the perverse" in organizational form, a Dostoyevskian hatchet in the brainpan of Western rationalism, so far out of the box that even the best of the Americans' three-dimensional thinkers—their think tanks of pipe-puffing geniuses sequestered in the bowels of the Pentagon—would never be able to come up with a workable counterstrategy. *What kind of people are capable of this? They're mad!* they would scream, fretting and conferencing as their fleets were scuttled and their sons and brothers died in terror and flaming agony. *Fighting like this and we're still only in the Philippines, for God's sake! What will they do when we try to invade Japan!?*

In the end it would come down to a brutal duel of national and civilizational will—the Japanese ability to absorb the systematic extermination of their young men versus the Americans' stomach for the sacrifice of their own. Ōnishi and growing numbers of flag-rank officers were increasingly convinced that, when it came down to such a contest, the Americans would blink first. For all of their steel mills and shipyards and skyscrapers and Western Union cables spanning the globe, there was still one gaping breach in their ramparts—Americans were skilled at the rhetoric of justifying their wars, claiming the cause of freedom or justice or individual liberty whenever it suited them, but there was no principle for which they were prepared to sacrifice *everything*. In the essence of their souls, they were pragmatists who fought to win as quickly and painlessly as possible. They preferred their heroes coming home alive to having them come home in boxes. Theirs was the bravado of gunslinger show-offs, the pearl-handled machismo of gangsters. Who did they think they were, flying into battle in high-performance aircraft emblazoned with paintings of naked women and cartoon characters? The Americans blasphemed the sacred art of war as much with their tastelessness as with their undeserved successes, and they were all the more despicable now that they were winning. Victory had to be seized from their grasp, whatever the cost. If they could not be made to lose, then at least they would never, ever be allowed to win. Not while a single Japanese was still drawing breath.

Push hard enough, sacrifice enough, and there would come a point when Washington would order its ships home. Once American voters knew what was happening to their sons, the politicians would have no other choice.

*Tokkō* seemed like the best chance for being able to push them to this point. But all those fine young men . . . all that blood . . .

And in whose name?

## five

# POSTER BOY

At 0300, there were two sharp raps on the door to the admiral's room. The door creaked open and yellow light spilled in from the hallway around a silhouetted head and shoulder. The admiral blinked a few times and Tamai's rugged features formed in the glare.

"Come in," the admiral said. "I'm awake."

"There've been some developments, sir," Tamai said. "While you . . . slept. We assembled and spoke to the NCO pilots last night, briefed them on the situation, and they all volunteered. . . . To a man, sir."

The admiral sucked in a sharp gulp of air, almost like a choked-back sob, then let it out in a low, forlorn sigh.

"To a man . . ." the admiral said.

"Yes, sir. We've also come up with a most suitable candidate for the *tokkō* unit leader. A young lieutenant named Yukio Seki. Naval academy man. Class of 'Forty-one."

The choice was inspired. Of course it had to be an officer, and better yet, a naval academy man. It had to be made to look like they were prepared to sacrifice one of their own—a strapping, heroic, capable, professional naval officer, not some farmboy crammed through flight training and hardly able to keep a control stick steady between his knees. There would no doubt come a time when it would be up to such innocents to carry the weight of the campaign, and perhaps sooner than most people thought, but that time was not here yet. This was a time for heroes.

49

Even among a politically docile populace well-conditioned by seven decades of sacrifice-intensive emperor-worship education, pumped up by Arima's Taiwan heroics and helped along the straight and narrow by 1920s "thought crime" legislation,[1] it was still inevitable that there would be voices—perhaps even in public—expressing doubt that the nation had to sacrifice the flower of its young men in such deliberate and decidedly irreversible fashion. It would be the navy's job to convince the nation that, indeed, it was just such sacrifice and nothing less that was required of the Japanese race in this, its darkest hour.

For this, they needed a ritual sacrifice—a Boy Scout to crucify, grieve over briefly, then deify. Seki seemed to fit the bill perfectly. He came from a lower-ranking ex-samurai family that had fallen on hard times after the Meiji Restoration; he was twenty-three—old enough to be taken seriously, but still young enough to break hearts; newly wed; captain of his junior high school* tennis team; modest and mildly introverted; highly intelligent; and devoted to his impoverished, widowed mother (he had attended the naval academy in the first place only because he did not want his mother to be burdened by tuition for a private school). Seki was a skilled aviator and experienced instructor for basic flight training at Kasumigaura, straight out of advanced flight school himself. He had seen some combat as a carrier-qualified pilot in the CBI theater flying Aichi dive bombers. His records showed high evaluations straight down the line from the academy on, with the only negative entries a few minor breaches of uniform regulations—long hair, shoes not properly shined— misdemeanors that could be written off to youth and human fallibility. So he was a bit of an individualist. All the better for the first fellow—the one everyone would remember after all of this was over—to have a little *ningen kusasa* ("whiff of humanity") about him. Seki had excellent qualifications, proven leadership ability, and, as the pièce de résistance, sizzlingly photogenic charisma.

The education system had done a wonderful job raising—no, *creating*— Seki's generation, snipping buds and turning branches with the patient guidance and loving care of a master bonsai gardener. These children were

---

*Compulsory education from the Meiji era until the end of World War II consisted of a six-year primary school program. Six-year middle school programs offered the equivalent of a modern-era high school education for white-collar job hopefuls and/or college prospects.

the fruit of a diligent, prudent, concentrated national effort to create an inspired, dedicated population base ever since Emperor Meiji's Imperial Rescript on Education of 1890. This was a factor often overlooked by students of modern Japanese history: the Meiji Restoration did not just bring about quantum leaps in the nation's technological prowess and economic might; far more profoundly, in the grand scheme of things, it placed the potential for greatness into the character of its commoners, teaching them that, contrary to what the Westerners preached with their poisonous and selfish liberalism, group loyalty and a properly deferential stance toward your superiors did not necessarily mean living on your knees. In the New Japan, rather, those values could be seen as a matter of honor and as a self-conscious, self-aware celebration of one's Japaneseness.

Anyone had to admit that it was an obscene waste to destroy a fine young man like Seki. Add some gray into his hair and wrinkles onto the visage staring up from the dossier page and you could be looking at the face of a dignified doctor who might cure cancer someday, create a vaccine for polio, make crippled children walk again. Perhaps you were looking at a professor who would inspire a generation of young minds passing through his classroom in a long and illustrious career. How about an artist who would be heralded the world over, spreading Japanese culture and bringing glory upon himself and his country? A progressive prime minister who would see the nation through the 1980s on a wave of prosperity? Someone's loving, supportive husband. Some lucky child's devoted father. A kind old man who doted on his grandchildren.

But on the orders of a blunt-nosed farmer's son from Hyōgo this beautiful young man's promising future would be turned into a flaming wreck and a mangled corpse, splattered over the deck of an American warship at six hundred kilometers an hour.

Now, *that* was truly breathtaking egalitarianism at work. Meiji's social reforms had not abolished the warrior caste—they had simply relaxed its membership requirements,[2] and for the Japan of 1944, this meant that there were only two kinds of Japanese left in the country: the emperor, who was the living, breathing essence of Japan itself, and then, on a perfectly horizontal plane immeasurably lower than His Majesty, an entire nation of modern-day samurai, active or reserve. "A sublime sense of self-sacrifice must guide you throughout life and death," the emperor's citizen-soldiers were told. "Think not of death as you push through with every ounce of your effort, fulfilling your duties. Make it your joy to do everything with all your spiritual and physical strength. Fear not to die for the cause of everlasting justice. Do not stay alive in dishonor. Do not die in such a way as to leave a bad name behind you."[3]

That was it—the Lord's Prayer of the new samurai; the crux of the whole "honorable death of the 100 million" mentality—which made it possible for a Hyōgo farmer's son to order a dashing young scion of the ancient warrior caste to his death and expect total obedience. It was this heady new elixir of populist pie-in-the-sky that was responsible for the *tokkō* phenomenon, not the kind of lower-cerebellum panic instinct that sent the civilians over the cliffs at Saipan. The difference was more obvious than might appear at first glance. A Western observer might be tempted to write off *tokkō* as some bizarre curio of Eastern thought and behavior—national character molded by ancient philosophies shrouded in mystery, or even an innate Japanese suicide gene. But *tokkō* had not arisen from such origins. Nor was it—contrary to the claims of the young Turks who had been clamoring for *tokkō* for years—a natural extension of samurai traditions. Rather, it sprang from a conscious elevation of devotion to duty and celebration of ethnicity to the level of state religion. This value system could have crystallized only in an industrialized, mid-twentieth-century culture, with all of the powers to mold mass opinion that well-organized compulsory educational systems, high-speed printing presses, the motion picture camera, and radio broadcasts provided its leadership. This banal reality was something that Japanophile Westerners—who tended to see only silky kimono sleeves, Zen proverbs, and misty mountain temples behind everything the Japanese said or did—would never understand, and that few Japanese themselves—holding on to their desperate, Orientalism-in-reverse belief in their cultural uniqueness that such Western stereotypes reinforced—would ever admit.

But Ōnishi understood. And while he did not accept most of the "official beliefs" proselytized for mass consumption at face value, he did believe in the sanctity of the ideals and institutions these beliefs were created to defend.

Despite what the academic fairy-tale spinners claimed, the Japanese race in 1944 was not an ancient one; it was one of the newest nations on the face of the planet. While other peoples still struggled to rise from the ashes of archaic, stultifying nobility systems, or threw away thousands of years of cultural identity on socialism, or staggered punch-drunk through the never-ending Darwinian fistfight of market capitalism, this new way—the Japanese way under His Majesty's benign and infallible guidance—implied a world of benevolence and wisdom where loyalty would be the sole measure of a man's worth. This was the way of the future, the only hope for a world of peace, harmony and, most importantly, order. With a little luck, young heroes like Yukio Seki might yet light that way to the "eight corners of the earth"* with the funeral pyres of their brave sacrifices.

These were soothing sentiments. But other voices still haunted the admiral.

What of the pain of the mothers who would lose these young men? How could anything justify that?

Not all that long ago, Lieutenant Seki had been a proud mother's fine little son. Mrs. Seki had wept with joy at her son's first tottering steps, played with the golden peach fuzz on the back of his sun-browned neck in the family's wooden bathtub, tickling the whorl of hair on the back of his scalp while his laughter rang high and sweet as an angels' chorus. She was the one who had dealt with all the diapers, dishes, laundry, and scraped knees, scrimping and saving to buy her boy a tricycle he wanted, or to get him some nice clothes for his formal elementary school photo. She was the one who had gotten a rash of goose bumps the first time she heard her twelve-year-old's voice crack and sound like a man's for a fleeting instant and fretted over the late hours he kept studying for his entrance exams. And finally, she was the one left standing alone on a gray, windswept railway platform watching with a mixture of sadness and pride as her uniformed young man, the object of all of her years of love, tears, and affection, her only child, the last vestige of her flesh and blood on the planet and the last surviving male of the proud house of Seki, was whisked off into the big, cold world to do great and wondrous things for his country.

---

*This quote is in reference to the official philosophy of *Hakkō ichi'u* ("eight corners of the earth in harmony under one roof," a metaphor for global control under Imperial rule) proselytized in Japanese propaganda since the 1930s to legitimize the nation's expansionist policies. It was one of the founding principles of the Greater East Asian Co-prosperity Sphere. See Edwards (2003) for an explanation of this expansionist propaganda imagery, and the ancient mythology creatively reinterpreted to legitimize it.

And now Ōnishi was about to sign orders that, in destroying this innocent woman's world by taking away everything she loved, would murder her just as surely as if he put his Nambu service pistol to her head and pulled the trigger.

Of course, people would say that only a man who had never known a parent's love for a child could do such a thing. Such talk would burn, but it would have to be endured for the sake of duty. For the sake of the country.

But then again, maybe such criticisms would be true. Maybe he deserved a little time twisting in the breeze, or tied to the roasting stake. The admiral himself could add readily to the list of charges against him in the murder trial his reputation would someday become; maybe he really was just an unhappily married, burned-out fifty-something with volcanic guts and chronic insomnia—a spiritually desolate old man who had not known any love since his mother's death over thirty years before. Childless, hopeless, unloved and unloving—it seemed a likely profile for the kind of man who could order tens, hundreds, thousands of young men to commit suicide on the pretext of duty, honor, country. "The only practical way I see of our accomplishing our mission will be to use special attack techniques. . . ." Whom was he trying to fool? Himself, first of all. Wasn't this really all just a big charade, part tantrum for blowing a war that had started out so well (or that should never have been fought in the first place), part morbid massacre fantasy, part power trip because it . . . because it . . . well, because it could be done? Affirmative to all the above. Damning evidence that the only convincing explanation for his decision was that he was a heartless monster. After all, how could a human being capable of love also be capable of giving orders like this?

Well, maybe that all depended on how you defined the word *love*.

The admiral considered himself to be full of love, just as much as the next man, maybe even more. But the love that burned in his heart was not the kind that a male felt for a female, or that existed naturally between a parent and a child. No, his was a love that only a Japanese man could experience. Love of emperor, of homeland, of culture, of blood.

Now, *those* were things worth dying for.

For a Japanese man of honor, there was no possible counterargument to these moral absolutes. Seki and his comrades had the opportunity to die glorious deaths while striking a grievous blow at the enemy, gaining immortality in the pages of history, and avenging the deaths of comrades and loved ones in the process. They would never have to know the bitterness of defeat, never see their wives, sweethearts, and sisters defiled by an occupying army of barbarians. The issuing of *tokkō* orders under such circumstances was an act of the most profoundly heartfelt love, faith, and mercy. While the admiral would never stop grieving for the young men he sent off to die, he would also never doubt the integrity and necessity of his decision or the righteousness of his cause.

Ōnishi handed Seki's dossier back to Tamai, pulled on his boots, and went downstairs to join his adjutants and the 201st staff at the map table on the first floor.

# FED UP WITH LOSING AND READY TO DIE

Dawn found the admiral and the other officers still bent over their maps. Mabalacat was socked in under a blanket of dripping humidity from a heavily overcast, ill-tempered monsoon-season sky. Although the weather was terrible—even dangerous—for flying, the 201st had put search planes up several hours earlier. Not surprisingly, no one had been able to get a fix on the Seventh Fleet's carriers, although they were believed to be operating somewhere off Samar Island, perhaps headed south for Leyte. Based on the premise that numbers would improve the chance of finding something, there was some merit to the idea of just sending up a reconnaissance in force, with the Zeros rigged for *tokkō* and ready to attack at first sight of the enemy. But what if they got lost in the bad weather, ran out of fuel, and had to ditch in choppy seas? What if, milling around the general area of operations with their eyes glued to the water looking for American flattops, they were jumped and mauled by Hellcats? An ignominious official debut for *tokkō* tactics would be utterly disastrous both in terms of morale and the future conduct of the war. News of a flopped operation here would go all the way to the top. Perhaps all the way to the emperor himself.

Ōnishi's decision was firm. No *tokkō* planes would take off from Mabalacat unless there were clearly identified targets. In the meantime, the recon planes would stay up and continue to search.

However concerned he was with getting results, the admiral was almost as worried about the effect of an interminable, excruciatingly boring morning on the morale of the fliers, which would be the ultimate anti-climax after all of last night's drama and passionate exhortations: brave hands of the NCO aviators thrust in the air under blackout lamps; what must have been young Seki's soul-searching, sleepless journey through the longest night of his life, no doubt tortured with imagery of his poor mother and young wife. Damaged morale, too, was to be avoided, but unlike bad weather or elusive American carriers, the admiral could do something about the danger of flagging spirits.

"Tamai," he said suddenly, "I want to speak to the volunteers this morning. And the ground crews. Everyone involved with the program. Call a formation for ten hundred hours."

At a few minutes before ten, Ōnishi, Tamai, Adjutant Moji, and the Nichiei News Service newsreel cameraman waited on the veranda of HQ while the admiral's limousine was brought around for the ride to Mabalacat Field. When the limo pulled up the driveway, its passengers were somewhat surprised to see that during the night, some orderly—no doubt following base vehicle camouflage SOP to the letter and not realizing whose car he was decorating—had given the Packard's shiny roof and hood toupees of thatched palm fronds and elephant grass, making the vehicle look like a giant duffer's divot with wheels. But there was no time to remove the offending foliage. It would have to stay.

When the entourage reached Mabalacat and the admiral stepped down from his shaggy Packard, all twenty-four *tokkō* volunteers were already lined up in front of the flight ops shack, with Seki front and center. Other 201st personnel formed up on the side of the clearing. A Rising Sun ensign snapped on the wind-sock pole, its colors somewhat subdued by the gray sky it fluttered against.

Commander Tamai received Seki's salute, did an about-face, and reported the 201st formed. The admiral mounted a wooden crate someone had placed at the head of the formation. He stood at attention while Tamai called out *"Keirei!"* and all present raised their hands to their cap bills in unison. Ōnishi held his salute longer than was customary, his hand trembling slightly as he looked into the eyes of each man lined in front of him. The longest gaze was reserved for Seki.

The admiral, still standing rigidly at attention, dropped the salute and cleared his throat. The air was charged with the unspoken understanding that everyone present was witnessing—and living—a scene destined for immortality in the pantheon of great moments in Japanese history.

"Japan is in grave danger," the admiral began. "Someone must come to her rescue, but it will not be admirals or generals or politicians, and certainly not senior officers like me. It will be fine, strong young men like you. Think of me standing humbly before you right now as the embodiment, if you will, of all one hundred million of your countrymen, asking for your help. Praying for your success.

"Having taken up this sacred task, you have all become young gods with no earthly desires anymore beyond the perfectly natural desire to know whether or not you have been successful in carrying out your missions and hitting your targets. As you are all about to head off into that long, good sleep, I am sorry to say that there will be no way of your knowing this for sure, and there will be no way for us, the living, to tell you. You may depart on your missions, however, secure in the knowledge that your deeds will be duly reported to a grateful nation. Do your best, boys. Do your best. . . ."[1]

The admiral began to say something else, but his words caught in his throat. Tears welled in his eyes and he choked back a sob. Sniffles could be heard from the ranks, and the newsreel cameraman present was so moved by the proceedings that he had forgotten to turn on his camera. There was a brief, somewhat tense silence among the men that Tamai ended, after a respectful pause, with a parade-ground-volume command for another salute.

"*Keirei!*"

Ōnishi returned the salute and stepped off of the crate to shake hands with each of the young aviators. Their handshakes were resolute. Some of the boys were stern-faced, while enigmatic smiles flitted across the faces of others, but there was no fear in their eyes—only thousand-yard stares tinged with fire, glossy with emotion from the admiral's speech and the existential weight of the moment.

For months now, these boys had been in the thick of one-sided combat conditions none of them had expected to survive. With the kill ratios the Americans were racking up of late, it seemed as if Japanese pilots were embarking on suicide missions every time they climbed into the cockpits of their battered planes, *tokkō* or not. But now, thanks to the wisdom and beneficence of Vice Admiral Ōnishi and the Combined Fleet general staff, they were going to be able to go out in a blaze of glory to return, with interest, some of the licks they had been taking for so long. This, more than any fatalistic somberness or stirring patriotism, was the dominant mood of the gathering—a paradoxically resigned eagerness. The unmistakable lure of empowerment was working its seductive magic on these boys. They were proud, fed up with losing, and ready to die.

With the ceremony at an end, Tamai ordered *"Kaisan"* ("dismissed," or "break ranks"), and the men went off to their respective ready areas, with two flight sections headed off to the eastern edge of Mabalacat Field, while the other two sections followed Seki to the western end.

The officers returned to the HQ building in the admiral's thatch-roofed limo. Ōnishi had Inoguchi write up official orders for posting on the HQ bulletin board and forwarding up the chain of command. The admiral read them over, penciled in some corrections, then handed the sheet over to Tamai. The orders read:

> **Item One:** In light of the current military situation, it has been determined that there is no alternative but to organize the 201st's twenty-six remaining Zeros into a *tokkō* unit. Thirteen of the planes will be assigned to actual *taiatari* missions, while the remaining thirteen will be assigned to escort. This *tokkō* unit will be divided into four flight sections, whose mission will be the destruction or at least critical disabling of the enemy escort carriers operating in waters to the east of the main area of operations if and when these forces should appear. This should be accomplished before the main elements of our surface forces are committed to the battle. The number of *tokkō* units will be increased as the combat situation dictates. The official name of the *tokkō* unit is the Shinpū Special Attack Unit.*

*The compound noun *Shinpū* is written with the Chinese kanji characters for "god" and "wind." Many readers will note that the word *kamikaze* employs these exact ideograms. Shinpū uses an *on-yomi* reading/pronunciation for ideograms intended to simulate their reading in the original Chinese, while "kamikaze" is a *kun-yomi* reading/pronunciation in which Chinese characters are used for ideographic meaning only and applied to Japanese words—*kami* (god) and *kaze* (wind)—which have existed in the Japanese language since before the adoption of

**Item Two:** The full resources of the 201st will be devoted to the successful completion of our organized *tokkō* missions, eliminating the enemy escort carrier targets by October 25 at the latest.

**Item Three:** Lieutenant Yukio Seki will assume command of the Shinpū Unit, effective immediately.

**Item Four:** The four flight sections will be named Shikishima, Yamato, Asahi, and Yamazakura,* respectively.[2]

So that was it. *Tokkō* was now official. There would be no turning back.

Ōnishi, Inoguchi, Tamai, and the other 201st staff officers worked through lunch at the map table, really just marking time, more than anything, waiting until they got a promising report from the afternoon's flight of recon planes.

At 1500 hours they got their contact. Escort carriers had been spotted

kanji in the seventh century A.D. The respective roles of *on-yomi* vocabulary items (usually compound nouns, verbs, and adjectives of two to four kanji characters each, often accompanied by particles in the Japanese *kana* phonetic syllabary) and *kun-yomi* words (basic grammatical structure and simple nouns, verbs, and adjectives) in the evolution of the modern Japanese language can be likened to the interplay of sophisticated Latin vocabulary and ancient Anglo-Saxon tribal tongues in the formation of modern English. *On-yomi* readings tend to imply erudition and sophistication on the part of the user, while *kun-yomi* readings imbue meaning with a homey, comfortable nuance harkening back to a rustic, idealized Japanese "good old days" era. To give a user-friendly example for the Western reader, imagine deciding to open a restaurant themed on the delicious bread you bake on the premises; whether you name your new establishment La Boulangerie or Granny's Bread Oven might be the determining factor in whether you have either BMWs with Ivy League bumper stickers or pickup trucks with shotgun racks in your parking lot on opening day. In using the characters for "god" and "wind" in the naming of the first *tokkō* unit, Ōnishi obviously wanted to evoke imagery of the fabled Mongol rousting "kamikaze" or "kami-no-kaze" of lore, but at the same time, give it a professional sharpness with the use of the *on-yomi* reading for the kanji. The actual use of the word *kamikaze* to refer to *tokkō* tactics and units was most likely either an Allied translator's or a Western journalist's mistaken reading of Shinpū. This misreading has stayed in the English vernacular ever since—and has subsequently entered the Japanese vernacular.

*These names are taken from the lines of a famous poem by late-eighteenth-century protopatriot and *kokugaku* "scholar" (I would translate his discipline as "inquiries into the nature of Japaneseness") Norinaga Moto'ori, extolling the virtues of Japanese culture and manhood. Both their origin and significance would have been familiar to any schoolboy in 1944 Japan. See Ogama (1996) and Befu (2001) for details on Moto'ori's career and his ideological influence on Japanese nationalism a century later.

where they had been expected, east of Samar, steaming south. The exact coordinates were hurriedly plotted onto the maps, the compasses came out, and the vectors calculated. The targets were at the extreme range of a bomb-laden Zero. If the planes arrived and could not find these targets, being able to return safely to base would be risky at best—downright impossible if they ran into combat either coming or going and had to push their engines at war emergency power settings for more than a few minutes.* Ōnishi felt that the odds, considering what was at stake, were too long. He cancelled the mission without asking for opinions. Although everyone present understood the logic behind the decision, there was a palpable air of disappointment in the room.

"Tamai, I'm heading back to Manila HQ this evening," Ōnishi said suddenly. "But I'd like to say good-bye to the boys before I go."

"Yes, sir," the XO replied, looking up from the maps.

"Where is Seki's flight right now?"

"Shikishima flight, sir? At the west end ready area."

"Let's go, then."

Adjutant Moji collected Ōnishi's papers and joined the admiral, Tamai, and the Nichiei cameraman in the limo. When they arrived at the ready area, they left the limo near a line of Zeros and found Seki and the six enlisted pilots of the Shikishima and Yamato flights sitting on the ground in a circle on a grassy ridge.[3]

"As you were, boys," Ōnishi said, cutting off Seki's *"Ki wo tsuke!"* (Attention!) before it even made it past the lieutenant's lips. "Carry on."

To the group's surprise, the admiral gestured for a break in the circle

---

*Accounts of *tokkō* aircraft being given only enough fuel for a one-way trip to their targets are fallacious and probably have their origins in Allied propaganda or sensational wartime/early postwar journalism, perhaps concocted to impress upon both the American public and the vanquished Japanese a sense of Western cultural superiority by playing up on a spurious "callous Japanese disregard for human life" angle. While Japan was certainly strapped for fuel in late 1944, it was even more desperately strapped for pilots and aircraft. Fully-gassed flights that failed to find their targets would be able to return to base and be available for new missions, while planes fueled for only a one-way trip would be gone for good, mission accomplished or not. Additionally, there were combat-effectiveness considerations: aviation gas remaining in fuel tanks gave a considerable boost to the killing and maiming capabilities of *tokkō* planes (basically turning them into giant Molotov cocktails) when they hit their targets, especially in the case of light fighter types like the Zero, which had a maximum bomb load of only 250 kg.

and plopped right down to join the fliers sitting cross-legged on the ground. There were twenty minutes or so of lighthearted banter about hobbies, hometowns, and sports before the admiral's sense of timing had him mulling over a fitting exit. The boys had work to do, and everyone was running out of small talk.

"Well," the admiral said, "good luck, boys."

As the group rose to its feet, Ōnishi asked for his adjutant's canteen.

"Let's say good-bye like they used to in older days," the admiral said, addressing the boys now lined up before him. There was no sake on hand for a toast, but a water toast—in the samurai *mizu sakazuki* (literally "water cup") ritual—was actually even more sacred, involving as it did symbolic cleansing of the warrior in mind and body on the eve of battle.

Ōnishi held out the aluminum canteen cap/cup while Moji filled it, then raised it in a toast to everyone present. His hand trembled slightly as he drained the cup, which was passed on to Inoguchi and Moji, then from Tamai and Seki to the rest of the fliers. When the junior member present finished his drink, Seki called his unit to attention and they saluted the admiral in unison.

"You're not saluting me, boys," the admiral said, raising his hand to the bill of his cap with a textbook forty-five-degree snap and not a sign of trembling left. "I'm saluting you."

The group disbanded quietly, with Ōnishi, the other staff officers, and the cameraman squeezing back into the limo to return to the HQ compound. An hour later, Ōnishi left Mabalacat for the long ride back to Manila, which was even quieter than the ride up had been. Not a word was spoken in the car until the admiral arrived at Manila HQ for the official First Air Fleet change-of-command ceremony with Vice Admiral Teraoka that evening at 2000 hours.


Morale was low at Mabalacat Field on the morning of October 25. The weather had been foul for days. Steamy, dripping heat made for sleepless nights, plagues of mosquitoes, and edgy tempers. On-again, off-again rain socked in the field for hours at a time, hampered the effectiveness of recon flights, and turned huge areas of the base into seas of black volcanic mud.

Combat results—or lack thereof—were not helping things, either. So far the Shinpū program had been a total flop.

Flights had been going out on *tokkō* missions since the twenty-first, but every one of them had come up empty: Targets were not where they were supposed to be; green fliers got lost in the fog (some never to return); flights were jumped by American fighters; engines broke down in midflight from Marianas gas, worn cylinders, or just poor maintenance, forcing planes to return to base in shame and bitter disappointment. Seki and his Shikishima flight had already been out on three of these abortive missions over the past four days, and their morale was bottoming out. But the worst experience by far had been after the first mission. They had gotten a dramatic send-off by the now safely returned Captain Yamamoto (hobbling on crutches, no less), solemn toasts with sake at a special, white linen–draped table, tears and cheers from the other fliers and ground crews, and a rousing group singing of "Umi Yukaba," the whole thing captured on celluloid by the Nichiei cameraman. Limping back to base a few hours later with nothing to report but fog, cloud banks, and empty expanses of Pacific had been the ultimate anticlimax— the most excruciating humiliation imaginable. Send-offs after that had become mercifully subdued. Everyone did their best to keep up a show of enthusiasm, but the overall mood on the base had settled into a routine of gray fear and numbing ennui. Death hung in the air now like the Mabalacat mist—an unpleasant feature of the landscape that no one seemed to notice anymore, the only excitement coming from the occasional Hellcat sweep over the field.

At 0725, Seki's flight bombed up and took off once again. The event went largely unnoticed by all but the ground staff immediately involved.

Making things worse for morale this morning were signs of the first cracks in the Sho plan. Reports were coming in about a terrible bloodletting in Surigao Strait several hours before dawn, but no one had any names or numbers yet. Details started coming in several hours after Seki had taken off, and the news was worse than anyone had expected; Nishimura's "southern pincer prong" had run head on into Kinkaid's Seventh Fleet battle line lying in ambush (and well stocked with armor-piercing rounds).[4] In the ensuing slaughter, Nishimura had gone down with his flagship *Yamashiro,* and the *Fusō* and three destroyers had also been sent to the bottom.* Adding to the mayhem and carnage, Shima's squadron, seemingly oblivious to the conflagration ahead, had blundered up the strait right behind Nishimura with no coordination whatsoever, and there had been an embarrassing collision between the heavy cruisers *Nachi* (Shima's flagship) and *Mogami* from Nishimura's element in the midst of all the confusion. *Mogami,* already on fire from the ambush, suffered grievous damage, slowed to a crawl, and was finally done in by American Avenger torpedo bombers around 0900 hours. Shima's ships had, however, managed to rescue some of Nishimura's men from the shark-infested waters of the strait and make good their escape, but all in all, the operation had been an unmitigated disaster. Taken alone, it was the most humiliating and lopsided defeat of Japanese line ships in a surface gunnery engagement in the nation's history. It would have to be avenged before the battle was out.

Meanwhile, Ozawa's decoy force had done its job well, although they were about to pay a terrible price for it. The potential prize of bagging Japanese carriers—most definitely on the endangered species list by late 1944—had proven too much for Halsey and Mitscher to resist, and they had committed everything to going after them. Task Force 38 was now hundreds of kilometers to the north of Leyte and too far to double back to arrive in time to help stop Kurita's force, which, according to the last reports, had made it through the now wide-open San Bernardino Strait and down the coast of Samar Island unopposed and was now within a hairbreadth of smashing its way into the gulf to destroy the main staging area of the invasion fleet.

The loss of the *Musashi* to American air on the way through the Sibuyan Sea was a blow, but Kurita still had more than enough seapower at his command to break through the perilously thin line of escort carriers and destroyers off Samar and blocking the northern approaches to the gulf—all that lay between the Japanese fleet and a stunning victory that could set the Allied war effort in the Pacific back by months, if not

---

*Not only did it spell the end of Nishimura and his force, but it also spelled the end of an era in naval warfare; the Battle of Surigao Strait was the last true battleship-to-battleship naval engagement in history. With the exception of mop-up operations against Nishimura's battered stragglers hours after the main battle, there was no use of airpower by either side during the engagement.

years, potentially even bringing the humbled Americans to the negotiating table with their hats in their hands.

Seki and his men had been thoroughly briefed on as many of these developments as were known by 0720, and they were well aware of the gravity of their mission and what was at stake. The young lieutenant, perhaps, was most aware of these factors, remembering his tactics classes at the naval academy, and how so many of history's greatest sea battles had turned on quickly seized opportunities posed by unforeseen developments, on mistakes and misfortunes, or even just on plain dumb luck. With determination and the right breaks, the Shikishima flight could score hits and take out some carriers. Five planes . . . that could mean five enemy carriers dead in the water with useless flight decks. . . . It could even mean five enemy carriers sunk! Any success by the Shikishima planes would mean fewer American aircraft over Kurita's flotilla. If the timing was right and luck was with them, it just might work. Operation Sho could still be salvaged.

Around 1030, a breathless runner from the western ready area telephone shack ran down the flight line, where Zeros of the new Wakazakura ("Young Cherry Blossom") flight were being gassed up to be ferried down to Cebu for evening strikes in Leyte. The runner's face was beaming. Success! He was bearing the first good news in many days. Planes from the Yamazakura and Asahi flights and the newly formed Kikusui ("Floating Chrysanthemum"*) flight had sortied from Davao† several hours earlier and had broken through the American combat air patrol (CAP) over the Seventh Fleet's screen, scoring hits on at least two escort carriers and setting them ablaze.

---

*This unit was named for the emblem used as the family crest of Masashige Kusunoki, a medieval samurai with a presence in Japanese lore similar to that of Nathan Hale in American history. He died on the battlefield regretting that he did not have more than one life to give for the emperor. See Turnbull (1996), p. 40.

†The Yamazakura, Yamato, and Asahi flights had been sent to the island of Cebu on the afternoon of October 20, then on to Davao Base on Mindanao Island on October 23 in order to be nearer the main area of operations. The Kikusui flight, one of the "expansion" units made possible by the open-ended wording of Ōnishi's standing orders for the Shinpū program, was formed on the evening of October 22 and sent to join the other flights at Davao the next morning. See Mori (1995), pp. 516–519.

The Wakazakura fliers, still numbed from the Surigao reports just minutes before, were electrified by the breaking news, and although they harbored some envy that others had beaten them to the honor of scoring the first Shinpū successes, this just made them all the more determined to get through and score even more spectacular hits. More than anything else, though, their prayers were with their young CO and the Shikishima flight, which would be close to reaching their targets by now. If anyone could get through to the American carriers, it would be Lieutenant Seki.

At 1045, as the shock of the first grim Surigao communiqué—followed so quickly by the elation of the Kikusui flight reports—was still being digested in command posts all over the Philippines, the Shikishima flight was clearing the last spiny, mist-shrouded mountain ridges of Samar Island at a stiff clip before breaking out over the Pacific. It was a Zen warrior's moment of the type that Seki had dreamed of since his days as a teenage midshipman. The doubts and despair about life cut short and everything that might have been, thoughts of his wife and mother that had ruined his sleep for the past four nights[5]—all that mental static had to be banished. In order for him to strike true and clean, his mind and eyes had to be clear. He was at peace with himself and at war with an enemy who had a flotilla full of fat, juicy targets waiting for the taking.

It was a good day to die.

The 1AF HQ communications room orderly knew what to do as soon as the cable from Mabalacat came through. Grabbing up the paper, he ran to Vice Admiral Ōnishi's office, knocked, and opened the door to find the admiral up and pacing, pallid-looking, beads of sweat dripping from his buzz cut to gather around the collar of his uniform shirt.

"Another report from Mabalacat, sir," the orderly announced. "Just in."

"Is it the Shikishima flight?" the admiral asked, wide-eyed. "Lieutenant Seki?"

"Yes, sir. I believe so. And details of this morning's strike out of Davao, also, sir."

Ōnishi snatched the typed cable from the orderly's hands and sat down at his desk, his brow furrowed as he pored over the news.

The first *tokkō* to make apparently successful hits were Zeros out of Davao from the Kikusui flight. The planes sortied at 0630 with the Yamazakura and Asahi flights. Soon after takeoff, one plane from the Kikusui flight was forced back to base, unable to retract its landing gear. A stupid maintenance error. Another two planes—one each from Yamazakura and Asahi—turned back with engine trouble shortly after that. Not even at the target yet, and nearly half the force was already out of the fight. Inexcusable. American CAP destroyed two more strikers on the way in, leaving two strikers to arrive over an element of American escort carriers at 0740. Two of the carriers were confirmed burning by one of the Kikusui escort pilots, the only man in the entire formation who made it back from the target area alive.

This was not the most auspicious debut the admiral could have imagined for the *tokkō* units, but still, two carriers for two Zeros. That was not bad. Not bad at all. He skimmed halfheartedly over the Davao administrative details to get to the Shikishima report.

The name at the top of the escort/witness action report—Warrant Officer Hiroyoshi Nishizawa—made the admiral sit up and take notice, and for an instant, a mean red jag of anger flashed through his head. What were they doing risking national heroes on *tokkō* escort missions!?*

But then again, this hadn't just been *any tokkō* mission. It had been *the tokkō* mission. The national will galvanizer. The one about which a proud and grateful populace would hear shortly.

The admiral read on.

Apparently, Shikishima flight had not been able to sneak in the back door quite as successfully as the Davao boys had. Although they managed to get under the radar umbrella, the American CAP made visual contact and vectored in on them less than a minute out, forcing Nishizawa and the escorts to fight a hole through the Hellcat screen for Seki and the other strikers to exploit. In the ensuing dogfight, Flight Officer Sugawa's

---

*Nishizawa was most likely Japan's leading ace of the war, with thirty-six confirmed and eighty-three claimed aerial victories. Landing their Zeros after the mission at Cebu, Nishizawa and the other surviving Shikishima escort pilots, Warrant Officers Honda and Baba, were killed the next day when the transport plane they were riding back to Mabalacat was shot down by Task Force 38 Hellcats (Inoguchi, 1958, p. 61). Nishizawa's loss was an enormous blow to Japanese morale, both military and civilian, equivalent in weight and effect to the grief experienced by the German nation after Manfred von Richtofen's combat death in April 1918.

Zero was hit by AA and exploded. Nishizawa accounted for two Hellcat kills* as the Shikishima strikers went into their final dives.

As the escorts had not exactly been in a position to observe at their leisure the events unfolding, there was no clear picture of what happened next. Under the circumstances, however, Nishizawa had done a reasonable job of relating what he could. Patching together various snippets and pieces of information from the other escort pilots upon their arrival at Cebu after the mission, he determined that one of the strikers had been downed by AA, but that at least four of the American carriers were hit, with one or two of them definitely damaged badly enough to be considered write-offs. There was no way to confirm how many of the stricken carriers had been sunk, but in keeping with Combined Fleet policy of late, it would not be untoward to report that all of them had gone down.

*"Yoshi, kore de nantoka naru,"* ("Okay, now things will start rolling,") the admiral muttered, leaning back in his chair.[6] He massaged his temples and let out a long sigh that was fatigue and relief in equal parts.

Four confirmed hits. In writing. Right there on the paper, and signed by a living legend, no less. That was good enough for anyone. Four escort carriers by Shikishima flight, another two by Kikusui flight this morning. Scratch six flattops. Declare another national day of celebration. The emperor and the nation needed some good news right now, and First Air Fleet had just provided some.


Twelve hours later, after all-night negotiations with Fukudome to create a large combined naval air command and greatly expanded *tokkō* force in the Philippines, the sobering statistics of losses from Operation Sho were still being tallied. The numbers were devastating: four aircraft carriers; three battleships, including the *Musashi*, which along with her superbattleship sister *Yamato* had been an icon of national pride; six heavy cruisers; four light cruisers; twelve destroyers; four subs; and, counting the planes on Ozawa's carriers along with numerous land-based units

---

*By most Japanese estimates, these kills were numbers 102 and 103, respectively, in Nishizawa's final official tally, although more than half of this total consists of unconfirmed scores. Sakaida (1998) cites Nishizawa's confirmed score at thirty-six.

destroyed in the air and on the ground by Task Force 38, Seventh Fleet's carrier planes and the U.S. Army Air Force, the greater part of the aviation strength of the Japanese navy. Leyte Gulf had indeed turned out to be another Actium, but victory had gone to the Americans.

The Japanese navy was all but finished as a conventional seagoing fighting force. *Tokkō*, which had provided the only glimmers of good news during the entire dismal Sho fiasco, was looking more and more like the only viable weapon left in the navy's arsenal. Vice Admiral Ōnishi was determined to do everything in his power to see that this was how the situation would eventually be explained to His Majesty. First the navy, then the army, and finally the entire nation would have to accept— then become—*tokkō* if there was to be any hope at all of the Americans being stopped.

This was a time for heroes—proud Japanese heroes—and before it all was over, there might very well be 100 million of them.

To be honored posthumously, of course.

## PART TWO

# ALL BOYS DREAM OF FLYING

## seven

# AN OLD MAN'S DREAM

March 2002—I am walking past the northern moat of the Imperial Palace grounds in Chiyoda Ward, Tokyo, headed for the headquarters of the Association of Former Imperial Army Officers—otherwise known in these parts by its traditional Japanese name, *Kaikōsha*. The Kaikōsha was originally established as an army officers' association in 1877. The year was auspicious for the new Imperial Japanese Army, seeing the service eliminate the last domestic armed challenge to Emperor Meiji's consolidation of national authority by neutralizing Takamori Saigō's Kyūshū-based Seinan samurai rebellion. However, the army's success was significant not only for its obvious benefits to the new regime in Tokyo. More crucially—and ominously—the victory also had the effect of propelling the army into a position of coddled favor and political prominence in the imperial government that it would maintain for the next sixty-eight years and relinquish only after the accrued consequences of its actions and policies had resulted in Tokyo and most of Japan's other cities being turned to ash.

The year also saw the Imperial Military Academy produce its first graduates, laying the foundation of the nation's officer corps. As the emperor's army grew in status and influence, so did the status and influence of the Kaikōsha. Membership in the organization soon became de rigueur for career army officers of all ranks, and by the early twentieth century, it had branches in every major city and army installation in Japan, as

73

well as in Korea, Taiwan, and other exotic locales in the empire's rapidly expanding portfolio of colonial possessions.

In addition to serving as a hybrid USO/officers' club/veterans of foreign wars/IMA Alumni Association, the Kaikōsha also functioned as a powerful lobby group for army interests, patriotic educational policies in the nation's schools, and improvements in government benefits for military personnel, dependents, and pensioners, among other issues. Given this tradition of political clout and the threat it posed as a potential *après guerre* rallying point for ancien régime militarists, the Kaikōsha—along with its naval counterpart, the Suikōsha—was one of the first *zaidan hōjin*\* abolished by GHQ at the beginning of the Allied Occupation. However, the association (and the Suikōsha) was not vanquished forever, but merely relegated to temporary dormancy. In 1954, with Douglas MacArthur's democracy babysitters already two years gone and the nation's sovereignty safely restored, the Kaikōsha resumed activities. Fifty years later, the association remains active and is, just as it was in "the good old days," almost exclusively the domain of old IMA grads.

In both its prewar and postwar incarnations, the Kaikōsha's Tokyo branch has always served as the organization's national headquarters, and despite several moves, it has never been farther than a good outfielder's toss from Yasukuni Shrine. The physical proximity is fitting, as many of the modern-day functions of the two institutions are intertwined, and in the case of the archiving of military records, actually shared. Like Yasukuni, the Kaikōsha's energies are devoted to: memorial services honoring army war dead; documenting and interpreting the nation's military past in a manner that will restore Japanese patriotic pride; facilitating the social activities of the rapidly dwindling ranks of war veterans; and maintaining its ongoing tradition of lobbying for right-wing interests in political issues. At present, the most critical of these ideological campaigns are for the reinstatement of national sponsorship and official recognition of Yasukuni Shrine (both privileges have remained abolished since the end of World War II, despite the return of Japanese sovereignty), and for the propagation of what is euphemistically known as "correct" Japanese history education in the nation's schools, particularly

---

\*A somewhat nebulous Japanese legal term loosely translated as "corporation," but which is usually applied to NPOs, schools, and political associations.

where curricula involve handling the interlinked subjects of the rise of Shōwa era militarism and what is generally referred to in right-leaning Japanese historical interpretations as the Great East Asian War of 1937–1945.*

The fundamental points of what could be called the "Yasukuni/ Kaikōsha Stance" (and the basic position of most other right-wing historical interpretation arguments) are:

- the Great East Asian War was the result of Japan being threatened by other powers, and the nation's actions constituted a legitimate defense of strategic interests;
- the war was fought to free Asia of Western colonialism/hegemony;
- the Nanking Massacre, POW slavery and vivisections, "comfort women" forced-prostitution policies, and other purported Japanese wartime transgressions either never happened or have been grossly exaggerated by "Japan bashers"—both domestic and foreign—eager to vilify the nation's conduct in the war for political purposes or possibly even financial gain (through reparations, etc.);[1]
- the current state of history education in Japanese schools is an unhealthy legacy of Allied Occupation policies designed to keep Japan eternally humbled and weak;
- the Tokyo International Tribunal to try Japan's "war criminals" was a sham trial of "victor's justice," and the men and women executed as a result of its verdicts gave their lives for Japan and thus deserve to be honored just as military personnel who died in combat;
- Yasukuni Shrine is the only facility in Japan that can legitimately claim to serve as a memorial facility to honor the nation's war dead in toto.[2]

---

*Understandably eager to distance Japan from the existence and deeds of wartime Nazi allies, defenders of Japan's conduct in the war prefer this term, which both politically and etymologically treats the European theater of the conflict as a separate war. It also underscores rightist Japanese attempts to portray the conflict as a war of liberation fought by Japan on behalf of Asia against Western imperialism. See Buruma (1995), Orr (2001) and Nathan (2004) for analysis of modern permutations of this mind-set.

"Incorrect" history, conversely, means any academic or educational inter-pretation that portrays the conduct and motives of the imperial armed forces during the war in anything less than a heroic and morally justified light, or that denies the status of Yasukuni Shrine as the nation's premier war memorial facility.

Controversy has always surrounded this stance, and while the Kaikōsha's views have never dominated public opinion in postwar or modern Japanese society, its voice has shown ironclad consistency over the years and has long had the ear of some of the nation's most powerful politicians. Given the emeritus status of so many of its nearly fourteen thousand members in business, political, and social spheres, the Kaikōsha's influence is greater even than its considerable size might imply. However, these numbers are dropping off sharply as infirmity and death from natural causes now begin to ravage the ranks of the last IMA classes.* The youngest full members are pushing eighty as of 2004, and there are no plans to "open the books" for a new generation of members. Barring any change in membership requirement policy that will bring new blood into the organization, the Kaikōsha is not much longer of this earth, and is destined to fade away like MacArthur's metaphorical old soldier when there are not enough members left to carry its torch.

Perhaps in light of the demographic realities facing the organization, it is fitting that the premises occupied by its Tokyo branch are consider-ably more modest than the grand stone palazzo—no longer extant—it called home until 1945. Tokyo's Kaikōsha is at present located on a bar-and restaurant-lined side street in Kojimachi, Chiyoda Ward, housed in a six-story building owned by a dentist who lives in a penthouse on the top two floors and drills teeth on the first. On the three floors in be-tween, the Kaikōsha has a canteen/club room, conference rooms, and administrative offices.

The façade and lobby of the building have had recent makeovers, with chrome, marble, and opalescent white tile (perhaps symbolic of the dental clinic's function?) making the structure appear to be much newer than it actually is. The building's true sixties soul, however, is to be encountered on the Kaikōsha-occupied floors, where as in all Japanese office interiors dating from the era, three or four decades of chain-smoking occupants

---

*The last class graduated in March 1945.

have coated every possible surface with a yellow nicotine patina that no amount of detergent and elbow grease can ever quite remove.

But despite the beige walls and linoleum floors, the space seems imbued with a nostalgic Camelot energy of happier times—of an era when Japan's economy was on a rocket sled of double-digit annual GNP growth and all was right with the world. Rounding corners and peering into open doors, one half expects to bump into Brylcreemed businessmen in blue serge suits, horn-rimmed glasses, and pencil ties on their way to Lockheed-funded geisha parties, or to see rooms full of uniformed, bouffant-coiffed office girls clacking away on abacuses and gigantic kanji typewriters.

The club room of the Kaikōsha on the second floor of the building has a small counter with stools, but most of its floor space is taken up by three or four round Formica tables ringed with Age of Aquarius airport-lounge swivel bucket seats. The walls are lined with the handiwork of artistically inclined members, mostly army- and IMA-themed oil paintings and military scale models in glass display cases.

Against the back wall, several pairs of cushy beige chairs face one another, separated by small glass-top tables and from the rest of the room by a wall of photosynthetically challenged rubber plants. One of the chair-table sets is occupied this morning by a small group of old smokers gathered around a Japanese chessboard. Apparently, a move in the game is being hotly contested, as the old men are engaged in a mixture of laughter and angry snarls. They do not take much notice of me when I park myself in one of the bucket lounge seats and order a cup of coffee from a mildly flustered middle-aged waitress. This reception is quite different from the one I got a month earlier, when I first visited the premises and people in the room looked at me like I had just walked down from the ramp of a flying saucer in a silver suit to utter *"Gort, Klaatu barada nikto. . . ."* Nevertheless, as the minutes go by, I am beginning to get some curious stares, and I feel some measure of relief when my interview subject—Toshio Yoshitake—arrives and we head off to a private conference room for our interview.

Toshio Yoshitake still has "the dream" sometimes—the one where he is back on the flight line of that bomb-cratered airstrip on Negros Island in the Philippines, sitting with the other army pilots under the palms in that same steel-gray morning rain, waiting for the weather to clear and the order to climb into the planes. Sometimes he forgets that he is an eighty-year-old having a fifty-eight-year-old dream, and blames the déjà vu he always feels here on crossed signals in a fatigued twenty-two-year-old brain. . . .

But tired or not, none of the young pilots on the flight line this morning is thinking much about sleeping. Anticipation and nerves keep eyes open and mouths firmly shut, the electricity of the moment paralleled in the metallic razz of sap-fattened bugs and the green whisper of light rain on foliage. There are occasional clinks and snaps of cigarette lighter lids, always followed by sighed exhalations of smoke. One pilot is leaning back against the trunk of a palm, looking at photos he has pulled from his pocket. The pilot next to him chews the stem of a long blade of grass as he gazes off to the east toward the twin volcanoes of Mandalagan and Silay, misty blue in the rain, beyond which lie American ships and destiny. The others just stare at their hands, down at the ground, or off into space, figures in a muted earth-tone tableau of young men quietly saying good-bye to the world.

Under the meditative weight of this somber lull, each lung-filling yawn or scratched cowlick is someone's small celebration and savored affirmation of a life that will cease to be in an hour or two. Socialized from boyhood to respect silence, these middle-class sons of rice farmers, schoolteachers, and small business owners share an unspoken understanding that this flight line downtime is probably the last chance in their mortal lives to be alone with their thoughts—to daydream, ruminate, fantasize, or just dwell on the white noise of rain-sizzle through palm fronds, the smell of wet grass, and the feel of warm sea air on their cheeks. There is no nervous banter. No pretentious blather or maudlin yammering. There has already been a send-off speech this morning, and there have been countless others in the past few weeks. No need for any more. *"Dulce et decorum"* lectures and pontifications on the meaning of it all are best left to the crickets in the grass.

Once in the cockpit, it will be all grim reality; the flight will be forty or fifty minutes of edgy boredom followed by a few seconds of screaming adrenaline rush through the American CAP and antiaircraft barrage to go over—then into—the targets. But Yoshitake should be able to handle the challenges he will face this morning. He is a graduate—as are the other four pilots in his flight—of the elite Imperial Military Academy (IMA), Japan's West Point. He has been superbly trained over the last three and a half years to build up an impressive repertoire of combat flier's skills. A qualified recon/assault pilot, he can skip-bomb moving ships and strafe targets with impressive accuracy, fly by instruments alone at night or in pea-soup fog, spot for devastating artillery barrages, and coordinate the movement of ground forces from the air. But today, very few of these skills will be called upon, and all of the years of sweat and effort expended on acquiring them will have very little bearing on the outcome of today's mission. Weather willing, he and the other pilots on the flight line this morning will turn over the engines of their bomb-laden, obsolete *Ki*-51 recon/assault planes and fly off into the sunrise to attack a supply convoy spotted heading for the main American landing area at Ormoc on the west coast of Leyte Island. And if all goes well, the fast-closing deck of one of these ships will be the last thing Toshio Yoshitake ever sees.

There is an irony, as in so many things about this miserable war, in Yoshitake's being here today. A whole string of ironies, in fact—broken-down engines, rough landings, rotten weather, overall bad timing, and the fickle rubber stamps of personnel pencil pushers—have linked up in a cause-and-effect chain that has determined that he must die on December 12, 1944, in the closing weeks of a lost campaign, the final year of a lost war. But the original ripples in the fabric of space/time that have resulted in this young man's being here go back much farther than the desk of an administrative officer in Fourth Army Air Force headquarters. The cause-and-effect trail leads back to the ambitions of a successful small business owner in late Meiji-era Japan.

Toshio Yoshitake was born Toshio Yamazaki into a family of traditional plasterers in Yamaguchi, a city on the southwestern tip of the main Japanese island of Honshū. The Yamazakis had been plasterers since at least the late Edo period. Grandfather Yamazaki had built the traditional family business into a thriving local construction firm in the years following the Meiji Restoration. He was a successful, self-made man—a living personification of the new Japanese dream at work. He was also determined that his own children would be the last generation of Yamazakis ever to hold a mortarboard or mix a tub of plaster. When not attending to the demands of his business regimen, he devoted his energies to supervising the education of his grandsons, sparing no expense for tutors and textbooks, even when things got a little tight during the Great Depression.

His efforts paid off in spades. Nearing his dotage, Grandfather Yamazaki could boast of two grandsons who were already field-grade naval officers. Another two grandsons were IMA graduates and career army officers. A fifth grandson, Toshio, was studying to take the IMA test in a year's time to follow in his older brother Takeharu's footsteps and fulfill his dream of being an army pilot.

For a boy growing up in early Shōwa-era Japan, the idea of being an army or navy pilot was better than being a movie star, a baseball player, and the prime minister all rolled up into one. Pilots got to fly around in fast planes and do death-defying stunts. They killed dastardly Bolsheviks and Chinamen and got medals from the emperor and their names in the papers so their parents and teachers could be proud of them. They wore sharp uniforms. They had movies made about them.

Toshio and his classmates had plenty of opportunities to see such movies. Throughout their elementary and middle school days, they had been marched down to the local theater by their teachers on a regular basis to watch films recommended for children's viewing by the Ministry of Education. The films were usually boring "yellow man's burden" harangues about the Japanese race's divinely ordained responsibility to enlighten and administer to the needs of its less fortunate Asian neighbors. These weren't good for much more than sleeping through, provided the teacher did not catch you.

If the films were crackling good combat yarns of the "handsome fighter pilot" genre, though, the whole theater went positively electric. Row after row of black-uniformed schoolboys with shiny pant seats and worn down geta soles would be sitting ramrod straight in their seats, as if their bodies were straining to join in the action on the screen, nodding along in unison with the stern exhortations of the narrator, tight little fists pounding on the armrests during the dogfight scenes, secure in the knowledge that the emperor's young war eagles—and thus Japan itself—were invincible.

All the boys dreamed of flying, but Toshio had an edge up on everyone. He had already flown. Not only had he flown—and he was careful whom he told about this, so as not to make his friends jealous—but he had actually held the control stick when the plane was in flight.

When he was twelve years old, his parents took him to Komagaya Airfield in Osaka, where his older brother Takeharu was stationed as a flight instructor. With the tacit approval of the base commander, Takeharu took his younger brother up in a bright cadmium-orange Akatonbo biplane trainer to buzz the environs and fly a few loop-the-loops and other aerobatic maneuvers over the field, much to his parents' horror. The experience had almost been intense enough for Toshio to require an underwear change after the plane set down, but it was also life-course determining: from that day on, he had his mind set on becoming an army pilot just like his older brother.

Toshio began the long and arduous process of securing an appointment to the IMA when he began the last year of middle school. There would be no opportunities for interviews to ace or influence won with admissions officers as a legacy candidate—everything would be decided by the same grueling battery of physical and academic exams every other applicant would take. The acceptance rate for applicants averaged about 5 percent every year, but Toshio, his grandfather, and his teachers at school had no doubts that he had the right stuff. An entire year would be dedicated to cramming for the admissions exams. Toshio was driven to succeed, and studied with unwavering determination and self-discipline. While his childhood friends frittered away their last year of irresponsible adolescence having fun or apprenticing for dead-end jobs, Toshio hit the books with his eyes on the skies.

In the midst of Toshio's studies, there was a development in his domestic situation that may seem unusual to Western readers, but which was quite normal for a middle-class family in prewar Japan. Some years earlier, Toshio's older sister had married into the Yoshitake household, a family of Buddhist monks who administered a temple in Yamaguchi City. The marriage was childless, so it was a perfectly reasonable request when, in Toshio's eighteenth year and right before his admissions tests for the academy were scheduled to begin, the Yoshitake family formally approached the Yamazakis to ask if they might adopt him as a son. Toshio had no intention of taking up a career in religion, but he would not have to worry about any monastic obligations—the Yoshitakes' childless son would take care of those, for the time being. Rather, the motive behind Toshio's adoption was so he could sire the next generation of Yoshitake heirs who would take over the temple and care for the old folks someday. Toshio would marry after his commissioning in the army, most likely with some girl of the Yoshitakes' choosing, then leave her in the temple compound with his adoptive family and be free to gallivant about the empire pursuing his military career for as long as he wanted. In the meanwhile, he would be expected to come home regularly on furloughs to attend to his child-producing duties.

Although the Yoshitakes were quite wealthy, as Japanese Buddhist monks generally are, life in their temple was austere and quiet. It suited Toshio's purpose at hand—the environment was perfect for the kind of rote-memorization studying he had to do for the IMA entrance exam. In February 1941, the peace and quiet and diligence paid off with a letter of acceptance from the IMA.

Toshio began his studies at the IMA in April 1941. He had an easier transition to the rigors of cadet life than most of his classmates. The time he had spent in the temple during his last months as a civilian prepared him well for the discipline he would need to endure the next three years. Moreover, his patient, sanguine, but not overly sensitive or emotional personality was also well suited for the harsh and often abusive environment at the IMA. His temperament enabled him to duck the blows he could avoid and bend with the blows he could not. He adopted a general policy of lying as low as possible, but when he or another squadmate screwed up and got caught, he took the group beatings his entire squad would be subject to without a whimper or a complaint. Overall, he was a model cadet. Outside of occasional weekend forays off campus with his squadmates to go down by the riverside and drink a little contraband wine from their canteens, he stuck to the straight and narrow. He kept his mind on his studies and off girls. He worked hard.

Three years later, on a bright, sunny spring day in March 1944, Toshio graduated from the IMA as Officer Candidate Yoshitake, assigned to Aviation Reconnaissance. Official commissioning as a second lieutenant would come later, after successful completion of the first portion of Recon Basic with thirty-nine other IMA classmates at Shimoshizu Airfield in Chiba Prefecture, on the eastern edge of the Tokyo megalopolis.

Three days after the start of this training, Yoshitake was introduced to the Mitsubishi *Ki*-51 Type 99 assault plane. The *Ki*-51 was a fixed-landing-gear two-seater design dating from the China conflict and was already woefully obsolete by this stage of the Pacific War. But to Yoshitake and his classmates, its 900-horsepower Mitsubishi Ha-26-II power plant sounded like rolling thunder compared to the 350-horsepower lawn-mower engines that pulled their Akatonbos around in Basic Flight School. The plane's bark, however, was worse than its bite. Like many prewar Japanese designs, the Ki-51's maneuverability was excellent, especially at low altitude and speed, but it was poorly armed and its maximum speed was no match for the American planes it now met in combat. Nevertheless, the plane was relatively easy to fly and forgiving in inexperienced hands.

Training on the Ki-51s at Shimoshizu was administered by a top-notch, combat-experienced faculty with excellent facilities at their disposal. The Marianas debacle had not yet seriously compromised Japan's petroleum supply, so aviation gas was still relatively plentiful. Subsequently, the trainees grabbed every minute of stick time that they could.

Instruction during the initial phase consisted mainly of aerial and ground tactics, signal and communication (both radio and visual), aerial photography, basic meteorology, and leadership. After this orientation period, the trainees were divided up into specialty groups. Yoshitake and fifteen other student pilots were assigned to ground liaison/artillery spotter pilot training. It was a good group—consisting entirely of IMA '44 classmates—and there were no slackers. The training was fulfilling and challenging, but these challenges often exacted a steep cost. During the following months, numerous accidents maimed and killed both students and faculty.

The worst accident occurred on the afternoon of May 27, about two months into the program, when Officer Candidates Tokumaru and Tomo-hisa Okujima collided while circling Kisarazu Field (Chiba Prefecture) in a landing pattern after a training flight was aborted in midmission for bad weather. The bodies of the dead students were returned to Shimoshizu the next day wrapped in silk from their own parachutes, and laid out for a wake in a hangar hung with special black-and-white-striped funerary bunting for the next day's formal funeral ceremony.

The school conducted a well-choreographed service. Retouched and blown-up photos of the deceased framed in black were displayed on an altar surrounded by attractive floral sprays. There were monks and incense and moving speeches by big brass, faculty, and classmates. In the emotional climax of the ceremony, the bereaved parents walked front and center to face the gathering. The fathers had white cloth-covered os-suary boxes hanging from their necks by white cloth straps. The boxes contained the cremated remains of their sons. The mothers were pre-sented with the retouched formal funerary portraits, which both women cradled in their arms. On cue, the group bowed deeply in unison before one of the fathers stepped up to the microphone stand, thanked the school for all it had done in allowing their boys to die honorable deaths in the service of the fatherland, and wished the faculty and student pi-lots the best of luck in combat against the foes of the empire.

A few weeks later, a box of adorable amulet dolls handmade by Okujima's younger sister arrived at the barracks. The dolls were sprin-kled with perfume, and there was one for each of the twelve surviving squadron members. The box contained two additional dolls—one each for Okujima and Tokumaru—with a note requesting that they be carried into battle when the squadron went into action. Yoshitake and the other pilots hung the dolls from the canopy slide latches in the cockpits of their planes.

Yoshitake and his classmates received their coveted *katana* samurai swords and commissions as second lieutenants in a modest ceremony on the morning of July 1. That afternoon they placed their kit bags and their pre-cious *katana* in the storage space behind their cockpit seats and flew their aircraft to nearby Chōshi Army Airfield, where they would spend the next few weeks studying aerial gunnery, horizontal bombing, aerial combat, and nape-of-the-earth flying.

Responsibility for the training of the liaison/spotter squad was handed over to Captain Kunio Takaishi (IMA '41), two senior lieu-tenants, and a sergeant pilot in late July. Takaishi had been on the north-ern China front for several years with the 54th Independent Air Group until the previous spring, when he had come to Shimoshizu for Aviation Recon Flight Leader School. Takaishi and the other instructors were combat-seasoned pilots whose experience and leadership would help guide the trainees through the difficult next phase of their training, which would concentrate on over-water long-range navigation, antisub-marine operations, convoy escort, dive-bombing, and low-level attack techniques. The final phase of the training would be the most hazardous

of all: instruction in recently developed antiship skip-bombing* techniques using a shiplike offshore reef formation as their target.

As the new lieutenants neared completion of Aviation Recon Basic, it
became evident that it was not mere coincidence that they were being
trained almost exclusively for an antishipping combat role. The trainees
became quite proficient in it and began talking among themselves that
perhaps they would not be used in a stale old recon role after all, but
would be flying their Ki-51s—which, after all, were also assault aircraft—
as an elite antishipping force to take on the inevitable American invasion
fleets that would be threatening the inner line of the empire's defenses
in coming months. Yoshitake and his classmates were told in no uncer-
tain terms that they would be sent straight into action as soon as they
finished the course, that their chances for survival were slim, and that
they would most likely be posted to the Philippines, where the Americans were expected to strike next.

The irony of this new mission profile was not lost on Yoshitake and his
classmates. For most of their IMA cadet careers, they had been indoctrinated to view Communism as the greatest threat to the nation. Accordingly, their practical training had concentrated on search-and-destroy
techniques for use against Chinese guerrillas or artillery spotting and
aerial recon for the massive land battles they expected to fight against
the Soviets in Manchuria someday. Even when the army took on extensive commitments in Southeast Asia and the Southwest Pacific with the
outbreak of hostilities with America and Britain, the IMA faculty looked
on this conflict with condescension—almost resentment—referring to it
as a "southern" or "oceangoing" matter that was better left to the navy
(who had started it, after all) while the army faced down the real threat
to the empire that lay in wait to the west and north.

---

*Skip-bombing was pioneered by U.S. Army Air Force units such as the 345th BG "Air
Apaches" in the Southwest Pacific in the early stages of the war as an effective—and extremely
hazardous to the attacker—method of attacking weakly armored merchant and transport shipping. An expedient tactic for fliers lacking extensive training in naval warfare (e.g., unable to
dive-bomb moving targets accurately), the technique involved flying at wave-top altitude and
using a standard high-explosive bomb like an above-water torpedo. Dropped close enough to
ensure a hit but hopefully far enough away to give the plane a chance to zoom away safely before detonation, the bomb would skip over the water like a flat pebble to bound into the side of
the target vessel and explode.

But like almost everything else the Japanese army had assumed or taken for granted in 1941, all of that thinking had been turned on its ear by 1944. Yoshitake and his classmates were going to be fighting Americans in a few more weeks—not raiding Chinese guerrilla camps or calling in artillery on Soviet armored divisions. Times had changed, and as usual, the army brass was far behind them and resenting being told to catch up.

# eight

## THE LIGHTS OF TALISAY

After a late October graduation furlough to say farewell—
perhaps for the last time—to loved ones in Yamaguchi,
Yoshitake returned to Chōshi, where he and his classmates were formally organized into an outfit designated Hakkō Unit 6*
under the command of Captain Takaishi. The other instructors on his
staff would stay on as regular pilots, with one of them, First Lieutenant
Yoshio Hosoda, doubling as unit XO. Hakkō Unit 6 would be deployed
immediately on "special assignment" to take part in the Leyte campaign,
which had opened up while Yoshitake and his classmates were home
on leave. No one in the new unit was exactly sure what "special assignment" meant. While some of the more pessimistically oriented pilots
surmised that it might be something along the lines of the navy suicide
attacks at Leyte that had been making such a big media splash of late,
Yoshitake and most of the other pilots guessed that the designation
could mean only that they were going to be an elite squadron of skip-
bombers after all.

In a briefing on the afternoon of November 5, the pilots of Hakkō
Unit 6 found out that the pessimists had been right. They were to be
posted to the Philippines with all possible haste for assignment to Lieutenant General Kyōji Tominaga's Fourth Air Army as *tokkō* raiders. On

---

*The *Hakkō* of the unit name refers to the first half of the "Japanese manifest destiny" *hakkō*
*ichiu* slogan.

the morn, twelve of the eighteen pilots, Yoshitake included, would go to Tachikawa Arsenal in western Tokyo to take possession of twelve brand new *Ki-51*s with a special new *tokkō* modification enabling the planes to carry 500 kg bombs (twice the *Ki-51*'s maximum safe bomb load). The group would then fly back to Chōshi, wait for the remaining six squadron mates to bring in their new planes, then depart for Pollack Airfield near Manila as soon as the flight orders came in.

The pilots of Hakkō Unit 6 spent the next two evenings in rowdy send-off parties, the first of these hosted by the Chōshi base commander, Brigadier General Takeshi Hattori. The second party was held the following night at the pilots' favorite off-post entertainment spot, the Itōya Inn. Special guests of honor were the mobilized local high school* girls who worked as grease monkeys in the Chōshi engine repair shops. Rounding off the guest list were several geisha, compliments of the house, who entertained the party with songs and dancing late into the night. The female guests were fully aware of what awaited their dashing young hosts in coming days or weeks, and as the festivities began to wind down, a contagious round of quiet sobbing began to work its way among the schoolgirls. One of the geisha barked at the girls to shut up, remarking that it was bad luck to end a party with tears. The tatami-matted banquet room fell into an uncomfortable silence.

Second Lieutenant Masamitsu Kataoka, an older classmate who had entered the IMA from the regular army as a prior service cadet, assessed the situation expertly and moved quickly to save the party from ending in disaster. Tying a towel around his head, he started a round of clapping in a traditional festival rhythm and waited for the others to join in before jumping up to do the comical *dojō sukui*† dance that was popular in Japan at the time. This got everyone laughing, and the party broke up on a cheerful note after Captain Takaishi was presented with a *yosegaki* placard signed

---

*Under the old Japanese educational system, a "high school" was equivalent to a junior college today. Students would have been from eighteen to twenty years old.

†"The Loach Scooper" dance: the loach is an evolutionarily quirky fish/lizard/eel-like creature that lives in the soil of tidal mudflats in many areas of Japan, propelling itself through the muck using its fins like legs. Not exactly a culinary delight of haute cuisine, the loach nonetheless provided an important and free source of protein in rural Japan until the modern era. The Loach Scooper dance is supposed to pantomime the futile efforts of a hapless *hyottoko* bumpkin clown trying to chase his dinner down in slippery muck.

by all the girls and decorated with now-common propaganda kanji idioms like *go'chin* ("screaming dive sinking") or *nikudan-hittchū* ("human bomb-shell never miss") beautifully penned in the girls' dainty calligraphy.

Early on the morning of November 8, the mildly hungover pilots of Hakkō Unit 6 left Chōshi in their brand-new *Ki-51*s for what was supposed to have been a two-day flight to Manila with rest and refueling stops on the way at Chiran Airfield in Kyūshū and Daitō Airfield in Taiwan. The first engine failure happened mere minutes after takeoff from Chōshi, and it only got worse from there. Two days stretched into nine and as many emergency stops before the last *Ki-51* sputtered into Pollack on November 17.

After a day of rest and aircraft maintenance, the pilots were invited to visit Fourth Air Army headquarters in Manila on the morning of the nineteenth for a special presentation from Lieutenant General Tominaga.* An open bay truck with armed sentries was provided for the trip to HQ. Yoshitake and his squadron mates were instructed to ride with their service pistols drawn and their eyes on the trees and shacks they passed. Several burned-out Japanese army vehicles along the sides of the roads leading to town showed what happened to those who failed to take the local guerrilla problem seriously.

*Welcome to exotic Luzon.*

On the ride in, explosions could be heard to the north in the direction of the Clark Airfield complex. A few moments later, columns of oily black appeared over the horizon. Pollack, of course, was in the same neighborhood, but it was a minor auxiliary base. The Americans would probably leave it alone. Everyone agreed that the smoke had to be coming from the Clark area bases.

When the pilots arrived at the venue, they were escorted directly to the general's office, where a media ambush lay in wait. As a pushy platoon of Army News Service and civilian Nichiei cameramen popped flashbulbs and shouted questions at the blinking, bewildered young men, Tominaga presented Captain Takaishi with a handwritten certificate penned in the

---

*Later publicly humiliated after abandoning his post and fleeing to Taiwan as the Americans closed in at the end of the Philippines campaign. His orders had been to stay and fight to the death. He survived the war. Hundreds of young army pilots he ordered on *tokkō* missions in the Philippines, however, did not.

general's own calligraphy announcing that Hakkō Unit 6 had been officially christened Sekichō Unit. The name, taken from the classical kanji idiom "steel heart stone bowel" (*"Tesshin Sekichō"*), dated from the days of the ancient Chinese philosopher Mencius, and was chosen to evoke the stalwart resolve and sturdy constitution of brave souls.

After the presentation, the general made the rounds with the pilots for photo ops before shooing out his guests with hearty backslaps and "Live up to your name, boys" comments loud enough for the reporters to catch. With their eyes still flashing purple from the press conference, the pilots were hustled out of the HQ and cut loose on the town for a nine-hour furlough. Downtown Manila itself was relatively guerrilla-free, but abductions and assassinations of Japanese personnel were not unknown. They were told not to wander off alone, to avoid unlicensed entertainment establishments, and to report back to HQ by 1900 for a reception with Lieutenant General Tominaga.

The party that evening was an eerily beautiful affair held in the courtyard of the Hiromatsu, an R & R establishment near 4AF HQ for high-ranking Japanese personnel either stationed in or passing through Manila. Great effort had been put into simulating the effect of a real Japanese inn here for the sake of homesick patrons. Outside of the scullery maids in the kitchen and other menial types, the restaurant was staffed entirely by Japanese girls, a swanky rarity in a colonial "comfort facility." Many of the rooms had tatami matting and sliding paper shoji doors. The wood-planked flooring of the corridors was well polished. Red paper lanterns were strung along the walls, casting a warm glow over the guests and the plates of sumptuous banquet fare as the sake flowed freely and laughter echoed into the night. Fireflies lit up the foliage ringing the courtyard like Christmas trees, adding to the festive atmosphere.

The next morning, after a pleasant stay in the best guest rooms at the nearby Air Corps Officers' Club, the pilots boarded the transport truck for the ride back to Pollack. When they arrived at the field, they found cleanup crews sorting out wreckage and filling in runway craters. The smoke and explosions they had seen and heard coming from the direction of Clark the day before had in fact been coming from here. Eight of the *Ki*-51s they had worked so hard to bring all the way down from Chōshi were now smoldering heaps, and another three were badly shot up, although not beyond repair.

The twentieth and most of the twenty-first were spent piecing together whatever could be salvaged from the wrecks and overseeing the repair of the damaged aircraft. On the afternoon of the twenty-first, Captain Takaishi was summoned back to 4AF HQ for an urgent meeting with Lieutenant General Tominaga. The other pilots had a pretty good idea of what this meant. The loss of the planes obviously derailed any plans to muster the Sekichō Unit in toto for a group mission in the immediate future, but repair work around the clock had gotten four of the machines back on line, ready to go. Things were beginning to accelerate now, and after all the hoopla in Manila, folks at the top would want to hear of big things from the Sekichō Unit while the media buzz was still strong. The army brass could not very well just sit around twiddling their thumbs waiting for new planes and whining about equipment problems while the navy grabbed all the headlines coming out of the Philippines, electrifying the home front with accounts of stirring self-sacrifice. The army was overdue for some favorable press.

That evening, Takaishi arrived back at Pollack long-faced and notably apprehensive. He called a meeting with his pilots in the billets, where he recounted details of the afternoon's meeting with the general. The young captain made the astonishing revelation that he had actually petitioned Tominaga for permission to let the Sekichō Unit contribute to the war effort in the skip-bombing role its pilots had been trained for instead of squandering them on one-time-only *tokkō* missions. The general— apparently still on a roll after the favorable press conference of the nineteenth—took offense at this request, denying it with the retort that it would not reflect well on the "spirit of *tokkō*" in the eyes of the service or the Japanese public for the Sekichō Unit's mission to be changed now that the story had been carried in the press back home. Takaishi told everyone that there was nothing to do except swallow their pride and follow their orders like good soldiers. He vowed to set the example by piloting the first plane into the target when they finally flew their mission.

In the meantime, there were flight orders for the next morning; Takaishi would lead Lieutenants Okagami, Ichihara, and Yoshitake in the squadron's four functioning aircraft and head for Bacolod Airfield on Negros Island for forward deployment. Negros was on the western edge of the Leyte main area of operations, so attack orders could come at any time. XO Hosoda would bring the rest of the squadron down to Bacolod as soon as the replacement planes arrived, but there was no guarantee that this would be soon enough for Sekichō Unit to all fly out together when X-Day finally arrived. The possibility of the unit being parceled out piecemeal on three- and four-plane *tokkō* missions was a heartbreaking scenario for the pilots, but as Takaishi reminded them, complaining about this was not a luxury afforded them by present circumstances.

About twenty minutes out of Pollack the next morning, the flight ran into bad weather and radioed for an emergency landing at a minor army airstrip near the town of Lipa in the southern suburbs of Manila. Yoshitake had been feeling a bit under the weather ever since waking up that morning. As he came into the landing pattern, his condition worsened so quickly and severely that he could barely move his arms or legs anymore. His head spun and he felt nauseated, but somehow he brought the *Ki*-51 down safely. By the time his wheels rolled to a stop on the runway grass, he was so weak and disoriented that he could not even unbuckle his seat straps. A ground crew helped him from his cockpit and took him to the base hospital shack, where he was diagnosed with dengue fever. If the illness had kicked in even a few minutes earlier, while the flight was still in the air, he probably would have crashed his plane upon attempting to land. As things stood, he was not in a condition to attempt very much of anything right now. He went flat on his back for the next few days, and watched from a cot in the Lipa hospital shack when Takaishi and the others took off for Bacolod without him after the weather cleared on the twenty-fifth.

Yoshitake was on his feet by the next day, and hitched a flight back to Pollack, where he was surprised to find Takaishi, Okagami, and Ichihara back with the others. Army Air Command in the Leyte area had determined that the army's 500 kg bombs, which had been designed for maximum antipersonnel fragmentation in land-based tactical situations, were not suited for antishipping use. From now on, all army *tokkō* aircraft would be armed with navy bombs designed specifically to explode after penetrating ship decks. The only problem, though, was that the army planes' bomb racks were not compatible with navy ordnance—not only antishipping bombs, but *any* navy ordnance—even general purpose high-explosive fragmentation weapons. This was a vivid illustration not only of the lack of standardization in Japan's war machine but also symbolic of the simmering eighty-year-old army-navy rivalry that had been such a hindrance to Japan's military efforts in every conflict it had fought since the Meiji era. The significance of these ordnance technicalities for the Sekichō Unit, in practical terms, was that there would be more downtime until the Pollack mechanics could jury-rig release mechanisms capable of handling the navy bombs.

Enough replacement *Ki*-51s arrived from Japan over the next few days for Takaishi to have eight planes on the flight line for a rousing send-off to Bacolod on the morning of December 3. Yoshitake rode in the backseat of Second Lieutenant Takao Ōi's aircraft, and was dropped off at Lipa to pick up his plane while the others flew on to their destination. Yoshitake was happy to find his *Ki*-51 still in one piece, but unfortunately, something had happened during the past ten days to throw the engine out of whack. Ōi flew on alone to Bacolod while Yoshitake waited at Lipa, once again dependent on the kindness of strangers to get his engine up and running.

Lipa mechanics spent the morning and early afternoon of December 4 running checks on the new Mitsubishi Ha-26-II engine they had installed in Yoshitake's plane in lieu of doing a time-consuming and possibly useless repair job on the original power plant. With the new engine given as good a check as time allowed, the plane's fuel tanks were topped off and a 500 kg naval bomb was slung under its belly for the 430-kilometer run down to Bacolod. Maintaining a decent cruising speed and barring more mechanical failure, the flight would take about ninety minutes. Aside from one slight heading adjustment over Mindoro Island to keep him over land a little longer, navigation would be a matter of maintaining heading and flying in a straight line.

Not that the flight would be a milk run—Yoshitake would be flying the whole ninety minutes unescorted and alone in a plane that would not last sixty seconds in a dogfight. Moreover, most of the trip would be made at dusk, with the last leg well after nightfall. Making matters worse, it looked like there was some weather moving in from the southwest, so there would be no room for navigation errors or distractions on the way down.

Iffy engine, lousy visibility, and lack of escort notwithstanding, there was no way he was going to miss this flight. It was imperative that he join up with the other Sekichō Unit members by evening. By now they were already set up in their forward combat staging area, so there was a distinct possibility that they would be going into action the following morning.

He had not come this far to meet death with strangers—and certainly not alone. The Lipa people had understood and respected that and gone out of their way to accommodate his wishes. He was thankful for their help, especially for the efforts of the mechanics, who had worked through the night without sleep to get his new engine up and running so he could make it to Bacolod in time to sortie with his comrades.

After a modest send-off by the Lipa base commander and some staff officers, Yoshitake received takeoff clearance at around 1600. He made the customary counterclockwise circuit of the field to gain some altitude and gave a final wing waggle to his hosts as he picked up a south-southeast heading, flying away into a cobalt-blue late-afternoon sky with the sun already low over the tree line on the west end of the field. In a few minutes he was out over water, alone, and feeling every second of it.

About fifteen minutes into the flight, just off the north coast of Mindoro, Yoshitake caught metallic glints sparkling in the upper right corner of his peripheral vision. He squinted for a better look and swallowed hard when he made out the distinctive twin tail booms of four American P-38 Lightnings, their unpainted aluminum finish a brash challenge to all comers, all silver and molten gold in the late-afternoon sun. Flying overhead in the opposite direction in a loose finger-four tactical formation, the land-based American army fighters had at least a thousand-meter altitude advantage. If they wanted him, they had him cold. Any one of the cannon-armed Lightnings could split-S, come up from behind with overwhelming speed, and chew the Ki-51 to pieces in a single pass. He wrestled with these unpleasant thoughts for an eternal minute or two of white-knuckled nerves until the P-38s faded away in the upper rear Plexiglas panels of his canopy.

He gave a long sigh of relief and wondered who or what—other than the amulet doll hanging from his canopy release bar—was to thank for sparing his life. Perhaps the Americans had not noticed his army-green camouflaged plane flying below their formation. Maybe they had merely passed him over as small fry not worth breaking up the mission timetable for. But in either case, he was damned lucky to fly away from the encounter with nothing worse than a good war story, a slightly damp flight suit, and a mild case of the shakes to show for it.

The Ki-51 soldiered on for a mercifully uneventful three-hundred-kilometer leg before hitting heavy cloud cover over Panay Island just as nightfall set in. Yoshitake had plenty of experience flying in low-visibility conditions, so it was no big deal at first, but things went south fast. Within a few minutes, a misty rain had cut visibility to zero.

Shortly after entering basic flight training, Yoshitake had learned about vertigo, that most lethal of mind games that can afflict a pilot on the stick. He was taught that low-visibility conditions encountered while flying at night and/or socked in by weather, especially when compounded by turbulence, were most likely to bring on an "episode." Even the most experienced flier was susceptible to vertigo—defined here as the basic and normally inalienable ability to distinguish up from down. If this happened and you panicked, it was only a matter of time—and not much time, at that—before your plane rolled, went into a dive, and finally augered into the ground.

These were not reassuring thoughts to be having just now, and Yoshitake groped for happier ones to hold back a kernel of panic he felt forming in his stomach—still manageable but there nonetheless—all too aware that if he lost control, he'd be lizard food before he knew what hit him, spread with the wreckage of his plane over a few hundred meters of triple-canopy jungle.

He had three options here: He could maintain present altitude and just try to fly straight and level. This would probably be the safest bet, but the chance of getting a little visibility warranted weighing alternatives. Another option would be to try to climb up and over the clouds—but there was no telling what all of this rainwater was doing to the engine, which was already getting stingy on rpms and was grossly overworked by having to pull the damned naval bomb around all afternoon. A stall right now would be fatal, so a power-draining climb was out. The engine would have to be nursed all the way to Negros.

The last option would be to drop altitude and try to get under the cloud cover. This would not help with the rain, obviously, but at least it would give him an outside chance of being able to see something on the ground—perhaps lights from a town—that he could use to guide him on his way. Then again, of course, there were dangers involved with this option, too. As he had no idea how far down cloud cover went, there was no knowing whether or not there would be an unwelcome piece of vertical terra firma—namely, a mountainside—waiting to greet him as soon as he managed to poke out of this pea soup. He could, of course, check the charts for mountain heights, then set a reasonable lower-altitude limit with enough clearance to fly over anything that might be in the way, but he really did not want to lose altitude right now. He was still too far away from Negros to go hill-slaloming in an overloaded *Ki*-51 with an undependable engine.

He finally opted, with some misgivings, to keep flying straight as long as he could, relying on his aviator's watch, airspeed indicator, compass, and map to tell him when he would be over water and it would be safe to try to duck under and out of the cloud cover. All that was left to do now was to keep his fear in check, rely on his instruments, and pray like hell that his fuel would hold out. Under perfect conditions, the *Ki*-51 had a range of about a thousand kilometers—twice the distance of tonight's flight—but there was no telling what the weather, headwinds, and, of course, the abnormal bomb loadout were doing to the engine's fuel-consumption rate.

Yoshitake checked his heading, watch, and map once more before gently pushing forward on the stick.

As the plane dropped out of the fog, perfectly flat slate-gray horizons fading to black appeared in all directions. He was over water, headed south-southeast. Negros Island would be coming up in a few minutes. The sooner the better, because the weather had taken a decided turn for the worse. The rain was now a torrential downpour that was battering the plane like hail on a tin roof, raindrop splashes turning the canopy into a shroud of colorless kaleidoscope glass. Visibility was nearly obliterated, almost as badly as before. The overloaded plane's center of gravity was all over the place, yawing the airframe this way and that. Trying to fly through this junk was like being blindfolded with surgical gauze and shooting whitewater rapids on a grand piano.

Crossing the Negros coast at low altitude, Yoshitake kept his eyes peeled for anything that even remotely resembled a landing strip. He headed for some flickering lamplights he could just make out through the driving rain and found himself over an airfield that looked more like a small lake than a runway. The lamps were arranged in the code symbol for "landing impossible." Another row of lights just below these formed an arrowhead shape pointing northeast. Yoshitake took the suggested heading and was over another field in less than two minutes. The lamps here ordered him to "land with caution," and more lights roughly marked the edges of a grass-and-dirt airstrip only slightly less soggy than the first one.

There was no way he was going to try to land in a swamp with this 500 kg bomb strapped to his belly. He circled around to find a spot to ditch the bomb and ended up dumping it, fuse unarmed, into a copse of trees at the far end of the field.

*Crap! All this way and all this trouble for nothing!*

He pulled the *Ki*-51 around into a landing pattern and lined up between the rows of runway lamps to bring her in. He dropped his landing flaps, eased forward on the stick to bring the plane into a proper glide path, and prayed, cutting the engine and pulling back on the stick to "flare" to near-stalling speed at the last moment before touchdown. The wheels hit the ground hard and the plane was instantly swamped in muddy brown water that went all the way up and over the canopy and even into the cockpit. A ground crew ran over to help the drenched Yoshitake out of the cockpit when the plane rolled to a stop. He was informed that he had landed at Talisay Airfield, five kilometers northeast of Bacolod. He was at the wrong airstrip.

Leaving his plane with the ground crew, he slung his kit bag and *katana* over his shoulder and reported to the base HQ officer in charge. *"Konna tenki de, shikata ga nai, ne,"* the officer said with a shrug. Getting caught in this weather was nobody's fault. The officer made the necessary entry about the bomb loss in the base logbook, then handed off the soggy second lieutenant to an orderly.

Yoshitake hopped a shuttle truck leaving for the main Bacolod area officers' billets, which were located in an old mansion in the town of Talisay. When he arrived, he found his squadron mates already there at a party in the mess hall hosted by the commander of the Second Air Division, Lieutenant General Sai'ichi Terada. Joining the gathering, Yoshitake had to endure some good-natured ribbing about his seemingly never-ending engine woes, but he was delighted and relieved to be with his comrades again, and they were happy to see him, too. Two more stragglers—Itō and Itoi—were due down from Pollack in the next day or two. When they arrived, the Sekichō Unit would be together again, at last. Hopefully, the brass would wait long enough for that to happen before cutting attack orders. It did not take long, however, for Yoshitake to find out that this was not going to be the case. There was a reason for the party, and a reason why the Sekichō Unit members were the guests of honor—they were going out on their mission tomorrow morning.

The party was joined by four lost-lamb stragglers from the Ichi'u Unit on engine-repair layover at Talisay and a semicelebrity guest, Corporal Yūji Sasaki,* who had been pulled from a shot-down bomber wreck as the sole survivor of the Banda Unit's disastrous first and last mission on November 12.[1] Now languishing in personnel paperwork limbo for reassignment to a new unit, the haunted young man sent with his body language a clear "leave me alone" message that his fellow guests, with few exceptions, were none too put out to accommodate.

With the notable exception of the taciturn corporal, who hardly said two words the entire evening, hosts and guests alike seemed to be in high spirits. There was plenty of sake, laughter, and the obligatory hometown culinary travelogues of which the Japanese are so enamored. Discussion of family, however, was strictly verboten, as was any intellectually weighty, overly sentimental, or sexual topic. Fallen comrades could be recalled fondly and mourned in passing during conversation, but there was no rumination over mortality itself or regrets expressed by the pilots over their own unnaturally accelerated and imminent demise. If the death that awaited most of the present guests within the next few hours or days was preying on anyone's mind, these concerns never saw air. Corporal Sasaki aside, everyone was careful to maintain a fairly convincing simulation of gaiety. A passing observer would have to be forgiven for mistakenly thinking that this was a festive celebration of some sort instead of the last supper of doomed young men.

The party broke up around midnight on an upbeat note. Laughter and slurred, off-key army songs echoed along the hallways of the old mansion as guests filed back to their rooms for a night that, for most of them, would feel interminable but would still be over far too soon.

---

*Fraternization between commissioned and noncom pilots in off-duty social situations was already a semiofficially recognized custom in *tokkō* units by this time, even in the rigidly stratified army, although in most cases keeping a subtle separation between the two groups.

**n i n e**

## ATTACK ORDERS

Yoshitake and his somewhat groggy squadron mates were awakened before dawn by orderlies with urgent news: Recon planes had spotted a large American supply convoy threading Surigao Strait and heading northwest, most likely for Ormoc. All Sekichō Unit personnel were to report to Bacolod ASAP for takeoff within the hour.

After gathering their gear, Captain Takaishi and the others boarded transport to the airstrip while Yoshitake phoned Talisay Field from the orderly desk and asked about the condition of his plane, which he planned to take for a hop flight to Bacolod in time to fly the mission with his comrades. The mechanic on the other end of the line broke the news to the young lieutenant as respectfully and gently as possible. Muddy water from last night's rough landing had completely fouled the engine and it would take several days to repair the damage. Yoshitake would not be going on the *tokkō* mission today. Numb with shock, his mind flashed back to Sasaki from the party last night; like that sad corporal, he would now have to spend some unspecified period of purgatory in a billet somewhere—probably this one—with the faces of his dead friends haunting his dreams. And in the end, he would die with strangers.

The tears fell bitter and hot as he hung up the phone. He did not even try to hide them from the orderly.

Yoshitake changed out of his flight suit and hitched a ride on the next truck to Bacolod. He arrived at the airfield just in time to find the other eight Sekichō Unit members, resplendent in full flight gear and Rising Sun *hachimaki* headbands, lining up at a long, white cloth-covered table in preparation for a sake toast with Lieutenant General Terada. A large and reverent audience of staff officers and enlisted ground crew had gathered to watch the proceedings. Many of the men held small Rising Sun flags. Several rear-echelon field-grade types strutted about with their hands clasped behind their backs, trying to appear important and involved. The whole event was being photographed by a Nichiei camera-man who walked around the venue taking shots from different angles. The pilots were asked to hold a pose with their glasses raised for a toast. For several more shots, they were asked to stand closer together and smile for the camera.

Yoshitake witnessed the proceedings in the grip of an emotional funk that was equal parts grief, disappointment, admiration, and envy. Tears came for the second time that morning as the Sekichō Unit boys filed past Terada for firm handshakes before trotting off to their planes. Nearly everyone else present was weeping, too.

Ōi, one of the last pilots on the handshake line, picked out Yoshitake in the crowd and ran over to him. Slapping Yoshitake on the shoulder, he pulled a small bottle of whiskey out of a flight suit pocket, took a slug, then put it to his friend's lips.

"I'm going to go on ahead of you, Yoshitake," he said, tears running down cheeks creased with a beaming smile bizarrely out of place on his normally stoic face. "And I'm going to put on a real show. Just you see. Don't be too late, okay?"

Yoshitake tried to speak, but could not. All he could manage was a nod. Ōi grinned back in response, his blood up and his face glowing with it. He drained the last of the whiskey in a long pull and smashed the empty bottle on the ground with a dramatic flourish before turning his back on the living and running off to join the soon-to-be-dead in their *Ki*-51s.

Engine ignitions fired sporadically and, one by one, the planes coughed to life on the flight line with thick puffs of black exhaust. Cries of *Banzai, Ganbatte* ("Do your best!"), and *Tanonda-zo* ("We're counting on you!") rose from the onlookers, who moved forward in a collective surge as the planes began to taxi for takeoff. Some well-wishers waved their caps or small Rising Sun flags. Others stood with their arms frozen over their heads in the banzai gesture, like sideline referees or cheerleaders in some sporting event. Yoshitake stripped off his uniform jacket and waved it over his head, screaming the names of his comrades as Mitsubishi engines roared into overboost for the takeoff run and the planes Doppler-shifted down the grass strip to rise up into the fragrant morning air.

As if lingering for an encore, the flight made several circuits over the throng of teary-eyed onlookers, tightening up the formation and corkscrewing for altitude to clear the saddle between Mandalagan and Silay to the northeast. When the last plane caught up, the flight straightened out into a file and flew away, the harmonic drone of eight Mitsubishis at full throttle fading out with a melancholy echo as the planes got smaller and smaller against a pastel-orange sunrise. Yoshitake kept shouting and waving until the airplanes disappeared over the horizon. As his jacket fell to his side in the deafening silence, he was overcome by the most profound loneliness he had ever experienced.

Temporarily without orders or assignment, he was free to go back to the officers' billets in town. After another call to Talisay to check up on his plane ("Nothing to report yet, Lieutenant. You just called an hour ago."), he made a beeline for his bunk to pull the blanket over his head and hide himself away until he felt like dealing with people again. He was not sure how long that would be, but he had four or five more hours until he would be expected to show up for afternoon mess, so he had at least that long to wrestle with his demons and grieve in relative solitude.

Half an hour into his long morning's journey into afternoon, he heard footsteps in the hallway stop by the door.

"Yah," a silhouette in the doorway said before entering the room.

Hearing a voice he had no business hearing, Yoshitake sat up like a shot as the hairs on the back of his neck went rigid. Blinking in disbelief, he realized that he was looking at his squadron mate Mitrugu Adachi, who had just taken off from Bacolod this morning, less than an hour ago.

*Impossible!* Adachi was dead—or at least supposed to be.

But here he was, in the flesh.

"Bet you didn't think you'd be seeing me so soon, eh?" Adachi said, his matinee-idol face twisted into a sardonic sneer. He threw his gear down in a heap and sat down on a bunk with his lowered head in his hands.

Yoshitake looked at the slumped figure before him with a mixture of joy at seeing his comrade again, pity because he knew exactly what the man was feeling right now, and relief because Adachi's unscheduled return meant that there would be a fellow Sekichō Unit buddy to pass this time in *tokkō* purgatory with. Yoshitake felt a bit ashamed of this last sentiment, but nevertheless, knowing that he was not going to be alone at the end was like feeling a ray of warm sunshine after weeks in cold gloom.

"Engine?" Yoshitake asked.

Adachi nodded, still avoiding eye contact.

"Don't worry about it," Yoshitake continued. "We'll make it next time."

The squadron mates stretched out on their cots and spent the rest of the morning reminiscing about better times. Combat reports of the morning's mission came in later in the day, but information about results was spotty. The escorts may have seen some transport ships hit, but they could not be sure. The only matter that could be confirmed was that Captain Takaishi and the others who had flown all the way to the targets were now gone forever.

Yoshitake and Adachi spent most of the next four days standing around and waiting for their engines to be fixed. They lent a hand when they could, but mostly they just spent their time talking, racked out on their bunks or running engine checks whenever the repair shop called with promising reports. Adachi's engine ran well, but Yoshitake was not happy with the condition of his own. It was spitting out more smoke that it should—even with Marianas gas—and was low on rpms and manifold pressure. Of course, the mud from that hard rainy-night landing was to blame. Yoshitake mentally kicked himself every time he heard its wheezing ignition system groan through another start-up test.

With crossed fingers, Yoshitake ferried the plane over to Bacolod on the afternoon of the seventh, trailing an intermittent stream of black smoke most of the way.

Itō and Itōi flew in from Pollack that evening, briefly bringing the Sekichō Unit contingent at Bacolod up to four members. The reunion was a welcome respite from the tedium of the previous seventy-two hours, but it would prove to be short-lived. Itō was ordered out on a solo *tokkō* mission the very next morning with no explanation and was never seen again.

Late typhoon-season torrential rain moved in early the next morning and fell virtually nonstop for the next seventy-two hours, completely shutting down all flight operations at Bacolod. While the precipitation certainly did not help with anyone's boredom issues, it was not entirely unwelcome. If the Japanese could not fly, it meant the Americans could not, either. Work on Yoshitake's engine could continue apace.

An orderly came around to the junior officers' rooms after mess on the evening of the eleventh. Orders had just come in from Bacolod: More American convoys were expected to be headed for Ormoc in the morning, and a *tokkō* mission would be thrown together and sent up, weather allowing, the moment anything was sighted. Yoshitake, Adachi, and Itōi from Sekichō Unit and two *Ki*-43 Hayabusa* fighter pilots, one each from Hakkō and Enshin units, respectively, were to report to Bacolod Flight Ops at 0600 as flight line standby pilots. A truck would be waiting in front of the billets at 0530 to take them to the airfield.

The Sekichō Unit pilots spent the rest of the evening talking and sharing a little sake before turning in around midnight. The rice wine did not help Yoshitake get much better than a miserable hour or two worth of restless sleep interspersed with visions of home, nocturnal visitations from dead men, and anxious glances at the glowing dial of his aviator's watch as the final hours of his life slipped away. Creaks throughout the night from the other pilots' cots told him that he was not the only insomniac in the room.

Yoshitake is groggy but tense on the shuttle truck to Bacolod this morning. The faces of the other passengers are drawn and tight in the blue-gray light, their eyes bloodshot. No words are exchanged on the way to the field.

The downpour of the past three days has tapered off to a light drizzle by the time the truck pulls up in front of the flight ops shack. Visibility is still lousy, but the horizon is going orange in the east and the dark blue ridges of Panay are emerging from the morning mist across the Guimaras

---

*The Nakajima Hayabusa was the IJA's mainstay fighter for most of the war, largely replaced in the last year of the conflict by the vastly superior Nakajima *Ki*-84 Hayate. See Bueschel (1997), Sakaida (1997), and Nohara and Mochizuki (2000).

Strait. The field is by no means socked in. When the sun comes up in another hour or so, it will no doubt burn the clouds away. After that, there is bound to be a mission.

Yoshitake is surprised to find that he feels relieved by this prospect. He is too heartbroken to fear death anymore. Most of his friends are dead, Japan has as good as lost the war, and he is sick and tired of being sick and tired about that. Death will be a release to be welcomed, not a mortal end to be dreaded. And if by dying like this he will be able to take down a few hundred of the enemies who have humiliated his country, then all the better. If he feels any fear or nerves right now, it is only a fear of failure, of letting down his comrades, or of having to return to base in shame again for some stupid reason or another, like engine problems or a fuel leak. That is just not an option this time. He'll ditch in the sea and ride his plane down to a watery grave before going back to those lousy billets alone again.

An officer is waiting on the porch of the operations shack as the pilots hop off the shuttle truck. Recon planes have spotted another American convoy heading for Ormoc. Assuming a takeoff time of 0700, the convoy can be intercepted in the Camotes Sea after threading the Canigao Channel. A mission will be on as soon as the weather clears, and corrected headings for the mission will be provided at that time. The pilots are ordered to aim for large troop ships to maximize American casualties. Warships—trickier targets—are to be left for the navy planes to deal with.

There is a short send-off speech and a subdued sake toast in the drizzle with Lieutenant General Terada (which the army public affairs officers and Nichiei folks obviously do not consider enough of a photo op to show up for), after which the pilots file off to their standby area under a row of palm trees by the flight line. The planes have already been gassed up and loaded out. There is nothing to do now but wait for the order to go.

The pilots take advantage of the downtime to be alone with their thoughts. The drizzle sizzles through the palm fronds. Bugs sing in the trees and grass. Yoshitake is struck by the feeling of being pinned like a collector's butterfly to this surreal and frozen Zen moment while time races on tirelessly toward conclusions everywhere but here. He shrugs off a weird déjà vu sensation, writing it off to nerves and fatigue. His thoughts turn to loved ones.

The somber flight line reverie is snapped when the attack order comes down from the flight ops shack a little before seven: takeoff immediately, assume heading of 095 to avoid lingering cloud cover over Cebu, then 085 until the American convoy is spotted. Just follow the headings and you will not miss the target, they are told. The Camotes Sea is so full of American ships this morning you can walk across to Leyte without getting your feet wet.

The pilots jog the short distance to their planes. Ground crews already have the engines warmed up and running. Yoshitake is amazed by the serendipity that the officer in charge of the flight line is Lieutenant Masuda, an old squadmate from academy days. There is a handshake and a brief conversational exchange over the engine noise, but neither schedule nor circumstances allow for any more than that. The men exchange a salute and shoulder slaps before Yoshitake climbs into the cockpit of his plane and guns the engine. Black smoke belches from the exhaust pipes.

Masuda jumps up on the wing of Yoshitake's plane and pops his head in the cockpit.

"Everything okay? You sure you can take this up today?"

"Okay. Ready to go," Yoshitake answers, after a barely perceptible delay. He is lying. The engine is low on rpms and giving only about 80 percent power. There is a lot of bomb under the plane and not nearly enough runway or engine power to get it up into the air, but he is not about to punk out behind a bad engine again. There have been enough send-off speeches and forced smiles for the benefit of farewell-party guests. Today is the day, and that's that.

Masuda understands without having to be told anything more, gives his old roommate a final slap on the shoulder, and hops off the plane to pull the chocks away.

Itōi, as the ranking pilot here, is in the lead of the planes taxiing for the runway. He goes into max revs and his Ki-51 seems to take forever to get off the ground. He just clears the trees at the end of the runway as Yoshitake, with a prayer on his lips, pulls a red knob on the instrument panel of his own plane to put the engine into emergency overboost.

The engine wheezes and coughs. The plane begins to roll over the bumpy, muddy ground, but not nearly quickly enough. A hundred meters of runway go by. Two hundred. The airspeed needle creeps across the indicator dial while the trees at the far end of the field get big way too quickly for comfort.

There is now more foliage than sky in the windscreen glass. Speed is still too low, but it's now or never. Yoshitake drops a few degrees of flap and swallows hard as he begins to ease the control stick back, bracing for a stall-out or, more likely, an impact with the trees. The plane bounds once. Twice. Once more and it is aloft, yawing to the right with overboosted engine torque.

*Trees!*

There is a loud *thwack* as the *Ki*-51 takes about half of the top of a palm tree off. The plane shudders under the impact, yawing even more and on the verge of stall-out, but somehow it stays up. The engine is none too happy about any of this, and is vociferous in its protest, but it is doing its job.

The flight forms up over the field and gets some altitude before assuming the heading for the first leg. Still only a few minutes out, Yoshitake's wheezing plane is streaming a thin band of smoke and already falling way behind the formation. Itoi and the others are pulling away. Their planes are rapidly shrinking into black dots in the windscreen.

There is no use getting too worked up about falling behind, although in an unexpected way it helps keep his mind occupied. The dominant emotions of the moment are impatience and determination.

Twenty minutes out, the formation is skirting a cloud bank over Cebu at about five thousand meters and turning into their attack heading. It is still somewhat overcast here, but the sky in the direction of the target area is sunny. Yoshitake, now at least two or three kilometers back from the formation, can still make out the other planes, but just barely. Black blossoms of smoke soon darken the horizon to the east. The Americans are putting up antiaircraft barrages. From the looks of it, there must be hundreds of ships out there. Yoshitake feels his pulse quicken.

*Just fly for the smoke puffs. That's where the ships are. They'll lead you right in.*

He zones everything else out and focuses on the smoke. His entire being is pulled forward toward the battle as the plane clears the coast of Cebu and heads out over a bright aquamarine sea shimmering in the overcast sunlight.

Every synapse in Yoshitake's nervous system fires instantaneously as a huge, shiny blue-black bat with white stars on its wings suddenly looms

up from out of nowhere directly in front of him, almost completely filling his field of vision.

*The trigger button! Press the trigger button!*

Yoshitake can hear the little voice echoing up from his cerebellum but
his hands are glued to the stick. He can't move a muscle.

The Hellcat levels off to the side and slightly in front of Yoshitake's
plane in a leisurely maneuver almost close enough to touch wingtips.
The pilot—a big, red-faced man who looks uncomfortably cramped in
his cockpit—fixes Yoshitake with an expression clearly readable as a mixture of disdain and pity before pulling straight up and away into a rock-
eting zoom climb. Yoshitake is just beginning to take it personally when
fist-sized, fluorescent pink fireballs start streaming by either side of the
canopy.

For the first time in the encounter, Yoshitake's reflexes kick in on cue.
He yanks the drop tank release lever to lose the bomb and the plane is
suddenly as light as a biplane trainer. He puts some of the *Ki*-51's fabled
low-speed maneuvering to the test to jink his attacker off his tail and
bring the fight down to the deck. By dropping his altitude to the wave
tops, he has lost his vertical options and most valuable spatial dimension
in terms of escape, but the faster bad guy, a second American fighter
that Yoshitake can make out as another Hellcat, is put at a disadvantage
as well. An experienced fighter pilot will give up a limb or two before
willingly surrendering speed at low altitude in a combat situation.
Therefore, if the American knows what he's doing, dropping speed to
pump lead into Yoshitake's tail at will is the last thing he is going to want
to do. His attacks will be limited to boom-and-zoom runs with a firing
window of only a few seconds at a time before he has to pull up to avoid
augering into the water. If Yoshitake can jink around enough during
these short attack runs and avoid stalling out, maybe he can buy time to
try to think of some way out of this mess.

The *Ki*-51 is scooting over wave tops and within sight of a tree-lined
island when its American tormentor comes in for another run. Yoshitake
braces for hits and a split second later the cockpit is filled with shattered
instrument panel glass, flying dust and debris, and the acrid smell of
smoke and aviation fuel. The engine sputters and dies. The *Ki*-51 is now
a powerless glider losing speed fast.

Something in Yoshitake's mind registers a black clearing in the palm trees past his starboard wingtip and he instinctively yanks the sluggish control stick to head for it. Spread out before him in splendor and glory is an asphalt airstrip cleanly splitting the jungle overgrowth in half. It is a heavenly choir moment, but way too early to join in the singing. He is rapidly running out of speed and altitude but still a good clip from the end of the runway.

He is too low to bail out, and ditching in a fixed-landing-gear aircraft is not recommended if he wants to keep his spinal column intact. His only chance is to make it to the runway. The water is changing color—going tan and shallow—but the end of the runway is creeping over the top of the engine cowling. Pulling back on the stick to try to get some altitude will just cause a stall.

The wheels hit hard a few meters from the end of the runway, on sand already sloping down toward the water.

There is a huge boom and suddenly Yoshitake is watching himself floating in a wooden boat in an upside-down black void. The sensation is not entirely unpleasant; nor is the smell of aviation fuel that fills the air. He does not register any pain or fear other than a vague loneliness and a desire for some light. He pulls at his harness buckle to reach for a patch of blue sand hovering somewhere over his shoulder, and the world falls on his head.

"Hitting my head like that snapped me out of it," Mr. Yoshitake says. "When I came to, I realized that I was hanging upside down in my plane."

I must have made a humorous expression of surprise here, because Mr. Yoshitake unexpectedly flashes big old-man teeth in a high-wattage grin I realize is identical to the one on the face of a beaming young man in wartime photos I have just finished thumbing through.

"I started digging around an open space on one edge of the cockpit," he writes in his wartime memoirs, *Nagai Hibi* ("Long Days"). "I heard voices, and then I clearly remember people actually jumping back in horror for a second when my head popped out from under the plane and into view. . . . About half of my scalp from just below the hairline had been lifted up and off my head."

Once they had regained their composure, Yoshitake's rescuers identified themselves as navy personnel. He was at a small naval airstrip on

Mactan Island. He was pretty banged up, but the injuries were not life threatening.

After recuperating in the first-aid shack on Mactan, he was sent back to Pollack Airfield, where he spent the next two months witnessing the military and moral meltdown of the Japanese occupation forces there and on the rest of Luzon Island. Riding on one of the last Japanese aircraft to leave Luzon, he spent the remainder of the war in Taiwan awaiting new *tokkō* orders that never came. He was repatriated in February 1946 after serving as a "volunteer" medic's assistant in the Taiwan countryside at the behest of local Kuomintang and Allied authorities.

So, did his traumatic experience over the Camotes Sea in late 1944 give him a lifelong fear of flying? Not a chance. He joined the Japanese Air Self-Defense Forces as soon as that organization was established, serving his country again as a military pilot and flight instructor for the next thirty years. After retirement, he started a successful aerial photography and mapping company, and continued pleasure flying in his spare time. His logged his last flight hours in 1993.

Yoshitake wishes he could still fly, but admits that his eyesight and reflexes aren't what they used to be anymore. He flies only in his dreams now. Usually, these are pleasant—soaring over the troubles and trivia of the earthbound world, high and free in the great blue. Sometimes, though—perhaps a few times a month for the last fifty-eight years, more when he is under stress—the dreams are not so good, and he is back on the flight line at Bacolod waiting for the order to get in the planes or flying toward those black flak clouds on the horizon. In the worst dreams, he is not flying at all, but running through the jungles of northern Luzon during a B-24 carpet-bombing raid over his position that kills half of the men in his new unit in seconds. But always—good dream or nightmare— he gets to meet once again with the best friends he ever had: Captain Takaishi and his IMA classmates in the Sekichō Unit. And along with the bittersweet joy of these regular nocturnal reunions invariably comes a feeling that maybe he was supposed to have died with his squadron mates. Maybe he had just cheated fate to survive that crash and last all these years to start a family, work in a fulfilling career, pursue hobbies, enjoy retirement, play with his grandchildren, watch sunsets. He has never really shaken this nagging survivor's guilt all this long half century, but he manages to cope with it one day at a time. One way to do this is to look at his life since that fateful day in 1944 not as something stolen but as a gift. It is a sentiment I will hear often in interviews with other *tokkō* survivors in coming months.

"I have lived twice," Yoshitake says. "I died in that plane crash, and was born again when I was pulled from the wreck. I'm not a religious man, but I have to think that something or someone decided to give me this time for a reason, and there is never a day that I do not feel grateful for it. Perhaps I have been living not only for myself all this time, but also to make up in some way for the long lives my comrades missed."

Yoshitake leans back in his chair to fire up another of the creosote-smelling Shinsei cigarettes he has been smoking throughout the interview. There is a faraway look in his eyes now, but there is a twinkle in them, too, like he is in on a secret that I, not present on his particular St. Crispin's Day, cannot be let in on until I have paid some more dues. It is a look you often see in the eyes of older men whose hearts, in Oliver Wendell Holmes's metaphor, were touched with fire in their youth. God and favorable defense treaties willing, Yoshitake and his seventy- and eighty-something former comrades-in-arms will be the last generation of Japanese ever to have it.

"I'll tell you what war is," Yoshitake says, almost as if he has been reading my mind. "It's a situation in which a person has absolutely no control over their own destiny. Everything is out of your hands. You can't stay alive when you want to, but you can't die when you want to, either."

# PART THREE

# THE ULTIMATE SMART BOMB

# ten

# THE YOKAREN CANDIDATE

I t is April 2002, and I am visiting Tokurō Takei's comfortably sunlit Japanese/Western-style home in Hamamatsu, Japan, for the first time. His wife meets me at the door with a deep bow, which I return with one of my own before handing over a gift-wrapped box of rice crackers and offering a stock Japanese apology for imposing myself like this. Mrs. Takei receives my gift with another bow and, as etiquette dictates, politely refuses to acknowledge my need to apologize. I remove my shoes in the ground-level foyer, and step up on to the raised floor of the house in my stocking feet. Mrs. Takei offers me the customary house slippers a visitor to a Japanese house will typically wear. I decline the offer on the valid grounds that my feet are too big for the slippers, and we share a quick if bashful laugh over this footwear conundrum while she shows me to the living room sofa.

I would guess that Mrs. Takei is in her late sixties or early seventies. She has the doe-eyed, rich caramel-brown variety of Japanese face that is often seen in her hometown of Okitsu and the other fishing villages squeezed between mountains and the Pacific Ocean on the coast of eastern Shizuoka Prefecture. It is a warm, sunny visage that conjures up forebears from milder climes than the tough Yayoi-culture rice farmers who sailed from the Korean peninsula two millenia ago to wrest control of the archipelago from the aboriginal Jōmon culture and leave the deepest footprints in the genetic makeup of modern Japanese.[1]

Any vestigial memory Mrs. Takei may have of her ancestors' multicultural experience is obviously not kicking in to help her to deal with welcoming a foreigner into her home. When not in motion plying me with green tea and cookies while we wait for her husband to come to the living room, she stands a few steps behind the sofa and just out of my field of vision. I can sense her nervousness, and am not sure if her taciturnity stems from fear and shyness or from her assuming that a language barrier will make any attempts at meaningful conversation a mutually embarrassing exercise in frustration. Accordingly, neither of us says anything. I sit on the Takeis' sofa looking at naval citations on the wall and plastic models of Zeros lined up on the bookshelves while Mrs. Takei maintains her vigil safely out of sight.

The cultural dynamic of silence at work here—which I have encountered thousands of times during my Japanese sojourn—is not particularly uncomfortable for me (although it may be for Takei-san, uninitiated as she is to visits from international men of mystery). Over the years, I have lost my quintessentially American fear of conversational lulls longer than a few seconds, so this particular silence does not faze me. Nevertheless, I am beginning to feel a tad guilty over Takei-san's obvious discomfort, so I decide to try to put my hostess at ease with a little demonstration of Japanese language ability. Etiquette gives me an in here—it will not be untoward for me to apologize once again for my rude intrusion (under the rules of Japanese etiquette you can never truly apologize too much for anything). The tit-for-tat torrent of stock platitudes my apology will trigger can be found virtually word for word in any basic Japanese conversation textbook, but then again, sometimes clichés can be reassuring, and I suppose this has as good a chance of breaking some ice as anything else.

"Please excuse my rudeness at imposing on your hospitality like this," I say. "And on a weekend, at that."

"*Iie, iie,*" Mrs. Takei says, fanning a hand in front of her nose in a Japanese gesture of denial often misinterpreted by Westerners as a reaction to some foul odor. "I'm the one who should be apologizing for our cramped house."

"No, no. It's not cramped at all. It's lovely. And your tea is delicious."

"I'm sorry about its poor quality."

"These cookies are good, too."

"It's just some local confectionery. Nothing special."

"You really didn't have to go to the bother of buying them just for me."

"Oh, no trouble at all."

Running out of things to say, we exchange a quick series of head nods—like bows from the neck up—just as Mr. Takei enters the room and rescues us from having to commit to another round of head-bobbing niceties.

Takei-san is a short, lean, and fit man of seventy-three, and although his hair is white, he still has most of it. His facial expression is dignified and a bit distant, not what I would call extremely emotive. But it does have one—or rather two—striking features. As we shake hands, I am taken aback by Takei-san's steel-gray eyes, which are as limpid and cool as puddles in a tin rain gutter under a cloudy sky. As eye color other than an oily ebony or a rich mahogany brown is extremely rare in Japanese, the Siberian seawater in Takei's eyes has my mind on the migrations of ancient peoples again.

However interested I am in this topic, though, I have not visited Takei-san today to discuss Japanese anthropology—well, at least not any more than it pertains to the mind-set of young men deliberately crashing their aircraft into things. But we must establish trust before we can reach a stage comfortable enough to attend to such meaty matters. And as the only man sitting on this sofa now who has not flown a warplane, or seen his friends killed in front of his eyes, or publicly repeated a vow to die for his country and meant every word of it, the burden of establishing this trust clearly falls squarely upon my shoulders.

It is apparent that Takei-san, at least at this point, does not quite seem to know what to make of me, and in his own masculine way, he is just as shy as his wife. As we go through our opening banter, he comes across as cautious, and, of course, he has every right to be so. Most *tokkō* veterans have had the experience of dealing with unscrupulous writers or researchers or journalists looking for juicy stories and conspiracy angles at one time or another, and many of these former warriors have been burned come publication time because they were duped into giving trust where it was not warranted. For my own interview to work, I have to prove myself worthy of the information I seek.

A skeptical war-veteran interview subject will ask in so many words—and squarely within rights—"Why should I let you in on this?" It is not so much a matter of "What am I going to get out of giving you this information?" as it is "Why should I trust *you* with interpreting my experiences accurately, on something this important?" I have been able to answer this question to most of my interview subjects' satisfaction during field research for this project, but I can never afford to be complacent, because no two approaches are the same, and each requires caution and tact. Some subjects want the questions fast and frank, while others take umbrage and clam right up under such a barrage, preferring their questions spoon-fed and gift-wrapped. But at either end of that continuum and everywhere else in between, the best way of steering an interview into a mood of candid comfort hinges on finding commonalities. Obviously, this is not always easily done when the parties involved are a seventy- or eighty-something Japanese combat veteran and a forty-year-old American who has heard shots fired in anger only in the Bronx.

I have often found that my ex–West Point cadet credentials can grease the hinges a bit with even the crustiest and most irascible of these old fellows. Admittedly, they are the only real military qualifications I can claim, but the brand-name value of the academy as the alma mater of His Royal Highness Douglas MacArthur still carries enormous weight with older Japanese, and it has opened more than one door for me during my career here. My stories about cadet life—especially plebe-year hazing—find an interested and even nostalgic ear with men of Takei's generation, and help establish those above-mentioned and elusive commonality bonds.

Another link, sadly, is that my being an expat New Yorker with family members and friends living on the island of Manhattan in our post-9/11 world also gives us a bond of pain, for I now share with my elderly Japanese counterparts the experience of having watched from afar—unable to help—as my home was attacked from the skies.

Takei-san and I talk about 9/11 for a while. In all of the discussions I have had with Japanese veterans on this topic, I have not picked up on the slightest shred of any "So, how did *you* like being on the receiving end for a change?" schadenfreude in their comments, and toward the American people they have expressed only feelings of sympathy, shared outrage, and solidarity. From many, I have also observed a sense of frustration at the constitutional restraints* that prevent the armed forces of their own country—a nation that profits handsomely from the commerce made possible by the current international order—from doing its part in the fight against the forces that would tear down that order with terror and chaos.

If Takei-san and his former comrades-in-arms harbor any negative feelings toward America in the aftermath of September 11, 2001, it is resentment against the American mass media for its culturally insensitive and historically ignorant likening of the mind-set and methods of Al-Qaeda with the Japanese *tokkō* program of sixty years ago. I find myself agreeing completely with Takei-san and other *tokkō* veterans who find the comparison both unwarranted and insulting, and wonder how the analysis of these media types could have missed the big picture so completely when it is as simple and clear-cut a matter as the difference between love and hate.

What Al-Qaeda's civilian suicide squads did to other civilians in the United States on September 11 was driven purely by the latter emotion. On their way to oblivion, these terrorists seek to inflict as much pain and destruction as possible on the triumphant order of secularism and rationalism that wrested control of the world from another cabal of superstitious, bearded zealots half a millennium ago.[2] With no hope of ever achieving final victory, the best they can do is to exact revenge in advance for their lost cause.

An argument can perhaps be made for parallels between the pathological mind-set of a Bin Laden and that of the more fanatic policy makers in Japan circa 1944–1945 by replacing fire-and-brimstone Wahhabist pipe dreams of global theocracy with the Japanese militarists' racial mysticism and revenge fantasies against Western hegemony. But none can be drawn—beyond the mere commonalities of flight training and willingness to die for a cause—between a Mohammed Atta and a Yukio Seki. What the Japanese *tokkō* personnel themselves did—at least at the rank-and-file level of the men at the control sticks of the aircraft—was done out of love of home and family, not out of theological abstractions and hate. Taking the liberty of imagining the 9/11 metaphor through a World War II

---

*Originally American-imposed, of course, when legal scholars from the MacArthur-led GHQ essentially rewrote Japan's constitution with the intention of declawing its military capability *ad aeternum*. Dower (1999) and Bix (2000) give the best English language interpretations of this process currently in print.

Japanese endgame perspective, the *tokkō* pilots were not the wild-eyed Koran thumpers at the controls of the 767s; they were the firefighters who knew the World Trade Center towers were doomed but ran up the stairways anyway.

In late 1944, American fleets were closing an iron stranglehold on Japan. By 1945, these forces had been marshaled into invasion fleets, and Takei, his comrades, and the entire population of Japan were told over and over through every information-dissemination organ at the disposal of the state that the men on those ships were hell-bent on rape, destruction, and nothing short of genocide.* It was only natural that young men with a strong duty concept, deep love of country and family, and insufficient worldly cynicism to doubt the spiel from on high would want to do everything within their ability to stop such an enemy force in its tracks.

*An armada of racist, murderous rapists is closing in on your homes! They'll rape and slaughter your mothers, sisters, and daughters in front of your eyes before your own slow, agonizing death unless you follow our instructions to the letter!*

For a panicked population that was incapable of doubting the integrity of their authority figures, who needed stronger exhortation to resort to extreme measures than that? The rank and file cannot be blamed for falling over each other in the rush to line up for *tokkō*. And if anyone should ever doubt that a campaign of misinformation for propaganda purposes was going on, consider that if the authorities had really believed that the American invasion force was going to be a million-man-strong KKK *Einsatzgruppen* of bloodthirsty sex maniacs, then Emperor Hirohito would have never okayed the surrender, nuclear-bombed cities or not.† Under such circumstances, an imperial order for the nation to fight on to the last man, woman, and child would have been entirely justified.

But the emperor did not issue such an order, thank God, because at

---

*And it should be noted that intercepted and subsequently widely publicized American propaganda did nothing to dispel these fears—at least the last two. For a detailed discussion of this process and its effect on Japanese military and civilian morale, see Dower (1986), pp. 246–248.

†The newest and most authoritative historical interpretations of Hirohito's wartime experience suggest that he had a much more active—if not dominating—role in guiding the war's conduct than had been previously believed. Readers interested in pursuing this topic are urged to read John Dower's *Embracing Defeat* (1999) and Herbert Bix's *Hirohito* (2000).

the bottom of his heart, he knew the Americans could be trusted, and I am sure he knew that if it ever came down to it, working with Democrats and Republicans would be a considerably more pleasant day at the office than cutting lumber in a Siberian gulag for commissars. Personally, I think he knew that all along. That he did not act earlier on his convictions and save millions of his countrymen in the process is something for which he can now be held accountable only to his Maker.

Of course, the emperor's instincts turned out to be right, and concurrent with Germany's and Italy's postwar experiences, the American-led administration of Japan that followed Hirohito's surrender proclamation was without parallel the most kid-gloved occupation of a vanquished nation in the history of warfare. The Japanese people today owe their lives to the wisdom of the emperor's decision, but they owe their prosperity to the unprecedented patience and generosity of former enemies. There can be no more damning argument against the racial pride mumbo-jumbo Japan's wartime leadership put over on an entire nation while cheering it on to the brink of self-extermination in the last year of World War II.

Takei-san nods throughout my monologue, but the gesture may be more Japanese politeness than wholehearted support. I am not sure if he agrees with me, but I do believe that I have at least convinced him that I have given these matters a lot of thought, and that gives us enough momentum to leave current events and historical theory behind us, and to begin talking about *his* war.

"Everyone likes to think that the *tokkō* pilots were happy to die for their country, but I don't think most of us were really like that," Takei-san says, when asked about his mind-set circa 1944–1945. "We did not want to die—at least not like that [i.e., in *tokkō* tactics]. We were not afraid to fight, but we wanted to come home to our families alive after the fighting was over. And nobody except for admirals and generals believed all that 'die for the emperor' business. We were fighting to protect our homeland and, most of all, our families."

"Do you ever feel that your life was deliberately spared for some reason?" I ask, recalling Yoshitake's almost theological explanation for his own survival.

"No, no," Takei-san says, mirroring the hand gesture of denial his wife made a few minutes ago. "I never really went in too much for that destiny stuff. I think I was just lucky; that's all."

Obviously, Takei-san is not someone most people would be tempted to call a very religious man, at least not in terms of religion having a significant presence in his daily life. Nevertheless, every New Year's Day he visits the local Shinto shrine with grandchildren in tow to pray for his family's health and well-being over the next twelve months. Shinto rites were also observed for his daughters' weddings, and in groundbreaking ceremonies for every office building, shopping mall, and hospital he helped put up during a lifetime in the construction business. As is the case with most of his countrymen, these rites are perhaps more reassuring affirmation of cultural identity and subtle reminders of the impermanence of worldly things than acts of religious devotion. However, when the transition to be marked is someone's passage to the afterlife, Takei-san's normal mode of healthy agnosticism is cloaked in the smoky incense and ornate mantle of Japanese Buddhism, and the prayers he will chant at a funeral along with the presiding monk and the other mourners are ostensibly offered in hopes that the soul of the dear departed will reincarnate on a higher plane than the one it has just left. Like most Japanese in similar situations, Takei-san may not believe—or even completely understand—everything he is repeating, but vague theology and incomprehensible ritual have never been problems with the variety of Buddhism practiced on these shores.

Buddhism's spread throughout Japan during the sixth century A.D. is a quintessentially Japanese story of cultural absorption and subsequent adaptation to local needs and tastes. Assuming a major nation-building role soon after its arrival, the religion served as a conduit for political philosophy, high culture, technology, and the kanji writing system imported from the Asian continent.[3] In its Japanese permutation, it has proved over the subsequent millennium and a half to be as jealous of its turf as it is flexible in its doctrine, withstanding the sands of time and several centuries' worth of Christian missionary activities without relinquishing hold on the professed faith of more than 1 or 2 percent of the Japanese population since Francis Xavier's frustrating tour of Jesuit duty in the country in the sixteenth century.

Buddhism's tenacious survival at the top has been made possible by the wind-sensitive political savvy of its prelates at key points in history, and their ability to shove the knife when confronted with rivals. The theological flexibility the religion demonstrated in its coopting of native Shinto animist beliefs and the ease with which it lends itself to spin-off cults and faiths has been another secret of its durability. But certainly its main tenet of *saisei* reincarnation has been the greatest part of Japanese Buddhism's appeal over the centuries for the hearts and minds of a rice-growing culture ill at ease with linear interpretations of time and more at home with cyclical concepts of life and death, sunrises and sunsets, the carousel of the seasons and the sensual distinctions each brings, every-one snug and comfortable in the knowledge that this is a world without major surprises or abrupt end, amen. For a farming culture, it is not the possibility of right or wrong pathways to ultimate destinations, but rather this assurance of predictable repetition that is most comforting.

Similar to the doctrine of other Asian creeds in the Mahayana tradi-tion, strict interpretation of the Japanese Buddhist cycle of reincarna-tion is karmic (although few Japanese believe this now), and the afterlife destination of a human soul is determined largely by what it did with the last corporeal vehicle of flesh and bones it was given a chance to jump into and take out for a test drive. At one end of the spectrum, for those rare souls patient and virtuous enough while alive to have achieved satori enlightenment—the Buddhist equivalent of a winning Powerball ticket—escape velocity from this plane of material illusion can be reached for an afterlife launch straight to truth and godhead. Thought along these lines has been coopted into the modern Shinto tradition holding that the souls of dead servicemen dwell for eternity in their heaven on earth amidst the cherry boughs at Yasukuni Shrine.

At the other end, for souls whose previous incarnations incurred insur-mountable bad karma by living particularly greedy, spiteful, or unchari-table lives, waits an indeterminate period of lonesome purgatory and earthbound wandering as *gaki* or *o bake,* the hideous but relatively in-nocuous phantoms and hobgoblins with which late-nineteenth-century proto-Japanologist Lafcadio Hearn was so fascinated, and which continue to play starring roles in the popular ghost stories of Japanese young and old. But the majority of us regular folks and run-of-the-mill lustful mate-rialists are sentenced to run the eternal karmic hamster wheel for untold aeons, shunting back and forth in constant transmigration between life and death, and will continue to do so until karma allows us to get off the ride once and for all.

A transmigrating soul slated for a return to this mortal coil could have drawn a cushier reentry point slot on the time-space continuum than an impoverished Japanese day laborer's home on the outskirts of a gritty regional industrial town in the first year of the Great Depression, but that was the hand dealt to the soul that became Tokurō Takei on February 10, 1929, in Hamamatsu, Shizuoka Prefecture. Tokurō was born the third child and third son in a string of Takei children that was soon to include a daughter and a fourth son. His parents were wise enough to have learned the importance of a good education after finding out firsthand what it was like trying to succeed in the world without one, and though the family finances hung perennially on a frayed shoestring, school tuition always got paid in full and on time. If the Takei children ever had reason to doubt the wisdom of occasionally having to go without new clothes at the start of the school year because their mother thought it better to spend the money on textbooks, all they had to do was look at the cracked calluses on their father's gnarled hands after a day of swinging an ax on a logging site or sorting leaves at a tea factory to appreciate their mother's sense of priorities.

When Tokurō graduated from elementary school in March 1941, most of his other classmates from the neighborhood opted—either from disinterest, impatience, or domestic financial straits—to close their textbooks once and for all after their successful completion of what Japanese law determined to be a sufficient compulsory education. Many of these boys had life tracks already plotted out as helpers and eventual heads of family businesses or as apprentices to craftsmen. Others secured employment right out of grade school with tiny but well-paying local manufacturing firms like Suzuki or Yamaha Motors, whose workers were putting in overtime to fill military contracts for small gasoline-burning motors used in field generators by signals and communication units with the army in the Chinese campaign.* With hostilities in China already four years old, and conflict with America and Britain looming on the horizon, Japan's wartime economy was gearing up into full swing, and Hamamatsu was enjoying a ride right up near the crest of this boom.

With work aplenty to be had, the temptation was great for Tokurō to

---

*This regional technological legacy in small motor production matched with a thriving local bicycle manufacturing industry led to a domination of global motorcycle production by these firms—joined by a postwar competitor, Honda—a mere twenty years later. The world headquarters of all three firms remain in the Hamamatsu area to this day.

grab up a plant job like so many of his friends and start putting some food on the family table. However, his parents would have none of this. Tokurō was going to make something of himself, and this future did not include pulling a drill press handle on a factory floor sixty hours a week or swinging a pickax in the hot sun all day for a living. After passing a moderately difficult entrance exam, Tokurō was enrolled in a five-year private vocational school to study engineering, a field in which his math and science ability seemed to indicate he might have a successful future. In the meantime, the family would scrimp and save to scrape together the entrance and tuition fees.

Never forgetting his obligation to his parents for sending him to school, and always keenly aware of the sacrifices they had to make to keep him there, Tokurō was a diligent student for the next two and a half years. But as the war with America dragged on, rumors about the impending cancellation of student draft deferments increased, and more and more young men from the old neighborhood started coming home from the war fronts in white ossuary boxes, Tokurō began to see less and less reason to stay in school. Although he was still at least five years below draft age,* it seemed likely that the war would still be raging when the inevitable *akagami* ("red letter"—draft notice) from the local draft board finally arrived sometime in 1948. In his adolescent logic, it did not make any sense for him to continue his studies and be a further drain on the family's finances when he was only going to end up getting drafted and killed in the war a couple of years later. There were also Tokurō's two younger siblings to consider. They might want an education, too, and his sister would need money when she got married someday. Thinking of their well-being was the clincher, and there was no longer any doubt in Tokurō's mind about what he should do. Without consulting his parents, he began discreetly looking into enlistment options.

Tokurō soon found out that, as a fourteen-year-old, his options were pretty limited. In fact, the only games in town were for pilot training programs that carried heavy service commitments after graduation. The army's Shōnen Hikōhei ("Youth Pilot") program could earn him wings as an army corporal pilot by sixteen, but it also carried a hefty fifteen-year service commitment. Tokurō had also heard rumors about the brutality

---

*Lowered from twenty to nineteen in 1943, then to seventeen in 1944.

of army NCOs toward trainees, which was another prudent reason to take pause and weigh options. The navy, which everyone knew as the gentleman's branch of service, had a similar Yokaren* ("Preparatory Aviation Training") program that could land him what was then the most glamorous office-with-a-view in Japan: the cockpit of a Zero fighter. The decision may have taken Tokurō all of several minutes to make. Yokaren it was, and if he did not get in, he would just stay at school and wait for the draft notice to come in a few more years.

No boy of his generation could ever forget the glory heaped upon the navy by the mass media, community leaders, and educators in the wake of the Pearl Harbor raid. Films and popular music sang the navy's praises, and schoolchildren sang songs in class about the nine *gunshin* (a fallen combat hero officially elevated to special posthumous deification as Shinto "war god") who piloted the midget submarines in the Pearl Harbor attack, and whose pictures were featured in newspapers, posters, and schoolbooks.[4] But the imagery of the Japanese fighting man that most captured the public imagination of adult and child alike in those heady days of Yankee-humbling victories was that of the boy-man Yokaren graduate Zero pilot, flying off of carriers in wind-tossed seas to vanquish the foe, like Momotarō the Peach Boy[†] off to subdue the long-nosed demons on Oni Island. There was not a boy in Japan in 1943 who did not spend some part of any given day daydreaming about flying a Zero and shooting down foreigners.

Full of patriotic determination to do his part for the war effort, and bound to go out—if he had to go out—as one of these glorious Zero pilots, Tokurō finally worked up the courage to discuss his Yokaren plans with his parents. Hesitant about their son's decision, but proud of his bravery and of the fine filial piety he demonstrated in his selfless desire to ease their financial burden, they had no choice but to give their assent. With the help of a local recruiting officer, they began the paperwork for Tokurō's Yokaren application in the spring of 1943.

---

*Syllabary acronym for *Hikō Yokarenshūsei*.

†This Japanese fairy-tale character is traditionally depicted as an immaculately conceived (sprung from a peach—that was his name, after all) boy with supernatural abilities who rids his rustic community of marauding *auslander* demons and banishes them from Japan. See Dower (1986), pp. 251–257, for accounts of how this fairy tale was "enlisted" into the Japanese war effort and used to legitimize expansionist aggression in Asia in the public eye.

The Yokaren program had held a romantic niche in the public imagination since its well-publicized inception in 1930, when 5,800 boys from around the country had competed for a mere seventy-nine slots—an acceptance rate that put even the vaunted service academies to shame. While horrendous combat attrition rates suffered by its aviators had since forced the navy to expand Yokaren to seven schools located throughout the country,* winning a slot in the program was still a heady accomplishment for a boy in 1943, especially if he had grown up in an impoverished or rural area without the educational advantages of well-heeled urban peers. The Yokaren acceptance rate had climbed from prewar single-digit percentages to 30 or 40 percent by the time Tokurō applied,[5] but the lowered admissions standards in no way lowered the prestige of the program in the public eye, and the distinctive seven-buttoned dress tunic and anchor-with-cherry-blossom collar badge of its cadets were instantly recognizable icons popularized in countless film dramatizations, musical references, and propaganda posters. When Tokurō received notice in the late summer that he had passed his academic ability tests and physical examination to win a slot at the Yokaren campus at Matsuyama Air Station, he was an instant hero in his hardscrabble Hamamatsu neighborhood.

As Tokurō enjoyed the last balmy weeks of his carefree civilian life, the season's blockbuster hit at the movie theaters was *Kessen No Ōzora E* ("Onward to the Final Decisive Air Battle"), a Navy Ministry–sponsored Toho Studios film starring superstar Setsuko Hara about the life of cadets at the Tsuchiura Naval Air Station Yokaren campus. The Japanese subsidiary of Columbia Records† enjoyed yet another smash hit in their successful catalog of propaganda songs with their recording of the film's theme song, "Wakawashi no Uta" ("Song of the Young Eagles"). The lyrics can be considered fairly typical of the genre:

---

*There were twenty Yokaren schools by the end of the war, each attached to a functioning regional naval air group at a campus bearing the base's name. For example, the Tsuchiura Yokaren was attached to—and under the nominal authority of—the Tsuchiura Air Group (KKT).

†Columbia Records remained in business in Japan—name unchanged—after the opening of hostilities, and went on to churn out some of the war's most effective propaganda music before switching quickly back to jitterbug and love songs in time for the GIs to arrive for the Occupation. Like many other American corporate subsidiaries trapped in Axis territory during the war, Columbia (now owned by Sony) continued doing business as normal in its host country and collaborating with the local war effort as it saw fit.

*Young blood of the Yokaren,*
*Seven-buttoned blouse, anchor and cherry blossom device.*
*To fly again today in the skies of Kasumiga'ura,*
*Amidst the roiling clouds of hopes and dreams.*

*Burning vigor of the Yokaren,*
*My arms are steel, my heart a ball of fire.*
*It's time to leave the nest and cross restless seas*
*To deliver a blow to the heart of the enemy.*

*I admire the Yokaren graduates who have gone on to war,*
*My blood is up when I hear of their feats of arms.*
*Training and more training to sharpen fighting spirit,*
*No enemy can prevail over Yamato Damashi.*

*Dauntless Yokaren,*
*Wings of will are wings of victory.*
*I want to send my mother a picture*
*Of the enemy ship I will sink.*[6]

In the closing days of the summer of '43, the song could be heard everywhere, and there was a hardly a person in the country immune to the charm of its macho-yet-cute imagery of rosy-cheeked boy warriors, eager to fight and just as eager to write their mothers regularly.

On October 1, 1943—the day before student draft deferments were canceled by national decree[7]—Tokurō arrived at Matsuyama Naval Air Station on the southwestern tip of the island of Shikoku to begin an eight-month-long basic aviation training course with 3,274 other classmates as a member of Yokaren Cycle Kō-13.* During the first six weeks

---

*There were three types of Yokaren, designated using the classical Japanese sequential nomenclature of Kō, Otsu, and Hei, respectively. Kō cadets were boys who had at least three years of postelementary school education, whether at junior high or vocational school level. Otsu cadets were boys who had completed only compulsory education. Because of the difference in educational background, the Otsu programs were longer, and their graduates were not promoted as quickly as Kō personnel. Hei cadets were from enlisted ranks of active servicemen, and were thus several years older than their Kō and Otsu counterparts. See Tagaya (2004) for detailed treatment of the Yokaren program.

of training, Tokurō and his classmates were constantly evaluated by the Yokaren faculty for flight aptitude, mental and physical toughness, and leadership ability. When this period was up, the cadets were divided into pilot and nonpilot (observer, radioman, etc.) aircrew groups, after which each group trained separately, pursuing conventional classroom studies in a science-focused academic curriculum, as well as more practical job-related skills such as basic aerodynamic theory, aircraft and engine maintenance and repair, and communication and signals (including semaphore flags and Japanese syllabary Morse code). Assigned to the pilot group, Tokurō found the classroom work challenging but not intellectually over-whelming. When combined with all the PE time set aside in the curriculum for building up young bodies and toughening young minds, though, the pace of a nonstop sixteen-hour Yokaren day could be brutal. PE sessions consisted of calisthenics and running for stamina, gymnastics with a lot of flipping and somersaulting to simulate the stresses and spatial disorientation of aerial combat, and long sessions of judo and kendo to heighten martial spirit and sharpen the eye. Despite the pressure cooker of cadet life—not to mention the lingering separation anxiety of fourteen-to sixteen-year-old boys away from home for the first time—there were few problems with insomnia at Yokaren. Most cadets were asleep before their heads hit their thin mattresses every night at taps.*

If any of the boys had shown up at the Matsuyama campus expecting to be behind the stick of a biplane trainer anytime soon, they were quickly disappointed. The closest thing to actual flight training they would get during the next eight months was in the cockpit of a wooden glider. Launched slingshotlike down a shallow-grade slope by cadets tugging on elastic ropes attached to the nose, the glider would give the trainee a few precious seconds of airborne stick time before sliding to a stop at the bottom of the hill, after which it would be tugged back up Volga boatman–style for the next trainee's turn. But even these decidedly modest glider sessions were few and far between, and most of the cadets' "flight training" consisted of hours spent in wooden chairs with jury-rigged pedals on a simple pivot and broom handle "control sticks" for the trainees to hold between their legs during their imaginary flights. For

---

*The Japanese and American versions of taps differ melodically, but are similar in length and tempo. Visitors to Yasukuni can hear it at regular intervals over the shrine's loudspeaker system.

"aerial combat training," a cadet would aim through a ring-and-post gunsight at a model airplane dangled by a classmate on the end of a string. Actual flying time in a powered aircraft would have to wait until after the cadets graduated from Yokaren and moved on to flight school.

By far the least beloved aspect of the training was the day-in, day-out regimen of corporal punishment arbitrarily meted out by the Yokaren faculty for the slightest infractions or shortcomings, real or imagined. This came as an exceedingly nasty surprise for boys like Tokurō, who had opted for the navy thinking they could avoid all those sadistic noncoms in the army they had heard so much about, and expected to be trained as cosmopolitan gentlemen warriors who wore crisp blue uniforms and never forgot to take time off for afternoon tea. Unfortunately, brass band accompaniment for formal dining was never more than a dream, and in the Imperial Japanese Navy of late 1943, the concept of group responsibility was as constantly drilled, slapped, smacked, and beaten into the service's basic trainees as it was in the army. The message was as simple and clear-cut as a sock in the gut: If one person screws up, everybody pays for it.

Some of the punishments were almost whimsical, if a bit embarrassing, such as being forced to recite nonsense or sing at loud volume in front of others, or being lambasted with eloquent streams of cuss words and withering put-downs by the NCOs. Other forms of punishment would have to go under the "cruel and unusual" category, like being subjected to interminable deep-knee-bend sessions, or having to hold an arms-extended push-up position for what seemed like hours, or being made to sit in tubs of ice water. And no one was ever safe from a sudden visitation of what the NCOs liked to call *ippatsu omimai*, or "a top o' the morning howdy-do," which was a full-force punch to the jaw of an unsuspecting trainee, sometimes for no apparent reason at all.

"You know we only hit you because we love you," a noncom would inevitably snarl over some sprawled teen who had just crumpled to the ground after stopping an out-of-the-blue haymaker. "But combat is one bad surprise after another. You have to get used to it."

"Human Seabag" was a bizarre version of something like musical chairs, in which cadets would have to jump and squeeze into the cubbyholes built into the wooden barracks walls where their seabags were normally stored. On command from an NCO, the boys would scramble over each other in a flurry of asses and elbows, stepping on faces, heads, stomachs in their rush to complete this human beehive routine. The more acrobatically adept boys could be in a tight fetal position in their cubbyhole within two or three seconds, but it did not matter. There were always slowpokes or guys with high cubbyholes who could not get in quickly enough. This would of course infuriate the noncom, and everyone would be ordered to line up against the ends of their bunks, stand on their tiptoes, and proffer their buttocks for yet another dreadful session with a wide, flat wooden cricket bat known as "the Morale Stick" or simply "the Paddle".[8]

Some NCOs began their punishment sessions with disclaimers of the "this is going to hurt me more than it hurts you" variety, but there were plenty of bastards who openly enjoyed what they were doing, not even bothering to hide their snide smirking or muffle their laughter as they let fly with punches or laid into Morale Stick sessions with gusto. But differences in the psychological profiles of the punishers aside, the noncoms were for the most part equal-opportunity abusers, and the black eyes and fat lips they meted out with such generosity were so commonplace that these injuries barely merited comment from either cadets or faculty members. And there were never, ever, any questions or even raised eyebrows from the few commissioned officers who flitted so infrequently and unobtrusively against the backdrop of Yokaren life. The campuses were noncom-centric universes in toto, and officer types for the most part steered clear of the details of their day-to-day operations.

Despite its gauntlet run of trials and tribulations, Yokaren was by no means a nonstop eight-month-long haze session of hell and privations for its cadets. One bright point in the cadet's otherwise austere lifestyle was the food situation at the Yokaren schools, which was downright luxurious compared to what the civilian population was beginning to have to deal with by late 1943 and early 1944. There was a well-stocked PX on the Matsuyama campus that the Yokaren cadets were allowed to use on Sunday afternoons, and the boys were paid a stipend that was sufficient to stuff their bellies full of sweets and other snacks if they were of a mind to use their precious few hours of weekly free time for this purpose. When family or friends came to visit from the outside world, any but the worst gluttons and spendthrifts usually had enough wherewithal and boodle on hand to press much-appreciated packages of precious goodies into the arms of guests before seeing them off at the gates.

Food was not the only escape the cadets had from their mind-numbing, backbreaking, and often infuriating daily routine. Even at its dreariest, Yokaren was interspersed with occasional happy flashes of fun and joviality, and most boys formed bonds with their fellow comrades-in-hardship that were as deep and loyal as those formed by men in combat. Perhaps, as many Yokaren graduates surmise sixty years later, that was just the point of all the harping, hazing, and misery in the first place. The program's organizers and administrators may not have been over-flowing with the milk of human kindness, but they knew how to take youths—some of whom cried themselves to sleep every night their first few weeks at the schools—and turn them into some of the most moti-vated and determined fighting men in the world in just eight months. The NCOs that dedicated themselves to making the cadets' lives hell knew that no matter how strong a warrior's patriotism might be, he would fight harder and face death more resolutely alongside brothers he has laughed and suffered with than in the midst of strangers with whom he has shared nothing.

Dying was a topic upon which Tokurō and his classmates were under-standably reluctant to spend much too much time dwelling, despite the *pro Mikado et patria mori* barrage of songs, movies, and rah-rah speeches Japanese boys of their generation had been exposed to from the crib up. But given the fact that they were now members of His Majesty's armed forces serving in the middle of the most savage war the nation had yet faced, the notion of death claiming many of them before they reached their sixteenth birthdays was not beyond the realm of possibility. While such a fate was horrifying to contemplate for boys whose chins had yet to know a razor and whose lips might never feel the brush of a girl's sigh, most embraced the notion that there was something glorious and ro-mantic about their imminent destruction as long as they were making this sacrifice for a cause that would ultimately prevail.

While this "cause" had somehow metamorphosed from Pan-Asian hegemony to a simple matter of national survival while everybody was too busy thinking about other things, this considerably more modest but infinitely more crucial military goal still seemed entirely within the reach of the Japanese fighting man. The Yokaren boys believed this in their hearts, and everything they read in the papers, were told by the radio, and saw in the newsreels reassured them that there was no reason to think otherwise. Taking the Japanese media accounts at face value, the Americans were reeling under blow after blow from the emperor's young war eagles, and would never be allowed to set foot on the Japanese home islands. The war might very well go on for years and years still to come, but Japan would not and could not lose. Defeat was unthinkable.

During a downtime bull session between training sessions one morning in early 1944, Tokurō Takei and his squadmates were let in on news that landed like a bombshell on their fragile eggshell minds. The instructor that morning was an NCO who was an object of intense hero-worship by the cadets. A dashing combat veteran pilot in his mid-twenties, he was one of the few laid-back members of the faculty at Matsuyama, and not surprisingly, the boys loved him and hung on every word he ever said. The conversation that morning had started with an innocuous enough query to the pilot from one of the boys along the lines of, "What is it like to be in combat?" The answer that followed was the first honest assessment of Japan's war record and present situation that the boys had ever heard.

"We're losing the war," the pilot had blurted, instantaneously wiping away his charges' admiring smiles.

Avoiding the cadets' eyes as he continued, the pilot explained the reason why there were now so many Yokaren campuses around the country, and so many more cadets. It was not because naval aviation was getting bigger, as everyone was being told. It was because they were losing so many pilots.[9] The situation was bad, had been headed south since the Battle of Midway almost two years earlier, and was only getting worse.

Battle of Midway? The boys had heard about it, but only in the context of a decisive rout of dastardly American aggression.

The NCO went on to describe the grim realities. Four carriers had gone down in the battle, he said. Hundreds of irreplaceable aviators were lost. He knew all about this, because he had been there, and seen it with his own eyes. And in terms of sheer numbers, what had happened in the meat grinder of the Southwest Pacific during the previous year had been even worse.

While this news was bad enough, the realization of how massively the public was being deceived by the authorities about the progress of the war was somehow even worse. Tokurō never really believed anything about the war he read in the papers, heard on the radio, or saw in the Nichiei newsreels after that. It was a devastating blow, and from that day on, his worldview took on a decidedly grayer hue.

## eleven

# I WANTED WINGS

On May 25, 1944, modest graduation ceremonies were held for the cadets of Yokaren Cycle Kō-13, Matsuyama Naval Air Station Campus. Out of 3,275 boys who had entered the Matsuyama program some eight months earlier, 1,180 were graduating as pilot candidates, and 1,610 as aircrew candidates. The other 485 boys who originally entered with the cycle had since fallen by the wayside through sickness, injury, or failure* to otherwise meet graduation requirements.

Tokurō's training company of 170 new pilot candidates, now officially designated as members of Flight Basic Training Cycle 38, shipped out the same day on chartered train cars for Ōmura Naval Air Station in Nagasaki Prefecture. At last, the boys were going to get that chance at the stick of an Akatonbo biplane trainer they had all been dreaming about for so long. They were going to be naval aviators. Headed for flight school!

---

*Unlike the Darwinian policies that doomed "washouts" in American pilot training and other elite training programs to military careers that could be metaphorically likened to "shoveling shit in Louisiana," in Patton's immortal phrase, the shame of Yokaren failures was only temporary. Administrators would recycle physically capable washouts to the next class group coming in, and these cadets would be given extra instruction until they succeeded. This "no member left behind" educational philosophy is a salient feature of the so-called Japanese group mentality Western observers—and Americans in particular—so often interpret as being robotlike, cold, and inhuman. What—if any—effect this approach may have had on overall ability and esprit de corps of IJN pilots vis-à-vis their American counterparts is interesting to contemplate.

However enthusiastic the cadets may have been about the start of their new careers as heroic aviators, they found out soon after arriving at their destination that it may have been a bit hasty to break out the white scarves and start growing handlebar mustaches. Although they had graduated from Yokaren, they had yet to graduate from hazing like "Human Seabag" and "the Paddle." New rank as petty officers third class notwithstanding, Tokurō and his classmates were about to begin another seven months of dreary same-old, same-old—haymakers to the unsuspecting and head games as usual for everyone. One significant difference between here and Yokaren, of course, was that this time the drudgery would be broken up into digestible chunks, with the exhilaration of stick time in the Akatonbos to look forward to in between.

The Akatonbos certainly lived up to the cadets' expectations as far as excitement went. There was never a dull moment in the two-seater biplane trainers—especially when sitting in the observer seat with a nervous classmate soloing* for the first time in the rear pilot's seat—and the danger the pilot candidates now faced daily was no longer just the NCO variety that put dental work, seating comfort, and young egos in jeopardy. There were flying accidents with alarming regularity, many of them fatal. One of the more horrific, which several Cycle 38 cadets witnessed from the ground, occurred when a pilot trainee was soloing with a classmate in the forward observer seat.

After a few circuits around the airfield, the bright orange trainer had climbed high in an Immelmann turn. Onlookers from below saw a black object fall from the now-inverted plane at the top of the turn, and there were shouts and gasps when everyone realized that the falling object was the plane's observer, flailing his arms as if some vestigial avian instinct was telling him to flap phantom wings. Whether through sheer panic or mere lack of time, the observer failed to deploy his parachute, and was dead before people on the ground reached his shattered body. When the understandably shaken cadet at the stick brought the Akatonbo down, he told his superiors that he had merely wanted to surprise his passenger

---

*In both IJA and IJN pilot training programs in the later stages of the war, time spent in the observer or "passenger" seat of an Akatonbo was counted in solo flight hour tallies for logbook entries to ensure that cadets could meet requirements for pilot qualification on schedule. This policy of "doubling up" also helped to conserve fuel and reduce wear on engine parts more desperately needed at the front than in rear-area training schools.

with some aerobatics, but in his enthusiasm, he had failed to notice that his passenger was not strapped into the cockpit.

As flight school entered its final weeks at Ōmura in late 1944, cadets of Cycle 38 had to start thinking about the postgraduation assignments they would formally request. Paradoxically, given this relatively advanced post-Marianas stage in the war, Japanese naval aviation offered a more bountiful variety of potential aircraft-type specialties for its fledgling pilots than ever before: There were medium bombers like the Isshiki Rikkō* ("Betty") and the venerable China War veteran Mitsubishi Type 96; many new types of high-performance attack planes, with the best examples being the Tenzan and Ryūsei torpedo bombers and the Suisei dive-bomber; single-engine seaplanes like the Kyōfu and giant flying boats like the Kawanishi Type 2; the high-tech, radar-equipped Gekkō nightfighters; hot new recon planes like the Sai'un—said to be able to outrun a Hellcat in level flight; and last but not least, the mounts of the navy's formerly hemisphere-dominating fighter branch, the legendary Zero and its superlative up-and-coming successor, the Kawanishi Shidenkai.[1] But despite this cornucopia of jobs and machines to choose from, the choice was a no-brainer for Tokurō and his classmates. They had not come this far to puddle-jump around the backwaters of the dwindling empire in seaplanes, or to languish in landlocked torpedo and dive-bomber units with the nation's carrier fleet now turning into extremely expensive coral reef at the bottom of the Pacific. As for an assignment to heavy bombers, well, that was about as exciting as being asked to drive buses. And who wanted to fly into combat with ineffective escort in large, slow targets whose only contribution to

---

*Isshiki Rikkō is short for Isshiki Rikujō Kōgekiki, or "Type-one land-based attack plane." The aircraft's most famous World War II deployments were during the brilliant Takijirō Ōnishi–planned mission that sank the British battleships *Repulse* and *Prince of Wales* off of Malaya in December 1941. Admiral Yamamoto was riding one when shot down over Buin in the Solomons in April 1943. Like so many other IJN designs, it had superlative range and good speed, which it enjoyed at the cost of sacrificing protective armor and self-sealing fuel tanks. The aircraft were called "Flying Lighters" by pilots of both sides of the conflict for their habit of exploding into fireballs as soon as they sustained hits in combat. See Yuzawa (1996) and Watanabe (2003) for more performance information on this aircraft. Davis (1969) and Hammel (1992) provide graphic assessments of the aircraft's performance from the perspective of Americans who shot it down.

the war these days was to fatten American kill tallies? With B-29s now beginning to grind the nation's population centers into bonemeal, there was only one kind of airplane that mattered anymore—the fighter.

Anticipating the overwhelming popularity of fighters as the most hotly sought-after assignment with the Cycle 38 cadets, the Ōmura faculty made every effort to ensure that sufficient numbers of candidates also opted for the less glamorous assignments. These units, after all, were suffering just as many casualties as the fighter jocks, and were thus just as desperate for replacements. While the administration of course had the authority to assign personnel as the service's needs dictated, common sense and experience said that it was better from a morale standpoint for the cadets to get assigned to their first choices whenever possible. In light of this consideration, something had to be done to lessen the appeal of the fighter branch for all but the most dauntless and motivated cadets.

Toward the end of Yokaren half a year earlier, the Kō-13 cadets had begun to overhear the expressions *tokkō* and *taiatari* at Matsuyama with increasing frequency. While the boys had a general idea that the tactics involved extreme danger, no one at their security clearance level in May 1944 was aware that they inevitably called for self-immolation. But the media blitz about Lieutenant Seki and the Shikishima flight at Leyte Gulf six months later finally brought all the dropped hints and snippets of scuttlebutt together, and what were formerly vague theoretical concepts and rumors now had a palpably grisly immediacy.

On the day in January 1945 when the cadets of Ōmura Cycle 38 were to submit their formal requests for assignment, the flight school commandant told the candidates that it was virtually guaranteed that anyone who volunteered for fighters was going to go "into *tokkō* units from which there is a zero percent chance of returning home alive."[2] But threats or not, nothing was going to change Tokuro's mind, and 60 out of his 170 classmates shared his convictions. The personnel office staff, shaking their heads with equal parts exasperation at the boys' stubbornness and admiration for their courage, eliminated first sons and only children* from the

---

*First sons and only children, in the traditional Japanese family model, are expected to assume responsibility for carrying on the family name and caring for parents in their dotage. The importance of this role is reflected in the special attention, respect, and privileges afforded such children both inside and outside of the family.

batch, whittling the original sixty down to thirty-eight. On January 11, after a short graduation speech by the Ōmura commandant, the fighter group boys bade farewell to their other classmates, gathered their gear, and spent most of the rest of the day going through tiresome outprocessing procedures like cleaning and returning gear to the quartermaster, and filling in combat insurance forms and next-of-kin notification cards with the HQ pencil pushers. That night they rode flatbed trucks to Ōmura Station. The boys were told nothing about their destination when they arrived, and still nothing when they boarded specially reserved passenger cars on an eastbound express train that night.

Once seated on the train, Tokurō nodded off quickly. When he opened his eyes again, it was morning and the train was just passing through Hamamatsu. The buildings were as drably industrial as always, but to Tokurō at that moment, savoring the scenery through the condensation-misted window glass, they were as breathtaking as a snowcapped Mount Fuji bathed in dawn sunlight. Realizing that he was probably looking at his hometown for the last time in his young life, he wished that the train would at least slow down enough to give him a longer look. But he was on an express, hurtling for points east. He craned his neck out the window to get as long a look as he could at Hamamatsu, getting small and sinking away into the cross ties.

The train pulled into Tokyo Station about three o'clock that afternoon. The new pilots were marched with their gear to the main gates of the Imperial Palace, stopped to bow in greeting, then moved on to pay their respects at Yasukuni Shrine, where they were reassured that they would "soon be resting for all eternity."[3] The march then continued through a couple of kilometers of downtown Tokyo to Meiji Shrine in Harajuku, where there was another group prayer.

As Tokurō had not grown up in a religious household, he was not particularly comforted by this detour pilgrimage, which smacked as much of self-administered funerary rites as it did of the invocation of divine providence. The ritual was the first of its kind he had experienced in his sixteen months of naval service, and the notion that the people in charge thought it important enough to take time out of a busy transportation schedule did not seem to forebode well for the unknown assignment that awaited the newly graduated pilots of Ōmura Cycle 38.

After a comfortable night's sleep on fluffy civilian futon mattresses in a Tokyo inn—perhaps the last time in their lives they would enjoy such luxurious sleeping arrangements—the boy petty officers were given a few hours of leave to sightsee. They were then marched back to Tokyo Station, where they boarded a train that took them to Sawara, a nondescript burg in Ibaraki Prefecture about fifty kilometers from the eastern edge of the Tokyo metropolis. From Sawara, navy flatbeds drove them deeper into the boondocks, where civilization's only toehold was a string of anonymous fishing villages dotting the Pacific coastline. As night fell, the small convoy negotiated unpaved dirt roads through an unappealing landscape of sand flats and scrub pines. If the navy had decided to build a secret base here for security measures, they could not have picked many places in central Japan more remote than this.

The convoy eventually came to a halt at a sentry gate, where a large wooden sign read, KAIGUN JINRAI BUTAI ("Navy Divine Thunder Unit"), 721ST KŌKŪTAI (KKT). A smaller, more clerically lettered metal sign over the gate read, KŌNOIKE NAVAL AIR STATION. Tokurō and his fellow truck passengers exchanged looks. Kōnoike? No one had heard of it. And what in the world did "Divine Thunder" mean? Was it some sort of Shinto reference? Did the name have something to do with the prayer visit to Meiji Shrine the day before? No one knew a thing, and answers would have to wait until the Jinrai NCO who ordered them off the trucks stopped yelling at them for showing up still wearing their old seven-buttoned navy-blue cadet uniforms. They were not at Yokaren or flight school anymore.

After calisthenics and chow the next morning, the newest petty officer pilots of the Jinrai Unit began in-processing. They were issued with new fatigues and flight suits, then assembled in a large wooden hangar, where a lieutenant gave the group a long, detailed, and brutally frank assessment of the current status of the Japanese war effort. The briefing ended with the officer expressing the notion that no one currently in uniform—and certainly not qualified naval aviators—should expect to survive the war. Maximum effort and supreme sacrifice might just be poster slogans for civilians, they were reminded, but they were words that navy men lived and died by, and it was time for all of them to show their families, their country, and, above all, their emperor that they were worthy of this honor and men of their word.

The collective mood of the chattering, chipper group of fifteen- and sixteen-year-olds who had filed into the hangar just a few moments before expecting to get Zero assignments now bordered on the morose. For most of the boys, this was the first time they had heard anything but pumped-up enthusiasm about the war coming from an authority figure, and they were visibly shaken by the talk. In addition to being told that their country was losing the war, they had also just been given what amounted to death sentences.

Tokurō and his old Yokaren squadmates still with the group had been clued in for almost a year now on the general gist of this talk, thanks to the Midway and Solomons revelations they had heard at Matsuyama back in early '44, but the newest awful details were still sobering nonetheless: the bloodletting in the Marianas; the loss of the last carrier task force in the IJN at Cape Engaño during the Leyte campaign; the impending fall of the rest of the Philippines; the inability to put up effective resistance against the B-29s. . . . Everything the lieutenant told them spelled doom and defeat for Japan.

In spite of the gloomy mood he had just created, the young officer's expression seemed strangely expectant. It was obvious that he was waiting for the right timing to lay on a punch line he knew was going to knock everyone back on their heels. Tokurō braced himself for the worst.

"I realize that what I have just told you may tempt you to lose hope in our war effort," the lieutenant said, clasping a lecturer's pointer in both hands behind his back. "Don't let that happen. What I am about to tell you should help make sure that it doesn't."

The lieutenant paused for effect, looking at the serious faces in the group while several noncoms started handing out small blank sheets of paper and pencils.

"The navy's weapons technicians have perfected the design of a topsecret superweapon that may very well turn around the course of the war," the lieutenant said, pausing briefly as a murmur buzzed through the assembly. "The navy needs volunteers to pilot this weapon. And that's why you are here. But I must tell you that nobody who sorties in the weapon will come back alive. Am I making myself understood? No one comes home alive. Before we go any further with this briefing, write your names on the pieces of paper you have just been given. If you agree to volunteer for the program, draw a circle under your name. If you would like to be excused and reassigned to other duties, leave this space blank."

The boys began scratching away on the memo papers, using each other's backs as writing surfaces. As they were all standing while they did this, it was easy to see what everyone else was writing. Tokurō saw the boys to his left and right draw large double circles—one inside the other*—so he did the same, mimicking the devil-may-care flourish they made as they signed their lives away. The brisk, almost nonchalant way Tokurō signed his own paper, however, was not a matter of postpubescent bravado or stiff-upper-lip resignation to his fate. Rather, it was more an expression of mild annoyance at being made to play along with what he felt to be a redundant—even insulting—gesture. The boys of Flight School Cycle 38 were still only in their midteens, but they were also Yokaren graduates, noncommissioned officers of the regular navy, and qualified naval aviators. What was going to be asked for next, a letter of permission from their mothers? Enough formality nonsense, speeches, and shrine visits, Tokurō thought. Just point the planes in the direction of the enemy and give the orders. Get on with it already.

The Jinrai NCOs collected the papers, and huddled in front of the group as they tallied the responses. Several boys had their names called, were pulled off to the side, and whisked away with palpable scorn by a disgusted-looking petty officer, never to be seen again. A moment later, the remaining boys were called to attention, and an important-looking older officer introduced as a naval aide to the imperial court read out a proclamation penned in His Majesty's own hand, exhorting the new pilots to do their utmost for the nation.[4]

With some of the boys still sniffling with pride and emotion in the wake of the impromptu proclamation ceremony, the group was marched out to the flight line, where they were halted in front of a large canvas tent open on one side. Inside, visible through the opened tent flap, was something that looked like a torpedo about six meters long with stubby wings, twin tail rudders, and a large wooden skid affixed to the underside. The wings and tail surfaces appeared to be made of fabric-covered plywood, with aileron- and rudder-control surfaces like those on their old Akatonbo trainers—cellulose-doped canvas stretched over a wooden framework. A cluster of three rocket nozzles was housed in the tail of the

---

*Common Japanese written symbol of strong approval or enthusiastic praise, often used by teachers on pupils' calligraphy practice sheets.

aluminum fuselage. Tokurō was probably not the only boy whose Adam's apple twanged once, hard, when he noticed that the "torpedo" also had a cockpit.

"This is the secret weapon that is going to save Japan," the lieutenant said, now using the lecturer's pointer. "The Project Marudai special attack craft. It's what you will be riding into battle as Jinrai pilots."

There were whispers and murmurs among the group.

The lieutenant waited for the murmuring to quiet down before continuing, explaining that Project Marudai had been so named in honor of the initiator of the project, Lieutenant Masakazu Ōta, a former transport pilot.* Approximately nine months earlier, after Lieutenant Ōta rotated back to Japan from duties in the Southwest Pacific, he approached the Aeronautics Research Laboratory at Tokyo University with a proposal for a dedicated *tokkō* weapon. Rough plans were drawn up, then sent to the navy's top technicians at the Aerial Weapons Research Lab in Yokosuka, where the engineering was hammered out, blueprints drawn, and prototypes built for testing. Since then, numerous test and training flights had been made, and the lieutenant could say from experience that the flying characteristics of the Marudai were excellent.

Obviously, the craft he flew—and that the new Jinrai pilots would soon fly—did not contain actual explosives. Sand was used for ballast where the explosives would normally be loaded in the warhead, which contained 1.2 tons of TNT in a combat configuration. It would be more than enough to take out an aircraft carrier or battleship in a single blow.

The weapon would be delivered to the area of operations slung under the belly of an Isshiki Rikkō mother plane. Released from an altitude of six thousand meters, the Marudai had an operational gliding range of thirty-five kilometers at full combat weight. If there was a sudden need for a boost in speed—for example, if pursued by enemy fighters over the target area—or if an extra two or three kilometers of range was needed when unpowered gliding range appeared insufficient to reach the target,

---

*Japanese code names for projects or proposals often use this *maru-* prefix + key element suffix nomenclature convention. *Maru*, which means "circle," refers to the circle actually drawn around the key element character when this nomenclature is written as a symbol. *Dai* in this case is taken from an alternate reading of Ōta's name.

these needs could be provided for by the pilot pressing ignition switches on the instrument panel in the cockpit either in sequence or in tandem to engage the three solid-fuel* rocket boosters located in the tail of the craft. Speeds up to four hundred sixty kilometers per hour were attainable by gliding alone, but if the rocket bottles were ignited sequentially, giving a total burn time of up to thirty seconds, that top speed could be boosted up to seven-fifty in level flight or even higher in a steep dive—far faster than anything the Americans had in the air. Once within two or three kilometers of the target with rockets engaged, no fighter could catch the craft, and nothing but a lucky AA hit would be able to stop it. And seeing how the frontal silhouette of the craft was only about the size of a beach ball, that would have to be a shot from a very lucky and very skillful AA gunner, indeed.

The lieutenant pointed at the venturi nozzles in the tail of the craft, explaining that these canisters were rocket-assisted takeoff boosters originally designed for new, larger attack planes like the Ryūsei to be able to operate from short carrier decks. Since His Majesty's navy was no longer conducting carrier-based flight operations, there were large stocks of these RATO bottles available for immediate use with Project Marudai. The briefing ended with the new pilots being told that their flights in Marudai trainer craft like this would begin after sufficient orientation in tokkō tactics and practice flights in conventional aircraft. Said training was to begin immediately.

Flight attack training began as soon as in-processing was completed. Ironically, Tokurō's dreams of becoming a fighter jock had finally come true, in a sense. The Jinrai's simulated tokkō dives were run in banged-up old Zero Model 21s, survivors from the early war years that had long since been relegated to home island training units. But despite the war-weary Zeros, it was obvious that the unit's mission was getting high priority, as it was being provided with enough gas to keep aircraft in the air almost constantly, and this at a time when other training units around

---

*This top-secret fuel was code-named FTD6, and was a mixture of 60 percent cotton fibrous stabilizing filler, 3 percent potassium sulfate, 7 percent mononitronaphthalene, and 27 percent pure nitroglycerin. (Kimata [2001], p. 34.)

the country were having to scale operations way back. From mid-January until well into late spring of 1945, Tokurō and his fellow pilots were in the air almost daily, logging more flight time than they could have ever dreamed of getting in a conventional outfit.

Tokurō made his first few attack-simulation flights in a special two-seater Zero "Type K" trainer with an experienced pilot on the other stick in the backseat. After a few of these chaperoned runs, he began flying the practice dives solo. Standard procedure was to take a Zero up to about three thousand meters, then cut throttle, nose over into a dive and buzz a designated "target" area of the airfield, where a junior officer would be sitting in a lawn chair with a notepad and binoculars, grading the runs. Angle of dive was generally between thirty and forty-five degrees, but with gravity and a three-bladed variable-pitch propeller pulling 2,700 kilograms of airplane toward trees, buildings, and an ensign in a lawn chair getting very large very quickly in the windscreen, forty-five degrees felt more like ninety. At the last possible second—preferably knocking the officer off his chair in the process—the pilot would pull back on the stick, slam the throttle forward, and power-zoom up and out of the dive to corkscrew around the field for altitude and another go. After landing, the pilots would assemble for a debriefing, where their diving approach techniques would be critiqued by senior pilots and officers in the training cadre.

While the Zero runs were breathtakingly dangerous, the single Marudai training drop each Jinrai pilot had to complete for full certification was the ultimate white-knuckler. Even with carrier-qualified, experienced pilots at the stick, the accident rate in the trainers was less than confidence-inspiring, with about one in ten drops ending in broken bones at best, or a dead qualified naval aviator at the worst.[5] After all of the officers and senior NCO pilots had been cycled through the training, the 105 junior Yokaren graduate pilots on the base began checking out on the craft. The training mission roster then followed date of arrival by group, and Akinori Asano, Takurō's Matsuyama and Ōmura classmate, was one of the first of the Cycle 38 pilots to ride the Marudai, although even he had quite a bit of a wait before the pilots scheduled for the first combat drops were all checked out.

On the day of his training drop, Akinori was given one final briefing on the flight line before boarding the specially modified Isshiki Rikkō bomber "mother plane" that would take the Marudai trainer up. The pointers were basic but vital:

*Remember, you're in a glider, not an airplane. The RATO bottles in the tail are empty, so you have no way of getting a power boost if you need it. Watch your airspeed, and don't stall out. Don't pull back on the stick. You'll be coming in at extreme speed, even with flaps down, so make sure you touch down soon enough that you don't run out of runway.*

Inside the mother plane, Akinori sat on his parachute pack facing forward, with the open canopy of the Marudai cockpit poking up through a bathtub-sized hole in the floor at his feet. This aperture was by no means airtight, and the sound added by the wind screaming through the opening as the bomber throttled up and went airborne only exacerbated the sixteen-year-old's anxiety at sitting on the edge of a trapdoor to precipitous oblivion.

When the plane reached the release altitude of approximately 3,500 meters, it maneuvered toward the optimum drop point. A minute or so out, a crewman helped Akinori into the Marudai, strapped him in, and gave the boy pilot a sharp salute before buttoning up the Plexiglas canopy. The apple-green cockpit of the trainer was a suffocating fit even for a modestly sized boy like Akinori, with a lingering smell of paint, plywood, and the sour adrenaline sweat of other pilots who had already taken their own wild rides in the craft.

With the Marudai banging around in the propwash and turbulence, the shrill whistle of wind around the canopy and the throb of the mother plane's engines were so loud Akinori could hardly hear himself being scared shitless. Strapped into this sensory-overload chamber, he focused his attention on the craft's spartan instrument panel, which consisted of a compass, airspeed indicator, altimeter, a rudimentary wing turn-and-bank indicator, and a signal lamp that would flash a "dot-dot-dot-dash"* signal before the Marudai was released on a final "dot."

The dark ruby signal lamp became Akinori's mandala as he tried to keep his mind from flip-flopping off into decidedly unhappy landing scenarios. He sucked in one last long breath, grabbed the stick in a death grip, and braced himself for the shock of release as the lamp glowed vermilion and the flash sequence began.

*Dot-dot-dot-dash . . .*

---

*Japanese Morse code for the syllable *Yo*, meant here as an abbreviation of *Yoi* ("ready"). (Asano, personal correspondence.)

The explosive bolt tethering the Marudai to the mother plane blew with a sharp, jarring *crack!* in sync with the last lamp flash "dot," and Akinori's breakfast slammed hard into his diaphragm. The dark interior and skull-rattling roar of the Isshiki Rikkō whooshed up and away, and the world was suddenly all blue and white and bright light, the only sounds now a soft whistle of wind poking through the joints in the canopy Plexiglas and Akinori's heartbeat in his throat. As the gravity acceleration of the drop leveled off into a constant velocity, riding in the craft gave less of a sensation of plummeting than it did of level flight, although repeated glances at the landscape coming up fast below reminded Akinori that he was falling almost as rapidly as he was flying, and that he had less than two minutes in the air before he had to figure out how he was going to put the Marudai on the ground in one piece.

Sobering reminders of time and gravity aside, the trainer was a joy to fly. The stubby wings gave it a roll rate like a fighter, but the twin rudder arrangement afforded excellent stability and minimal yaw. Akinori put the craft through its paces, making the most of his two minutes of airborne freedom rolling, banking, and lining up various imaginary targets on the ground through the ring and post in front of the windscreen that served as the Marudai's sighting system. The craft flew straight and true toward anything he aimed at. When the moment of truth came, he could put this thing right down the funnel of a ship if he wanted to.

By the two-minute mark, altitude was less than one thousand meters but airspeed was a blistering 460 kph. Akinori banked the trainer through a series of turns to bleed off some speed before settling into a glide path for the tree-bordered patch of grass on Kōnoike Auxiliary Field 2 that served as the special Marudai landing strip.* This was the most crucial stage of the descent, and everything here was timing and depth perception: keeping proper descent rate; watching approach angle; knowing when to drop the flaps (which had only two settings—up or down); and getting the craft on the ground with enough runway to work with. Dropping the flaps too soon would result in a stall, but deploying them too late would make the landing speed excessive. In one common accident

---

*The reason for using a tree-lined strip was to conceal activities there from the prying eyes of observers—and possible spies—lurking outside the perimeter fence of the high-security installation. (Asano, personal correspondence.)

pattern, the Marudai would crash-land when the pilot panicked and pulled back on the stick in an instinctive braking attempt, causing the craft to flip over backward and crush its occupant when the canopy collapsed. The most common mishap, however, was when the momentum of a high-speed landing would simply end up carrying the craft past the far end of the runway and into the trees.

Remembering everything he had been taught in the preflight lectures, Akinori waited until he was about a kilometer out before dropping flaps. The Marudai decelerated rapidly, but airspeed was still 200 kph when the wooden landing skid hit the grass. Akinori's fate now depended solely upon the friction between the landing skid and the grass runway stopping the craft before it careened into the trees.

After covering almost the entire 2,500-meter length of the landing strip, the craft finally shuddered and scraped to a stop in the shadow of the scrub pines at the end of the runway. Akinori's adrenaline buzz gave way to a profound and ecstatic relief at being alive, and his sweat-drenched flight suit suddenly felt as heavy as lead. Closing his eyes and catching his breath, he heard the *putt-putt* of a small motor in the distance. The sound got louder until a ground crewman on a navy-blue motorcycle with a sidecar pulled up and helped him out of the cockpit. He rode in the sidecar back to the command post on the main base and reported the results of the drop to the CO of Ōka* Section One, Lieutenant Akira Hirano. After his report, he went back to the barracks, flopped on his bunk, and savored the fact that he was alive to enjoy the moment. Dying could wait for another day.

---

*The official name for the Marudai craft was Ōka ("Cherry Blossom"), and it was the latter nomenclature that was used in press releases after the Jinrai Unit began combat operations in March 1945. However, according to Mr. Takei, most pilots called it "Marudai" until the end of the war.

# twelve

## AMENITIES

W hen not buzzing airfield buildings in mock suicide dives, Marudai pilots led leisurely and comfortable lives compared with the daily grind and stresses of an aviator in a line unit engaged in regular combat. The permanent KP duty that Tokurō, Akinori, and their Ōmura classmates were assigned to as junior personnel on the pilot roster was no fun at all,* but other than that, compared to Yokaren and flight school, they were living high off the hog. Best of all, they would never again have to deal with the kind of arbitrarily abusive discipline they had known as Yokaren and flight school cadets. They had considerable amounts of free time on their hands and wallets fat with flight and hazardous-duty pay riding on their hips.

The boys had so much money, in fact, that they were often pressed to think up ways of spending it. Unlike the situation at Yokaren and Ōmura, they did not have to pay for most amenities anymore. As *tokkō* personnel, they were given what would be considered "luxury" items as standard-issue rations. Hefty slabs of rich chocolate, packs of cigarettes,

---

*Japanese naval and army personnel did not "serve KP" in the sense traditionally abhorred by generations of American servicemen. In rear area posts such as Kōnoike, such duties were performed by specialized kitchen staff, and "KP" for Tokurō and his peers consisted of lugging full rice and stew pots prepared in the kitchen down to the barracks, then bringing the empty pots and cans back to the kitchen after chow (there were no "mess halls" on Japanese posts—personnel usually ate in their barracks or at their duty stations—the youngest personnel would drag the food cans around to wherever someone was waiting for chow).

and small bottles of Nikka whiskey were handed out a few times a week, as were emergency aviation rations,* which were stockpiled in literal mountains of boxes in the base dry goods storehouse. Bottles of wine and sake were distributed every few days, a policy which led directly to Tokurō—like so many of his peers—finding out the hard way that he was alcohol intolerant. Having never drunk anything more than a tongue tip's worth of his father's sake as a child, he was at a bit of a loss as to what to do when issued his first bottle of wine at Kōnoike. All doubts aside, appearing to be a sissy in front of his barracks mates was not an option here, so he slammed down the whole bottle in minutes flat, then promptly passed out. What he experienced after regaining consciousness at reveille the next morning was harrowing enough to make him resolve never to drink like that again, and he made it a practice from then on to trade away his booze to veteran pilots in the barracks who had no need for their candy and confectionary rations but who sometimes needed a little liquid assistance in keeping their bad dreams at bay.

Although only fifteen or sixteen years old, Tokurō and his classmates were treated as adults and, like other Jinrai pilots, given a lot of leeway as far as minor infractions of uniform regulations or military protocol lapses. For example, the majority of Tokurō's group began smoking cigarettes after their arrival at Kōnoike, regardless of the fact that they were four or five years under the legal limit of twenty years of age for such adult recreation. But just as the boozing in the barracks was overlooked, the Jinrai command staff and cadre recognized the absurdity of demanding adherence to naval smoking regulations from young men in the uniform of their country who would be asked to die in coming months. If these boys were prepared to die like men, then it seemed only fair that they be allowed to smoke and drink like them, too.

The relaxed atmosphere of the Kōnoike culture—in such stark contrast to the grisly reality of the Jinrai mission—carried over into the highly egalitarian tone of relations between officers and enlisted flight personnel, which were relaxed even by *tokkō* standards. Mutual respect among pilots of all ranks and ages precluded excessive reliance on military protocol to maintain professionalism, and the use of less than rigidly formal language

---

*These packs contained several thousand calories worth of caramels and were intended to be used as pilot survival rations. They were normally found in emergency medical kits on aircraft.

when addressing superiors—a lapse that would have resulted in an on-the-spot howdy-do to the kisser in most any other naval or army units—was generally tolerated at the base. Not surprisingly, the morale of the Jinrai's personnel was quite high, even by elite naval aviation standards.[1]

The two officers most responsible for establishing and maintaining this almost paradoxical combination of professional pride, relaxed atmosphere, and high morale were the Jinrai CO, Captain Motoharu Okamura, and Commander Gorō Nonaka, CO of the 711th Hikōtai (HKT), the Jinrai's main attack element. Both officers were highly experienced combat veterans and products of the Imperial Naval Academy. But despite their Etajima pedigrees, Okamura and Nonaka were not martinet sticklers for details and regulations; nor were they too proud or haughty to receive and appreciate feedback from their subordinates—even from the enlisted ranks. Experience in the field had shown them that uptight attention to trivia and ignoring the opinion of their men were detrimental to morale and performance under the stresses of combat. And if any of the seventeen other INA men[2] on base holding key positions in the chain of command thought otherwise, Okamura and Nonaka would see to it that they either quickly got with the program and learned to grin and bear it, or transferred out before they could do any damage.

One INA graduate who needed no urging to approach his subordinates with a relaxed attitude was the easygoing Lieutenant Hirano, whose even temperament and good communications skills were probably why he was pulled from the Jinrai combat roster and put in command of Ōka Pilot Section One, which had just received a consignment of thirty-odd Yokaren fifteen- and sixteen-year-old PO3s straight out of flight school. Hirano was joined by a cadre of seven naval reserve ensigns whose skills as potential educators were also held in esteem by Jinrai HQ, and these eight officers were ordered to stay behind at Kōnoike to see after their fledglings' training needs when the main attack element of the 721st flew south for deployment in Kyūshū on January 20. The lonely reality of being left out of the fight, combined with saying farewell to comrades and fast friends for what might very well be the last time, had the Section One cadre members suffering something of a dip in morale. Adding to the gloom, a thunderous silence prevailed on base in the absence of the charismatic and wildly popular Commander Nonaka, who had taken with him to Kyūshū his beaming smile, tea ceremony utensils, repertoire of joyfully shrieked profanities, and the replica samu-rai war banners he often used as motivational props. But Hideo Suzuki, one of the ensigns in Section One, came up with an idea for countering the blues afflicting Lieutenant Hirano's cadre members. The ensign, a native of the entertainment and hot springs resort of Atami, Shizuoka Prefecture, considered himself to be an expert in matters of rest and recreation, and he approached the mustachioed but still rather naïve young INA graduate one day during these late January doldrums with some measure of confidence in his plan.

"You know, Lieutenant," Suzuki began, "submariners always get great R and R after they come back from a combat mission, don't they?"

Hirano blinked at the non sequitur for a moment.

"Yes. I suppose they do. So?"

"Well, Lieutenant, wouldn't you agree that Ōka pilots are just as elite as submariners?"

"Uh, certainly. Unquestionably."

"But we won't be coming back from our missions."

"No, I don't suppose so."

"Well, sir, it just doesn't seem fair, and you know it isn't healthy for us all to be cooped up on this lonely base all the time. Who knows what kind of effect all this gloom might be having on our fighting effectiveness?"

"Hmm . . . I agree that is a matter of some concern," Hirano said, blinking some more, twisting his mustache a bit. "But you know I can't authorize any leave. The base is top secret, and so is our unit. There's no precedent at Kōnoike for personnel taking leave. Nobody has left since we came here in November, outside of official business or a family emergency."

Suzuki had not yet begun to fight.

"Well, that's just my point, sir. Begging the lieutenant's pardon, don't you think it would be good for our morale if we *could* get out of here for a spell? Maybe to a hot springs resort somewhere? I have family connec-tions in Atami. I can set it up. And there wouldn't be any security risk if we all go together. You'll be there to supervise us, after all."

"I don't know, Suzuki, I don't know. I'll take it up with command at the next COs' meeting, but don't get your hopes up."

One night a few days later, the lieutenant showed up in the officer pi-lots' quarters wearing a big smile.

"Pack your bags, boys. We're going to Atami tomorrow," Hirano said to cheers. "And the navy is paying for everything."

After several days of geisha carousing and hot-spring steaming in Atami on the navy dime, the officers returned to Kōnoike satiated and refreshed. Outside of the immediate improvement in junior officer morale, the Atami junket had the long-term beneficial effect of establishing precedent in the Jinrai organization for weekend leave, which Captain Okamura subsequently decided to limit to officer personnel on twenty-four-hour passes good from Saturday to Sunday afternoon. Ever painfully aware of the true nature of their mission, despite the plentiful creature comforts on base, a lot of the pilots made every effort they could to hit the pleasure quarters of Tokyo on weekends and satisfy biological urges that, under the circumstances, were perfectly understandable.

While the young man ultimately to thank for everyone else's pleasure-seeking opportunities was himself certainly not immune to their allure, being within eight or nine hours' rail travel from home proved to be the greater temptation for Hideo Suzuki. The ensign's priority was getting boodle from the lavishly stocked Kōnoike PX to his family in Atami, who, like civilians everywhere in Japan, were seriously hurting for foodstuffs by early '45. Suzuki would try to get out every weekend he could with a big suitcase packed to bursting with bean jam cakes, preserves, whiskey, chocolate, cigarettes, and other luxuries. He would spend all but a few hours of the twenty-four-hour passes riding on crowded trains or making the interminable series of tiresome connections at stations to and from Atami, but he always thought it was worth the trouble to see his family's smiling faces every time he arrived home with his bag of goodies and, more important, with himself still in one piece. Playing out that scene again and again, as many times as he could get away with it, was something Suzuki never tired of, just as he never tired of trying to stretch every hour at home into a small eternity.

It is November 9, 2002. Hideo Suzuki is sitting across from me at a banquet table. He is lean and long-faced for a Japanese of his generation, with large eyes deep-set and intense behind a high-bridged nose. His is almost a Levantine face, and it would not be incongruous on a man named Irving or Sal sitting on a park bench in Brooklyn, chomping on a green cigar while he bragged about his grandchildren and complained about his gallbladder. His shiny eighty-year-old head is fringed with snowy white hair, and this imbues him with an aura of Ebenezer Scrooge at first glance, but his surface crustiness is confirmed as benign by the deep smile creases in his cheeks and the laughter he lets out frequently. It is not the nervous laughter Japanese often display to smoke-screen uncomfortable situations, but sincere and straight from the belly. He refuses to suffer fools gladly and will not hesitate to speak his mind when he thinks someone is out of line. It is clear that he is at the point in his life—which must be wonderfully liberating for this former warrior of the rigid Japanese corporate culture—when he is no longer obligated to camouflage his feelings for appearance's sake. He seems breezily contented with this state of being.

We are in the rear dining room of a large, multistory restaurant in Yokohama's Chinatown, venue of the annual Jinrai reunion that has ended about an hour ago. Some of the decorations from the event are still up, and the backdrop for our table is a large imperial navy battle jack—the Rising Sun radiant with sunbeams—nearly as big as a garrison flag, taking up almost an entire wall. We are joined at our table by other Jinrai veterans, including another Waseda alumnus, Tokuji Naitō, who was also Suzuki's flight school classmate and one of the second group of naval reserve ensign pilots who arrived at Kōnoike in December 1944. Naitō-san was a lit major at Waseda, and the bookish orientation suits his mien. His bald pate, narrow eyes, and enigmatic smile give him the countenance of a Buddhist abbot. If we were in a one-on-one situation, I might half expect him to hit me up with a few Zen riddles. He is an introspective, intellectual type, meticulous in speech and manner. I imagine these traits must have served him well in his career as a Tokyo municipal bureaucrat.

A decidedly Falstaffian and incandescent Akinori Asano is also here, emitting high-amplitude wavelengths from the far-red end of the spectrum. He has just finished his "the time I rode the Marudai trainer" account in a performance well seasoned with appropriate sound effects and hand and body gestures. The story garnered some chuckles and remarks in a "Can you believe they put us in those things?" vein from the other old men at the table.

"How many drops did you make?" I ask naïvely.

Evidently, I have triggered some kind of stock sequence about to be played out here, because everyone at the table suddenly looks at Asano-san expectantly.

Asano-san assumes an expression of exaggerated umbrage, his head weaving slightly side to side. In an instantaneous and somewhat surreal mental connection, I recognize what I am seeing as Ralph Kramden a nanosecond away from threatening Alice with the moon.

"You only had to do it once," Asano-san huffs, and several men join in to complete the couplet, almost on cue: *"And once was enough!"*

The table breaks out into loud guffaws now, and I feel my ears turn red. A middle-aged waitress clearing dishes from another table steals a look at us. I sense that she wants us to leave. But she is going to have to endure a few more war stories before that happens.

Naitō-san is the only person at the table not laughing.

"I almost crashed on my own drop," he says, oddly dispassionate, perhaps trying to rescue me from my temporary embarrassment. "I went into the rough at the end of the runway. Luckily, I missed the trees."

The conversation takes a turn through time and landscapes, war and peace. The mood at the table becomes somber. Faces and places are recalled, and Suzuki and Naitō muse on the losses that ravaged the ranks of the Ōka reserve ensigns.

"You know, we came *this* close to getting completely wiped out," Suzuki-san says.

"Just as promised," he adds with a tired chuckle.

Suzuki-san chuckles alone, though, and I wonder if the semantic significance of his remark is responsible for the slightly uncomfortable silence that sits over the table now. He has not claimed, as many Japanese veterans are wont to do, that it was "the war" or "the Americans" or "the times" that should be held responsible for the death of his comrades. Instead, what has just been suggested—or at least this is what my nonnative speaker's ears have picked up—is that it was the onus of obligation implied in the "promise" that had done the killing.* Without the nod of an

---

*Suzuki-san's comment in the original Japanese was: *"Dakara, hotondo, yakusoku do-ri ni korareteshimatta."* Readers knowledgeable in Japanese will note that responsibility is tactfully vague in this passive utterance.

expectant benefit receiver—without agreement from the second party—
a "promise" is still merely a proposal. If the pilots assumed some portion
of the responsibility for their self-immolation upon rising to the *tokkō*
battle cry, then the rest of the responsibility was shouldered by everyone
else who agreed with the idea—who expressed gracious thanks and sent
the boys off with speeches and fanfare, never thinking to lift a finger to
stop what was happening or even wonder aloud if there were reasonable
alternatives to this slaughter.

In the case of the Ōkas, none of the young men who drew circles on
their ballot papers for *tokkō* slots at their training bases really knew what
they were getting into until they took a walk down to the flight line at
Kōnoike and saw the winged torpedoes for the first time. And by that
point, it was too late and they were too proud to turn back. They were
young and brave and wanted to help win the war—or at least turn back
the American onslaught and "win the peace"—any way they could. The
code of loyalty socialized and drilled into them from childhood demanded that they leave the details of how that could best be accomplished up to their superiors. The Japanese state in those days had a
ready supply of millions upon millions of young Japanese men like this.
Tokurō Takei, Akinori Asano, Hideo Suzuki, and Tokuji Naitō were four
of them, and at one point in their lives, they felt the best way to serve
this state was by agreeing to become human bombs.

## thirteen

# LOOKING FOR A FEW GOOD WAR GODS

I n September 1943, Hideo Suzuki was only a few weeks away
from his war-accclerated graduation* from Waseda when his
attention was drawn to a Navy Ministry notice posted on a campus bulletin board. Recruiters scheduled to visit the college were looking
for naval aviator officer candidates. Like many of his classmates, Suzuki
was facing imminent and somewhat less-than-welcome conscription into
the army upon the completion of his studies.† Understandably, he was
quite receptive to options at this time, and the course outlined on the
navy poster seemed to offer him a much more glamorous and considerably more comfortable way of serving his country than tending to Mon-
golian ponies as a buck private on the Manchurian border, colder than a
well digger's ass nine months out of the year, scorched and fly plagued
the other three.

Suzuki made it safely to the navy recruiter's desk and had his name on
the dotted line before the army could get its hooks into him. The Waseda
men, Suzuki and his classmate Tokuji Naitō who now joined him, passed
their flight physicals and paper exams for the program with flying colors.
They were in naval uniform before the month was out, reporting for duty
as cadets in the thirteenth cycle of the Kaigun Hikōka Senshū Yobigakusei

---

*In a peacetime curriculum, they would have graduated the following March.
†Suzuki had already received and passed a preliminary physical clearing him for cavalry service,
which at this point in the war probably would have meant Manchurian border guard duty.

155

("Naval Aviation Specialized Training Reserve Student Course") at Mie Naval Air Station near Nagoya on September 30, 1943. The "Yobigakusei" course—as it was called in abbreviated form—was like a Yokaren for officer candidates,* combining the basic training needed to turn soft college boys into fearless warriors with the accelerated, intensive instruction in basic aviation subjects necessary to get the cadets ready for flight school. Cadets were commissioned as naval ensigns upon successfully meeting graduation requirements at the end of an eleven-month-long training cycle.

After finishing Yobigakusei in July 1944, Suzuki and Naitō went to flight school at Tainan NAS on the southern tip of Taiwan. When midterm branch destinations were handed down, Suzuki was assigned to carrier attack planes, which meant that he would be expected to handle either the big Ryūsei torpedo planes or the equally bulky Suisei dive bombers the navy was now using. Naitō, on the other hand, had been lucky enough to win a slot in fighters. After getting his wings in October, he could look forward to a job in the front office of a Zero or, even better, of a snappy new Kawanishi Shidenkai armed with four devastating 20 mm cannons, powered by a humongous eighteen-hundred-horsepower engine and purportedly superior to the Hellcat in speed, climb and roll rates, and maneuverability. He would be able to knock some Americans down in such a mount. In the meantime, while preparing for future battlefield glories, the aviator candidates put in the prerequisite Akatonbo stick time together and struggled to survive being parboiled in the sun and steam of a Taiwan summer and eaten alive by carnivorous mosquitoes.

One night in August, an unscheduled assembly was called after evening mess. The cadets and faculty proceeded to the base *budōjo*,† where they found Lieutenant Commander Shunsaku Takahashi (INA '18) waiting to address them. At forty-nine, Takahashi was perhaps a bit long in the tooth to still be languishing at his present rank, especially for an Etajima man, but he seemed to have enjoyed a rewarding career nonetheless. In addition to being the Tainan Flight School commandant, he was also a

---

*It may help the reader to envisage this course as a World War II Japanese version of what Richard Gere was put through in *An Officer and a Gentleman*. See Kaigun Hikō Senshū Yobigakusei Dai 14 Ki Kai (2001) for participants' recollections of the program.

†Literally "martial arts place," in this case the standard judo/kendo gymnasium found on any established Japanese military or naval base.

published poet and the lyricist of Polydor Japan's wildly popular 1940 propaganda hit "Getsu, Getsu, Ka, Sui, Moku, Kin, Kin" ("Five Day Work-week in the Navy: Monday, Monday, Tuesday, Wednesday, Thursday, Friday, Friday"), a kitsch masterpiece about the joys and wholesome rigors of naval life that had since entered the national pantheon of perennial pop favorites.* If Takahashi's naval career itself had been something less than stellar, he could certainly take pride in having achieved immortality as a lyricist in his lifetime.

Normally a peppy, fire-'em-up, type, Takahashi was not his usual self on this particular evening. He was sober-faced and somber-toned. His eyes were red, as if he had just finished having himself a good long cry in private before splashing some water on his face to compose himself. Whatever it was he had called everyone to talk about, it was obvious that he was dreading it.

After the assembly was formed, Takahashi suddenly ordered all only children, first sons, and fathers to leave the premises, instantly reducing the ranks by about 30 percent. The other pilots and trainees waited in silence until the excused personnel were all gone. When the door closed behind the last man out, Takahashi stood up on a calisthenics leader podium and began talking about the exceedingly sorry state of the war situation.

"As we speak a secret superweapon that could turn the tide of the war is in the final stage of development. Just one of these will be powerful enough to sink a capital ship. We need volunteers to *put their lives on the line* and operate these weapons."†

There were raised eyebrows among the cadets as the euphemisms flew fast and furious but the grim message gradually sank in.

"Everyone already knew by that point that 'put your life on the line' meant 'sacrifice your life,'" Suzuki-san recalls. "There wasn't a lot of subtle nuance involved there."

"The enemy is closing in," Takahashi had continued. "We must defend

---

*This was yet another monster propaganda hit for the Japanese subsidiary of a Western record company. Over sixty years after its debut, the ditty remains a favorite for drunken karaoke carousers, usually of the businessman type to whom the song's message of cheery yet selfless dedication to dreary work no doubt has an immediate poignancy.

†*Inochi wo kakete* in the original Japanese, which can also be translated as "risk one's life" or even just "give it one's all."

the home islands and turn back the Allies. High command believes that these secret weapons are the only way to do this. The weapons are now in the final stage of development. Those who pilot them will lose their lives. Nevertheless, the navy needs volunteers for this program. This is strictly voluntary. But keep in mind that in volunteering, you could help turn the tide of the war."

The assembly was dismissed and the pilots filed out of the martial arts hall. But where they would have normally been BSing and laughing as they made their way back to the barracks, tonight they were meditative and silent.

Suzuki did not even make it back to the barracks to think things out. He sat down right outside the entrance to the gym, stared up at the night sky, and tried to sort out what he was going to do about what he had just heard. Back in his quarters for the lights-out head count, he still had not made up his mind.

Takahashi had told the pilots they had three days to respond, and Suzuki ended up taking nearly every last minute of that time to think it over. In the end, though, the idea that his country was losing—and losing badly—was decisive. Adding to his determination was the element of panic thrown into the equation by the imagery of a senior officer like Takahashi having to come to the men like that and ask—almost plead—for volunteers instead of just giving orders. An act so incongruous with navy tradition could only foreshadow pain ahead. Things had to be really, really bad if they had come down to something like this.

Suzuki thought about the oath of loyalty to emperor and country (which were supposed to be one and the same entity, really) he had taken when he entered the Yobigakusei program, and once again when he accepted his commission as an ensign in His Majesty's navy. He figured that he and his comrades had sworn away any right or claim to their own lives the moment they put on a navy uniform. Their lives belonged to Japan now, and if fulfilling their duties to the best of their abilities meant dying for the country, then so be it.

At the time, Suzuki and the other Tainan flight school trainees were still raw and green and many hundreds of flying hours away from achieving proficiency as pilots in the highly specialized tactics of their respective conventional aviation branches. Under such circumstances, Suzuki desperately needed to believe that the new wonder weapon—whatever it turned out to be—offered an honorable alternative way for him to keep his promise to the country and make the most significant contribution to the war effort possible given his limited capabilities. One man's sacrifice to take out a fleet carrier or a battleship? Magnificent. Thinking things through this far, he seemed to have no other choice but to volunteer. He handed in his circled chit to Lieutenant Commander Takahashi.

Suzuki had always hated to think of his family constantly worrying about him. Maybe it would be better for all concerned to just end things quickly. That way his family's suffering—and his own—would be lessened. He figured he was probably going to die, one way or another, before the war was finished. Why settle for that death being on someone else's terms? Why leave it to fate—perhaps even dying without knowing it was going to happen, like in an accident, or getting caught in a sudden air raid, or shot down by Americans on a conventional mission? Whatever this "superweapon" was, if it was as good as promised, it was a golden ticket to being able to go out in a blaze of glory. Suzuki signed up for the "special attack" program with a clear conscience, confident that he would bring great honor to his family and, most important, make his mother proud.

Eighty-year-old Suzuki-san laughs somewhat forlornly here—a slow *huh-huh-huh* with some Eeyore in it—as he recalls the naïveté of an idealistic young man who took it for granted that his mother would share in his heroic sentiments.

"Of course, I don't think there's a mother in Japan now who would think such a thing, but back then, things were different," he says, still with some forlorn chuckle in his voice. "A mother, at least with the face she wore in public, was obliged to appear happy and grateful to the emperor and country for giving her son such a fine way to die. Of course, even back then, I'm sure that in their hearts all mothers wanted their sons to come home alive. But they couldn't express such things to anyone outside the family. It would be considered defeatist and unpatriotic."

While mothers at the time may have secretly prayed for their sons' safe return home, they were publicly encouraged to pray for their honorable death in battle. Citizens' committees, Army Reservist Association branches (Zaigō Gunjindan),[1] school boards, and other local propaganda organs urged families in their communities to prepare *kamidana* or *butsudan*\* in their homes, and honor their *living* sons in uniform as they would a deceased family member. The message was clear: Your son is gone forever. Live with it. A grateful nation shares in your pride.

Under a constant audiovisual bombardment of such imagery and messages through cinema, music, newsprint, posters, and communal agitprop, the populace seemed to fall sway to this mass psychology. It was not uncommon for mothers in urban areas—where there were always neighbors within earshot—to send their boys off to war saying, "Don't let me be the only mother on the block to not have a son in Yasukuni."[2] Neither was this nihilism limited to civilians. Sentiments like, "Don't worry, I'll be home safe and sound" were rarely heard from servicemen sons leaving for war. The salutation, "Please think of me as already dead"[3] was a common one in the strictly censored letters they sent home after arriving at the front.

Iwao Fukagawa, a former IJA *tokkō* pilot, suggests that the mechanism at work behind such expressions was rooted in the smothering bonds of mother love that dominate the psyches of Japanese children—especially sons—for their entire lives.[4] Worried that the emotional restraints of wanting to stay alive for mommy's sake would hamper her son's devotion to duty when the bullets started to fly, a Japanese soldier's mother was freeing her child—as well as herself—from this pressure when she exhorted him to come home from the war as a pile of ashes in an ossuary box.[5] This thinking possessed a certain merciful if convoluted patriotic

---

\*Suzuki, personal correspondence. *Kamidana* and *butsudan* are home altars for Shinto and Buddhist worship, respectively. In mid-twentieth-century Japan, most homes would have had both, with the *kamidana* being the domain of actual deities, both natural and ancestral, who watched over house and family, theologically similar in importance and function to Lares in ancient Roman homes. The *butsudan*, however, was less of a place for communication with deities than it was a place to mourn and report news to recently deceased (within one, perhaps two generations) family members. The idea that the soul of a son in uniform could be addressed in both places seems to suggest that combat death would jump a recently departed soul several generations up the ancestral line to be put on a level with older ancestors as household protectors. That the death was incurred while ostensibly in the emperor's service would also give robust Shinto legitimacy to such early deification. The *gunshin* institution, of course, is the best and ultimate example of this process. While many Japanese families paid lip service to such rites, the degree of actual faith involved is impossible to estimate with any accuracy. They could perhaps be more reasonably considered as expressions of patriotic devotion than as religious observance.

logic on the level of individuals, but moved into the realm of stark banality when institutionalized for mass consumption as the war dragged
on and Japan's prospects became irreversibly bleak. Patriotism was gradually morphing into the chrysalis of a national death cult, and by late
summer 1944, as the government and media thumped the post-Saipan
"honorable death of the 100 million" drum with ever-increasing ardor,
this cocoon was beginning to split open and show mesmerizing flashes of
dun wing.


Hideo Suzuki's career path detour from elite Waseda University man to
human glider bomb was fairly representative of the first group of seventeen naval reserve ensigns selected for the Jinrai program back in early
autumn of 1944. At a Waseda reunion many years later, Suzuki heard an
interesting anecdote from a former classmate who had worked during
the war as a clerk in the Navy Ministry's public affairs office in Tokyo.
One day in late summer of 1944, the clerk was delivering the day's out-
box contents to the ministry message center. Although he was not supposed to even glance at the documents he handled, he had a bad habit of
doing just that, and on this particular day, an asterisked name on a long
personnel list caught his eye. The line read: *Suzuki, Hideo; Naval Reserve Officer Aviation Class 13; Waseda University Class of 1943; Hometown Atami, Shizuoka.*

The clerk's eyes ran down to the bottom of the sheet to find the as-
terisk notation, which read: *Deemed suitable for special attack program
and subsequent* gunshin *status. Gunshin?!* Why use that phrase when
nobody on the list was dead yet? And what in the world did "special attack" mean, anyway? As far as anyone in the navy PAO knew, that was
just a phrase used in lurid propaganda copy for press releases about
phantom news events, but there it was now on a personnel department
memorandum, being used to refer to actual operations. His curiosity
now piqued, the clerk stole a look at a memorandum paper-clipped to
the list. It read:

> To public affairs office, select seventeen candidates from this
> list your office deems most suitable for *gunshin* status—after
> thorough personal background checks—from the standpoint

of propaganda value. Preference should be given to individuals from elite universities and/or sons of socially prominent families. By order of the Minister of the Navy.[6]

The clerk went back over the list of candidates, and sure enough, all of the asterisked names were of graduates of Waseda, Keiō, Meiji, Rikkyō, and other elite private universities or public teachers colleges. *Gunshin* designation meant that the navy either expected or intended for all these young intellectuals and rich boys to die. And why an odd number like seventeen? The clerk passed the sheaf of documents on to the message center with his questions unanswered, filed the event away in his memory under "anomalous PAO memorandum," then promptly forgot about it for the next thirty years.

He remembered these strange documents only when he met Hideo Suzuki—alive and thus spectacularly unqualified for *gunshin* status—at their college reunion in the mid-1970s. His thirty-year-old questions were answered when he found out that Suzuki had been in the Jinrai, and Ōka suicide bombs were what the term "special attack" had referred to on those documents. Also, the odd number of seventeen *gunshin* candidates was rounded out to twenty on the first Jinrai pilot roster by the inclusion of three INA graduates. Ironically, although fourteen of the seventeen reserve ensigns in the original group went on to die in Ōkas,* there were so many other aviators and other personnel dying in *tokkō* missions in other branches by the time they finally went on their own that they never received their *gunshin* recognition, and, in fact, died never having known that they had once been considered for the honor.

In late August 1944, Suzuki and sixteen fellow *gunshin* candidates graduated from Tainan Flight School blissfully unaware that the committee meetings and rubber-stamp thumpings of bureaucrats and PR specialists in the Navy Ministry were deciding their collective and individual fates. They had no idea that the nature of their service would be any different from those of their other Tainan classmates, and just like

---

*Only one Etajima man—Lieutenant Kentarō Mitsuhashi, INA '42—died in combat as an Ōka pilot Jinrai Butai Senyūkai (1997).

everyone else, their shooting war would begin as soon as they arrived at line units for advanced on-the-job training in their respective aviation branch specialties. In fact, things would get so hot and heavy from the get-go that Suzuki even forgot—as hard as that is to believe—about his volunteering for *tokkō* in the first place.

The hard facts of the Battle of the Philippine Sea in June meant that large numbers of carrier pilots suddenly had no carriers from which to operate, and the few flight decks that were left could not be given over to training newbies. Even though Suzuki had signed on for carrier-borne attack planes, the logistical realities of the times resulted in the navy assigning him after graduation to a landlocked Nakajima B5N2 torpedo bomber* unit attached to the 953rd KKT, an antisubmarine flying boat outfit on an anonymous rock in the Pescadores, a small archipelago in the straits between Taiwan and mainland China. Sub contacts were rare, the natives were friendly, and the days long and languid. Had Suzuki been a dedicated slacker, the posting might have seemed a perfect place to sit out the rest of the war in relative peace and quiet. It might have, that is, until six weeks later on October 12, when Halsey ordered Task Force 38 to begin pounding Taiwan and the islands around it with the combined air strike capability of an armada of seventeen fleet carriers.[7] Suzuki's war had suddenly become very real and noisy indeed, descending into a chaos of frantic antisub patrolling, dodging American fighters, and hunkering down in bunkers and slit trenches when air strikes hit the base.

The worst of the American storm blew over in a few days, but sporadic harassment continued for weeks. On November 3, a "five-minute warning" siren sounded in the 953rd KKT base. Personnel ran out to the jetties and flight line to hustle the unit's torpedo bombers and seaplanes into camouflaged revetments before the Hellcats arrived on the scene. Standard operating procedure was for the pilots or senior ground-crew people to get in the cockpits and steer with the rudder pedals while others pushed the planes (or in the case of the flying boats, pulled them with rope towlines) into their respective revetments. Suzuki was just climbing into the

---

*The Nakajima B5N2 torpedo bomber—woefully obsolete by 1944—is today best remembered for its role in the Pearl Harbor raid.

cockpit of his plane when one of his noncoms ran up, pulled him out by the shoulder, and told him to seek cover while he took care of the plane.

A few seconds later, the air was filled with snarling radial engines as machine gun rounds started tearing through the area, sending up geysers of spray, runway gravel, splintering wooden planks and pilings, holing the airframes of the seaplanes lined along the quay. The Hellcats had come out of nowhere, and a hell of a lot quicker than five minutes since the siren warning. It had been more like one.

Suzuki's plane was hit and went up in flames. The noncom scrambled out of the cockpit but was cut down in another hail of .50-cal rounds from a strafing Hellcat while most of the unit watched from an air raid slit trench, helplessly screaming for their comrade. Suzuki started to get out and help, but others in the trench pulled him back in. Flames were now sweeping through the area, fueled on aviation gas, ammo, and pier wood, engulfing the planes at the docks and on the runway flight line. There was nothing anybody could do.

After the fire had subsided enough to get through to what was left of the squadron's aircraft, Suzuki and others found the noncom still alive but badly burned. With a bullet hole in his back and a massive exit wound that had blown out most of his abdomen, he managed to hold out for five agonizing hours in the base infirmary before slipping away. The bodies of three other ground-crew members were pulled from the wreckage burned beyond recognition.

This experience scarred Suzuki (who continues to have nightmares about it to this day), yet it also gave him even greater determination to die well when his time came. He was filled with gratitude for the noncom who had died in his place trying to save his plane. But in another sense, owing such an obligation to another human being was unwelcome and unbearable. How was he supposed to live with that kind of baggage on his soul?

That evening, after the noncom's death in the infirmary, Suzuki was summoned to the base command post and handed orders that had just come in from Taiwan Seaplane Operations HQ. Suzuki opened the envelope and realized that Taiwan HQ had not issued the orders—they had merely passed them on from higher up. He swallowed hard when he opened up the cablegram and found out just how high "higher up" meant. The orders read:

NAVY MINISTRY                          12 OCTOBER, 1944

ENSIGN HIDEO SUZUKI, 953RD KKT, WILL REPORT TO
HYAKURI NAVAL AIR STATION, IBARAGI PREFECTURE, NLT
2000 HRS, 15 OCTOBER, 1944, FOR SPECIAL
ASSIGNMENT.

BY ORDER OF THE MINISTER OF THE NAVY,
ADMIRAL MITSUMASA YONAI.[8]

Special assignment? What did that mean?

Suzuki got a high-wattage surge down his spine and an instantaneous misting of forehead sweat when he suddenly remembered the volunteer paper he had handed in two months earlier at Tainan. Special assignment? That could only mean Special Attack! *Tokkō!* It did not seem possible, but he had actually forgotten about all of that business. Had not thought of it in weeks, probably not since the air raids started.

Suzuki looked at the orders again and got another jolt. They said he was supposed to be at Hyakuri—wherever the hell in Ibaragi Prefecture that was—on October 15. That was almost three weeks ago! There was bound to be a serious shitstorm waiting for him at the end of all this.

"What happened with these orders?" he asked the HQ orderly. "Why did they take so long to get here?"

"Look at the date, sir. They came in the day the raids started. I guess they got misplaced in all the excitement."

"Think they'll buy that at my court-martial?"

"Don't worry about it, sir. I'm sure Taiwan will square it away for you."

As Suzuki packed his seabag back in the barracks, he rationalized to himself that at least the orders would get him back home to Japan one last time, even if it was only to face administrative punishment. Given all the horror he had seen and emotional baggage he had taken on today, that did not seem too big a price to pay for the privilege of getting out of here. Perhaps the orders could not have arrived with better timing.

After finishing outprocessing the next morning, he reported one last time to pay his respects at unit HQ, and was sent off by the base CO with a hearty "Good luck" and a slap on the back, glad to be leaving and even happier about going home.

As Suzuki's orders were already three weeks old, the attached official rail itinerary was now useless. This meant that he would have to make it all the way to Hyakuri by wit and guile alone. With the dust hardly settled from the American raids and now the Philippines about to go all to hell, there was no telling how long it would take him to make his trip. He figured that when he finally arrived at Hyakuri, he could be as much as a month late.

Getting back to Taiwan was as easy as hopping a liaison flight to Tainan. The real problem was how to get from there to Japan. Someone at Tainan said he knew of a destroyer about to leave for Japan, but even a sea voyage of a couple of days was too long with the kind of orders he had hanging over his head. Only a plane would do, so he decided to wait, but once the destroyer was gone, so were his other transport options. He ended up spending nearly a week at Tainan trying to bum a ride until finally chancing upon a plane with an empty seat for him. It was a big Type 2 flying boat packed stem to stern with ossuary boxes carrying the remains of recently cremated naval personnel—mostly air raid casualties being sent back to their homes in Japan.

Suzuki spent the five-hour flight up in the cockpit with the pilot, who by happy coincidence was a hometown junior high school buddy, and tried not to dwell too much on the other "passengers" in the back. But he could not help but think of them as the plane pulled into its final approach at Ibusuki, Kagoshima Prefecture, flying past the stately, Fuji-like slopes of Mount Kaimon-dake and over the pine-fringed white beaches of the Kyūshū coastline. Although the boys in the white boxes were also making their final trip home, they had been cheated out of getting to see its beauty one last time.

At Ibusuki, Suzuki boarded a train to start the final rail leg of his journey to Hyakuri. His worries about rail accommodations were unfounded, and the orders in his pocket greased every potential choke point in the journey, jumping him straight to the head of every railroad station ticket line that got in his way. But even with smooth connections, it still took him two days just to get off of Kyūshū and make some decent headway up Honshū. Sleep did not come easily—if at all—in the long hours of racket and jostling on the crowded trains, but there was plenty of time to think about what lay ahead. Too much time, maybe.

Headed north on the Tokaidō line and still a few hours out of Tokyo, the train slowed down to make a stop in Atami. It proved to be too much for Suzuki to resist. Figuring that he was already almost a month late and that a few more days could not get him into much more trouble than he was already in, he grabbed his seabag and squeezed his way off the car, which was rapidly filling up with more passengers. Of course, what he was doing was wildly impulsive, irresponsible, and unprofessional—not to mention illegal—but really, what were his superiors going to do about it? Put him in a plane and make him crash it into a ship? He was a *tokkō* pilot visiting home for the first time in thirteen months and probably the last time in his life. If anyone was going to dare to give him crap about that, well, they could just go to hell.

When Suzuki rounded the last corner on the walk home from the station, he saw his mother dressed in earth-toned *monpe* work pajamas, bent over a dusty truck garden in the front yard of the family inn, weeding and pulling sad little tubers from the sandy soil. Suzuki stood at the front gate in silence for a few seconds, soaking in the details of this scene for future memory reference, remembering days when his mother would dress in a gorgeous kimono to entertain guests and VIPs in this same garden among carefully tended flowers and bonsai plants.

"Mother," Suzuki said, self-conscious of the frog in his throat. "I'm home."


Suzuki ended up staying for two days. His family did not pester him about the details of the last thirteen months of his life, and he saw no need to tell them about the nature of his next assignment or about the technically illegal nature of his visit. When not welcoming visitors at home or paying respects to neighborhood notables, he passed the hours stretched out on the tatami of his living room with his family members' voices and the smells of home in the air, trying not to imagine what the room would look like when they held his funeral here in a few more months.

Leaving on the morning of the fourteenth, Suzuki did a good job of keeping his composure as he said his good-byes, vowing to himself to get home at least a few more times. After all, it was not like Ibaragi was on the other side of the planet. Just eight or nine hours by train, tops. If he could get off on a couple of weekend passes before his sortie, there was no reason this had to be his last visit home. As he boarded the train at Atami, he tried very hard to hold on to these happy thoughts.

Getting to Hyakuri was another exercise in hours of lugging a seabag through maddening crowds, and adding insult to injury, he was told upon his arrival that the "Special Attack" people had moved on to a new base deeper into the countryside two weeks earlier. He hung around to wait for a liaison car that would be making a run out to the base—someplace called Kōnoike—in a few hours.

After a spooky nighttime drive through pine barrens and magnificent desolation to reach Kōnoike, Suzuki was spooked even more when he saw the sign over the main gate of the base.

"It was a big sign, in beautiful, professionally done calligraphy," Suzuki-san recalls sixty years later. "But when I read what was written on it— Jinrai—I thought, 'Divine Thunder'? What kind of kooky outfit have I gotten myself involved with here?"

What he saw when he reported in to the officer on duty only confirmed his suspicions. When he entered the HQ shack, there was some kind of ceremony going on in a back room. The astringently sweet, meditative smell of funerary incense filled the air, and he could hear Buddhist chanting.

"What's going on?" Suzuki asked.

"Lieutenant Kariya—one of the Ōka flight leaders—died in an accident yesterday," the OD answered. "That's his wake."

"Ōka?"

"Yeah. Ōka. *Sakura no hana.* Cherry Blossom."

"An airplane?"

"You'll find out soon enough, Ensign. Welcome to the Jinrai. Now pick up your gear and go report to the CO," the OD said. He pointed at the date on Suzuki's orders. "And you've got some explaining to do about this."

Suzuki walked down the hall, pausing briefly to bow toward the stranger's wake before knocking on the door of the CO's office. When a voice inside told him to enter, he opened the door to find a rather small, thinly mustachioed captain in his late forties at a desk covered with paperwork. The captain received and returned Suzuki's salute, then told the ensign to stand at ease.

"Who the hell are you?" the captain asked.

"Ensign Suzuki, sir. Reporting for duty."

"Ah . . . yes . . . the AWOL fellow."

"Sir? I was told that Taiwan would contact you with—"

"We haven't heard a damn thing from Taiwan," the captain said, cutting Suzuki off. "Would you mind telling me what took you so long getting here?"

Suzuki began to go through an accurate accounting of the massive disruption caused by the American raids and about his actions and movements over the last month, conveniently leaving out the small detail about the two days of unscheduled home leave.

"Quite a journey," the captain said, gesturing for Suzuki to stop before the explanation was finished. "Thanks for making such an effort to get here."

The captain stood up from his desk.

"Welcome to the Jinrai," he said, pumping the ensign's hand. "I'm Captain Okamura, the CO here. Hope you are a quick study. You have some catching up to do."

Suzuki made his way to the reserve officers' billets, which, like the rest of the buildings on post, were quickly-slapped-together plywood structures so new they still smelled of lumberyard and wood stain. When he stepped inside, he realized that all of the other ensigns inside were faces from Tainan, including one of his best friends from flight school, Saburō Dohi. It was a happy surprise, one of his first in a while.

Saburō Dohi was a reserve ensign out of a public teachers college in Wakayama Prefecture. Before answering the same navy recruiting poster message that had lured Suzuki and Naitō into the "gentleman's service," he had been training to become an elementary school teacher. Like so many others before and since who have been paradoxically attracted to a profession that requires standing in front of a roomful of people and talking all day long, Dohi was a painfully shy introvert— what these days would be called a "nerd." However, as nerds can often be, he was an intriguingly profound thinker who, in a one-on-one situation, could be an engaging conversationalist with someone who had invested the time to become his friend, especially if the topic was something he could get passionate about, like literature or philosophy. Suzuki had spent many hours talking with Dohi in Taiwan, so he was the first person he approached to start filling him in on details about the Kōnoike ropes.

The next morning, on his way to report to Commander Nonaka, flight ops boss of the Jinrai, he walked by the flight line and caught his first glimpse of an Ōka. His reaction was similar to that of Takurō Takei two months later—and of virtually every new pilot who laid eyes on the craft for the first time.

"I couldn't believe they actually expected us to fly in *that*," Suzuki-san remembers. "To me, it just looked like a torpedo with wings stuck on the side and a cockpit dug out of the middle."

Unlike enlisted pilots, Suzuki's officer rank afforded him the luxury of voicing his concern about his new mount.

"That looks like a bomb, for crying out loud," he yelled at one of the enlisted technicians servicing the bright orange craft.

"Well, sir," the technician answered, "probably because that's exactly what it is."

For the rest of the day, Suzuki familiarized himself with his new environment and found out what he could about the glider bomb he was being asked to fly. Scuttlebutt had it that the design kinks in the craft had yet to be ironed out. Until the technical people could figure out what was wrong with the Ōka's flight characteristics—other than the unfixable flaw of having the descent rate of a dropped brick—there would be no more test drops, and no more new pilots getting checked out anytime soon. The lowdown was that nobody was really sure if the Ōka worked or not, as Kariya's spectacular accident in front of visiting Navy Ministry dignitaries the day before had demonstrated so dramatically.

The next major setback was strategic rather than technical. A few days after Kariya's crack-up, a technical team figured out that the trainer mishap had been due to a problem of frozen lines preventing the proper distribution of water ballast during flight. Sand was exchanged for water in a new mock-up and this was successfully tested.[9] The training drops resumed, and new pilots were checked out daily. The Ōka design had been vindicated—at least for now—and as preparations for the Jinrai to come online moved into the final stages, Imperial General Headquarters was eager to get it into action to see what kind of damage it could do. By the end of November 1944, the Americans were in the process of chewing up His Majesty's armed forces in the Philippines, and every bit of available firepower was needed to remedy this situation, especially after the surface fleet debacle at Leyte. Ōnishi's *tokkō* tactics—the only happy news to come out of the theater in weeks—had shown what one little Zero with a 250 kg bomb could do to an American carrier. Now it was time to see what 1.2 tons of TNT moving seven hundred kilometers an hour could do to one.

First order of business was to get the initial production run of factory-fresh Ōkas from the Yokosuka Aircraft Works (attached to the Navy's Aerial Weapons Research Lab) to suitable forward-area naval installations. It was decided that the huge base at Kure, with its extensive arsenal facilities and torpedo storage capabilities, would be the ideal staging point for stockpiling Ōkas. Although the navy could not be certain where the Allies' next big push on the home islands would be made, it seemed reasonable that large caches of standby Ōkas stored in Taiwan and on the southern tip of Kyūshū would pretty well cover the most likely sea approaches, and Kure's location in Hiroshima Prefecture would be convenient for keeping Jinrai elements in either one or both of these potential campaign theaters logistically supported.

On November 27, the supercarrier *Shinano*—so new her hatches had to be kept open to ventilate drying paint fumes—left her berth in the Yokosuka Naval Yard for the first time and moved across the harbor to dock at Yokosuka Arsenal. There she was loaded with a consignment of fifty Ōkas, support technicians, and six Shin'yō suicide motorboats bound for Kure.[10] The *Shinano*'s keel had originally been laid as a sister ship to the superbattleships *Yamato* and *Musashi*, but a prudent midconstruction conversion to compensate for the navy's disastrous losses at Midway resulted in the world's largest aircraft carrier being built instead over her massive frame. At nearly seventy thousand tons, she dwarfed her largest American counterparts, and was the largest warship ever built until the debut of the giant American flattops of the 1950s.[11]

After taking on her precious cargo, the *Shinano* left Yokosuka with an escort of three destroyers to begin her maiden voyage to Kure. Unbeknownst to the officers and crew of these ships, their convoy had been spotted almost as soon as it had gotten under way. Its spotter—and now stalker—was the USS *Archerfish*, a submarine originally posted outside the entrance to Tokyo Bay on lifeguard duty for downed air crews from the war's first B-29 raid on the capital three days earlier. Having completed this assignment uneventfully, and with no rescued airmen to bring back to safety, the *Archerfish* was free to lurk and pick up targets of opportunity. But no one on the boat had expected something as juicy as a Japanese supercarrier.

The *Archerfish* trailed the southwesterly zigzagging *Shinano* with great caution for several hundred kilometers before putting four fish into her off the coast of Wakayama Prefecture on November 29. The great gray maiden slipped under the waves eight hours later, taking most of her crew and passengers and all of her top-secret cargo to a watery tomb. Survivors were picked up by the *Shinano*'s escort destroyers and quarantined for security reasons on Mitsuko Island in Kure Bay, Hiroshima Prefecture, until January 1945.[12]

Operating from the stance of "what the pilots don't know can't hurt them," Kōnoike command made sure news of this latest catastrophe was kept strictly need-to-know, and it never left the HQ shack. But the loss of the Ōkas—while painful and demoralizing—was not insurmountable. The Yokosuka works would have another large batch of the structurally simple aluminum-and-wood craft ready within a couple of weeks.

With shock waves from the *Shinano* loss still reverberating in the cloistered top-floor offices of the Navy Ministry, a veritable stream of brass made morale visits to Kōnoike during the first few days of December, indicating the vital importance of the Jinrai in upcoming campaigns and the high expectations IGHQ had for the unit. The black limousine parade began on December 1, when Combined Fleet C-in-C Admiral Soemu Toyoda (INA '05) arrived for an overnight stay with crates of ceremonial headbands and *tanto* short swords for the Jinrai pilots. He was also bringing perhaps the best possible morale booster: a sense of purpose. This came in the form of an attaché case full of orders and maps for Captain Okamura outlining the Jinrai's first scheduled operational deployment.

Before attending to ceremonial duties, Toyoda and Okamura went to the latter's office in base HQ, drew the blinds, and went over the details of the Jinrai debut mission. IGHQ wanted sufficient numbers of pilots, support personnel, and Ōkas on standby in Takao, Taiwan, and the Clark Airbase complex in Luzon in time for the Jinrai to hit American capital ships in Leyte Gulf on December 23. Okamura assured the admiral that his men and equipment would be up to the task.

That afternoon, the four Ōka pilot sections—a group of about two hundred men in total*—were assembled in a hangar and addressed by a visibly emotional Admiral Toyoda. Tears brimmed in the admiral's eyes as he spoke, then ran down his cheeks for all to see as the pilots were called up one by one to receive their headbands and short swords. Suzuki was one of the first to be called front and center. The admiral shook his hand and thanked him. Next, an aide handed the admiral a white cotton headband stenciled with a red Hinomaru circle in the center and flanked by the kanji characters *jin* ("god") and *rai* ("thunder") penned in black. In an oddly intimate posture—almost an embrace— Toyoda tied the headband on Suzuki's bare head. The men then stepped back from each other, exchanged deep bows, and the admiral handed over a ceremonial short sword in a handsome orange-and-gold brocade pouch.

Deeply moved as everyone else had been by the weight and dignity of the ceremony, Suzuki went back to the barracks uplifted, full of purpose, and eager to examine the treasure he had received from the admiral. The short sword was an elegantly minimalist piece of Japanese craftsmanship. Both scabbard and haft appeared to be carved from the same block of blond, unfinished wood, wound at both ends with sword guards of coiled rattan strip. The haft of the weapon was inscribed with the kanji characters *go* and *koku* ("defend" and "country," respectively) and the scabbard bore Toyoda's signature, all in the admiral's accomplished "grass hand"† brush calligraphy. Judging from the elegant outward appearance of the item, Suzuki expected to find the fine handiwork of a traditional swordsmith inside the scabbard. But when he drew the blade,

---

*Only the officers and a fraction of the enlisted men were checked out on the Ōka trainer— and thus qualified for a combat mission—by this point.

†"Grass hand" or *sōshu* is a cursive calligraphy style that, at its best, can seem paradoxically and simultaneously highly stylized and spontaneous. Originated by classical Chinese poets, the style requires many, many years of training with a calligraphy brush to master and has traditionally always been viewed in Japan as a sign of great erudition and impeccable taste. Suzuki (1959) provides several good examples, especially plate 22.

he found that it was just shiny stainless steel, like a parade bayonet, all flash and useless for anything but a fancy letter opener.

"It was obviously mass-produced," Suzuki-san recalls. "Many years later I found out that the swords we got were from the same batch given by Admiral Miwa to the Kaiten human torpedo pilots at Ōtsushima a few weeks earlier."

Visits to Kōnoike by Admiral Koshirō Oikawa, chief of naval general staff, and Navy Minister Admiral Mitsumasa Yonai followed in rapid succession. There were the prerequisite speeches, proclamations, and citation presentations, and the dignitaries got to see some training drops (successful this go-around). Morale was up, especially with rumors of upcoming action making the rounds in the pilots' barracks.

By mid-December, one new batch of thirty Ōkas had been successfully run from Yokosuka to Kure, while another fifty-eight had made it to Sasebo in Nagasaki Prefecture. The next step necessary for the December 23 combat debut to be kept on schedule was to move the Ōkas to forward-deployment areas, and the carriers *Unryū* and *Ryūho* were slated for this ferrying mission. The *Unryū* headed for Manila Bay on December 16 with the Kure Ōkas. The *Ryūho*, which had originally been scheduled to ferry the Sasebo Ōkas to Takao, Taiwan, was instead ordered to head directly to the Philippines as well in light of the rapidly souring situation in the Leyte region.

On December 19, about one-third of the way through her journey to Luzon, the *Unryū* was sunk with her cargo of thirty Ōkas by torpedoes from the USS *Redfish*.[13] This prompted emergency orders from the Navy Ministry for the *Ryūho* to change her destination back to Taiwan to unload her Ōkas at Takao, where they languished unused for the remainder of the war.

The actions of American submarines had by now resulted in the first 138 Ōkas off the assembly lines being removed from the war effort—either collecting dust in Taiwan or growing barnacles at the bottom of the Pacific. The Japanese navy could not afford any more losses like this, so the decision was made that from here on in, Ōka surface transport operations would be confined to overland rail and truck hauling and quick cargo ship dashes through the relative safety of Japanese home waters. The Jinrai's combat operational range would be limited by how far their Isshiki Rikkō mother planes could fly from home island bases, so this meant that the plan for seeing what the Ōkas could do in the Philippines would die as an unrealized pipe dream. But from a strategic viewpoint, this new deployment picture was not necessarily an entirely undesirable development. When the American invasion fleets eventually showed up off the Japanese coast—and no one in His Majesty's navy higher than an ensign now doubted that they would—it would be best to have the as-yet-untried superweapons close at hand.

Word about the carrier sinkings, Ōka shipment losses, and the canceled combat debut gradually filtered down through the ranks during the last dark weeks of December, and by the end of a markedly subdued New Year's 1944–45, morale at Kōnoike was bottoming out. Spirits picked up some, however, in the flurry of activity on the base that followed orders for Captain Okamura and Commander Nonaka to take the first detachment of Ōka pilots and Isshiki Rikkō mother planes to Kanoya NAS in Kyūshū. Kanoya was the location of the Fifth Air Fleet HQ of Vice Admiral Matome Ugaki, and Nonaka's 711th KKT would be operating there as an elite independent command answerable only to Captain Okamura and the admiral himself.

There was a big flag-waving send-off for the Kyūshū-bound detachment on January 20, 1945. After speeches, songs, handshakes, and backslaps for the departing heroes, the big, lumbering Isshiki Rikkōs and their Zero escorts climbed up and away into the cold, clean Ibaragi air, and the hearts of every man left behind on the tarmac went with them. As the droning of the engines faded away into the cold, brackish Pacific breeze, gloom once again descended on Kōnoike.

The Jinrai orphans stranded at Kōnoike slowly settled back into a comforting—if dull—routine. Hideo Suzuki tried to stay busy organizing R & R trips for the officers and spent a lot of time shooting the bull with his best buddy, Saburō Dohi. Tokuji Naitō was still learning his way around the unit after a month on base and, like the batch of fresh-faced teenage petty officers who had also just arrived on the scene, getting used to the feel of a Zero control stick in his hands. During downtime—which was plentiful—pilots could drink and smoke if they wanted to and stuff their faces with chocolates, caramels, and canned goods when not chowing down on three squares a day from the excellent Jinrai kitchen.

All creature comforts, including sleep, were well taken care of. Things were so cushy, in fact, that a pilot might almost forget there was a war on.

But the war had not entirely forgotten Kōnoike.

The one hundred or so Jinrai personnel still left on the base had become accustomed to B-29 activity overhead in the two months since raids out of Saipan by the big bombers began hitting targets on military and industrial targets in the Tokyo area. The American bomber formations often passed over southern Ibaragi and the vicinity of Kōnoike in their egress from Tokyo-area bomb runs. But until the afternoon of January 27, the planes were no more than faint engine noise and orange contrails in setting sunlight, and the men who flew them were faceless.

At about two in the afternoon on January 27, B-29 V-Square-27 *Rover Boys Express* of the 499th Bomb Group, 73rd Bomb Wing out of Saipan, had just passed over Mount Fuji at an altitude of thirty thousand feet and was headed for the day's target, the Nakajima aircraft engine factory in Musashino, Tokyo.[14] The bombardier had assumed his customary squat at the Norden bombsight and was just beginning to nudge his fly-by-wire toggle to line up for the bomb run when his Plexiglas office in the B-29's distinctive "greenhouse" nose disintegrated in a hail of 37mm cannon fire from an IJA twin-engined *Ki*-45 high-altitude fighter.[15] Three other crewmen were killed in subsequent *Ki*-45 passes. With cabin pressure thus catastrophically compromised, the surviving crewmen were exposed to 250 mph airspeed-fed winds at minus fifty degrees Fahrenheit. The remaining seven crewmen managed to keep "Rover Boys" aloft long enough to fly clear across the Tokyo metropolitan area and out into the Ibaragi countryside before the plane began to break up.

Raymond "Hap" Halloran—navigator of the stricken plane—recalls the last moments of the last flight of *Rover Boys Express*:

*I went into what I would describe as a state of denial,* he writes, *sort of like a bad dream. This couldn't be happening to us Rover Boys in V-square-27. We delayed parachuting over Tokyo—hoping for a miracle. I even ate a turkey sandwich from our lunch box* [in a psychological state of] *denial and trying to create some normalcy in our B-29. I was frightened and prayed for help from God. I finally parachuted through the front bomb bay—bombs still in—and did a long free fall—estimate 22,000 to 24,000 feet—to avoid extreme cold and lack of oxygen.*

Abandoned by its surviving crewmen, the flaming remains of *Rover Boys Express* came hurtling out of the afternoon sky to smash into the sleepy village of Ikisu, a tight cluster of fishermen's huts squeezed into the narrow strip of beach dune between Kōnoike base and the Pacific Ocean. Seven Ikisu residents were killed by the debris, sending the hamlet into an uproar.[16]

All seven of the *Rover Boys Express* jumpers' parachutes functioned properly, and the crewmen landed at intervals of several hundred meters in a straight line along the Ikisu beach southwest of the base. So far, so good, but things took an unhappy turn as soon as their boots hit the dunes, where they were almost immediately set upon by mobs of frenzied, bereaved villagers and beaten with fists, shovels, and ax handles. Two crewmen died from the beatings, and the others were close to death before local police officers and Kōnoike personnel arrived on the scene to whisk the bloodied Americans away to be interrogated.*

Tokurō Takei was milling about with squadmates near the base HQ trying to get a glimpse of action when one of the Americans—a tall man—was brought in. Unlike the reactions of the villagers, the boy NCOs displayed more of an excited fascination than any personal animosity toward the Yankee (who may or may not have been Hap Halloran), and there was more gawking and nervous tittering over the man's large frame and long nose than there were vengeful remarks. For some of the pilots, especially the ex-farmboys in the unit from deep rural areas, the crewman was the first Caucasian they had ever seen who was not on a movie screen or in a magazine spread.

The map case the crewman still had strapped to his leg was even more of a jaw-dropper than its owner, but not for its contents. Rather, the material it was made out of was what made it an item of such dumbfounded scrutiny. No one at Kōnoike—top-secret, high-tech weapons base that it was—had ever seen anything made out of clear PVC before. The case was passed around for the rubberneckers to inspect. Although

---

*H. Halloran, personal correspondence. Halloran would go on to spend seven months as a POW—including a miserable day on display in a cage at Ueno Zoo. He also spent several months with an illustrious cellmate: Major Gregory "Pappy" Boyington of USMC Black Sheep Squadron fame. Readers interested in more information about Halloran's experiences are urged to avail themselves of his memoirs, *Hap's War*. The book is available through his Web site: http://www.haphalloran.com/.

Takei marveled at the texture and characteristics of this amazing—almost otherworldly—material, he also remembers experiencing a worrisome sense of technological inferiority as he handled it.

"I thought, Wow, these guys are really way ahead of us," Takei-san recalls. "Just a little thing like a flexible transparent plastic pouch. But it said a lot about the relative strength of our two countries. I think we all felt some of that."

A few hours later, Kempeitai military police* arrived at Kōnoike to round up the map case crewman and his surviving comrades and whisk them off to Tokyo for interrogation and imprisonment. The evening's excitement soon faded from memory, and Kōnoike returned once again to its routine of training drops and abundant free time.

The *haruichiban*† blew its annual single loud trumpet blast to herald the arrival of spring weather a few weeks earlier than usual in 1945—always the sure sign of a long, hot summer just a couple of more months down the road. Following behind the high-pressure pocket pushing this messenger wind was a thousand-kilometer-long mass of warm, wet air roughly paralleling the coastline of Honshū. This low-pressure front promptly parked itself right over the Pacific coast of the Japanese home islands in mid-February, bringing with it days of rain and mist.

In the dreary predawn of February 17, more than just bad weather was lurking off the coast of Japan. Cloaking his armada in this fog and drizzle with the guile and cunning of a ninja assassin, Vice Admiral Marc Mitscher had brought the full striking power of Task Force 58‡ to

---

*An IJA branch of service similar in political and counterintelligence functions to the Nazi Gestapo, while also responsible for a conventional military police role. See Harries (1991) for more information on its function.

†"First spring wind," a powerful blast of southwesterly wind that whips through Japan every year in late February or early March on the leading edge of the massive, humid low-pressure warm front that banishes winter weather from the archipelago for the next nine months.

‡"The Fast Carrier Task Force was composed of four task groups under the overall command of a vice admiral. Depending upon the fleet commander (Admiral Halsey with the Third Fleet or Admiral Spruance with the Fifth Fleet), the carrier striking arm was designated Task Force (TF) 38 or 58. The designation changed whenever the fleet commander alternated for planning purposes. Heimsteidt, http://boracay.vasia.com/ddivers/ph_history.htm.

within 100 kilometers of the Bōsō Peninsula and 220 kilometers of Tokyo without being spotted by Japanese patrol planes. And in a double stroke of pure luck for the Americans, radar facilities in Chōshi, Chiba Prefecture, and Shirahama, Shizuoka Prefecture, that were responsible for guarding the southeastern air and sea approaches to the capital were both temporarily inoperable due to technical malfunction on this particular morning.[17] Japanese air defense had been caught with its pants down.

At 0600 hours, when Mitscher gave the nod for the first attack wave of rocket- and bomb-armed Hellcats and Corsairs to be launched, the entire island of Honshū was laid open like a banquet spread for the American marauders. It must have been a moment of sweet revenge for the curmudgeonly vice admiral, who in this most definitely non-PC era was both famous in the American media and beloved in the navy as an inveterate, unforgiving, and utterly unabashed Jap hater, whose colorful and often anatomically graphic racist epithets in regards to his foe were perhaps rivaled only by those of his sometime boss, Admiral William Halsey.[18]

Outside of the mission objective of temporarily sating the wrath of Mitscher, the raids now on their way to Honshū had strategic and tactical aims as well. Strategically, it was hoped that they could achieve a psychological effect along the lines of the Doolittle raid nearly three years earlier[19]—panicking the residents of the Japanese capital and stirring up the IGHQ like a smoked-out beehive. This would not be another antiseptic raid by massed B-29s bombing from altitude, but real in-your-face, barnstorming aggression—single-engine fighter-bombers buzzing the rooftops, clipping clotheslines, and shooting up anything that moved. It was hoped that the shock value of the raid would create enough anger and chaos to divert Japanese attention from the American surface fleet movement and buildup presently under way in the Bonins in preparation for the Iwo Jima invasion that would kick off in two more days.

The tactical objective was to neutralize as much enemy air strength as possible in order to downgrade counterattack capability available for the Japanese to send south when the invasion actually started. The more Japanese aircraft left in smoking heaps on Honshū bases this morning meant fewer planes available for *tokkō* attacks on carriers and packed troop ships off Iwo Jima two days from now. There was not a single Leyte and Lingayen Gulf veteran in TF 58 who had to be sold on that arithmetic, or who was not praying godspeed and good hunting for the glossy dark-blue fighter-bombers now heading northwest at five hundred kilometers per hour.

Thirty minutes after Mitscher's launch order and 250 kilometers northwest of the wet flight decks of Task Force 58, Tokurō Takei and three other squadmates were lugging Ōka Pilot Section One's empty aluminum mess pails back up to the Jinrai kitchen when Kōnoike's air raid siren ripped open the dawn calm with a long, climbing wail. Having only ever heard the siren during drills, for a few moments the boys stood frozen in place with their pails by their sides, looking at each other while they waited for their brains to work and tell them what to do next. But when a gull-winged Corsair emerged from the slate-gray morning mist with a sinister whine of whistling superchargers and began to let loose with its .50-caliber machine guns, the mess pails hit the ground and the boys made a mad dash for the nearest tree line.

Their hiding place was on a slight rise, so it afforded a panoramic view of the airfield, where all twelve of Kōnoike's remaining Isshiki Rikkōs were lined up like tombstones, fully fueled and ready to go for the morning's scheduled formation flight training. Panting from fear and their hundred-meter dash to safety, the boys watched in slack-jawed disbelief as one of the bombers went up in a spectacular orange fireball under the Corsair's guns.

"The flames lit up everything," Takei-san remembers. "Everything that had been bluish gray a second before was now yellow and orange. If the scene hadn't been so horrible, I would be tempted to call it beautiful."

A second Corsair motored in, guns ablaze, followed by a long succession of others that formed a kind of Lufbery circle doing laps around the field, their pilots apparently paying little or no mind to the few stingy tracer streaks of small-caliber AA fire the base managed to put up. One Corsair at a time would drop out of the loop, swoop down to strafe the Isshiki Rikkōs on the flight line, then climb back up to join formation before the next plane came strafing in behind him. The process looked so leisurely and routine it could have been a gunnery range training session.

After ten or twelve passes, Kōnoike's flight line was a wall of towering flame. The Corsairs stuck around to shoot up a few buildings on base before winging off back into the morning mist from whence they came. As the base air raid siren wound down from its frenzied, undulating shriek to one last melancholy, dying moan, a sad, chaotic cacophony could be heard wafting up from the airfield. There were hoarse shouts for firefighting details to be formed, and anguished cries as the dead and wounded were tended to.

Still hunkered down in the scrub pines and trembling with fight-or-flight adrenaline, Takei and his friends watched the scene wordlessly, sniffling back tears of shock and rage.

"I've never forgotten the bitter frustration of that moment," Takei-san says. "And never experienced anything like it since."

Takei was not alone in his chagrin. But the operational and logistical repercussions of the raid were even worse than the emotional and morale damage it caused. The Americans had destroyed every last one of Kōnoike's twelve Isshiki Rikkō mother planes. Replacing them would not simply be a matter of placing an order with Mitsubishi or borrowing bombers from other units. The planes they had lost were specially modified for carrying Ōkas, and the only mechanics and technicians capable of making the conversions from stock Isshiki Rikkōs were all down in Kyūshū with the combat detachment and could not be spared. With no mother planes, the Kōnoike detachment could no longer make Ōka trainer drops.

It was a bitter setback for the Jinrai. Not only had the American raid ripped the heart out of Kōnoike by taking out its facilities, but in stomping its training capacity so decisively, it had really taken away its very raison d'être. Captain Okamura eventually sent two reserve Isshiki Rikkōs back up to Kōnoike so that training drops could resume, but the gesture was really more symbolic than practical. Two mother planes were only enough to restore the trainer drop rotation to a fraction of its former pace. This meant that the Jinrai could no longer count on the kind of replacement pilot numbers they had planned on being able to get from Kōnoike once combat operations started.

When all was said and done, it had taken only a few minutes of enemy strafing runs and Kōnoike was now effectively out of the war.

"You've got to watch out for those early-morning air raids," Takei-san says with a barely perceptible smirk. "Remember Pearl Harbor."

**fourteen**

# FLIGHT OF THE THUNDER GODS

W hile Okamura, Nonaka, and the others at Kanoya were concerned about Kōnoike's predicament, they had more pressing concerns. First and foremost, they had to prepare for their combat debut, which nobody doubted was imminent. The Americans had now taken Iwo Jima, and either Okinawa or Taiwan would be their next logical target. But in either case, as a visibly excited Admiral Ugaki constantly reminded Okamura, the enemy would at last come within striking range of the Jinrai, and he and everyone else in naval high command were expecting big, big things from the Ōka.

When American movement in the third week of March made it clear that the next big push would be coming in Okinawa, Ugaki and Okamura began brainstorming the appropriate deployment scenarios. Recon aircraft were constantly kept aloft scouring the East China Sea looking for a target valuable enough on which to stake the Jinrai's all-important debut. After several false alarms and flying starts, recon planes made a solid contact on the morning of March 21, spotting an American force of three carriers and support ships 350 kilometers south of Kyūshū on a heading of about 145 degrees.[1]

The ships were TF 58 elements that had participated in the massive March 18–19 raids that had clobbered Kyūshū and Inland Sea region air bases—including Kanoya—in preparation for the upcoming Okinawa invasion. Some of the vessels had sustained *tokkō* aircraft and conventional weapons damage during the raids, most notably the carrier *Franklin*, when a Zero crashed through her flight deck and exploded amidships, causing over a thousand casualties. *Tokkō* escorts and conventional attack planes had returned to their Kyūshū bases after their counterattacks with electrifying (if inaccurate) reports of carriers sunk and others with shattered, useless flight decks. Ugaki, in yet another disastrous example of his characteristically wishful thinking, bought everything he was told at face value and grossly overestimated the damage the Americans had suffered. He was under the impression that the force spotted on the twenty-first was a column of crippled stragglers, and would thus be unable to mount a combat air patrol in strength sufficient to stop a Jinrai raid. If this were indeed the case, the Isshiki Rikkōs, even with a modest escort of Zeros, would be able to ingress close enough to release their Ōkas and score crushing hits on the Americans. There might never be another opportunity this good to send the Ōkas into battle. The time to strike was now. Ugaki believed that today was going to be the day of the big payoff, and expected nothing less than a brilliant victory to be able to report to Toyoda.

Okamura and Nonaka did not agree with the admiral's assessment of the American combat air patrol capabilities, and thus could not share any of his optimism for the chances of the mission's success. Topping the list of reasons not to be cheerful was that Fifth Air Fleet Flight Ops had told them that there were only going to be fifty-five Zeros available for the escort[2]—thirty-two of the Jinrai's own fighters plus another twenty-three from other units in southern Kyūshū that would rendezvous with the main force en route.[3] Moreover, many of these planes were in various states of disrepair and most were going to be flown by green pilots just out of flight school. They would be useless if the force ran into a determined American combat air patrol. Unless they could achieve near total surprise, the 711th HKT was going to be flying into its own massacre.

Okamura and Nonaka were painfully aware of the potential disaster that lay ahead, and had laid out good reasons for postponement during the staff meeting that had just finished, but their honor as officers meant that they had no choice but to follow Ugaki's orders and go through with the mission when he dismissed their misgivings as unfounded. For the last item during a hurried session at the planning tables to go over the final operational details of the mission, Okamura—with reservations—yielded to Nonaka's insistence on flying the lead Isshiki Rikkō into battle. Neither of the men, by this point, doubted that the assignment would be fatal. They shook hands, then left the ops shack and walked down to the flight line, where Nonaka had choreographed in advance a scene that must go down in history as one of the classic moments in gloriously doomed military exploits, right up there with the Foreign Legion's bayonet charge at Dien Bien Phu, the Light Brigade at Balaclava, and Pickett's Charge.

All 160 pilots and aircrew who would be participating in the main attack element were standing tall in formation along the flight line under the late-morning sun as *jindaiko* war drums, which Nonaka had borrowed from a local Shinto shrine just for the occasion, thundered out martial rhythms dating from antiquity. Nonaka's beloved reproduction samurai banners—Masashige Kusunoki's *Hirihokenten* pennant from the Battle of Minatogawa in 1336 and the *Nanmu Hachiman Daibosatsu* Minamoto clan battle flag immortalized in the medieval Gempei War—trailed multicolored streamers in a stiff breeze. Front and center in the place of honor, the fifteen Ōka pilots who would be flying the mission were wearing spotless uniforms and the pristine white headbands they had received from Admiral Toyoda in December. At their head was the ranking Ōka pilot, Lieutenant Kentarō Mitsuhashi (INA '42), with a white pouch around his neck containing some of Lieutenant Ben Kariya's ashes.[4] The Ōkas' first victim would also be participating—at least in spirit and corporeal dust—in its first combat sortie.

After Admiral Ugaki emerged from his fortified command bunker to join the ceremony, Okamura gave the 711th the most rousing send-off speech he could muster without breaking down in tears. Still, there were few dry eyes when the Jinrai CO gave a final salute and the pilots and crews broke ranks to run to their aircraft with loud and lusty warrior yells, exchanging shouted farewells and encouragement with the throngs of onlookers who lined the field. Nonaka's last words as he headed off for his command plane referred to the battle that resulted in the defeat and death of his personal hero, the legendary samurai Masashige Kusunoki.

"This is Minatogawa," a glassy-eyed, glowing Nonaka had been heard to say to no one in particular, already half slipped into a state of preself-sacrificial beatitude. No one who witnessed the scene would ever forget that he made the remark with a wistful smile on his face.[5]

At 1135 hours, sixty-six twelve-hundred-horsepower Sakae engines in a total of forty-eight aircraft coughed to life on a signal from the control tower. The Zeros—now whittled down to thirty from thirty-two by engine failures—took off first to wild cheers. But the biggest roars from the on-lookers were reserved for the takeoffs of the three command Isshiki Rikkōs and the fifteen mother planes with light-gray Ōkas slung under their bellies. When the final lumbering bomber crawled into the air, the massive formation circling the field straightened out and headed south. The cheering continued until the last echo of droning thunder from the formation's engines faded away. As the crowd broke up and other personnel returned to their duties, Ugaki and Okamura walked off in the direction of the command bunker to begin their long day's vigil in the radio shack.

Approximately three hours later, radarmen in the American carrier group picked up the first contacts of a large formation of unidentified aircraft approaching from the direction of Kyūshū. The carriers *Hornet* and *Belleau Wood* wasted no time putting up a CAP of forty-eight Hellcats split into high- and medium-altitude elements to meet the bandits.[6] When the Jinrai planes finally came into view, the Hellcats already had the tactical picture sewn up. While the medium-altitude Hellcats waded into the ranks of the top-cover Zero escorts—which had been even further depleted by engine failures on the way down from Kyūshū—the high-altitude CAP element peeled off into long, diving attack runs on the Isshiki Rikkōs farther below.

Anyone who has watched a History Channel documentary or two on World War II air combat has most likely seen at least a few seconds of American gun camera footage from the slaughter that ensued. I would imagine that documentary editors favor this particular collection of footage for the almost Hollywood quality of its pyrotechnics. The photographic record has left us with some grainy imagery of cool explosions, but film cannot begin to evoke the feeding frenzy of devastation the Hellcats wrought on that March afternoon so long ago.

Fire belched from the engine nacelles of the Isshiki Rikkōs almost the instant the first .50-caliber rounds began perforating the aluminum airframes of the Jinrai planes and the flesh of their crews. Unarmored, non-self-sealing fuel tanks exploded, turning aircraft into giant torches within seconds. Catastrophic structural failures led to wings collapsing and tumbling away. The big bombers lurched at sickening angles with the deadweight of the useless Ōkas still slung under their bellies, shuddering under hits before disintegrating in midair.

The 711th never had a chance. The engagement was all over in less than twenty minutes.

By the time the last shred of Japanese airframe fluttered down into the East China Sea, fifteen Ōkas, eighteen Isshiki Rikkōs, and ten Zeros had been destroyed. One hundred and sixty men were dead. One American Hellcat was lost.[7]

As this massacre unfolded, Ugaki and Okamura had been in the radio shack for nearly three hours now, standing with a crowd of staff officers, pilots, and clerks that surrounded a radio set. Close to the attack force's ETA of 1500 hours, the radioman's Morse ticker registered a single, enigmatic "mission cancelled" message.* After that, dead silence.

Late in the afternoon, the few shot-up Zero stragglers that were the only survivors of the debacle began landing at Kanoya. Their eyewitness reports confirmed everyone's worst fears—the devastation had been total. The force had not gotten anywhere near being close enough to drop the Ōkas before all of the bombers were shot down. Nonaka, the other section leaders, all of the Ōka pilots, and everyone else who had been on an Isshiki Rikkō were lost, along with over half the escort fighters. Nobody else was coming back.

The enormity of the disaster only became more emotionally crushing as the initial numbing shock wore off, the evening wore on, and every man in Kanoya was left alone to face a long night of brokenhearted bitterness. By most accounts, Admiral Matome Ugaki was the most despondent of them all, and was never the same man again after being told the news. Perhaps the smiling faces of the Jinrai pilots were projected in

---

*Japanese air-to-air and air-to-surface vox radio was unreliable throughout the war, and the army and navy primarily depended on Morse code for radio transmissions during air operations.

his mind's eye when, less than five months later on August 15, he ignored the surrender announcement and disobeyed his emperor's orders for the only time in his life to fly the final *tokkō* sortie of the war.*

From a morale standpoint, no one could accept another debacle like the March 21 outing, and Ugaki waited ten days before committing to another sortie with the Ōkas. And this time around, he was going to keep his gamble small. On April 1, the second Jinrai attack force left Kanoya with only three Isshiki Rikkō/Ōka strike teams. Although small, the mission saw the Jinrai's first successes, with the American battleship *West Virginia* and three transport ships damaged.

Ugaki—a brave but never rash or daring man—refused to allow the minor successes of April 1 go to his head, and he waited until April 12 for just the right conditions to order the next Ōka attack. He was, however, emboldened enough on this day to up his ante to eight Isshiki Rikkō/Ōkas.

On the afternoon of April 12, eighteen-year-old Radio Operator Third Class Charles Stanford was at battle stations in the "radar shack" of *Mannert L. Abele*, a Task Force 54† destroyer on picket duty with several other "tin cans" at Radar Patrolling Station 14 ("Sugar Charlie"), about seventy miles northwest of Okinawa in the East China Sea. The job of the picket destroyers was to protect the American invasion fleet by keeping a constant radar search vigil over the area of operations, and vectoring in CAP to intercept anything deemed a potential threat. Since the introduction of *tokkō* tactics by the Japanese, this function had taken on crucial importance. Since the start of the Okinawa campaign, it had become a matter of life and death.

Veterans of fierce action during the defense of the Iwo Jima invasion fleet, the *Abele*'s radarmen were good at their jobs—experts at the

---

*See Hoyt (1993) for an account of this incident, plus detailed biographical information on Ugaki. Ugaki's wartime diary has been translated into English and is available under the title *Fading Victory: The Diary of Admiral Matome Ugaki 1941–1945*, Pittsburgh, PA: University of Pittsburgh Press (1991). This is highly recommended for valuable insights into this complicated, sensitive man's thinking.

†Rear Admiral Morton Deyo's Task Force 54—not to be confused with Mitschar's TF 58—was tasked with providing naval gunfire and cover for the Okinawa landings.

arcane art of IFF (Identification Friend or Foe). When Stanford picked up a large formation of unidentified aircraft approaching from the northeast at a range of 286 miles, the well-oiled human machinery of the radar shack clicked into gear:

*We went to battle stations five minutes later after satisfying ourselves that the threat was real*, Stanford writes fifty-eight years later. *Captain [Alton E.] Parker called down to the radar shack, instructing us to advise "Delegate Base" (command post for the sixteen destroyer picket stations surrounding Okinawa) of our radar contact. . . . They scrambled additional aircraft immediately. We had four Hellcats under our direct control but had released them earlier to check on other "bogies" who were closer to the Hellcats position than our incoming contact.*[8]

In short, Sugar Charlie's dedicated CAP was too far out to get back to help before the bogeys arrived, assuming the contact maintained present speed and heading. Whatever the planes were and whoever was flying them, they were coming in, and there was nothing Stanford and his shipmates could do now but wait for them to show up and play their hand.

At about 1340, the first of the Japanese attackers—three obsolescent Aichi Val dive-bombers—appeared over Sugar Charlie, where they were made quick work of by the AA crews of *Abele* and the other ships on station. By 1400, however, another fifteen to twenty Japanese planes were swarming overhead, circling the American ships like sharks in a feeding frenzy. At about 1440, a Zero with *Abele*'s number jinked AA fire to crash her amidships, knocking out the engine room and leaving the destroyer as good as dead in the water.[9]

About five minutes after the Zero strike, three Japanese heavy bombers were observed approaching from a distance, then turning away before closing any further. A moment later, the *Abele*'s survivors and AA gunners on the other ships caught a split-second glimpse of something they had never seen before. Visible only as a light gray streak against a light gray horizon, a missile of some sort came whistling in at extreme speed and wave-cap altitude, cracking the *Abele* with a tremendous explosion right above the waterline and nearly splitting the ship in half. Stanford and Captain Parker were the last two men to leave the ship alive.

Within minutes, the *Abele* slipped under the waves. But the Jinrai was not through with her crew. As Stanford and those shipmates still able treaded water, clutching for dear life onto anything that floated and kicking at the sharks that were beginning to gather, two of the Jinrai's escort Zeros barreled in and began strafing and bombing the *Abele*'s survivors.[10]

**fifteen**

## ECHOES OF THUNDER

O n April 14, Suzuki and Naitō and about forty other Ōka
pilots were flown from Kōnoike down to Kanoya to replace the steep operational losses of the previous three
weeks. When news of the March 21 debacle reached Kōnoike, the pilots
there shook off their initial sadness and disappointment with the ration-
alization that there was no accounting for the fortunes of war. The only
thing the pilots could do was to give it a better showing when it was their
turn to strap into the Ōkas. But no one on the April 14 flight to Kanoya
had any idea when they were going to be given a chance to prove their
mettle.

The plane from Kōnoike had barely rolled to a stop and its passengers
lined up on Kanoya's tarmac before the pilots were to go on standby for attack orders. The directive was given by a flight ops staff officer with about
as much tact and emotion as if he were ordering a bowl of noodles in a
restaurant.

"Have you ever heard the expression, 'I felt like ice water was poured
down my back'?" Suzuki-san asks me. "Well, that is exactly what I experienced when we got that standby command."

Naitō-san laughs and nods when he hears this description.

"I couldn't believe that we were going to be sent out so soon," he says.
"I thought we'd at least have a little time to mentally prepare ourselves.
But it was not really a 'fear' kind of shock, more a feeling of being not
quite ready for this. You know how people say, 'My life flashed in front of

my eyes'? Well, in that moment that's exactly what I experienced. . . .
Like there was a slide show of faces and places in my head. I think I was
really saying good-bye to those people and things. But I did not have
much time. I had to say my good-byes quickly. After that, though, I experienced a kind of calm and thought, So, this is it. I'm dead. Well, now I
guess I don't have to worry about dying anymore."

A few minutes later, as the stunned pilots were going through the final checks on their gear, the flight ops officer swaggered up to the group
once again.

"Stand down," he said, with just as much nonchalance as his previous
utterance. "Pick up your gear and report to personnel for billeting."

That night, the pilots were told about the April 12 sinking of the
American destroyer. The news electrified the group, but Suzuki's excitement was tinged with loss when he heard the name of the man who had
piloted the Ōka. It was his best friend, Saburō Dohi. Still, Suzuki could
not help but be proud of his friend's success, and most of all, of his
bravery.

"I talked later to the pilot of the Isshiki Rikkō that carried Dohi's Ōka
on that mission," Suzuki-san says. "He said Dohi was so cool and collected that he napped most of the trip down from Kanoya. They had to
wake him up to get him into his Ōka when they closed in on the drop
point."

Naitō had one more close call on May 6, when his mission was canceled on the flight line. The Isshiki Rikkōs' engines had been gunning
and the Ōka pilots were walking toward their planes when the stand-
down order came. For the next two months, Suzuki and Naitō were left
off the attack rosters, attending instead to the lonely vigil of watching
their buddies fly off on their missions, never to return. During those surreal weeks of send-offs and long hours of contemplation on the subject
of their imminent demise, the young men gradually came to terms with
their fate. This grim determination, however, would turn out to be unnecessary. They could not have known it at the time, but their war was
already over.

The Jinrai's war ended on June 22 with a failed four-plane mission to
Okinawa. In the end, the Ōka never lived up to expectations, having
sunk only the *Mannert L. Abele* and damaged six other American vessels
for the loss of 375 Isshiki Rikkō crewmen and fifty-five Ōka pilots.[1]

The final months of the war were even more anticlimactic for Takei, Asano, and their other Kō-13 classmates stranded at Kōnoike. They sat out the rest of the spring of 1945 in a training regimen that steadily slowed as the fuel situation worsened. During the long, hot summer that followed, training ground to a halt as the last precious drops of the nation's aviation fuel stocks were ordered set aside exclusively for *tokkō* missions.

After the surrender, the young petty officers were demobilized quickly. They now had to sort out the rest of their lives as fifteen- and sixteen-year-old veterans of a war that had devastated their country and overturned the entire value system of its people. The boys were destined to bear the brunt of the backbreaking labor that would be required over the next twenty years to rebuild a nation that had been destroyed in the previous two. In many ways, their hardest days and toughest challenges were still to come.

"When I went back to Hamamatsu, I enrolled in junior high right where I had left off before Yokaren," Takei-san says, now grinning as he approaches the punch line of the anecdote. "But there was one major problem. The school didn't have a roof anymore. Every time it rained, classes were canceled."

It is September 13, 2002, and Takei-san and I are riding the Shinkansen home after attending the last annual meeting of the Zero Fighter Pilots' Association (Takei-san qualifies for membership, having trained in the plane). The association officially disbanded today—its members too old and far-flung throughout the archipelago to keep up their annual congregation. From now on, activities will be informal, and carried out mostly by newsletter.

Perhaps the finality inherent in today's ceremony has the normally taciturn Takei-san in a philosophical mood, for he is now regaling me with stories about his life after the war. I am not asking anything. Just listening and nodding.

Takei-san talks about how he finished up his studies, got his engineering qualifications, and began his rise through Japan's rough-and-tumble construction business during the exciting and turbulent years of the postwar economic growth period. He talks a little about fishing, his postretirement passion. Toward the end of his monologue, however, his tone becomes pensive. He begins to talk about raising a family, and about how, during his busiest years, he lost touch with his wife and children for a while, even when they were all living under the same roof. He has devoted the years since his retirement to making up for lost time and trying to refurbish these relationships, but the going has been slow and not always easy.

"I grew up being told that a father was supposed to be strong and silent, and that working hard for the family was the only thing really expected of him. Emotions and tenderness for the children, sitting down and talking with them about school and troubles and worries—all that was supposed to be the mother's job. That was the way it always was, and it seemed to work just fine when I was a kid."

Unbeknownst to his generation until it was almost too late, the dynamics of the Japanese family had changed, most radically and critically in the terms of the role of the father. And, to use Takei-san's metaphor, there was no user's manual to help them through the transition.

"Now I see that I was wrong," he says to the window glass. "I wish I had another chance to redo those years. I would have spent more time with my family . . . helped my wife out a little more than I did. . . ."

Silence returns, but it is not uncomfortable. We are tired, and quietly staring out the window seems as good an idea as any for passing the rest of the journey home. A night landscape whips by the window at two hundred kilometers an hour, all glittery industrial plant, neon-blazing pachinko parlors and mammoth, Orwellian apartment blocks stretching as far as the eye can see, everything strung with bridges, honeycombed with underpasses and tunnel entrances. I realize that 90 percent of everything I am looking at right now—including the magnificent train on which we are riding—was built and paid for with the hope, sweat, and youth of men like Tokurō Takei. Was it really only this generation's war dead who ended up sacrificing their lives for Japan?

# PART FOUR

# A SOLDIER'S SCRAPBOOK

# sixteen

# BRIGHT-EYED BOYS FROM THE PROVINCES

I wao Fukagawa is slightly stoop-shouldered, but he has the vigorous presence of a man still in the prime of life, with a full head of bushy white hair and small eyes as lively and animated as his foghorn voice. He bears a strong resemblance to Warren Oates, if you can imagine what the actor might have looked like if he had managed to reach eighty relatively intact.

Every minute of the nearly half a century the stentorian Fukagawa-san spent as a business executive is evident in his hurried but economical movements, and in his voluminous but measured speech, which is what a linguist or computer programmer would call "semantically dense." Nary a breath is wasted, and every utterance is task-oriented. No matter the topic, Fukagawa-san speaks excitedly and with unqualified conviction— one moment a football coach motivating his players before a big game, the next a mother lecturing her children about dressing warmly in cold weather. Although I do not always think everything he says necessarily merits such conviction—especially when the subject of "correct" history is broached—I find his attitude refreshing and his energy contagious, and there is a confidence-instilling sincerity in everything about him. His is a vanishing breed of Japanese male, imbued with an undeniable quality of what my grandparents' generation would have called "sand."

As we begin our interview in a tatami conference room at Kaikōsha— the veterans' club venue where I will interview Toshio Yoshitake a month later—Fukagawa-san arranges his papers and appointment book (open to today's date, of course) just so, everything spread out before him within easy arm's reach, the lower edge of each item parallel to the edge of the table. No sooner have I asked my first formal question of the interview than Fukagawa-san is off and running, summarizing his brief but dramatic career in military aviation by reading from a sheaf of notes itemized in chronological order and broken down by unit and air base location. I can barely get a word in edgewise, but I have no problem with that, and it is obvious that Fukagawa-san has no problem with the arrangement, either. In the meantime, the recorder is running, and it will catch everything.

Iwao Fukagawa was born the second of three brothers on January 18, 1923, on the outskirts of Saga City, a manufacturing center in northwestern Kyūshū in what was once the old samurai province of Higo. Although his father, Yonekichi, liked to talk about the proud samurai heritage of the region, the Fukagawas were originally of peasant stock, hailing from deep in the Kyūshū mountains, and Iwao and his siblings were the first generation of the family born in an urban environment. Yonekichi had worked very hard to make that possible.

In his own youth, regional primogeniture traditions meant that Yonekichi—as the youngest of four sons—would not be expected to devote his life to caring for his parents in their dotage and looking after the family homestead. Sharing the fate of his next oldest two brothers, he was also cut out of any claim to his father's estate, which would go lock, stock, and barrel to the eldest son. But the flip side of this de facto congenital disownment was that Yonekichi was free to seek his fortune wherever and however he chose to do so. After completing elementary school, he exercised this freedom by leaving the family farm and heading off to Ogimachi on the outskirts of Saga City to apprentice as a carpenter.

The boy was a quick study, skilled with his hands and blessed with keen business sense and political savvy. His day-to-day activities were fueled by a vigorously extroverted temperament, a robust hard-work ethic, and lofty ambitions that, in his case, even an unwelcome year of army conscript duty failed to derail. Returning to Saga after his stint, he continued to hone his professional chops while establishing the network of contacts and customers that would help him set up his own sawmill, lumberyard, and woodworking factory by his late twenties. By the time his second son, Iwao, was born in 1923, Yonekichi was already on his way to becoming a successful businessman and a leader in his local community.

Although Yonekichi Fukagawa was by no means a highly educated man, he believed himself to be a wise one, and thus eminently qualified to instruct his family in the ways of the world. A favorite after-dinner activity in the Fukagawa household was for Yonekichi to gather his children in front of him in the living room and tell them school-of-hard-knocks diligence fables and stories about how tough his own life had been as a child and young man, especially during his hand-to-mouth apprenticeship years.

"The goddess of fortune dangles a golden opportunity before a person at least once in a lifetime," he was fond of saying. "And success goes to those quick and brave enough to reach out and grab that chance. Be decisive, children. Don't be afraid to take chances. Don't go through life staring off into space, waiting for good things to fall into your lap."

Yonekichi's go-getter attitude and lifelong drive for self-improvement were reflected in his choice of a marriage partner. From the perspective of a man of his background, his beautiful bride, Tsuma*—one of the few women in the community to have completed any education beyond elementary school—was what would today be called a "trophy wife." In many ways, she was symbolic not only of his notable accomplishments so far, but more important, of the ascent he wanted his family's social status to take in the future.

Tsuma was a real nurturer—"the gentleness specialist of the house," in her son's words—a quiet, reserved, supportive woman who never raised her voice or did or said an unkind thing to anyone. Unlike Yonekichi, she was not one for opinionated pontification and lectures, but although she rarely expressed her desires openly, she shared her husband's ambitions for the family's future and his enthusiasm for their children's education. An accomplished flower arranger and calligrapher, Tsuma also felt that culture and refinement were prerequisites for the social

---

*Readers with Japanese ability may do a double-take at this name, which also happens to be one of the Japanese words for "wife." Fukagawa-san himself is not sure of the origins of this naming.

status her husband had in mind for their children, and were thus just as essential for life training as practical academic subjects and Horatio Alger fables. She believed that it was best to begin this well-rounded education as early as possible, and toward this end, sent her children to a nearby Christian kindergarten that enjoyed the patronage of other well-off families in the community. The tuition was not cheap, but Tsuma felt that no corners should be cut when it came to making sure her own offspring spent their formative years around a "better" type of children.

Classes at the kindergarten were taught in fluent but heavily accented Japanese by an old-maid German missionary named Frau Winter, who laced her lessons with a healthy dose of Lutheran dogma that never really caught on with the children or their families, the Fukagawas included. But religious affiliations or not, everyone became a believer at Christmastime, when *die Frau* would organize her charges into a chorus to sing carols and perform pageants in phonetically memorized German. Iwao enjoyed her Christmas productions so much that he continued participating in them well into his elementary school years, although this stopped after neighborhood boys clued him in on the inherent sissiness of candlelight handbell recitals and singing "O Tannenbaum" in an elf costume. Convinced of this wisdom, Iwao stuck to less masculinity-threatening activities like baseball and marbles from then on.

Playing "war" with friends was another favorite activity for Iwao, and it was encouraged by teachers at school and other adult figures in the community, including his own father. Like many other self-made Japanese men of his generation, Yonekichi Fukagawa saw a military career as a quick, honorable, and surefire way for his sons to elevate not only their own but the collective family social status as well. Putting his sons through either the naval or military academy would do the trick nicely, propelling them up and out of Ogi-machi and as far away from the family sawmill as they could get. Yonekichi made no secret of his ambitions for his boys, and often discussed with his oldest son, Tadao, the merits of attending the army's IMA prep school Yōnen Gakkō (literally "Army Youth School") program. Yōnen graduates were guaranteed automatic acceptance to the IMA after their three-year courses of study, and a Yōnen pedigree was generally considered to be a necessary ticket on the fast track to general's stars. Family hopes were high when Tadao sat for entrance examinations to the program in early 1933.

Iwao never forgot the shame and disappointment in the Fukagawa household when Tadao failed his exams, and he vowed to avenge the family honor when his own turn came by succeeding where his brother had failed. The nail-biting drama of cramming and test batteries were repeated five years later during Iwao's fifteenth spring, but this time, the family's hopes were realized. Iwao passed his exams and matriculated to the Yōnen Gakkō Hiroshima campus in April 1938. It was a heady honor for a sawmill operator's son.

While Iwao's social background as a craftsman's son would have made his entry into Japan's warrior elite difficult even forty or fifty years earlier—and outright impossible another thirty years before that—it was very much representative of the "new" samurai being produced in Japan's naval and army service academies in the early decades of the twentieth century. This was especially true of the IMA, which was an organizationally rigid but much more socially egalitarian institution than its naval counterpart at Etajima. Since the closing years of the Meiji period, IMA graduating classes were increasingly dominated by sons of Japan's provincial petit bourgeois—a nascent social stratum that had proved early on, as in most other nineteenth-century experiments in nationalism, to be the most loyal and patriotic in its support of the Japanese nouveau regime.[1] While all but three out of 158 members of the first IMA class in 1877 were of samurai descent—with the class dominated by cadets from landed-elite families with large estates in the old Satsuma and Chōshū clan bastions of western Japan—samurai descendants made up only 15 percent of the class of 1931, when the majority of the academy's cadets were from middle-class origins and hailed from far-flung regional urban centers and agricultural areas.[2]

This demographic shift in the makeup of the officer corps was encouraged by the army, which saw a wide home region and social class distribution for its membership as a factor that, working in tandem with the burgeoning Army Reservist Association (Zaigō Gunjindan), would help the service consolidate its popular power base and political influence. Moreover, as intellectual dallyings in socialism and democratic movements centered in the Tokyo area became particularly conspicuous in the post–World War I years, the army—whose ideology was increasingly influenced by a German-inspired school of thought known as Japanese Romanticism—saw boys from outlying regional areas as being more wholesome and "purely Japanese" potential officer material than their more cosmopolitan Tokyo counterparts, who were traditionally suspect of squandering their energies on the capital's pleasures and clouding their minds with subversive Western thought. Bright-eyed boys from the provinces like Iwao Fukagawa attracted to military careers in Japan's interwar years were seen as fit, pure-hearted, fiercely patriotic, and expected—when the time came—to be unflinchingly prepared to die for what they believed in.

These long-term social and regional shifts in army junior leadership development paid off in unexpected ways, eventually producing a faction of officers who were unfettered by old clan loyalties and who tended to regard the army as the supreme arbiter of the national and imperial will in most political matters. They would go on to assume a praetorian guard–like influence in the capital during the tumultuous twenties and thirties, when their senior ranks engineered the nation's swing toward militarism, and a cabal of hotheads from their younger ranks very nearly toppled the parliamentary government with a coup d'état attempt in February 1936. During the war that resulted in large part from this militaristic adventurism, the last generation of torchbearers—Iwao and other 1940s IMA graduates—would end up bearing the brunt of cleaning up the mess, with many making the ultimate sacrifice as *tokkō* pilots in the final months of fighting.

Of course, the fury and destruction of war Iwao would face was still years away when he began his military career as a fifteen-year-old cadet in 1938. Even though the China war was already going on at the time, few Japanese felt that it had much bearing on their lives, and in the case of the Fukagawa family, no one was particularly worried that Iwao— despite his chosen career path—might have to be involved in this or any other war someday. Iwao gave the possibility even less thought. Even as a teenager, he had a pragmatic, work-the-problem approach to life, and he tended to concentrate his efforts on the tasks at hand. Whatever was going to happen in the future would happen, and could be dealt with when the time came. It did little good to worry about what might be when there was work to be done *now,* and for the time being, Iwao had that work cut out for him as a new cadet in the Imperial Japanese Army.

Like future IMA classmate Toshio Yoshitake, Iwao was also temperamentally well suited to survive and thrive in this environment of extreme regimentation and frequent hardship, but for different reasons. Where Yoshitake was highly adaptive, good at bending with the breeze, and adept at ducking punches, Iwao was more of a Ulysses Grant type—a bullheaded hard charger who always took his punches squarely on the chin. He banged away 100 percent at everything he did, whether it was academic work, military training, or the school's daily PE regimen of kendo fencing, judo, and gymnastics.

The young cadet's martial spirit and fighting vigor did not escape the attentions of his instructors, and Iwao was often chosen to give kendo exhibition matches for VIPs visiting the Hiroshima Yōnen campus, such as the delegation of Hitler Youth members and Nazi officials who toured the facilities during the summer of 1939. His greatest honor, however, was when he was tapped for a bout to be held for the ultimate visiting VIP—none other than Emperor Hirohito himself.

"I was very nervous," Fukagawa-san remembers some sixty-five years later. "But it was quite a thrill when I won. His Majesty watched very carefully, commenting when someone made a good move or parried a blow skillfully. You could tell that he knew something about kendo . . . that he knew what to look for."

After an exemplary Yōnen Gakkō career, Iwao matriculated without incident and on schedule in April 1941 to the IMA main campus at Ichigaya, Tokyo,* where he would pursue a fourteen-month core-curriculum academic course before being sent to his appropriate service branch school to finish up his cadet training. Like so many of his classmates, Iwao had his heart set on aviation. These ambitions came crashing to earth, however, when he was diagnosed with high blood pressure at his flight physical and sent to the infantry instead. Although bitterly disappointed, Iwao—true to character—shrugged off the setback and put his efforts into succeeding at being an exemplary infantry cadet, just as he had succeeded in everything else the army had thrown at him so far.

After graduating from the core-curriculum course in June 1942, Iwao

---

*IMA '44 was the last class to study at the Ichigaya campus. The core-curriculum campus was shifted to Zama in Kanagawa Prefecture (present-day Camp Zama—a joint U.S./Japan Self-Defense Force base) in October 1941.

and his classmates were sent out on a three-month Cadet Troop Leadership Training* program to serve with actual line units as apprentice officers. In Iwao's case, he was assigned to the 210th Infantry Regiment, a Chinese Expeditionary Force unit that was composed mostly of conscripts from Kofu City, Yamanashi Prefecture, and the Yokohama metropolitan area.† As Iwao and his other classmates assigned to summer duty with the unit soon found out after their arrival at the unit's northern China base camp, 210th's area of responsibility happened to be in a combat zone. The cadets were given a firsthand reminder of this fact when they came under fire from Chinese troops during a visit to the front line one day to observe an assault on a Kuomintang base.‡

Outside of the shooting incident, Iwao enjoyed his temporary duty in China, and even got to do some sightseeing in the nearby town with classmates on days off. While there was plenty of guerrilla activity in the area, this was mostly limited to sabotage and nighttime skirmishes in the countryside. The Japanese had firm control over urban concentrations and major roads, and as long as Iwao and his friends stuck to these areas, the only danger they faced was the unwelcoming stares of the locals.

The children were friendly, though, and Iwao always carried a big bag of sweets for the inevitable kiddie crowd that would mob him, begging for candy, whenever he ventured off-post. Iwao enjoyed this attention, and never experienced with the local children the halfheartedly guilty sense of "invader consciousness"§ he usually felt when he was around Chinese adults. The children also kept him from dwelling too much on a strategic situation that even a nineteen-year-old cadet could see was hopeless.

"I always felt that high command didn't really know what we were supposed to be doing there," Fukagawa-san rues. "The place was too big

---

*For ease of understanding, I use here the USMA terminology for equivalent training undergone by West Point cadets during their junior-year summer.

†IMA '44 was the only class sent to overseas units for CTLT, although the assignments were limited to China, as theaters where combat was being engaged in with the Americans were considered too hazardous.

‡The practice of bringing IMA cadets along to observe combat operations was soon canceled when reports of this particular incident reached high command in Tokyo. Even Japan's formidable propaganda machine would have been hard-pressed to explain a cadet getting shot during a training mission.

§Fukagawa-san renders this as *shinryakusha ishiki* in Japanese.

for a nation of Japan's limited resources to occupy. We committed troops to China without a clear goal and, most crucially, without a victory scenario plotted out. It was a no-win situation. Like Vietnam for the Americans."

Cadet Fukagawa returned to the Zama campus in September 1942 a bit more wizened and worldly for his efforts, but he wasted no time settling in to begin classwork for the Infantry Officer's Course. Although he now had a much more realistic mental grasp of the realities of the war, he nevertheless still believed that Japan's cause to protect Asia from Western encroachment was just, and that she would prevail in the end. Thus, he thought nothing particularly untoward about the announcement in late fall of that year that cadets previously disqualified for aviation for medical or physical reasons would be given another opportunity to apply for a branch change. Unfettered by any particular loyalty toward the infantry, Fukagawa jumped at the chance, and was overjoyed when told that he had made the cut this go-around. He transferred to the IMA aviation branch campus in Toyo'oka, Saitama Prefecture, in January 1943.

Fukagawa and his fellow transfer cadets assumed that their good fortune was due to dramatic increases in the size and importance of aviation in the army's battlefield role, and they interpreted this as an exciting and promising development in terms of the nation's striking power. They had barely more information about the combat then raging on Guadalcanal and throughout the Solomons than the average newspaper-reading civilian, and were blissfully unaware of the horrific attrition of army pilots in these battles that was in fact most responsible for their being able to make it over the now considerably lowered bar to qualify for flight training.

The cadre officers at Toyo'oka did not talk much to their charges about the progress of the war. Obviously, morale issues dictated that troubling news—an increasing supply of which was available as 1943 progressed—be carefully screened for cadet consumption. However, it would be unfair to imply that any failure to keep the cadets informed with constantly updated reports on the nation's military fortunes was entirely due to some campaign of misinformation or deception on the part of the administration. More than anything, ignorance of the news was probably a matter of simply being too busy. With a crushingly tight schedule otherwise exclusively dedicated to learning basic piloting skills in the Akatonbo and aeronautical theory in the classrooms, the cadets had little energy and even less time to worry about much else than their studies and training, let alone combing newspapers and scuttlebutt for niblets of truth about the world beyond the academy gates.

As the March graduation date approached for the class of '44, it was time for its members to select their aviation specialty branches. At the unchallenged bottom of the list were recon, liaison, and ground attack, which were the most common destinations for those not lucky enough to get picked for one of the two perennial favorites, fighters and heavy bombers. These last two specialties each had their own reputation among the cadets, with fighters generally seen as being best suited for the individualistic jock crowd—boys long on guts but not brains—while bombers were seen as appealing to a more plodding, exacting, and intellectual variety of pilot.

As in the air forces of other countries, the great fighters-versus-bombers controversy over which branch had tactical primacy in the skies had yet to be resolved in Japanese army aviation. And although the almost exclusively defensive posture of Japanese airpower in the last eighteen months of the war would render the argument moot and relegate most of the nation's multiengined medium and heavy bombers to transport duties, the bomber branch was nevertheless still considered the best career path for a young professional with his eyes on general's stars someday.

Fukagawa weighed his own choice carefully, but in the end, his not-often-indulged romantic side got the better of him. After his graduation on March 20, he received a three-day pass and travel orders for the Army Fighter School at Akeno, Mie Prefecture, Kita Ise Annex Air Base, where he would undergo the roughly half-year Fighter Basic Course.* Like most other cadets who chose this path, he had done so because he thought a fighter plane would afford him the best chance to strike a blow against the enemy that was threatening his country. Some fourteen months later, IGHQ would concur with Fukagawa's opinion, but the methodology they would suggest was something this young pilot could never have imagined in the spring of 1944.

---

*In Japanese terminology, this is called *Otsu-Shū*, or "Phase A" training.

Fighter Basic began with a few weeks of diagnostic shakedown flights on the Akatonbo as the first step in evaluating individual trainee abilities. Remedial training was assigned as needed, and the students moved up to stick time on actual combat aircraft when they were deemed up to the task by the Akeno cadre. Fukagawa's first experience flying a fighter plane was at the controls of a Nakajima *Ki-27*, an all-metal, late-thirties monoplane design that had been effective against the Chinese and Soviets in Manchuria seven years earlier but was suitable only for training—and barely, at that—by 1944.* But to Fukagawa and his classmates, the type's obsolescence did not diminish in the least their thrill and pride in being able to solo in a fighter, and it was not long before most of the trainees—Fukagawa included—were walking around Kita Ise in expensive aviator sunglasses with all the swagger and aplomb of veteran aces.

Personal kit was a matter of pride for the cadets. Unlike enlisted men, whose gear was almost entirely government issue, officers—and officers-to-be—were responsible for buying their own uniforms, and there were subtle individual differences in taste and quality for these items. In Fukagawa's case, his proud father had splurged on him during his last home leave before IMA graduation during New Year's 1943–44, buying him a pair of high riding boots (which only commissioned officers could wear), a tailor-made dress uniform, and, as the pièce de résistance, an officer's *katana* handcrafted by one of the most famous swordsmiths in Kyūshū. Fukagawa was too afraid to ask how much the sword had cost, and the blade soon became the envy of his classmates.

When Fukagawa flew down to Chita Peninsula in southern Aichi Prefecture for two weeks of live-fire gunnery range training at the end of June, he brought along the new dress uniform and sword he would need for his July 1 commissioning ceremony and formal commemorative photograph. Intensive training continued throughout the summer, but there was considerable free time between flights and technical seminars, and as lieutenants, the trainees were free to do as they pleased after instruction every day. All of this freedom of movement was a bit of a culture shock for the IMA graduates, and this was especially true for Yōnen Gakkō products like Fukagawa, who had only recently emerged into the

---

*Some *Ki-27*s were used as *tokkō* aircraft when things got really desperate in 1945.

daylight of reality and hormones after a total of six years in the monastic he-man woman-haters club of army cadet life. Perhaps wishing to ensure that this newfound freedom did not go to the trainees' heads, the Akeno administrators were careful to make sure there were plenty of wholesome, stress-releasing outlets for their charges' excess energies. Group trips to the seaside—usually nearby Yokkaichi Beach in Aichi Prefecture—were one form of activity organized for this purpose. Other amenities included excellent chow, a well-stocked PX, and other concessions on the base.

Officers' privileges meant that the lieutenants—if not on duty— were able to venture off-post each weekend from Saturday afternoon to Sunday evening. One such excursion that is particularly fresh in Fukagawa-san's memory was a late summer day trip he made with several classmates to Kameyama, Mie Prefecture, a nearby town famous for its pleasant weather and beautiful scenery. Stepping off the wood-burning bus at their destination, the lieutenants were intrigued to see two beautiful and well-dressed young women standing ankle-deep in a small river running past the bus stop. Judging from their clothing and light complexions, they appeared to be from the city—Fukagawa guessed Nagoya. In any case it was clearly evident that they were not local farm girls, and were thus eligible candidates, under army social conventions, for some harmless flirtation with dashing young officers. Excitedly expecting some rare female conversation and at least a nice leg show for their troubles, Fukagawa and his buddies walked over to investigate and make their move, then were stunned into silence to see that rather than bathing their tootsies in the water, the girls were washing yams they had just pulled out of a field somewhere and were eating them raw, on the spot. As for the obviously famished girls, they were either too busy gnawing away at their rude morsels to realize that they were being watched, or they were merely ignoring their audience out of shame for their own less-than-elegant situation. Whatever the case, the young officers walked away without saying a word, although the encounter was the subject of concerned conversation on the bus back to Kita Ise that night.

"That was a real eye-opener. We didn't realize things on the outside had gotten that bad," Fukagawa-san remembers. "We had always gotten plenty of food at the academy and at Akeno, and the farmers around the base seemed to have enough for themselves, so we were completely unaware of the food shortages that were beginning to hit the cities by then. We all said to each other, 'We can't let things get any worse than this.'"

# seventeen

# FIGHTER JOCK

By September 1944, the Akeno Fighter School administrators—under pressure from higher-ups to deliver new pilots to the front as soon as possible—were beginning to screen talented trainees for accelerated graduation and immediate posting to the elite 200th Fighter Regiment in the Philippines, where combat was expected to be imminent. Fukagawa and his classmates were by then learning to fly the army's mainstay Nakajima *Ki*-43 Hayabusa fighter and were well aware of the evaluation process under way. Everyone knew that the number of students selected would be small, and competition was as fierce as spirits were high. The pilots' motivation was also stoked by knowledge that a posting to the 200th FR would mean stick time on the *Ki*-84 Hayate, the hot new next-generation Nakajima design. All of the pilots dreamed about flying the machine, so there were a lot of long faces at Kita Ise when the very short list of *senbatsu* ("final cut roster") pilots to be sent into combat ahead of schedule was posted on the flight ops bulletin board.

"I was crushed when orders didn't come through for me," Fukagawa-san recalls. "And extremely envious of the boys who got picked. I would have given anything to have gotten to go with them, and still regret to this day that I didn't."

Sentimental regrets aside, Fukagawa-san, after a long career in business management and personnel administration, is a sharp judge of character and thus able to be objective about his disappointment. Regarding his elite *senbatsu* classmates, he remembers them as a breed apart in terms of flying ability, and also distinctly separated into two general personality types. One group—probably the numerically dominant of the two—was of the rather standoffish, athletically talented, narrow-eyed-killer Chuck Yeager type most people have in mind when they conjure up imagery of hotshot fighter jocks. The other group, interestingly enough, was of what might be called a "performing artist" temperament—good-natured, extreme extroverts who were clearly in their element in the air and eager to show off their breathtaking flying talents at any and all opportunities.

Fukagawa-san's close friend "Shin-chan" Ishiyama was of the latter type, but his natural talents at the stick were not enough to keep him alive for long once the bullets started flying in the Philippines. Out of nineteen pilots in the *senbatsu* group, seventeen others were to share Shin-chan's fate before the Leyte campaign was finished.

"Experience is as important for a fighter pilot as natural ability," Fukagawa-san reasons, "because it makes you cagey. If you go into combat with just ability alone, like the situation the *senbatsu* pilots were thrown into, you are made quick work of by experienced enemy pilots. And the Americans the 200th FR faced in the Philippines were the best in the world. They knew all the tricks."

After the *senbatsu* send-off at the end of September, the remaining trainees spent their last month of Fighter Basic on TDY at Miyakonojo Air Base in southeastern Kyūshū, where there would be a final round of evaluations by the Akeno cadre. The training itself concentrated on technical points such as formation flying and combat tactics, and when it was over, the trainees were assigned wherever and however the army felt their individual talents could best be applied. For most of the 338 IMA '44 pilot trainees, this meant a frontline unit assignment. Nearly half of them would die by war's end.[1]

In Fukagawa's case, however, his evident leadership abilities had been recognized early on in the program and were evidently considered more important than the contribution his piloting skills could make to the war effort. Instead of being sent to frontline units with other classmates, he and a select group of similarly evaluated graduates were given slots for enrollment in the next three-month Flight Leader School cycle at Akeno, which would start at the beginning of December. Normally, postings to this program were reserved for captains with several years of line—and preferably combat—experience, but such personnel were in woefully short supply in IJA aviation by the fall of '44. Combat losses at the captain and major levels meant that in coming months, green second lieutenants would be leading flights and even squadrons into battle. The army had no other choice but to let lambs lead other lambs to the slaughter.

Given this crisis in junior leadership, the least the army could do was give the Akeno pilots as much stick time as possible before sending them into the fray. During the monthlong lull before the beginning of Flight Leader School, Fukagawa and his classmates were put to work as ferry pilots while they waited for their training cycle to begin. This duty consisted of flying fighters that had passed final army evaluation at Akeno to frontline units around the country and in forward areas like Taiwan and the Philippines. From a training perspective, the flights had the side benefits of providing the pilots with valuable experience in long-range/over-water navigation and formation flying.

By late November, Fukagawa had several successful domestic overland shuttle hops under his belt, and was deemed ready to participate in an over-water mission to ferry a large formation of Hayabusas to the Philippines. The flight plan called for rest and refueling stopovers at Miyakonojo, Yontan Air Base at Okinawa, and Taichū, Taiwan, before reaching the final destination at the Clark Airfield complex. The flight itself was tiring but uneventful until the planes were taxiing to begin the hop for the last leg from Taiwan to Clark. Fukagawa's engine started spewing oil, and was soon putting out so much smoke that it completely obliterated all forward and lateral vision. Correctly judging that the best course of action was to get his stricken plane out of the way as quickly as possible, Fukagawa nonetheless failed to notice the proximity of another aircraft to his plane. When he swung his Hayabusa around to pull it off the runway, he put his port wingtip directly into the spinning prop of the other aircraft. Both planes were total write-offs.

To the pilots' surprise and immeasurable relief, no one got particularly angry with them for pranging their kites. After a mild dressing-down and some resigned head shaking, they were told to find their own transport back to Akeno and sent on their way. They ended up hopping a Ki-67 heavy bomber back to Japan a few days later, laden down with souvenirs of Taiwan bananas and brown-sugar rock candy that were much appreciated by their comrades at Akeno.

Although Fukagawa-san still blushes a bit whenever he recalls the accident, he has also taken some comfort over the years in thinking that the mishap may have saved the lives of two pilots waiting to make attack sorties in the Philippines. Moreover, Fukagawa's life was probably saved as well—the Leyte campaign was raging unabated at the time, and many of the other pilots on the ferry flight to Clark were ordered to stay on with fighter units in-theater as replacements, only to die in combat. Others were killed when their transport plane back to Japan was jumped by Hellcats and sent into the South China Sea.

In the final days of November 1944, Akeno was abuzz with the latest news and rumors from the Philippine front. Not surprisingly, most of the scuttlebutt was troubling, and although the press was trumpeting Leyte as a stunning Japanese victory,* Fukagawa and his classmates were given fairly accurate accounts of the swan song of Japan's surface fleet in the October 25–26 battles. The news was enough to convince all but the most unhinged optimists that any chance of winning the war was gone, and that "winning the peace"—i.e., fighting the Americans to an honorable stalemate—was the best that could now be hoped for.

News of the navy's Shikishima flight taiatari attacks during the Leyte battles provided one spark of hope in all of the doom and gloom. The pilots had first heard about taiatari tactics as official army policy in early November, after the Fugaku and Banda tokkō bomber units were dispatched to the Philippines and squandered in underescorted attacks. Although that particular piece of news had been disheartening, the navy "special attacks" were showing promise. Fukagawa was convinced of the basic merit of the taiatari concept, and in discussions on the topic, he and his fellow pilots at Akeno felt that tokkō was atarimae—perfectly understandable, given the circumstances—and they were eager to kick in and do their part, especially after hearing that IMA classmates at the

---

*Mainichi Shimbun, October 28, 1944. Front-page headlines reported seven American aircraft carriers sunk. In reality, American carrier losses at Leyte amounted to one light and two escort types. The light carrier Princeton was lost on October 24 to land-based conventional aircraft attack. The escorts were both from Sprague's Taffy 3, and both went down on October 25: Gambier Bay was lost to shellfire from Kurita's attack force, and St. Lo was, of course, sunk by Lieutenant Seki's Shikishima flight tokkō attack.

other army fighter school in Mito, Ibaraki Prefecture, were already being organized into *tokkō* squadrons.

The Akeno pilots would not have to wait long to prove their enthusiasm. One night in late November, an impromptu formation was called in the IMA '44 officers' quarters. Forming a long file in the narrow corridor of the single-story wooden structure, Fukagawa and the other thirty or so residents of the barracks were addressed by the Akeno CO.

"Things have not been developing well for us on the war front," the CO said, pacing up and down the line, the floorboards creaking in the silence between his words. "Therefore, high command sees no choice but to employ body-crashing tactics against the Americans. Anyone who wants to volunteer for this, take one step forward."

Despite all of Fukagawa's mental preparation in previous weeks for the eventuality of such a moment, the suddenness of its arrival left him momentarily blank. There was no time to mull over a response, and in any case, the atmosphere in that tight hallway was too tense for anyone to speak up even if they had made up their mind not to go. In such a situation, standing in ranks and in full sight of one's peers, it was absolutely inconceivable that a Japanese officer—especially an IMA graduate—could have ever stood fast and refused to "volunteer."

"I don't even remember telling my feet to move," Fukagawa-san recalls of the moment. "It was like a strong gust of wind whooshed up from behind the ranks and blew everyone forward a step, almost in perfect unison."

Satisfied with the response, the CO nodded with a kind of grim relief, informed the pilots that their names would be added to official *tokkō* rosters, then turned on his heel and walked out into the night. The episode was never mentioned again, and Fukagawa was too busy training to think much about the ceremony's significance during the next few months.

The Flight Leader course at Akeno officially started on December 1, 1944, with instruction concentrating on formation flying, bomber interception, and other aerial combat tactics. Also included in the training regimen—somewhat ominously—were simulated diving attacks on stationary ground objects. But while the *tokkō* runs were only simulated, the bomber interception drills were most decidedly intended to be on-the-job training, and for the task, the pilots were given their first rides in the highly touted Hayates.

Beginning in January 1945, the anti-B-29 patrols were flown mainly over the Nagoya area, as this was the metropolitan area closest to Akeno. While the trainees never ran into any Americans during these patrols, the missions gave them much-needed stick time on the new Hayates.

The Hayate was a quantum leap in Japanese fighter design—a beautiful airplane that more than lived up to all of its hype to deliver as advertised. Powered by a Nakajima Ha-45 engine delivering up to eighteen hundred horsepower on a war emergency power setting, the plane was fully 100 kph faster than its Hayabusa predecessor, and more important, had an almost 20 kph edge on the American Hellcat. Highly maneuverable, with excellent climb rate and diving speed (crucial for prudent escape from an unfavorable combat situation), the plane also provided decent armor to protect its pilot, which was a rarity in Japanese military aircraft at the time. Another confidence-instilling feature of the design was its main armament of two 12.7 mm (equivalent to American .50-caliber) and two wing-mounted 20 mm cannon, which gave it enough firepower to knock anything up to and including the mammoth B-29 out of the sky. For the Akeno trainees, their introduction to the plane was something akin to a religious experience.

"I'll never forget the first time I opened up the throttle all the way and heard the takeoff roar of that big engine," Fukagawa-san recalls with a distinct gleam in his eyes. "There was nothing like it. We felt omnipotent in that plane. Everyone was saying 'Bring on the Hellcats!'"

As Fukagawa and his classmates accumulated flight hours in the Hayates, most of them seem to have conveniently forgotten about their *tokkō* pledge, instead believing that they were destined for postgraduation assignments to lead fighters into combat with line units. Reality for most turned out to be distinctly less glamorous. In Fukagawa's case, orders were cut for him to return to his old barracks at Kita Ise field to begin duty as an instructor on Akatonbos at Flight Basic. No previous teaching experience was necessary—the sheer numbers of college student volunteers the army was beginning to push through its Tokubetsu

Sōjū Minarai Shikan flight program* were beginning to swamp the regular cadre there, and they needed all of the qualified pilots they could get to help pick up the instruction slack.

The Tokubetsu Minarai program—or Tokusō, as it was usually abbreviated—was created in late 1943, when the official cancellation of college draft deferments presented the army with a tempting new pool of potential flight candidates to compensate for the alarming attrition of pilots it had suffered over the previous year of combat in the Southwestern Pacific. A two-birds-with-one-stone combination of OCS and rudimentary flight training, the four-month crash course (too often literally so) was designed to produce combat-ready army reserve officer pilots from students straight out of civilian universities, teachers colleges, and higher-level vocational schools. Not surprisingly, its graduates were notorious for their often less-than-exemplary piloting skills, and experience soon proved the majority of them to be little more than cannon fodder when sent out on conventional combat missions. By early 1945, as Japanese air doctrine shifted decisively toward *tokkō* tactics, most Tokusō graduates were being sent directly to *tokkō* units. Many hundreds died during the Iwo Jima and Okinawa campaigns, and the vast majority of those not sacrificed in these battles were pooled as reserve *tokkō* pilots for the apocalyptic "Hondo Kessen" battle to come when the Americans invaded the home islands.

During his three-month stint as a flight instructor at Kita Ise, Fukagawa did his best to keep his mind on the task at hand and off of the postgraduation fate that probably awaited most of his students. In this sense, the workload was mercifully busy, and by the end of a typically exhausting and often terrifying training day of student stall-outs and lousy landings, it usually took all of the strength he could muster just to climb out of the observer's cockpit of the Akatonbo.

Late in the afternoon of May 3, 1945, Fukagawa finished a hair-raising day of wingtip-bumping formation flights with his students and went back to the barracks even more exhausted than usual. He had just stretched out on his bunk in his favorite posttraining posture when his roommate, Shigeharu Arai, poked his head in the doorway and told him

---

*The phrase, translated literally, is "Special Hands-on Flight Officer Training Program." See Nagatsuka (1972) for a personal account of the program from a trainee's perspective.

that their CO, Major Kanezawa, wanted to see him immediately. He bolted upright and ran to the HQ shack as quickly as he could, still in his sweaty flight suit.

In 1995, when the Association of IMA '44 Graduates compiled a class history of their air operations in the war, Fukagawa wrote down the following recollections of that afternoon:

> After knocking on the CO's door, I entered and reported for duty. For some reason, I remember the room as dark and shadowy. I stood there at attention for a while in front of the major's desk, where he sat in silence for an uncomfortably long time. Finally, he spoke.
>
> "Tomorrow, you are to report to the Akeno main campus," he said, as if he had to struggle to get each word out. "They are organizing more *tokkō* units. Do you understand? *Tokkō*."
>
> "Understood, sir," I said, and snapped a salute. Major Kanezawa returned it and dismissed me. As I walked back to the barracks—much more slowly than I ran there!—I thought of all the heavy hitters who had already gone on *tokkō* missions, never to come back. People like Koretoshi Wakasugi, who had graduated first in our IMA aviation class. I figured if *tokkō* was good enough for someone like him, it was good enough for me. I lay down on my cot, staring at the ceiling in a daze and trying to think things out, when Arai stuck his head in the doorway again.
>
> "Hey, Gan-san," he said, using my nickname. "Did you hear? They say we're all going *tokkō*."
>
> We stared at each other for a few long seconds before he went on his way without another word.[2]

Fukagawa-san does not recall being particularly overwhelmed with fear or regret at having just been given orders to die, or even pity at the thought of the sadness his death would bring to his family. Rather, the predominant emotion he experienced as he processed the enormity of the news was an oddly comforting sense of relief. By this point in the war, nearly half of his IMA aviation classmates had been killed in operational accidents or combat, with many of the latter casualties the result of *tokkō* missions. He counted some of his best friends among the dead.

"For months, I had felt incredible frustration at being left behind, spinning my wheels with those trainees at Kita Ise while my classmates were in combat, fighting and dying," Fukagawa-san tells me. "I remember thinking, So it's finally come to this. . . . All right then. Let's do it already."

On the morning of May 4, Fukagawa and his classmates were trucked to Akeno, where they were formed up in the courtyard of the main HQ building with a large group of reserve officers and enlisted pilots. Some big shot from area command issued formal *tokkō* orders to the assembly in a practiced, polished speech before surrendering the podium to an adjutant, who began reading names off a roster in groups of six. When Fukagawa's name was called, he formed up front and center with a squad of five other pilots—two reservist second lieutenants and three corporals. He had never seen any of them before.

Another staff officer approached the group, informed them that they were now the 197th Shinbu Unit, and that Fukagawa was their commander. The officer then marched them around the corner of the HQ building, where a photographer was waiting with a camera and tripod. After a formal snapshot of the group was taken, the staff officer walked over, shook each pilot's hand, and said "Thank you for your cooperation in volunteering to make this *tokkō* unit possible." As the group was marched off for administrative paperwork in the HQ building, another group—ostensibly the 198th Shinbu Unit—was being formed up on the photographer's bleachers. Fukagawa noted that his old IMA friend Shūzō Fuji'i was standing front row center.

Soon after assuming his new command, Fukagawa was struck by the fact that until now, he had never been away from other Yōnen Gakkō or IMA personnel at any point in his seven-year military career, and that his new situation would require adjustments in his worldview and leadership style. From his perspective, the men in his command were quasi-civilians, and when giving explanations and orders to them he would not be able to rely on the system of common values and shared knowledge operant when interacting with fellow IMA men. Of course, the same was true when teaching raw college kids how to fly an Akatonbo, but that was hands-on activity. Communications were simple, intuitively obvious and direct, and his authority was reinforced by the students' knowledge that if they did not follow his instructions to the letter, they might not walk away from the consequences alive.

But now, Fukagawa would be living, bathing, eating, and training with his men twenty-four hours a day until their sortie orders came in—whenever that turned out to be. He would be counting on them as much as they counted on him. There was no time anymore for ceiling staring and posttraining naps. He was the *taichō*—the boss—and his job was to lead and take care of his men. The supreme test would come later, in the unit's single combat sortie.

Fukagawa sized up his pilots as they settled into their training and barracks routines at Kita Ise and established a rapport with one another. He was relieved to find out that his two reservist lieutenants were not Tokusō products, but rather had come up through the much more thorough and professional Kanbu Kōsei officer candidate program* and had received standard flight training. One of the reservists, the cheerful Lieutenant Tadatoshi Makino, was a teachers college graduate from rural Fukui Prefecture. His classroom experience would prove useful during instruction phases of training.

The other officer—Lieutenant Toshio Abe—would also serve as the unit XO. The son of a Kawasaki Heavy Industries executive, Abe was a cosmopolitan Tokyo swell who had graduated from the Department of Engineering at Waseda University. Although his piloting skills were somewhere between mediocre and awful, he knew his way around a teahouse and was only too happy to share his knowledge about the wonderful world of women with his comparatively naïve squadmates. More important, though, he had a warm, human-touch leadership approach most IMA types—Fukagawa included—were both incapable of and uncomfortable with.

"I may have been the *taichō*, but Abe was the 'mother' of the unit," Fukagawa says, remembering his subordinate and close friend. "Abe was less demanding of people and more familiar with human nature than I

*This was the army equivalent of the navy's Yobigakusei program attended by Ōka pilots Hideo Suzuki and Tokuji Naitō.

was. He cared for the other pilots' mental and physical well-being, always offering an ear for their problems or a kind word of encouragement when they were feeling down. His presence in the 197th was a perfect complement for my leadership style. He added to our unit cohesion immeasurably, and I learned a lot watching him that helped me later in life, in different leadership situations."

The unit's performance was also enhanced by the high quality of its three enlisted men—Corporals Shinji Bandō, Kazuhiro Makiuchi, and Tatsuo Yabuta. All were honor graduates of the army's Shōnen Hikōhei pilot training program, which had been started during the early thirties, when military aviation mania was sweeping the country in the wake of the Manchurian Incident. Similar in both function and popularity to the navy's Yokaren system, competition for slots in the three-year program was as stiff as its fifteen-year mandatory postgraduation service commitment.

Schooled at several air base campuses throughout the country, Shōnen Hikōhei trainees entered as fifteen- or sixteen-year-olds and graduated as highly proficient eighteen- and nineteen-year-old corporal pilots. Some flight cadets with proven scholastic and leadership ability were given shots at IMA appointments, but most graduates were sent directly to line units and—in later stages of the war—straight into combat in either conventional or *tokkō* roles.

The 197th's new corporals lived up to the excellent reputation of the Shōnen Hikōhei program and were, in Fukagawa-san's words, "real hotshot pilots" who flew like angels. Unlike their commissioned squadmates—who often bounced their Hayates all over the field when coming in for landings—the corporals always touched down on three points at once when they came down. Often, the officers found themselves swallowing their pride and asking for pointers on flying techniques. But as far as Fukagawa was concerned, there was nothing untoward about this at all, and thus no need to worry about bruised egos. In his book, such personal concerns took distant backseats to effective training, and if anybody had any knowledge or experience that would improve unit performance, it did not matter what rank insignia the teacher wore on his collar. Military protocol was always respected, of course, and proper tone was maintained between the unit's officers and enlisted men, but the camaraderie the squadmates felt for one another as pilots and their dedication both to the 197th and to its CO were what really made the unit special, in Fukagawa-san's opinion.

In 57-*ki Kōkūshi,* he describes the effect this kind of rapport had on the morale and performance of the unit:

> I trained my men hard, but they never let me down. And when we did formation flying, we were tight. We would take up and form over the field to turn, climb, and dive as one, wingtip to wingtip, communicating our thoughts just by the merest glances at each other's goggled, helmeted faces.*
>
> As the hard days of training continued, I knew that my men were ready for anything. But around this time, we began to hear rumors that the army was beginning to run short of *tokkō* aircraft, and that there was a possibility of our unit having to be parceled out piecemeal for sorties. One of my pilots, Corporal Bandō, addressed me directly about this.
>
> *"Taichō,"* he said. "If my plane can't fly on the day of our mission, I want you to let me ride in the fuselage of your plane so you can take me along."
>
> I was touched by Bandō's purity of spirit, sincerity, and bravery, especially as I knew that he was battling with the same fears of death that we all were. Knowing that one of these days I would have to order him and the other pilots in the unit on the mission that would seal all of our fates was an emotional burden I could bear but never get used to. As a leader, it was a thankless position to be in.[3]

While the grim nature of their impending first and last combat mission was never far from their minds, Fukagawa never once asked his subordinates what they thought about *tokkō.* To do so would have been bad for morale, and just as critically, it would have reflected poorly on his "moral fiber" and abilities as a leader. If the unit was to function at its best, he

---

*This is a reference to the quasi-supernatural *ishin denshin* telepathic nonverbal communication said to have existed between well-trained Japanese pilots (in many popular *Nihonjinron* folk anthropological treatises, this is claimed to be a unique and innate talent of the Japanese race). See Peattie (2001) for more discussion of this topic in a military aviation context.

could not allow his men to have such doubts; nor could he ever appear to have any himself.

"My father always told me that if you believe in yourself, you can do anything," Fukagawa-san says, "and that even if a leader doesn't know everything, he has to pretend that he does!"

Looking back, Fukagawa-san surmises that without six of the world's best fighter planes and five excellent pilots under his command, such self-confidence would have been impossible for a twenty-two-year-old who did not even have to shave every day.

"I was so proud of my men," Fukagawa-san recalls. "I thought that leading them into battle would be a fine way to go out. I had no regrets about dying if it was going to be like that."

Like any competent military leader, Fukagawa recognized that unit pride was just as important a factor in maintaining the morale of his men as their confidence in his leadership abilities. Accordingly, when command encouraged the Shinbu units operating out of Kita Ise to come up with distinctive unit names and insignia to paint on the tails of their Hayates, he gave much thought to the matter. The planes, after all, would be carrying the pilots to their deaths, so something tasteless on their rudders just would not do. But while the lieutenant may have had a good handle on the workings of military psychology, his IMA education had not given him much of a foundation in artistic creativity, and he kept coming up with blanks when it came to this particular task. And try as they might, the lieutenants and corporals in the unit were of no help, either. There were a few proposals when the squad discussed the subject, but they were all hackneyed Japanese versions of "mom and apple pie" patriotic kitsch or stock samurai imagery that had already been overplayed in government propaganda.

In the midst of the 197th's collective creative conundrum, the Kita Ise *tokkō* barracks were visited in mid-May for a PR newsreel shoot by a Nichiei cameraman who had just been in Chiran a few days before. Fukagawa and the other pilots had read the papers and were generally aware of what was going on at the Kyūshū *tokkō* base, but they were eager for more information when they heard that the cameraman had just been there. The Nichiei man's impressions of the base were somewhat at odds with what the newspapers were portraying.

"I'll tell you this much," the cameraman said. "It sure is a relief to be out of there. I couldn't leave quickly enough."

"Why?" Fukagawa asked.

"Because I just didn't think I could take the atmosphere down there much longer," the cameraman answered. "There are all these send-offs and speeches. Then they line the boys up, have them face in the direction of their hometowns and sing farewell songs to their mothers before they leave for their missions. It's too sentimental and maudlin. I like it much better up here in Kita Ise. You guys are cheerful."

As the cameraman posed his subjects for a series of shots around the barracks, he noticed that, unlike the other Shinbu units on the base, the 197th had no unit emblem by the doorway of their dayroom. When Fukagawa explained the fix they were in, the cameraman smiled.

"Actually, I'm pretty good at this," he said. "And I've helped a lot of *tokkō* units on other bases with ideas.

"Looking at such cheerful fellows as yourselves," he continued, "I think you should have a symbol that fits your mood. Happy, brave, resolute . . . Hey, how about Momotarō?"

A few of the pilots were at first taken aback by the suggestion that they use a fairy-tale character as the unit symbol, but after a short discussion the naysayers were won over. The imagery was perfect. Momotarō—the heroic "Peach Boy" of legend who saved his homeland from marauding demons (long-nosed, blond, kinky-haired demons, it should be added)—was every Japanese kindergartner's hero. Now Momotarō would be flying a Hayate to vanquish some more blond-haired demons! With Fukagawa's enthusiastic approval, the cameramen whipped out a pencil and paper and drew up a tail emblem design on the spot.

Corporal Yabuta—who had some sign-painting experience—looked at the sketch and was confident that he could render it on the planes with no problems. After Fukagawa gave the final okay, the corporal ran off to scrounge up some paint. Black, white, and red would be a rich enough pallette for the job, and those colors were readily available in the maintenance shop storeroom. Within a couple of hours, all of the 197th aircraft were sporting the tail art, and everyone who saw the cameraman's (and the corporal's) handiwork declared it a masterpiece. Everyone— that is—except for the base CO, who came storming out of the flight ops shack looking like he was ready to stomp somebody flat.

"What the hell do you think you're doing, painting a woman on your planes like that?" he thundered. "Who do you think you are, Americans?"

Admittedly, the painted faces were pretty and adorable enough to be mistaken by an inartistic and judgmental eye for some form of pinup cheesecake, and had they in fact been so, the CO would have arguably been within his rights to lambaste such flagrant and gaudy effrontery to Japanese martial machismo. But after the imagery was explained, the now rather red-faced officer joined everyone in declaring his wholehearted approval of the artwork. And no one, of course, was happier than the Nichiei man, shooting footage of the scene that would be viewed by millions of people around the country in a few days' time.

Inspired by the tail art and the basic plotline of the Momotarō story, Fukagawa came up with the unit name "Seiki Unit," which employed the kanji characters for "subdue" and "demon." Tapping theretofore untapped and unknown reserves of literary talent, he even came up with a unit poem* that cleverly parodied the verse forms used in the classic Japanese fairy tale:

> *Mukashi, mukashi, sono mukashi*
> *Oni wo taiji shita Momotarō*
> *Umarekawatte, umarekawatte*
> *Yanki wo taiji!*
> *Yaruzo, ossoro!*
> *Seiki Tai!*

> A long, long time ago, and even longer ago than that,
> Momotarō the Peach Boy
> Made quick work of the nasty demons.
> But now he is back, oh, yes, he is back,
> To make quick work of the Yankees!
> We'll do it, huzzah!
> Seiki Unit!

The poem was duly written up in classy calligraphy and posted over the entrance to the 197th barracks.

---

*Fukagawa-san refers to this as an *uta*—which usually means "song" in Japanese, but can also mean "poem" when, as in this case, the piece is meant only to be recited rather than sung to a melody. Poem courtesy of Iwao Fukagawa.

The pilots were also wont to chant alcohol-emboldened renditions of their squad *uta* when they partied with geisha off-post on Saturday nights. The preferred establishment of the 197th Shinbu—and also that of their frequent drinking partners in Second Lieutenant Fuji'i's 198th—was an army-licensed teahouse in the nearby town of Kuwana. Army licensing meant that the teahouse was obliged to give special preference to military personnel, and was in turn exempt from alcoholic beverage and foodstuff rationing. Consumption of either commodity was limited mainly by the amount of money their army clientele wished to spend, and the *tokkō* pilots were always loaded.

As a twenty-two-year-old lieutenant, Fukagawa was earning a flight and hazardous-duty-pay-boosted monthly salary that was close to three times what most white-collar managerial level workers twice his age made. And with no lodging or food expenses, the pilots' huge salaries were pretty much all gravy. Some of the fliers sent money home or contributed to patriotic fund-raising drives (unlike American war bonds, these were actual cash donations to the state), but many—with newfound appetites in wine, women, and song no doubt motivated by the Damoclean presence of *tokkō* orders perpetually hanging over their heads—blew money on nightlife prodigiously.

The 197th Shinbu was no exception. And while it would have been difficult for Fukagawa and his men to eat and drink away all of their cash, the teahouse also offered various and tempting nongastronomic methods of draining one's wallet. After being shown the ropes by Lieutenant Abe, everyone became an old hand at the necessary protocol.

During the spring of 1945, the army determined that the monotony of barracks life was having an adverse effect on the morale of *tokkō* personnel. In an attempt to counter this, it instituted a program of cyclically rotated billeting for its pilots in conjunction with civilian communities and religious institutions near *tokkō* bases around the country. Under Kita Ise's version of the new program, each Shinbu unit would spend one week in their regular barracks, and another week billeted in seminar facilities at a nearby Buddhist temple. For the final week of each cycle, the units would spend their nights as guests in local homes.

When army authorities asked for volunteer host families, farming households with children tended to be approached first, not only because their dwellings were usually large enough to accommodate multiple guests at a time, but also because they were thought to provide a more wholesome spiritual environment. The main purpose of the program, after all, was to solace the pilots in their last weeks or months of life and give them something more tangible and immediate than wrinkled letters from home and wallet photos to remind them for what—or for whom—they were supposed to be dying. What better iconography for this purpose than a friendly farm family with a brood of cute kids?

This billeting was also intended to heighten patriotic awareness of the war effort on the part of the host families, which would hopefully spread from there to the local community as a whole. The host families knew perfectly well what their guests' job title implied, and they were always careful to avoid any household conversational topic that might inadvertently stumble into talk about death or personal plans for the future. And while the families extended to the pilots all of the warm hospitality they could manage, there was always a certain amount of emotional distancing between host and guest that, for obvious reasons, was in the best interests of both parties to maintain. But the presence of young women in host households often had a way of skewing this delicate arrangement.

Once he knew he was going *tokkō* back in November of '44, Fukagawa told himself that he would never fall in love, and more importantly, never let anyone fall in love with him. It would not be fair for the girl, and moreover, a pure-hearted warrior had no business fooling around with women. Nevertheless, during the late spring of 1945 he allowed himself—in spite of his conscience—to became somewhat more than just friendly with the daughter of a host family. Photos and love letters were exchanged.

One summer Sunday when he was walking off-post, he saw the local Defense Women's Association* practicing bamboo spear defense tactics

---

*The Kokubō Fujinkai was a somewhat more plebeian and populist version of the Women's Patriotic League (Aikoku Fujin Kai), and with a much larger membership. I use "League" in my translation of the latter organization's Japanese name to imply its more elite status. See Smethurst (1974) for a detailed explanation of the class issues involved in this matter.

in a local park.* He noticed his girlfriend among the trainees, chanting and spear thrusting in unison with the group. Right then it hit him all at once—the whole reason for *tokkō*, and why it had to succeed. The nation's warriors had to die to the last man, if necessary, to keep things from coming to the point where those plucky but helpless little housewives and schoolgirls would be running down to the beaches to try to hold off American landing craft with those bamboo spears. Such a scenario could not be allowed to come to pass, and it was this awful fate for the nation that the *tokkō* would fight to prevent. At that moment, Fukagawa lost any lingering doubts he might have had about the necessity of *tokkō*. And although he eventually outgrew his infatuation with the host family's daughter, he never forgot that scene in the park, and the resolve it gave him to go all the way when his time came. The nation expected nothing less of its fighting men.

Fukagawa was not the only *tokkō* pilot at Kita Ise getting love letters. As the war entered its final grim months, the *tokkō* community was fairly inundated with the attentions of what would today be referred to as groupies—in this case, womenfolk of a surprisingly wide age spectrum who tried to befriend and/or enter into romantic relationships with the pilots, harboring for the doomed young fliers an intoxicating mixture of romantic infatuation, patriotic gratitude, and maternal instinct–fueled pity. Those too far from the bases for actual visits sent articles of clothing like embroidered flying scarves or handkerchiefs, photos of themselves in frilly dresses or knockout kimonos. The most popular items by far, however, were the sackfuls of gushing love letters and poems that arrived at the barracks addressed "To Whom It May Concern," these literary efforts often written in—or otherwise daubed and decorated with—the authors' blood.

A very, very small number of pilots more mired in the muck of worldly desires than their more stalwart comrades were not beyond taking advantage of this female attention.† But the vast majority of the fliers were

---

*Inevitably aiming at the practice dummy's crotch—this was purported to be the strapping, bulky Americans' most vulnerable weak spot. It is reasonable to assume that the targeting of this area also had symbolic meaning, given the Japanese regime's constant warnings to the female populace that the approaching Americans were violent satyromaniacs.

†An IMA '44 classmate of Fukagawa's—who will remain unnamed—survived the war and ended up marrying one such "fan."

either too naïve and inexperienced with the opposite sex or too proud of their constantly reinforced status as Japanese Galahads to give much—if any—attention to girls. Moreover, Fukagawa-san recalls that there was a popular superstition among *tokkō* personnel at Kita Ise that pilots involved with women had training accidents, the rationale being that the female Shinto *ten'nyo* angels who were scheduled to be the pilots' eternal companions after their *tokkō* dives would look down from the heavens, get jealous of the human girls, and cause the pilots to crash in order to keep the objects of their divine affections out of the meaty clutches of their mere mortal competition.[4] A more practical viewpoint on the issue held by many of the base personnel was that it was probably psychologically undesirable to socialize with women—or even close family members—because such distractions could cause potentially disastrous lapses in concentration when pilots were in the air.

As at any air base running constant training flights, the danger of such disastrous lapses was always present at Kita Ise. On the morning of June 1, 1945, Corporals Bandō and Makiuchi were practicing touch-and-gos on the runway while Fukagawa sat at the small flight ops tent referred to as the *pisuto*\* with binoculars and a notebook, watching the proceedings and critiquing his pilots' performance. Although attentive to what was going on in the air, Fukagawa did not feel any particular apprehensiveness as he watched the planes fly their clockwise, lozenge-shaped circuit around the field, lining up for landing approaches, lightly touching down on the airstrip, then throttling back up and returning to the pattern. It was a standard drill reinforcing elementary landing, takeoff, and banking techniques that even a pilot straight out of Flight Basic should have been able to handle in his sleep, and the monotonous consistency of the corporals' performance threatened the observers in the *pisuto* with a rather boring morning. Fukagawa was kicking back in his canvas director's chair and enjoying a warm breeze on his face when he saw one of the planes suddenly stagger and sideslip as it pulled into a turn with its landing gear and flaps down.

---

\*After the French *piste* ("runway"). Unlike the Japanese navy, whose aviation arm was influenced by prewar British advisers (see Peattie [2001] for an enlightening exploration of this relationship), Japanese army aviation tradition owed much to French advisers invited to Japan immediately after World War I.

*"Throttle!"* Fukagawa screamed to no one, raising his binoculars to his eyes as he bolted up from his chair.

If the plane had been a little higher, the pilot might have been able to pull off a recovery, but it was not to be. With a heartbreaking lurch, the Hayate stalled, dropped like a rock, then disappeared in a blossom of orange flame and billowing black smoke. An eyeblink later, a loud boom rent the air and hit Fukagawa like a punch to the solar plexus. Instinctively, he dropped everything he was holding and started running toward the smoke column as recovery vehicles whipped by him, spewing dust and dirt. By the time he reached the crash site, the charred body of nineteen-year-old Kazuhiro Makiuchi had already been pulled from what was left of the Hayate.

"Losing Makiuchi like that was by far the worst thing that happened to me in the army, and I still have nightmares about it," Fukagawa-san tells me. "After the war, I tracked down his family in Wakayama Prefecture to apologize for the accident and pay my respects. But when I got there, I found out that only his older brother had survived the war. Of course, I think the brother had every right to tell me to go to hell, but he didn't. In fact, we still keep up correspondence to this day, exchanging New Year's cards and at least one long letter a year."

But despite whatever emotional closure he might have gained from his Wakayama pilgrimage, the accident has haunted Fukagawa-san for the last six decades in waking moments as well as his dreams.

"I don't know how many times I have run that crash through my mind, trying to figure out what went wrong," Fukagawa says. "Of course, no one will ever know for sure, but after all of these years the best theory I have been able to come up with is that Makiuchi may have forgotten for a second that he was at the stick of a Hayate, and not one of the light Hayabusas he had been training on all those years in the Shōnen Hikōhei program. The Hayate was a very heavy-framed aircraft . . . the whole airframe built around that big engine . . . and it had a much higher stall speed than the Hayabusa. But if Makiuchi had been in a Hayabusa, he would have made that last turn no problem."

Minutes after Makiuchi crashed and burned, however, Major Kanezawa had suspected other factors at work in the accident. After cracking Fukagawa in the jaw for losing a man and an aircraft, the major—suddenly businesslike—asked if Makiuchi had received any visits from family members of late. Fukagawa replied that he had not.

"You know, sentimentality makes you lose concentration," the major said matter-of-factly. "There have been army studies on this . . . other cases where family visits can be directly traced as the cause of poor pilot concentration, which in turn resulted in fatal accidents. Keep your men's minds on their jobs, Lieutenant. And that goes for yourself, too."

By early June, the Battle of Okinawa was entering its endgame phase. But *tokkō* operations were still pouring men and machines into the conflagration, and the 197th Shinbu had been expecting sortie orders any hour of every day for nearly a month. Although the unit's morale had been high throughout this period, the waiting was helping no one's nerves, especially in the wake of Makiuchi's death. One way the pilots prevented flagging spirits was to write home regularly.

As soon as Yonekichi and Tsuma Fukagawa received the letter from their son telling them that he had been named the commander of a *tokkō* flight, they decided to get to Kita Ise any way they could. But deciding to go somewhere in Japan beyond the range of one's own two feet and actually being able to go there were entirely different matters in June 1945. Even with sufficient funds, domestic travel by this point in the war was an extremely iffy business, especially by rail, and tickets were nearly impossible to get without connections and/or official orders. Regardless of the difficulties they knew they faced, the Fukagawas marched down to the Saga City stationmaster's office with youngest daughter Teruko in tow and Iwao's letter in their hands. Touched by the appeal and honored to help the family of a *tokkō* pilot, the stationmaster produced the desired tickets. The Fukagawas reached Kita Ise twenty-four hours later on the rainy afternoon of Saturday, June 9, 1945.

Fukagawa and his pilots received the visitors in the unit's dayroom. A *Mainichi Shimbun* reporter looking for human-interest stories at Kita Ise on this particular day wrote up his observations of the Fukagawa family's visit and other activities on the base. The article is translated and reproduced here in its entirety:

## Warm and Happy Families of the Divine Eagles

(PART TWO OF A TWO-PART SERIES)

### By Army Correspondent Yanoi

*Photo caption: Surrounded by visiting family members, brave* tokkō *pilots enjoy homemade Abekawa-style rice-cake confectionary.*

JUNE X, 1945, OXOX AIRBASE: There is nothing *tokkō* pilots hate more than bad weather, and you can see that in the rain-soaked faces of the boys clambering on the truck that will take them from the flight line back to their barracks.

"Dammit, another day late for Okinawa," says Unit Commander Second Lieutenant Nogami,* with only a towel bandana to keep his head dry.

The imagery of the grumbling, rain-soaked lieutenant boarding the truck proves to be too much for recent Shōnen Hikōhei graduate Corporal Nakane, who jibes "So says Prisoner Number One as he boards the truck back to his cell. . . ."

This gets a hearty laugh from the other pilots, but Lieutenant Nogami stubbornly refuses to share in the mirth. This is out of character, actually, as the lieutenant is almost always bright and cheerful as he leads his men through their training, not wanting to delay even for a minute their sortie orders, when they will at long last spread their wings in Okinawan skies. It is merely the knowledge that this rain puts off that glorious moment one more day that gives the lieutenant a gloomy and pensive expression.

Suddenly, Lieutenant Nogami addresses this rain-soaked reporter.

"1945 is the year all of the heroes die, isn't it? It

---

*Nogami—another IMA '44 man—was CO of the 196th SBT.

has seen Mussolini and Hitler go out, and the end of the European war. So whose turn do you think is next?"

Waiting for my answer, the lieutenant stares at me with an intense gleam in his eye.

"Chiang Kai-shek?" one of the young corporals ventures naïvely but sincerely, temporarily derailing the lieutenant's spell.

"No, dummy," Lieutenant Nogami shouts. "You! Me! All of us! Japan's numberless, nameless young heroes, that's who! But you know what? This will also be the year of Japan's final victory. Isn't that right, Mr. War Correspondent?"

I nod vigorously, but in silence.

Lieutenant Nogami now faces his men.

"Listen up. We will have classes in night navigation after mess. Got it?"

While the pilots are at mess, I walk around the barracks area, visiting the quarters of various units. The barracks entrance of Second Lieutenant Fukagawa's unit features a picture of Momotarō the Peach Boy, and below that, written in a broad, masculine hand, is the unit's fitting name—Seiki Tai. The unit's pilots are just as young and dashing as their hero, eagerly awaiting the moment when they will bravely and resolutely sally forth into battle.

Today, there are special visitors in the barracks. Lieutenant Fukagawa's parents and younger sister have come from very far away to see him and his pilots.

"We rushed to get here as soon as we got the letter from our son telling us that he had been selected to be a *tokkō* flight leader," says the proud father of this Divine Eagle, understandably at a loss for fitting words as he regards the fine, gallant young man his son has become.

"Eat, eat," says Lieutenant Fukagawa's mother,

passing around the red-and-white Abekawa rice cake confectionary she has made for the pilots and brought all the way from home.

Watching this scene, I cannot help but feel that all that is noble and strong in Japan is right here before my eyes.

In the barracks next door, Nogami's unit has begun its night-navigation seminar. The lieutenant is holding a model airplane and explaining some point of tactics to a rapt audience whose young eyes burn with determination, following the model airplane's every move and turn with the piercing gazes of hawks. The young men know that they will have only one chance at the enemy, and thus every precious second of their training counts.

Second Lieutenant X, a graduate of the elite Fukuoka Business High School,* informs me that he has left a sister behind on Okinawa.

"Even if it means not sleeping for three or four days straight, I want us to finish up our training and sortie as soon as possible," says the lieutenant. "It we tarry and miss our chance to contribute to the battle, how could I ever make it up to my sister, who is fighting so bravely on Okinawa, even as we speak?"

"I am filled with pride and joy to be able to be a warrior who will get to die such a glorious death," says Lieutenant X, who also attended graduate school at Aoyama Gakuin in Tokyo. "I will not fail to sink an enemy ship. The other day when I was getting my hair cut, the barber said, 'A *tokkō* unit is more than just a *hisshi* [willing to risk lives in performance of duty] unit . . . it's a *kesshi* [resigned to dying in the performance of duty] unit, isn't it?' That was the first time since becoming a *tokkō* pilot

*Present-day Fukuoka University, a campus of the national university system.

that I really thought about the significance in the difference between the two terms."

Just shy of twenty years old, Corporal X is another Shōnen Hikōhei graduate.

"I felt so proud of myself when our *tokkō* orders came through. I thought, 'Now I can finally hold my head up when I see my old Shōnen Hikōhei classmates.'"

No doubt the other young Divine Eagles can identify with the corporal's heartfelt but humble expression of pride.[5]

That evening, Fukagawa called on his parents and sister at their room in the Yamada Ryokan, a nearby inn. The foursome sat on the tatami matting around a small table, with the men drinking sake and smoking and the women making thin tea and well-intentioned but halfhearted attempts at small talk about Saga and absent family members. Tsuma and Teruko did a decent job of appearing cheerful, but Yonekichi was having none of it. Uncharacteristically moody and quiet, he only became more so as the night dragged on and the women's attempts at "normal" conversation inevitably died quick and merciful deaths under the surreal pall that hung in the air. Try as they might, no one around the table in the little hotel room could banish for more than a few moments at a stretch the thought that they were gathered as a group for what would probably be the last time. In a few more weeks—possibly even a few more days—Iwao would be nothing but a memory and a *butsudan* photo.

At blackout curfew, Tsuma drew the curtains to the room as per regulations. The single electric bulb hanging from the ceiling was shrouded with black cloth that let a forlorn beam of dim light trickle down onto the table and tatami matting in the middle of the room. Somebody yawned, and Yonekichi—in one of his few utterances of the entire evening—suggested that they all go to bed. Then, in the next breath, he said something that Fukagawa had not heard since he was a preschooler.

"Iwao," Yonekichi said, too shy to look his son in the eyes but still with a strong father's authority in his voice. "I want you to sleep next to me tonight."

There was an embarrassed silence for a moment as Fukagawa, his mother, and sister exchanged looks in the low light, stealing glances at Yonekichi, now a slightly hunched silhouette raising and lowering the red glowing cherry of a lit cigarette in a corner of the room. Fukagawa broke the spell of the moment with a comment along the lines of his being a grown man now who did not have to sleep with his parents to keep away the hobgoblins at night. As he chuckled alone at his own attempt at levity, his mother stood with surprising alacrity and tugged him by his uniform sleeve out of the room and into the inn corridor.

"Iwao-chan," Tsuma said in an urgent whisper, sliding the room door shut after one last glance inside to check on her husband. "You know what kind of man your father is, and how hard it is for him to express tender feelings. And I know you're the same way. But can't you see what he is trying to say? Can't you understand what he must be feeling right now?

"I'll tell you some things that happened on the way up here to see you," she continued. "Before we left for the train, your sister picked a bunch of beautiful blue azaleas for you in our garden. But when your father saw them, he flew into a rage, and screamed, 'Azaleas are for funerals! Your brother's not dead yet! Throw those damned funeral flowers away!' Of course, Teruko cried. It was a wretched scene, but I could say nothing, and your father was still fuming and stiff-lipped when we got on the train.

"Hours into our journey, your father still had not said a single word. When I asked him what was the matter, he said, 'I have loved and worked hard for my boy all his life. Now they're going to make him disappear like a puff of smoke.' He said it loud enough for everyone sitting near us to hear. People looked at us strangely. Luckily, there were no policemen on the car, or who knows what might have happened?

"Iwao-chan, now you know how your father feels. Can you find it in yourself to show your father some affection in return? Just for tonight— forget that you are a big, strong soldier. Be his little boy one last time."

That night, for the first time in many, many years and the last time in his life, Iwao Fukagawa fell asleep holding his father's hand.

## eighteen

# BELT OF A THOUSAND STITCHES

I t is November 2002, and Fukagawa-san and I are staying in a municipal community center in Yokohama for an overnight study session to catalog the contents of his wartime photo albums and scrapbooks. While time-consuming, the work is not as daunting as it sounds—I have already scanned the photographic materials and old newspaper clippings into my laptop, and cataloging the material is a simple matter of clicking through the images with the pocket digital voice recorder on and Fukagawa-san giving the play-by-play. My elderly friend is obviously delighted with all of this "high tech," and we keep a brisk pace as he tries to find the words for the torrent of memories brought on by all these pictures of old comrades long dead, family scenes, children, Hayabusas and Hayates, smiling young men with sunglasses on their heads and samurai swords on their belts.

I click the right arrow key on my laptop, and suddenly we are looking at the famous shot taken by the *Mainichi Shimbun* reporter when the Fukagawas came to visit their son at Kita Ise. Fukagawa-san tells me to pause for moment, and is suddenly pensive.

"My mother didn't know how much food we already had," Fukagawa says, pointing at the table spread in the picture, "and I didn't have the heart to tell her that she needn't have gone to all the trouble of bringing those rice cakes for us all the way from Kyūshū, especially when I knew they were already running low on food themselves. The other pilots and I were enormously touched by their gesture, and we gave them a big bundle of canned goods, candy, and cigarettes when they left. Of course, they insisted that they didn't need it, but we insisted that they take it. Finally, they did.

"My father did not have it in him to come see me again," Fukagawa-san continues. "It was just too painful. Look at the picture. You can see he's the only one in the group not smiling. This picture really says a lot, doesn't it?"

"Did anyone else come to see you?" I ask.

"My mother and Teruko came up one more time, a couple of weeks later, to bring up a *senninbari* they stitched for me."

The *senninbari* (literally "stitches by a thousand people") was a talisman belt worn by most Japanese servicemen in the nation's wars since the Meiji era. Generally a plain cotton-muslin waist sash decorated with patterns of dotlike stitches sometimes arranged in a connect-the-dots picture of a tiger,* it also usually featured auspicious and/or otherwise symbolic kanji characters to protect and bring glory upon its wearer in battle. The custom began as a housewives' superstition during the Sino-Japanese War of 1894–95, but had spread nationwide by the time of the Russo-Japanese War ten years later. By the Second World War—like so many Japanese folk customs and new "traditions"—the belts had assumed semireligious iconic status, and collecting stitches on street corners from female passersby became a major daily occupation for Women's Patriotic League and Defense Women's Association members and mothers, wives, and sisters of servicemen about to be sent off to war. The activity was a common sight on street corners throughout the country from the late 1930s until the last days of World War II.

The requirement that the belts bear stitch dots by a thousand different women was representative of the tradition of powerful supernatural femininity/mother/fertility iconography—common among other animist agricultural cultures, as well—that was the backdrop for superficially hypermasculine Shintoism. Covering the wearer's navel, the *senninbari* was symbolically a placenta or umbilical cord remnant—a manifestation of mother love in fabric. It was a spiritual tie between mother and son, and thus collaterally, a magical link between female nurturing and male strength.

---

*Tiger imagery was used after the popular Japanese belief that the fierce animal always found its way back to its lair, no matter how far it ranged during its hunting activity.

As their magic power was imparted through female touch, the belts were never washed, which in less than sterile combat conditions often meant that they became terrariums for various unwelcome flora and fauna.[1] Nevertheless, Japanese servicemen were extremely proud of the belts, although they jealously guarded them at all times from the eyes of other men.* This was due not only to the inappropriateness from a warrior machismo standpoint of expressing open sentimentality for a female—even for the sacrosanct mother figure Japanese men were normally encouraged to worship—but because it was thought that the very glances of other males could drain or sully the female magic in the belts, rendering them ineffective.

Given that the major function of the *senninbari* was, ostensibly, to bring its wearer home from war safe and sound, there would seem to be a degree of contradiction involved in giving such a talisman to a *tokkō* pilot. Tsuma and Teruko were aware of this as they collected their one thousand stitches on Saga street corners, but they rationalized the gesture by telling Fukagawa that the belt was meant to bring him home safe and sound—if only in spirit.

When asked if he has preserved this treasure, Fukagawa-san tells me that he has, and that it is now on permanent display with other items of his wartime personal kit in a Japanese cultural museum near Budapest, Hungary. His *katana* sword, however, is too important to trust to anyone outside of the family. And although he did not have any sons, the sword will someday pass on to his oldest grandson.

As a visit to the busily and happily cluttered study in his Yokohama home will confirm, Fukagawa-san is an inveterate hoarder. In addition to the above-mentioned items, he has an enormous and historically significant collection of other military/wartime mementos. All of his pictures and newspaper clippings, his flight suit, his cadet cap from the IMA, even his parachute harness—he has saved almost everything from his warrior days, with the sole exception of something he has regretted losing for the last six decades: the *hanayome ningyo* ("bride doll") his mother and sister handmade for him and also brought up on their second and last visit to Kita Ise.

---

*Shinto tradition, Japanese folklore, and even imperial court protocol is filled with examples of such "not to be looked upon" taboos.

The giving of *hanayome ningyo* to sons and brothers in uniform was very popular among mothers and sisters of Japanese servicemen during the war, especially for families of *tokkō* pilots. The sentiment behind the gesture was rooted in the expectation that many boys were going to die before they had a chance to marry human brides (or *all* boys, in the case of *tokkō*). In giving them doll brides, it was felt that a mother could experience at least some of the joy of seeing her son married off. More supernatural variations on the theme also afforded roles to the dolls as afterlife companions for dead servicemen, almost like Egyptian tomb-figures or Chinese terra-cotta warriors.

Fukagawa-san recalls seeing some pilots around the Kita Ise *tokkō* barracks displaying bride dolls from home at the head of their bunks and saying good night to the figures when turning in after lights-out. But the young Fukagawa thought this sort of behavior spectacularly wimpy and maudlin—not to mention morbid—and he was having none of it. When his mother and sister presented him with the doll, he was grateful for the gesture, but also nothing short of mortified with embarrassment. Ten minutes after seeing his family members off at Kameyama Station, he gave the doll to the daughters of a local innkeeper and never saw it again. He would soon regret this.

"After I got back to the barracks and read the letter my mother had also given me, I realized that she had intended for me to take the doll with me on my *tokkō* sortie. Of course, I wasn't about to return to the inn and take the doll back from the children I had given it to. But I sure did regret that. I've regretted it ever since."

"Do you still have the letter from your mother?" I ask.

"Yes," Fukagawa-san says. "But it's in another scrapbook I haven't seen for years. I'll try to find it for you."

We continue clicking through the photo scans, which are arranged in rough chronological order. At one point in the series, Fukagawa starts appearing in civilian clothes. Fukagawa-san tells me to stop and back up one frame, to a shot showing himself in full flight gear next to an adolescent boy in army cadet uniform.

"That was taken with my little brother Nobuo in my backyard the day I arrived home after the war's end," Fukagawa-san says. "My father said he wanted one last picture of us in uniform. I'm in my flight suit, and Nobuo is in Hiroshima Yōnen Gakkō uniform. He has a *hibakusha te chō*

("Atom Bomb Victim's ID Card"), you know. He was in Hiroshima the day after the bomb was dropped, returning to school after summer leave. When he arrived at Hiroshima, though, there was nothing left of his school. They sent him straight home again. Luckily, he never had any side effects from exposure to the radiation."

We come to a picture of a smiling, strapping, twenty-something Fukagawa in a dapper straw fedora.

"Those are the clothes I rode the train home from Kita Ise in," Fukagawa-san says. "The *tokkō* pilots were given priority for demobilization, because the authorities were afraid we might do something rash, so we got to go home pretty early. In fact, I was home even before the Americans started arriving.

"That soon after the surrender, no one . . . especially officers . . . wanted to be seen in public in uniform. I traveled in a civilian shirt and wore that hat, but my pants and boots were military. When the train slowed down to pull into Saga Station, I took my uniform tunic and hat out of my suitcase and changed right there on the train car so I could arrive home looking like a soldier."

When Fukagawa rounded the corner of his home street that late August morning, he caused quite a commotion in the old neighborhood. Everyone knew he had been assigned to *tokkō*, so his sudden appearance was almost like seeing a ghost walking down the street. After this initial shock, however, neighbors began to call out to him in welcome. As for his family, they already knew from an earlier letter that he had survived and was on his way home, but this did not mean that there was no joy in the Fukagawa household when he darkened the doorway.

"Most people talk about what dark, sad times the postwar was for them," Fukagawa-san says. "But that wasn't true in our house. My parents had three sons in uniform and all of us survived. The night I came home, all of the family members were together for dinner for the first time in many years. And I'm not ashamed to say that we all wept with happiness, man and woman alike. Lost war or not, that was one of the happiest moments of my life."

The conversation turns to the postwar era, when Japan's economy was in shambles and a way of life and value system were gone forever.

"My first job after the war was working in a displaced-persons relocation center in a storefront near Saga Station," Fukagawa-san says. "That was very therapeutic. I felt like I was helping Japan get back on its feet. I did this for about six months, then helped a childhood friend with a small trading company for a few years after that. After a while, though, I started to feel like I was just spinning my wheels. I needed to move on.

"I remembered something they taught us at Fighter Basic. . . . When you find yourself in a chaotic situation, climb for altitude. With altitude, you can get a better take on what's going on around you, then pick the exact spot and timing for your return to the battle. Well, I applied this thinking to my own situation in postwar Japan, which was certainly chaotic. I was already in my mid-twenties, and still had my most productive years ahead of me, but I didn't have all the time in the world, and I felt like I didn't know where I was going as long as I stayed in Kyūshū. So, just like my instructor at fighter school always told me to do, I climbed for altitude. In my case, this meant heading for Tokyo."

Fukagawa packed up and headed for the big city in 1948, never looking back. But his struggles were only beginning. GHQ demilitarization policies meant that his once-elite IMA credentials were not worth the parchment on which they were printed. At least officially—on paper—he had finished only an elementary-school-level education. But Fukagawa, always the fighter, pushed on, got qualified for university entrance exams by going to night school, and eventually graduated from the well-regarded Chūo University in 1952. He has lived in the Tokyo/Yokohama metropolis ever since, marrying a Kyūshū girl nine years his junior in 1953. He now has a daughter and three grandchildren—two boys and a girl.

Fukagawa-san recently retired from a nearly fifty-year-long business executive career, and fills most of his days pursuing hobbies with his delightful and lovely wife. The rest of his time is taken up with the various IMA and Akeno Fighter School alumni, Kaikōsha, and veterans' group activities he has been involved in since the 1980s. He has spent two-thirds of his long life in a land of peace and prosperity, but has never forgotten about all of the friends and comrades he left behind—who did not get to enjoy the peaceful and prosperous Japan he has been able to call home for the past half century.

The direction the conversation is taking reminds me of something I have heard in a prayer at the Setagaya Kan'non Buddhist temple, which has a chapel devoted to the memory of army and navy *tokkō* pilots. It is the venue for monthly meetings of the Tokkōtai Senbotsusha Irei Heiwa Kinen Kyōkai or, as this is usually abbreviated, Tokkō Zaidan. It is a memorial-cum–historical association whose members consist mainly of *tokkō* veterans, surviving family members of *tokkō* pilots who died in the war, and the odd American expatriate Japan scholar. In the prayer in question—which is chanted at the beginning of each monthly memorial gathering—there is a reference to the sacrifices of the *tokkō* pilots as being largely to thank for the rest of us being able to live in "this peaceful and prosperous Japan."[2] While it would of course be unrealistic—not to mention culturally uncouth—to expect people to gather in a downtown Tokyo temple once a month for the last fifty years to sing the praises of Douglas MacArthur, GHQ reforms, and massive postwar American aid packages, I have long found this "it's all thanks to the *tokkō*" line baffling. But the operant logic here, as Fukagawa-san explains it, is all about the surviving postwar generation's psychological need to pay back the *tokkō* pilots' sacrifices the only way they could without a shooting war going on anymore. They had to sacrifice their own lives to rebuild Japan from the ashes of defeat and make sure that a disaster like World War II never befell the nation again.

Fukagawa-san—now with a bit of stridency in his voice—goes on to explain that he feels that the dead *tokkō* pilots also saved Japan in that they were able to preserve some of Japan's pride in defeat.

"A race without pride will soon lose its nation," he says.

He believes that the pilots were fighting for this at the end, when everyone knew the war was lost but flew their sorties anyway, and that in this sense, their missions were successful. The pilots were the epitome of integrity, purity of spirit, and courage—the finest young men the country has ever produced.

"Any great nation is made and sustained by such young men. This is a universal given."

I ask him if he thinks this spirit is still alive in Japan—if the nation still has such human resources at its disposal.

"Yes, that spirit is still here, just hidden now. These qualities are in our genetic makeup, even though the people in charge of educational policy in Japan seem to be doing everything they can to destroy them."

* * *

Fukagawa-san calls me in March 2003 to tell me that he has something very important to show me. After a long search, he has finally found his mother's wartime farewell letter (written, obviously, without knowing that she would go on to spend another thirty-five years knowing that her son was alive, happy, and healthy). The item is too important to trust to the mail system, so he wants to hand it over in person.

We meet a few weeks later at the Shinkansen waiting lounge at Hamamatsu Station. Fukagawa-san is passing through Hamamatsu on his way home from an overnight excursion to a hot-springs resort with some old IMA friends. The drinking and laughing last night went far past his normal bedtime of nine o'clock, so he is a bit road weary.

We order some coffee, and while we wait for it to arrive, Fukagawa-san rummages through his blue Naugahyde overnighter and customary collection of plastic shopping bags before coming up with a crumbling black leather-bound scrapbook.

"I hadn't seen this in nearly forty years until the other day, when I dug this out of my closet. I don't think I had seen it since I built my house, and that was in the sixties."

I thumb through the scrapbook, and it is indeed a treasure trove of wartime newspaper clippings. There are a couple of pieces about the Se-kichō Unit—classmate Toshio Yoshitake's old outfit—and one of the articles even has a picture of the dolls the pilots flew into battle with hanging from their canopy latches.

There are pictures snipped from magazines and propaganda leaflets. Letters and postcards from home. But the real treasure in the book—what Fukagawa-san has called me here to hand over—is his mother's letter. It is written in a beautiful and accomplished grass-hand calligraphy on a long strip of letter scroll, a form of stationery that is almost never seen anymore in modern Japan. The letter itself is crumbling along its edges and folds. Most of the damage is due to the effects of time and paper acidity, but physical wear and tear is also a factor. As Fukagawa-san explains, he kept it in the breast pocket of his flight suit during many a sweaty training session, and planned to carry it there—over his heart—when he made his final sortie.

The letter seems imbued with an energy that makes my fingertips tingle as I handle it. Declaring my inability to make my way through all the elegant and almost Arabic swirls of the grass-hand, I hand it back to Fukagawa-san so that he can read it for me.

*Looks like rainy season is upon us again.*

*It certainly sounds like you are training very hard. We were all shocked speechless to hear about Corporal Makiuchi's death. He sounded like such a nice young man. But you can take comfort in knowing that he has now joined the gods protecting our country. He is an angel watching over the Seiki Unit.*

*Every morning since coming home from our last visit to your base, I have gone down to the river behind our house and ritually bathed before going to the local shrine to pray for the Seiki Unit's success in battle. I pray that the gods give each one of you boys the chance to sink an enemy aircraft carrier. It will be a fine and glorious death.*

*Whenever I visit the shrine, though, I can't help but remember how you also used to go there so faithfully as a boy, praying to be accepted into the military academy. When I think of that, and all of the other things you have done to make me so proud of you, hot tears never fail to come to my eyes.*

*It is hard to believe it has already been twenty-two years since we welcomed you into the world, Iwao. You have always been a source of pride for our family—always so diligent and hardworking, never accepting failure without a fight, studying from early morning until late at night every day. Remember the alarm clock we bought for you to put on your desk when you were studying so hard to get into the Yōnen Gakkō? Maybe you didn't know it, but I was awake every hour that you were, and many times when you weren't. Sometimes I would find you fast asleep at your desk, and I would leave a little treat in your desk drawer for you to find when you woke up.*

*I could never get over how cheerful you seemed as you worked and studied, but never so serious that we couldn't share a laugh or a light moment once in a while, like the time we stood in front of the window looking out at the rain and sang*

# A TIME FOR HEROES

*St. Lo* explodes after being hit by Yukio Seki's Zero, October 25, 1944.

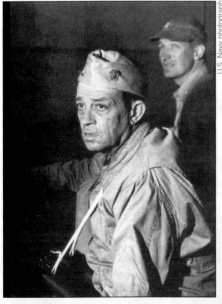

Rear Admiral Clifton Sprague, USN, in his favored air boss chair perch, from where he could observe flight operations on the carrier deck

Admiral Takijirō Ōnishi, the father of the *tokkō* program, as a captain in China, late 1930s

Yukio Seki at Mabalacat, most likely before the first
abortive sortie on October 21, 1944

The Shikishima Unit gets a big send-off, probably also October 21.

# ALL BOYS DREAM OF FLYING

Sekichō Unit (still Hakkō Unit 6 at this point) at Chōshi Airfield before deployment flight to the Philippines, November 8, 1944. Toshio Yoshitake is kneeling in second row, far right.

Masamitsu Kataoka dances "The Loach Scooper," Bacolod, December 4, 1944. Yoshitake—still soaked from his rough landing at Talisay—is sitting on the windowsill, smoking.

Pilots of Hakkō Unit 6 check final flight plan to the Philippines in posed army publicity shot taken at Chōshi, November 8, 1944. Yoshitake is the third pilot from the right.

Posed shot of Chōshi flight line salute from Captain Takaishi, November 8, 1944. Yoshitake is at center, facing camera.

Posed shot of Captain Takaishi addressing pilots before attack sortie from Bacolod, December 5, 1944

Sekichō Unit *Ki*-51 heads for the Surigao Straits and destiny, December 5, 1944.

Fourteen-year-old Tokurō Takei, standing a in light-colored uniform with family members on the occasion of his sendoff for Yokaren training, September 1943. The flag display is a gift from the local neighborhood association. Note his father's *kokuminfuku* civilian mobilization uniform.

Official Yokaren graduation group portrait for Tokurō Takei's *buntai* training section, May 1944. The average age of the boys was fifteen.

Takei's official Yokaren graduation portrait. The cherry blossoms symbolize the brevity and beauty of a young life soon to be sacrificed for Emperor and country.

A pensive Akinori Asano at Kōnoike, spring 1945

Saburō Dohi—Hideo Suzuki's close friend and the pilot of the Ōka that sank the destroyer *Mannert L. Abele*

Restored Ōka rocket bomb on display at Iruma Airbase Museum

Tokuji Naitō hoisting a celebratory sake bottle before shipping out to Kanoya, March 14, 1945

Official propaganda portrait of Hideo Suzuki, December 1944. This photograph would have been used in newsprint and patriotic posters in the event of Suzuki being given posthumous *gunshin* ("war god") status.

Ōka pilots leaving Kōnoike for Kanoya, March 14, 1945. Hideo Suzuki is at center, behind the smiling pilot facing the camera.

# A SOLDIER'S SCRAPBOOK

The Fukagawa family, circa 1938. Iwao is kneeling at far right, in IMA Yōnen Gakkō uniform.

Fukagawa during down time on Kita Ise flight line, autumn 1944, clearly enjoying the aviator's sunglasses he is now authorized to wear

Fukagawa, center, with fan, and fellow junior officers at their favorite off-post tea house, Kita Ise, summer 1945

Fukagawa's family visits Kita Ise base, June 10, 1945.

*Hanayome ningyo* "bride dolls"—afterlife spouses for the souls of servicemen who died single—today line the wall of the main waiting hall at Yasukuni Shrine.

Corporal Bandō applies "Momotarō the Peach Boy" tail art to one of the 197th Shinbu Unit's *Ki*-84 Hayate fighters.

197th Shinbu Unit official photo, May 4, 1945. Front: Lieutenants Makino, Fukagawa, and Abe. Rear: Corporals Yabuta, Makiuchi, and Bandō.

Nadeshiko Unit volunteers serving pre-attack sortie tea to Army *tokkō* pilots in a Chiran defiladed barracks, spring 1945

Nadeshiko Unit volunteers pose with army *tokkō* pilots, spring 1945

Nadeshiko Unit volunteers give cherry bough send-off to Ten-Gō attackers at Chiran Airbase, April 1945.

Shigeko Kaneko and Haruo Araki on date, Tama River, Tokyo, circa 1936

Shigeko and Haruo on date chaperoned by Fumi, Lake Haruna, circa 1943

Posed photo of Haruo (second from left) going over sortie flight plans, Chiran, May 10, 1945. The distinctive roof of a *sangakuheisha* defiladed barracks is visible through the pine trees.

Photo from the same posed session showing Haruo and other pilots admiring headbands made for the Yūkyū Unit by female high school students from northern Japan. The *hinomaru* circles and lettering are penned in the girls' own blood.

Tadao gives his baby brother, Fumitake, a ride in a wagon, circa 1929.

Tadao Hiroshima rides tall in the saddle on a tricycle presented by an Osaka uncle, circa 1930.

Tadao (rear left) and Fumitake (rear right) visiting the famed Aviation Shrine in Kyoto Prefecture with younger cousins to pray for Tadao's success in the upcoming Yokaren program entrance exams, February 1943

The inseparable brothers: Tadao and Fumitake Hiroshima at the zoo in Nara during Aviation Shrine trip, February 1943

Left: Tadao's father, Mankichi Hiroshima, during a visit to Kajiki Naval Air Station, Kagoshima Prefecture, June 1945

Right: Tadao with his mother, Haruō Hiroshima, during Kajiki visit. It will be the last time the Hiroshimas see Tadao alive.

Tadao resplendent in naval aviator's uniform with life vest and *tokkō* headband. This is the photo that Dr. Hiroshima carries with him wherever he goes.

# TORPEDOMEN IN TWILIGHT

Toshiharu Konada, second from right, with his Kaiten *buntai* section, Ōtsushima, spring 1945

"Kikusui" symbol on conning tower of restored Kaiten at Yasukuni Shrine Museum showing the twelve-petaled floating blossom. The original would have employed the sixteen-petaled blossom of the official Imperial household crest.

Harumi Kawasaki, standing at far left, with his Kaiten *buntai* training section, Hikari, spring 1945

Kaiten at Ōtsushima with top surface painted white for training operations in shallow water

Short sword presentation ceremony at Ōtsushima, late 1944. Toshiharu Konada is in the front row at far left.

Kaitens on occasion of first Kikusui Unit sortie from Ōtsushima, November 8, 1944. Note crew members brandishing *katana* samurai swords.

Kaitens lashed to sub deck, November 8, 1944

Aftermath of Kikusui attack on USS *Mississinewa*, Ulithi Atoll, November 20, 1944

# THEN AND NOW

Yoshitake

Takei

Fukagawa

Chiran girls

Shigeko

Dr. Hiroshima

Kawasaki

Konada

Main altar at Yasukuni shrine

Massive steel *tori'i* gate of Yasukuni Shrine. This is a postwar incarnation, the previous gate having been melted down for strategic resources late in the war.

*Tokkō* statue in front of the Yasukuni Shrine museum

Author M. G. Sheftall (rear) with *tokkō* veterans at a reunion, 2004. From left: Tokurō Takei, unidentified Jinrai Unit vet, Tokuji Naitō, Hideo Suzuki, former squad commander Akira Hirano, and Akinori Asano.

the "Rainy Day" nursery rhyme you used to like so much as a toddler.

Oh, Iwao, what a joy you were for us. You can't imagine how we felt when your letter arrived from the base telling us that that cute, precious little boy we once knew is now a tokkō flight leader. Our emotions were even more complex and intense when we got to meet you at the base—so sad on one hand that we will be losing our son, yet so proud of the fine young man you have become. There were so many things I wanted to say to you but didn't because I know that what you are doing is for the good of the country. It took so much effort for me to smile in front of you and your men as I said, "Go off and do your best." I couldn't say what I really felt, and it was all I could do to stop myself from shouting out, "Iwao-chan," calling you like I used to when you were a little boy.

As the proud Japanese mother of a Divine Eagle, I could not show you my tears when I gave you the hanayome ningyo. All of us in the family poured our hearts and prayers into that doll as we made her, and I held her in my arms like a baby when I took her to the shrine to be blessed by a priest. We want you to carry her into battle with you. Don't think of her as just a doll. Think of her as your real bride, and know that your father and I have asked her to watch over you and take care of you, and to give you strength in your moment of truth, making sure that you sink an enemy carrier. She will follow you into death, and accompany you on your journey to eternity. As I held her in my arms at the shrine, I thought she was so precious and adorable, but my heart became strong and proud when I gave her to you, because at that moment I realized that you are not my cute little boy anymore, but a man with a mission that will be known around the world. When you make your attack, you will show the enemy of what stuff Japanese men are made. Even as a child, you used to say, "I'm going to put the name Fukagawa in the history books." Well, now you are really going to do that after all.

Fall like a beautiful cherry blossom for the emperor, and take strength in knowing that you will not be going alone.

*There are one hundred million of us behind you—every one of us a tokkō warrior, too. If the enemy invades Kyūshū, we will fight him just as hard as you have, and I will surely avenge your death.*

*Be sure to get a carrier. We are all praying for the success of the Seiki Unit. Please pass this message on to your men: TO ALL SEIKI UNIT PILOTS: Thank you for working so hard for our son, and graciously overlooking his shortcomings.*

*I am also writing letters to the families of your men. Hopefully, we will all stay in touch, and perhaps even meet in person someday.*

*Iwao, if you have a chance and if your final forward base is close enough, please try to come visit one last time before your sortie. If you can't come to us, we will do everything we can to come see you and be there for your send-off. If we can't be there in person, though, we have prepared big Hinomaru flags for all of us to wave from our rooftop, so please try to fly over the house one last time if you can.*

*Recently, there has been much on the radio about tokkō missions, and our ears prick up every time there is a special bulletin, wondering if you were involved or not. In any case, we will try to make it to your base and send you off with warm smiles.*

*Take care of your health and exert all of your energies toward accomplishing your mission.*

*Your Mother*
*June 15, 1945*

I pretend not to notice the tears welling in Fukagawa-san's eyes as he finishes the letter, then smooths out the scroll paper like a monk preparing the Shroud of Turin for another decade of climate-controlled storage. As he performs this ritual, I wonder if he is thinking the same thing I am— that in another destiny, this letter would not exist. It would have burned up in a Hayate, or been blown into molecules against the deck of an American troop ship instead of lasting for sixty years tucked between shoe boxes in the back of an old man's wardrobe closet.

Fukagawa-san carefully folds the letter up along its yellowed, crumbly creases, puts it back in the album, then hands the album over to me. The sentimental look in his eyes is gone in a blink, and he is an army officer again.

"Don't lose this," he says, with a chuckle that nevertheless has some push behind it.

I slip the scrapbook album into my book bag and remind myself to keep a tight grip on it, for today it is heavier than usual. It contains a life.

We shake hands and exchange salutes—a quick ceremony that gets a few curious looks from otherwise busily scurrying passersby. Then the stoop-shouldered Fukagawa-san does a crisp about-face and stomps off into the Brownian motion of the Friday evening rush with his stiff, vaguely Nixonian shuffle, his crusty-but-benign Warren Oates face thrust forward like the prow of an icebreaker to clear a path through the crowd.

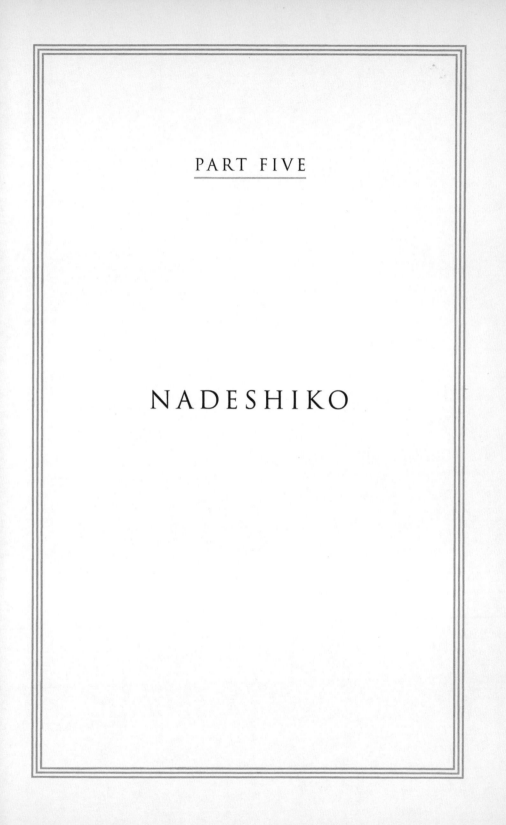

PART FIVE

NADESHIKO

## nineteen

# BAND OF SISTERS

Kyūshū is the southernmost of the four main Japanese home islands. While the climate of the heavily developed and industrial northern half of the island bordering the Inland Sea is temperate, its more agricultural southern half is semi-tropical. Jutting out into the South China Sea, southern Kyūshū catches the full brunt of the Kuroshio Current, a perennial stream of latitude-ambitious seawater from equatorial climes that keeps the weather balmy from October to May, positively steaming from June to September, and rainy year-round. Despite poor soil, the climate supports the cultivation of sweet potatoes, succulent fruit, flowers, green tea, and, with effort, rice. It also makes the region a popular retirement destination for winter haters (who do not mind a lot of rain) from colder areas of the country, and a preponderance of palmetto-fringed roadways and marine sports–themed amusement parks reinforces this "Japanese Florida" image.

While the climate may be appealing to meteorologists and rheumatism sufferers, and the active volcanoes dotting the area draw seismologists from around the world, Kyūshū's craggy terrain features are deserving of the scrutiny of military historians—especially those enamored of "what if " conjecture. The area was slated to have been the main battlefield for the opening rounds of Operation Olympic, the invasion of the Japanese home islands scheduled to begin in November

1945. If that invasion had actually taken place, the island's spiny topography and soggy rice paddies would have made maneuvering and logistics an absolute nightmare for an army in the field, with the thirty-degree-sloped, heavily foliated mountain ranges threading the area providing a defense-in-depth network of natural fortresses perfectly suited for guerrilla ambushes and hunkered-down fanatics. In any scenario short of quick Japanese surrender, casualties on both sides of the fighting would have been appalling.[1]

Equally unpleasant to contemplate is the stress already war-weary American GIs would have been subjected to by such prolonged, bitter combat in this treacherous terrain, watching buddies cut down over weeks and months of grim struggle against a maddeningly determined foe, and the malice this could have engendered in the hearts of these Saipan, Iwo Jima, and Okinawa veterans against a people and culture they already considered to be something less than human and, therefore, psychologically that much easier to exterminate. Estimates that the resulting destruction in this region alone would have been at least a tenfold magnification of the horrific Operation Iceberg— where some 12,000 Americans and over 200,000 military and civilian Japanese were killed during the American invasion of Okinawa— are probably on the conservative side. That such a bloodbath did not come to pass is one of the few happy notes in the history of the Pacific War.

But the historical significance of Kyūshū certainly does not begin and end with its almost-role as a backdrop for seven-figure body counts and apocalyptic culture clash. Long the most important conduit to the Japanese archipelago for migrations, trade, and cultural contacts from the Asian mainland, the island is the setting for the ancient Nikon Shoki and Kojiki racial and national origin myths adroitly popularized in postrestoration Japan to legitimize central authority under the imperial government.[2] In the early twentieth century, passionate nativists and nationalist anthropologists like Kunio Yanagita and Tetsurō Watsuji, troubled by what they saw as the danger of Japan's inadvertently adopting Western social values in the country's headlong modernization rush, were fond of affording Kyūshū status as a cultural repository of timeless national essence. It was seen as a region where harmonious agricultural life was closest to the spiritual core of the nation's soul and the ideal natural state of its people.*

As militarism began to gain momentum in the 1930s, much was also made of the island's samurai heritage—especially that of the former Kagoshima fiefdom of the Satsuma, the warrior clan famed as the fiercest and most patriotic (read "most xenophobic") in feudal Japan.† This martial heritage readily lent itself to propaganda efforts in the last year of the war, when the government began to lay the spiritual groundwork for maximum defensive effort against the American invasion expected to make a beachhead in the region. The symbolism was lost on no one when they were reminded that Kyūshū was the setting for the original *kamikaze* of legend that swept away a Mongol invasion fleet in 1281, especially when the old Satsuma holdings around Kagoshima in the south began turning into what was basically one gigantic *tokkō* base in early spring 1945.

Steamy climate, rugged terrain, traditional Asian crossroads function, and reactionary warrior heritage—all are reflected in the character of the Satsuma descendants living in present-day Kagoshima Prefecture, who are among the most conservative yet paradoxically most personable residents of the archipelago. Kagoshima natives tend to be stereotyped by other Japanese as easygoing, with a slow-burn temperament that nevertheless blazes fiercely when finally and fully aroused. If true—and there may be some historical basis to this stereotype—it is a trait of which potential invaders and other uninvited visitors remain ignorant at their own peril.

Kagoshima's history as an ancient Asian migrant melting pot is clearly

---

*Actually, an extrapolation on this line of thought applied at a national cultural level colors Japanese diplomacy and trade policy to this day. Former Prime Minister Yasuhiro Nakasone, influenced by Watsuji's theoretical model, has long been one of its major proponents, and is fond of referring to Japan as a "warm, wet, cooperative" culture of rice farmers as opposed to the "cold, dry, competitive" Western primeval-hunter cultural legacy in explaining innate Japanese aversion to unregulated trade, among other diplomatic, political, and economic logjams vis-à-vis Western countries. See van Wolferen (1989), Hashimoto (1998), Scheiner in *Mirror of Modernity* (1998), Befu (2001), and Oguma (2002) for further details of this ideology.

†Ironically, the Satsuma samurai were also the most resistant to centralized authority, and it was a renegade samurai rebellion led by Kyūshū demigod Takamori Saigō in this very part of Japan that gave Emperor Meiji his biggest headaches when he was consolidating his power in the 1870s.

evident in the spectacularly varied physical appearance of its people. The full Japanese spectrum of Asian facial types is well distributed throughout its population, but if there can be said to be a classic "Kagoshima" look, one need only look at a daguerreotype of the large-eyed, full-lipped visage and powerful physique of legendary renegade samurai Takamori Saigō to get a perfect example. When visiting the area, one notices many people it is not difficult to imagine could be Saigō's descendants, with warm facial features in common with Okinawan cousins to the south, but stocky, barrel-chested builds that speak more of cold north Asian steppes than balmy tropics.

Not surprisingly for a region with such a rich genetic potpourri, Kagoshima is renowned for the beauty of its women, who are traditionally referred to as *nadeshiko*, after the wildflower (wild pink, *dianthus superbus*) that thrives in the region. The tough *nadeshiko* flower, with its ability to blossom even in sunless spots and rocky soil without losing its beauty, is cherished as an age-old symbol of purity and quiet endurance in adversity. During World War II, when propaganda organs were searching for appropriate imagery to push acceptance of the mobilization of schoolgirls into wartime work details, the flower's combination of beauty and grit seemed order-made for poster visuals and catchphrase sloganeering. Thus the phrase *Yamato nadeshiko* was born, with the addition of one of the ancient names for Japan—*Yamato*—effectively deregionalizing the imagery for application to chaste, patient, diligent young women nationwide.[3]

This ideological usage of *nadeshiko* was so effectively disseminated, in fact, that it remains in wide use today, mostly by middle-aged and elderly men in the context of lamenting the Westernized emancipation of women in modern Japan to the detriment of more traditionally passive Japanese models of femininity. But even these chauvinistic old pessimists hold near and dear to their hearts the belief that "good old-fashioned Japanese girls" still exist where the inspiration for the modern stereotype/manufactured archetype originated—in the sleepy farming communities nestled deep in the mountains of the Satsuma Peninsula on the western shore of Kagoshima Bay.

These days, the most visited of these remote locales in undoubtedly Chiran, a town located about twenty kilometers north of the windswept slopes of Mount Kaimondake, an active volcano on the shores of the

South China Sea. But an explanation for the recent surge in tourist interest in Chiran is not to be found in any preponderance of nubile
*nadeshiko* among its female population. While the town has been be-
sieged by busloads of day-trippers in recent years, these visitors are not
eligible bachelors who have made a pilgrimage to look for doting, docile
brides.

Nor do visitors come in search of fun and sun. Chiran is not now—
nor has it ever been—a place to spend a rollicking good Saturday night.
And outside of day-trip tourism and tea farming, there is nothing particularly robust about its economy that might attract serious investment in
the area. Rather, judging from all outward and empirically measurable
signs, it would appear that the town is taking a slow country stroll into
oblivion that its residents do not seem all that riled up about trying to
stop. Chiran's population peaked at 19,639 in 1965 on the demographic
tidal wave of Japan's first postwar baby boom, but has since dropped to
13,846 in 2001, and the average household size has gone from 3.8 to 2.5
family members during the same time frame.[4] Data on average age has
been kept for only the last ten years or so, but one walk down the town's
main drag tells you that things here are headed the way they are in rural
districts all over the country—the population is shrinking and graying
with alarming rapidity.

The secret to Chiran's recent popularity as a tourist destination lies
not in its present or future, but in its past. Times were not always as se-
date as they are now, and from early spring to early summer 1945, when
Chiran was the location of the Imperial Japanese Army's main *tokkō* hub
airbase during the Okinawa campaign, the town was the scene of some of
the most intense pathos—both spontaneous and ritualized—to be found
in any theater of World War II. It is remnants and echoes of those dramatic times, more than anything else, that Chiran's typically humbled
and somber-faced visitors—over a million of them in 2001[5]—have been
coming to see and hear in recent years.

In the summer of 2001, Chiran native Reiko Akabane (née Torihama), a successful Tokyo restaurateur who splits her time between the
capital and her hometown, made a significant contribution toward re-
creating some of the tragic yet dramatically charged atmosphere of Chiran's wartime experience when she helped finance the restoration of an
old two-story clapboard restaurant and inn in the center of town called

the Tomiya Shokudō. In addition to being Mrs. Akabane's birthplace and home for the first twenty years of her life, the Tomiya Shokudō was also the only off-post civilian facility in wartime Chiran approved by local air base authorities for use by *tokkō* pilots as an R & R spot and a place to receive loved ones who came to see the pilots off for their final sorties.*

This decidedly melancholy wartime history has made the Tomiya Shokudō one of the most famous structures in this region of Japan. The building—now a museum-cum–*tokkō* memorial—has been the subject of numerous books and articles in recent years, as well as a movie, *Hotaru,* which is based on a conglomerate of various wartime legends and anecdotes set at the inn. Starring the legendary Ken Takakura—Japan's Clint Eastwood—the film was released in 2002 to considerable box-office success, a development that resulted in an exponential increase in "*tokkō* tourism" to Chiran.

Frequent *tokkō* survivor reunions and other *tokkō*-oriented media events held at the Tomiya Shokudō keep the seventy-two-year-old Akabane constantly shuttling back and forth between her two Tokyo-area Kagoshima-themed restaurants and Chiran. Further complicating this hectic lifestyle is the never-ending stream of interview requests she must field from reporters, writers, and scholars. With her unique personal background, matronly handsome daughter-of-Satsuma looks, and ever-colorful candor, she is a popular interview subject for TV and print journalists, and the history she witnessed and participated in as an adolescent is of incalculable value to historians researching both the *tokkō* program and home-front conditions in wartime rural Japan.

In addition to her personal attributes and qualifications, the harsh reality of demographics probably comprises another factor in Mrs. Akabane's media appeal. In a phenomenon similar to one currently being experienced in post–*Private Ryan* America, Japan is rapidly running out of World War II combat veterans just as renewed interest in the war is becoming evident among younger media audiences. As America has suffered in recent years the loss of such fighter pilot legends as Francis "Gabby"

---

*\*Tokkō* had become publicly accepted and institutionalized enough by this point in the war that such personal involvement by family members and other loved ones was common. For more on this phenomenon, see Takagi (1973), Satō (1997), and Akabane (2001).

Gabreski and Joe Foss, old age is also ravaging the ranks of Japan's aces and other wartime headline makers, and it has all but wiped out the generation old enough to have held influential policy-making and major command positions during the war. In the not-too-distant future, relative "youngsters" like Reiko Akabane will be the only surviving witnesses of Japan's wartime experience left to tell their stories in the first person.

And in the meantime, Mrs. Akabane is getting plenty of practice for this torchbearer role.

Aging and simple arithmetic mean that the next decade will see exponential increases in the rate of the youngest combat veterans—men who were in their high teens and early twenties during the war—answering that final roll call in the sky. Whenever I talk to these old warriors, I am immensely proud that they have deemed me worthy of their precious time, but I never quite shake what I can only call a sense of melancholy urgency in knowing that every day, hour, and minute they are willing to spare for me counts. Like Dustin Hoffman's bedside interviewer in *Little Big Man*, I hang on every word, constantly checking to make sure my recorder is still running, always careful not to breathe too close to the microphone, ever aware that I am in the process of recording history about as pure and unadulterated as it comes and that I cannot afford to let a single word of it get away.

However, I do not experience this awestruck melancholy, if you will, when I talk with Reiko Akabane, who is after all only ten years older than my mother (and Mom is eternally dark-haired and thirty-something in my mind's eye). Reiko-san—as she likes to be called—had barely begun puberty by the end of the war, and although she is no spring chicken, she is no frail crone, either. Her vitality allows me to have a more relaxed, unhurried feeling when we speak, and I take great comfort in the fact that this is a woman who keeps up a work and traveling schedule that would lay low Colin Powell or Bill Gates. From all appearances and evidence, Reiko-san will no doubt be just as busy and healthy as she is now for many years to come. She is fit, mobile, charismatic, and in possession of a spectacularly detailed memory. An interviewer lucky enough to get an audience squeezed into Reiko's busy schedule could hardly ask for a more ideal subject.

No matter how busy Reiko-san may be with her business activities and historical research cooperation, there is one personal event for which she always manages to make time—the monthly Tokyo meeting of the Chiran Nadeshiko Kai ("Chiran Nadeshiko Association"). The members of this informal group are childhood friends and schoolmates from Chiran who, like Reiko, have lived in the Tokyo metropolitan area since the postwar era or, at the latest, the nascence of Japan's economic takeoff in the late 1950s. These get-togethers are extremely important for the women, not merely because of the bond of seven decades of friendship and memories, but because of shared wartime experiences that, in their own way, were every bit as harrowing, dangerous, and magnificently courageous as those of any frontline infantryman or combat airman.[6] During the last year of the war, the girls performed grueling and often hazardous duties under enemy fire in the service of their country, and if William Shakespeare and Stephen Ambrose can speak of combat camaraderie as forming a "band of brothers," then the Chiran Nadeshiko Kai can certainly be called a "band of sisters," as its members are war veterans in every sense of the word.

The bond of loyalty and friendship the women share has stood the test of time to last, in Reiko-san's words, "through thick and thin." Most of the veterans' associations mentioned in this book cannot boast of group histories even half as long as that of the Chiran Nadeshiko Kai. The political atmosphere during the greater part of the postwar period was not conducive to organized public activities by Japanese war veterans, especially by members of a long-stigmatized group like ex-*tokkō* personnel. As a result, most of these groups have realized robust membership levels only within the last decade or two, as survivor's guilt, the lingering shame of defeat, and unwelcome memories lose their emotional tug-of-war with nostalgia and remembered camaraderie.

In sharp contrast to the social dynamic that muzzled male Japanese veterans for so long, the six members of the Tokyo branch of the Chiran Nadeshiko Kai have been meeting on the last Friday of each month for nearly fifty years. For their sessions, the women gather at one of the members' homes to have some tea and cakes, laugh at their memories of each other as gawky teenagers, tell the same stories over and over to inevitably laugh and cry in the same places, then go home to their families in the evening with the same warm glow of camaraderie they knew as naïve and pure-hearted country girls in 1945. Over the span of half a century of living in the great Tokyo urban sprawl, these Kagoshima expatriates have tended to their ritual of loyalty and friendship with unflagging devotion to watch one another grow up, then watch one another's children grow up, and now cluck and coo over pictures of one another's grandchildren.

In May 2002, I had the honor of being invited to one of these reunions to conduct a group interview and collect material.

May 31, 2002, is unseasonably hot, even for central Japan. When I step off the train at Saitama City station in Tokyo's northern suburbs, an electronic news billboard thermometer reads 28 degrees Celsius (82.4 degrees Fahrenheit). The humidity is not intolerable—yet—but it is getting there, and the combination of bright sunshine, middle-aged metabolism, and a heavy shoulder bag full of camera equipment and notebooks has me mentally congratulating myself on opting for an aloha shirt this morning instead of the button-down shirt and necktie I had originally planned to wear.

This month's meeting of the Chiran Nadeshiko Kai is being held at the home of Shōko Nagasaki (née Maeda). After a white-knuckled pedal-to-the-metal ride through twisting backstreets in the passenger seat of her son's car, I arrive at the venue. I am early, but Shōko-san does not seem to mind, and graciously accepts the gift of eel cookies* I have brought from Hamamatsu.

"Ah, Unagi Pai," she says. "These are famous. Everyone will be delighted to have some of these today."

The Nagasaki home is a classic sixties Japanese mixture of traditional and Western elements. A green-tiled entranceway leads to an interior dominated by warm wood and dark earth tones, which gives the space a mellow, meditative atmosphere I would imagine Shōko-san's husband, Kazunori, finds very conducive to his writing. A bookcase in the living room is filled end to end with his collected published works. Nagasaki-sensei is Japan's foremost authority on persuasive public speaking and the author of thirty-five books on the subject, several of them best sellers. I inquire about the man of the house, and am not particularly surprised to be told that he is busy in his study writing book number thirty-six.

---

*Not a misprint. "Unagi Pai" are a confectionary made from powdered eels (yes, *eels*), butter, flour, and sugar. They are a famous souvenir product of the Hamamatsu/Lake Hamana region renowned for their rich taste and supposed stamina-improving properties.

The tatami-floored main parlor of the Nagasakis' home opens out onto a charming Japanese garden about as big as the room it faces. A row of opened cat food tins in one corner of the garden explains the faint ambient soundtrack of meowing and mewling I have been aware of since entering the house. A line of questioning posed as tactfully as possible reveals that Shōko-san, evidently, is the neighborhood "cat lady," and she informs me with not a small measure of pride that in addition to keeping two house cats, she is at present attending to the dietary needs of upward of a dozen regular feline visitors who are free to come and go, loaf, frolic, and leave calling cards in her well-tended garden as they please.

"My husband used to complain a lot," Shōko-san says with a sly smirk. "But I refused to give in. The cats stayed, and now I think he likes them. Of course, he would never admit that."

Shōko-san is about as physically and temperamentally different from Reiko-san as two best friends from the same hometown can get. Vellum-skinned, articulate, and rabbitlike, she is a diminutive Katharine Hepburn to Reiko-san's hard-laughing and occasionally pushy Anna Magnani mama bear. As the other members begin to arrive and I get a chance to observe the pecking order a bit, I also realize that Shōko-san is the big intellectual in the room. She is not in anyone's face with it, but the authority is there nonetheless, and while Reiko-san is unquestionably in control of the conversational flow and speaking order, all eyes turn to Shōko-san when information is in doubt or somebody wants confirmation of the accuracy of an anecdote. Most tellingly, when she speaks, the others invariably stop talking and listen.

Another obvious but unassuming authority presence in the room is the tall and regal Kayoko Mori. When I ask who the leader of the group was when the girls were growing up, everyone points to her.

"She was the class president five or six times running," Shōko-san says as the others nod.

"But I was always the class secretary," Reiko-san interjects, with a note of stridency that brings on a round of laughter.

Someone makes a quick comment in Kagoshima dialect that I cannot understand. A rapid-fire exchange of more of the same leaves me even farther behind in the dust. Reiko-san—ever the attentive emcee—picks up on my predicament immediately.

"You know," she says, "we're doing our best today to speak standard

Japanese for your sake. If we were talking the way we usually do to each other, you wouldn't be able to understand us at all. Even our own children can't follow when we really get rolling."

The group belly laugh that follows this remark is explosive and tinged with reed and metal, just this side of cackling.

As I watch and listen, I find myself charmed by the warmth of the women's smiles, the melody in their lilting Kagoshima intonations, and their constant banter of jibes and laughter as they fuss over the lunch preparations. Although the women are old enough to be my aunts, it takes no effort or stretch of the imagination at all to see them in a Chinese cultural-revolution-poster-girl milieu as flush-cheeked fourteen-year-olds in pigtails, patched cotton *monpe* trousers, and rumpled middy blouses, cheerfully singing as they fill in bomb-cratered runways or camouflage airplane revetments. There is, of course, some sadness and even a measure of banality in that imagery, but there is undeniable beauty in it, too, as there always is in naïve, innocent bravery. This aspect, I believe, is shared with the *tokkō* mystique, and I think that getting a monthly recharge shot of that stalwart yet innocent glow—or at least a sufficiently stimulating recollection of it—is part of why the Nadeshiko Kai exists.

Watching the women like this, I cannot help but ponder the breakneck pace and staggering enormity of the changes they have seen and experienced in their lifetimes. They huddled in air raid shelters and scrounged for food as teenagers, and never tasted butter or wore anything on their feet other than wooden geta until they were almost twenty. In their thirties and forties, they bought their first cars and televisions and refrigerators. Now they live with cell phones and broadband Internet service. They use credit cards on overseas vacations with their families. Their children attended universities and have gone on to attain positions of importance in the second-largest economy in the world. They splurge for their grandchildren's Nintendo software and treat them to take-out pizza. In a sense, the Chiran Nadeshiko girls are personifications of Japan's journey over the last sixty years—human time capsules living in the twenty-first century but still carrying memories and even physical legacies from an era so inconceivably different from our own it could have happened on another planet.

*    *    *

Reiko Torihama, Shōko Maeda, Kayoko Mori, Fusako Mori, Mutsuko Miyake, and Yuri Kuwashiro were born when Japan was still reeling with the initial shock of the worldwide Great Depression. Joblessness, fore-closures, and deflation hit rural areas like southern Kyūshū especially hard. On the national level, burgeoning militarism was beginning to ap-ply a heavy-handed influence in politics, education, and many other as-pects of Japanese society. Army adventurism and profiteering on the Asian continent had flared up into open combat in Manchuria, and as a result, Japan was becoming increasingly isolated on the international stage. In two more years it would quit the League of Nations to complete its isolation and seal its fate, dooming Reiko-san and her classmates to a life without peace until they were in their teens, and to third-world living standards until they were pushing thirty.

The Nadeshiko Kai girls grew up with institutionalized militarism and simmering Asian conflict as accepted facts of daily life. Of course, the adults in their childhood landscape talked about what was going on in China—especially when all-out warfare erupted after the Marco Polo Bridge incident in 1937—but it was always in the context of something read in the newspapers, happening far away. Shōko-san remembers a flag-waving train depot send-off for a male cousin going off to fight in China, but cannot recall anyone ever mentioning what happened to the boy after that. Occasional word-of-mouth news about the son of some family in town getting killed was enough to remind everybody that there was fight-ing going on, but it was not the stuff of posters and songs and food rationing.

The residents of Chiran got their first inklings that big changes in their lives were on the way when it was announced that the Imperial Japanese Army wanted to construct an annex air base for the Shōnen Hikōhei program on the outskirts of town in early 1941. Unlike the Japan of today, where citizen action committees can delay public or pri-vate construction projects for years or even decades with protests and haggling, opposition to a governmental policy decision was not some-thing that was tolerated by the authorities in early Shōwa Japan. In Chi-ran's case, the army people arrived to survey the plot they wanted, came up with what they thought was a fair price, tracked down all of the af-fected landholders, and made them an offer they could not refuse.[7]

By fall, there were orange Akatonbo army trainers constantly buzzing overhead, and on Sunday afternoons the streets of town were thick with fresh-faced fifteen- and sixteen-year-old flight cadets who had big smiles for all the girls and pockets full of spending money to throw around like there was no tomorrow.

The new base brought undeniable benefits to the local economy, and Reiko-san's mother, Tome Torihama, certainly welcomed the boost in patronage that the Tomiya Shokudō was enjoying as a result. But like many other town residents, she found unsettling the simple fact that the army had determined it necessary to build an airstrip in a remote burg like Chiran. Were there not enough big military bases on the coastline and around big cities already? Why disrupt life in a peaceful little farming village unless the army was so desperate for more bases it had run out of better places to build them?

"We knew a major war was in the works from around that time," Reiko-san recalls.

If anyone doubted this by late 1941, all they had to do was pick up a paper to be convinced otherwise. Although no one the girls knew had a radio, newsprint was available everywhere, and throughout the summer and fall of that year hundred-point headlines using phrases like "strategic materials," "oil embargo," and "A-B-C-D encirclement"* played up unfamiliar new bogeyman roles for America and Britain, countries that were still supposed to be friendly the last time most people in Chiran had checked. At school, the girls were told by their teachers that trouble was on the way, but that it was nothing the emperor's army and navy could not dispose of with one hand behind their backs. Thus there was more excitement than surprise when news of the Pearl Harbor raid was announced. The nation was assured that the emperor's war eagles had sent the American fleet to the bottom of the Pacific. Most people assumed that the war was already won.

What the Chiran girls remember most from this heady time was the teacher-orchestrated group euphoria at school over the news that one of the "Nine Gunshin" midget sub pilots from the raid—Lieutenant

*"American-British-Chinese-Dutch."

Masaharu Yokoyama—was from Kagoshima.[8] Schools across the prefecture were ordered by the board of education to have students write commemorative *tanka* poems for Yokoyama and submit them for a contest.* An official commemorative song was later written for Yokoyama and sung regularly at assemblies in Kagoshima schools.

"He was so dashing," Nadeshiko Fusako Mori recalls, as someone hums a bar or two of his song in the background. "Like a movie star."

Despite Chiran's holiday mood in December 1941, things were a little more sober in Shōko Maeda's household, where her grandfather—who had spent seventeen years in Seattle as a young businessman—was livid about what he saw as the government's insane decision to go to war with America.

"Do those people in Tokyo realize what they've gotten us into?" he had thundered. "How are we going to win a war against a huge, affluent nation with limitless resources?"

When Shōko-san noticed posters like LUXURY IS THE ENEMY and A DROP OF GASOLINE IS A DROP OF BLOOD going up around town soon after the war started, she began to think that her grandfather might be right, after all. But doubts or not, she followed the example of friends and neighbors in doing her work, avoiding objective comments about the war, and trying to at least give the impression that she believed everything she was told.

Shōko, although gifted with a precocious intelligence, was nonetheless still a child of eleven or twelve. The idea that she might have been the only person in the community other than her grandfather with the political savvy to pick up on occasional glimpses of frightening reality like this is of course preposterous. There were others who knew things were not quite as peachy as the papers would have them believe. But like Shōko-san, these skeptics also knew well enough to keep their mouths shut about their doubts, and were careful to keep up the appearance of believing that there was nothing to worry about and that Japan was going to win the war. The times behooved taciturnity, for to speak one's mind in public when one's opinion conflicted with the official line was to risk

---

*Tanka* are like haiku, but with thirty-one syllables instead of seventeen. They are also not stylistically limited to seasonal themes, like the shorter haiku, so are better suited for commemorative poetry.

social ostracism at the least, if not arrest for sedition after being reported to the police by neighborhood informants, who were only too eager to drop a name to get on the good side of the local authorities.*

Most Chiran residents, however, did not lose much sleep over doubts about the war. They slept the sleep of the innocent, secure in their belief that what the authorities told them about the war was gospel. But they cannot be completely faulted for buying the government line at face value. Their optimism was as much a matter of lack of information as lack of cynicism. Unlike city dwellers, who had greater access to alternative (and thus illegal) news sources, citizens in remote areas were completely dependent on official organs for the dissemination of war news.

In wartime Japan, war news through official channels passed through two layers of filters before being made public: the top layer consisted of imperial GHQ and public relations officers at the Army and Navy Ministries, who made the initial choices about what the public should or should not be told about, and concocted official whoppers where appropriate. The second layer consisted of cautious editorial staff and line-toeing journalists well seasoned in self-censorship who phrased this filtered information as patriotically—or vaguely, if the circumstances called for smoke-screening—as possible. The third and last line of information defense was manned by the thousands of government censors at police bureaus and public prosecutors' offices who scanned advance "review" copies of publications for sensitive information, seditious undertones, or lèse-majesté.

Chiran's schoolteachers did their part by keeping the discussion of war developments vague and to a minimum, seeing their duty as educators more constructively performed in organizing scrap metal drives† and putting their charges through a healthy daily regimen of close-order drill and group singing of patriotic songs. The students memorized books full of anthems about hot young blood and sacrifice, and might be forced to sing them at any time during the day. The musical activity the Chiran

---

*This informant function was usually performed by neighborhood merchants in the Army Reservist Association or housewives in the local Defense Women's Association (Kokubō Fujinkai).
†The national government took over the collection of scrap metal by official decree in 1944. All pots, pans, and other metal utensils were declared the property of the state and collected from communities by local authorities. Coins were also removed from the national currency system and replaced with paper notes (Bunkazai Kamisu [1995], p. 20).

girls remember most clearly—and with the most distaste—was the constant singing of "Umi Yukaba." Starting rather early in the war and continuing right up to the bitter end, children and teachers alike stood at rigid attention to sing it at the top of their lungs every day at outdoor morning assembly and any other time the student body was gathered for an event.

"Any occasion they could possibly think of, the teachers made us sing that song," Reiko-san recalls. "Oh, how we hated it."

I ask if this was because the girls understood the barely veiled suicidal message in the song's lyrics.

"Not at all," Reiko-san says. "We had no idea what we were singing, but we knew that we were sick and tired of it, whatever it was."

The other women nod emphatically.

"Whenever I hear that song now it brings back so many bad memories," Shōko-san adds to another round of nodding.

## twenty

# THE NADESHIKO UNIT

As the singing and scrap metal drives dragged on, signs that no one could miss or ignore anymore began to appear in the community suggesting that the war situation was not necessarily developing to Japan's advantage. One obvious indicator was that the number of funerals for young servicemen from the town increased dramatically. Another message was purely lexical, but telling nevertheless: The language in the papers and slogans in the posters became more strident and tinged with desperation. The change had been so gradual as to be barely noticeable at first, but by late 1943, as the food situation got tight and rationing became stricter, few people could have missed the significance of there now being a preponderance of flowery death euphemisms and more talk about "sacrifice" and "resisting to the end" in the media than about "winning the war" and "Asia for Asians."

In March 1944, a harbinger of bad tidings on the home front came along that not even the thickest-skinned optimist could misinterpret. In that month, the Ministry of Education announced in a national emergency decree that regular academic lessons at junior high and high schools across the country were hereby canceled for the duration of hostilities to free up adolescent labor resources for the war effort.

Chiran Girls' School was not exempt from the wartime requirements of the state. When its students began the new school year in April, they were informed that they would be organized into a "volunteer" work detail unit. In honor of the blossom featured on the school crest and in hopes that the girls would live up to their honor as maidens of Kagoshima, their group was named the Nadeshiko Unit.* The sixteen- to eighteen-year-olds of the upper three class grades were packed up and sent off to Nagasaki, where they would spend the next seventeen months working at the big Mitsubishi Heiki Seisakusho torpedo factory. The lower three grades, which included Reiko and Shōko's new third-year class, were deemed too young and vulnerable to be separated from maternal supervision, and were instead put to work in or close enough to town to be home for a bath and bedtime every night. With all of the local boys twelve or older committed to the war industry or military service, and schoolgirls, small children, housewives, old people, and war invalids the only other potential workforce groups now available in any kind of numbers, the local military authorities came to depend on Chiran's pool of able-bodied twelve- to fifteen-year-old girls as the prime source of volunteer labor in town.

For the next year, the girls did little else but dig. During harvest season, this meant pulling spuds, radishes, and tubers from the ground in the sort of agricultural drudgery to which the farmgirls were well accustomed, but the rest of the time they were excavating roomy and well-furnished bunkers and air raid shelters for the army in the local countryside.† These high-ceilinged spaces were dug underground or into chalky hillsides, and the work was dangerous, exhausting, and above all filthy. The girls dug for months with little rest, and wearing no protective gear other than *bosai-zukin* padded hoods (not much more than floor cushions tied over the head). Luckily, there were no cave-ins, and other than calloused hands and sore shoulders, the worst indignity the girls suffered was the dirt that constantly fell into their faces, eyes, mouths, and clothes as they dug.

---

*Flower-themed names for mobilized female student units were common during the war. Along with Chiran's Nadeshiko Unit, the most famous—and undoubtedly most tragic—of these was the Himeyuri (Scarlet Lily) Unit, a detachment of nursing students mobilized for combat aid stations in Okinawan caves who committed suicide with hand grenades rather than allow themselves to be captured by the marines who invaded the island. Survivor testimony indicates that rather than patriotic sentiment, urging by armed Japanese soldiers in the caves and panicked fear of rape and murder at the hands of the Americans formed the strongest motivation for the suicides.

†Many of these were intended to serve not only as bomb shelters, but also as long-term underground defense facilities to be used when the American invasion came.

"I swear, some of those bunkers we dug out were big enough to hold a house," Reiko says.

"And when we finished digging," Kayoko-san adds, "they'd make us cart in sand and foliage to camouflage the shelter entrances."

The shelters—and the residents of Chiran—got their baptism of fire on March 18, 1945, when the airfield and environs were shot up by American carrier fighter-bombers.* These attackers were not the first enemy planes the townspeople had seen—B-29 formations had been passing overhead at altitude on the way to Kagoshima City and other industrial centers like Yahata, Kurume, and Nagasaki farther to the north since the previous summer—but it was the first time that Chiran was the Americans' intended target, and the Hellcats hit it hard.

"Some villagers were killed hiding in their slit trench bomb shelter during that first raid," Reiko says. "But even with an air base there, we didn't get a single airplane up to defend against the raiders. This was when I really knew that things were not going our way."

Shortly after dawn on March 27, the girls arrived at school for work detail in their usual *monpe* work clothes. Principal Utō and one of their young teachers, Miss Chosa, had the students form up as they always did before marching out to the day's worksite. On this day, however, Mr. Yamaguchi—the head of the local board of education, Army Reservist Association bigshot, and town hall *heiji kakari* military liaison chief— was there, too. It was the first time since the formation ceremony for the Nadeshiko Unit almost a year ago that their activities had been graced by the presence of such a VIP.

After lining up and singing "Umi Yukaba" en masse, the girls were told to run back home, change out of their beat-up work shirts and into their normal school uniform sailor middy blouses, and then come back on the double. When everyone had formed up again, the teachers and liaison officer marched the squad of eighteen students down a path through the woods behind the school. None of the girls had ever taken the route before, so they had no idea where they were being led, outside of a vague directional awareness that they were walking toward the southwestern corner of the air base. But that was impossible. Everyone

---

*This raid was conducted by the same Task Force 58 element that was the intended target of the disastrous first Ōka sortie from Kanoya NAS three days later on March 21.

knew the base was strictly off-limits—even as army volunteer workers, the girls had never set foot inside its gates. Yet as they continued their walk through the woods, they were led past an AIR BASE PERSONNEL ONLY sign without breaking stride. Just as the girls were beginning to look at each other quizzically, the drone of a large number of engines, faint at first, could be heard overhead. The sound got louder, quickly.

"Take *coverrrr!*" Mr. Yamaguchi shouted.

Already seasoned air raid veterans by now, the girls knew what to do without further explanation, and they instinctively darted off into the trees and bamboo on either side of the path. As Reiko and Shōko huddled together in a thicket, they both penciled SAYONARA on a bamboo trunk. They had no idea where they were being taken, or if they were going to get bombs dropped on them at any moment. Maybe they were being taken off to be shot for stumbling onto some big army secret. For all they knew, this really was "sayonara."

The engine drone from above became loud enough for the girls to feel in their chests. Looking up, they watched as a silver-glinting, contrail-streaming flight of twenty or thirty B-29s passed over.* As they watched the malevolent beauty of the bomber formation, they heard another loud engine sound, much closer and moving toward them on the ground. Just then a big army truck rumbled down the forest path. Riding in back was a group of pilots in Hinomaru headbands who smiled and waved as they passed, jostled as the flatbed bumped along toward the airfield. The girls had no way of knowing it at the time, but the pilots they had just seen were on their way to the flight line to take part in the first *tokkō* sortie from Chiran.

"I remember the look Reiko and I exchanged at that moment," Shōko-san says. "Living in Chiran, we had seen plenty of pilots before, but never pilots with headbands like that. We had only seen pictures of them in the newspaper, in articles about *tokkō*."

When the high-altitude B-29 formation was gone, the girls and their escorts continued walking deeper into off-limits territory, following the path from which the truck had emerged. After a few minutes, they arrived at the bottom of a long, curving rise of packed-dirt-and-log steps.

---

*This may have been a (the) formation that mined the Shimonoseki Straits between Kyūshū and Honshū on this day.

Climbing these, they reached a tranquil forest clearing domed with tall-trunk pine boughs softly rustling in the breeze. Mr. Yamaguchi halted the group in front of what looked like a small hamlet of half-buried log cabins, each with a few steps leading down to entrances below ground level. These structures were what the army called *sangakuheisha* (literally "triangle barracks"), so named because the sleeping quarters were sunken for defilade against flying bomb shrapnel, and the only portions poking up over ground level were the sloped roofs.

A sergeant standing in front of the entrance to one of the *sangakuheisha* explained that taking care of this barracks area and whoever happened to be staying in it would be the girls' responsibility until further notice. Their main duties would consist of doing laundry in the nearby river, cleaning and sweeping, bed making, meal and tea serving, and making sure that the foliage used for camouflaging the *sangakuheisha* was kept fresh and green. If the need for other duties arose, these would be explained as necessary. Finally, it was stressed that under no circumstances were the girls to tell anybody else—not even their own mothers or other family members—about the nature of their duties on the base.

In a little while, another truck came along the forest road from the direction of the airfield, but this was full of mattresses and blankets rather than pilots. A scrappy supply corporal put the girls to work immediately, trundling the bedding from the road up to the pine clearing, then down into the damp, dark, unpainted interior of the *sangakuheisha*. The mattresses and blankets were laid out on tatami sleeping shelves lining both sides of the slat-floored corridors running the length of the barracks. There would be very little storage space for personal effects and no privacy at all for the pilots who had to sleep down here. There would not be much fresh air, either, as the only ventilation came from the sunken entranceways at either end of the hut. Steel helmets and canteens—presumably one set per sleeper—lined the walls, hanging on wooden pegs. The overall effect was like a slave ship with clean sleeping linen.

Although Reiko and Shōko had already surmised from their morning truck sighting that the "guests" who would be staying in these dank barracks were *tokkō* pilots, the girls could not confirm this until that afternoon, when a formation of Hayabusa fighters landed at the base and the men who had flown them in arrived at the *sangakuheisha* compound. But as these "men" jumped from the back of the truck, still in their flight suits and carrying small canvas kit bags, the girls were surprised—shocked, even—to see that the pilots were in fact boys of seventeen or eighteen and not the hardened professionals they had always assumed were flying the nation's warplanes into battle. The boys did not really seem heroic or dashing at all. Rather, they had a kind of innocent purity about them, free of worldly contamination. They were almost glowing—as if they were already halfway to heaven and happily resigned to their fate, answering the girls' whispered queries about their mission with beaming smiles.

This particular group of pilots was only the first of many that the girls would serve at the *sangakuheisha* compound. The normal rotation of groups through Chiran could be anywhere from one or two nights to up to a week if attack sorties and/or incoming flights were delayed by bad weather or other unforeseen problems.* Although both the pilots and the Nadeshiko Unit members were under strict orders forbidding fraternization, it was only natural that with adolescent boys and girls thrown together in a stressful environment redolent with pathos, danger, and constant reminders of mortality, some measure of emotional bonding was going to occur. These bonds grew stronger the longer a particular group stayed at Chiran, reinforced by long and languid interludes of downtime when the girls finished their chores early and were free to socialize with their "guests" for the rest of the day until the truck came along to take them home in the evening.

Statistically, the pilots broke down into two basic demographic groups—commissioned ex-college students in their early to mid-twenties from urban backgrounds, and mostly rural, working-class enlisted men still in the eighteen-to-twenty range. Many of the former were accomplished intellectuals and budding literary talents straight out of liberal arts programs in the best universities of the land. They often had their own reading material and preferred to keep their faces buried in their books the entire time they were in the barracks. Shōko had a temperamental affinity for these types, and liked to read her own favorite books—usually poetry—aloud for them. Some of these brainy young men were also trained teaching professionals fond of gathering the girls

---

*Unlike the navy, the army did not send up *tokkō* flights in poor-visibility conditions, likely due to army pilots' notoriously underdeveloped navigational skills, especially over water.

under the pine arbors to give lectures—not without some measure of showing off involved in their performances—on subjects like medieval Japanese literature or European modern art that left their captive audiences scratching their heads, but deeply impressed nonetheless. However, the majority of the girls tended to bond with the enlisted men, who were closer to their own age and social background. The teenage pilots liked to sing and play games and were more interested in spending their last hours and thoughts with a soft, winsome face and a sympathetic feminine ear than in holding forth in weighty conversations about the meaning of it all.

Although the girls were aware of the importance of the pilots' missions, and felt an enormous responsibility to help these young men and boys be as happy and comfortable as possible in the last days and hours of their lives, it was impossible to be completely objective about their work in a situation this emotionally loaded. As time went on, and the girls became quicker at making friends, feelings of sympathy and duty became complicated with the wrenching pain of knowing that they would have to say farewell to each new group of friends who briefly flitted into their lives before disappearing forever.

And in the meantime, out of earshot of anyone who was not a Nadeshiko Unit member, the girls would pray for rain. But no matter how heartfelt and earnest their pleas for inclement weather, the inevitable hour of sad parting would arrive when the attack orders came down and it would be time for the current group of *tokkō* boys to leave. On the morning of a sortie, the girls, many holding bunches of wildflowers to press into the hands of their favorite pilots, would go down to the airfield flight line. There, they were often accompanied by pilots' family members who had traveled to Chiran and received special permission from the base commander to see off their sons, brothers, and—on rare occasions— husbands. Although all onlookers and well-wishers—including family members—were under strict orders not to shed tears under any circumstances, these orders proved impossible to enforce, and the sobbing and crying out of the names of loved ones would always rise to a crescendo as the engines of Hayabusa fighters or *Ki*-51 assault planes gunned up for takeoff.

While pilots' family members who made it to Chiran had to go endure the agony of a send-off only once, the Nadeshiko Unit girls had to go through a barely less devastating version of it over and over again, day in and day out, without rest or reprieve. And no matter how often they participated in these farewell rituals, they never became inured to the pain. Things could have been a little easier to bear, perhaps, if there had been any time to grieve together as a group, but this was impossible, because they would have to go back to the *sangakuheisha* immediately after each send-off to get the barracks ready for the arrival of the next group coming. The floors would be swept, new bedding laid out, tears wiped dry, and best smiles put on before the next trucks bumped down from the airfield and another ten or twenty beatific boys in flight suits would amble up the trail to the barracks compound with innocent smiles of their own.

For most of the girls, the real grieving didn't come until years later. And every one of them still has dreams and the occasional crying jag about their wartime service to this day.

"If fourteen- or fifteen-year-old girls in this day and age experienced the kind of long-term grief and stress we went through that spring they would be getting psychological counseling right now," Shōko says. "But we didn't get anything like that. People didn't think like that back then. That doesn't mean the scars aren't there, though."

## twenty-one

# FIREFLIES

D uring the last week of March and the first five days of April 1945, the Imperial Army and Navy joint *tokkō* command finalized preparations for Operation Ten-Gō. While the Nadeshiko girls were sending their young heroes off in flights of ten or twelve at a time with flowers and song, hundreds of new *tokkō* pilots and aircraft from around the country streamed into Chiran and every other army air base and naval air station in southern Kyūshū to go on immediate standby for "Kikusui 1"—Ten-Gō's first attack wave.

Meanwhile, five hundred kilometers to the south, on and under the decks of Admiral Spruance's Fifth Fleet warships, a different group of young heroes went about the business of their war with the same resolution as their Japanese counterparts, albeit without the benefit of bouquet-bearing teenage cheerleaders. Spruance's men had long since become experts at the job of invasion support, and for the first five days of the Okinawa operation, it was looking like things here were not going to be any better or worse than anything else they had faced to date. Of course, there had been a steady pace of a dozen-odd suicider attacks a day ever since they had arrived off Okinawa, but these were spread pretty thin over an armada the size of the Fifth Fleet. And the fact that no ships had been lost so far during the course of the operation was reassuring proof not only that the Fifth's luck seemed to be holding out, but, more important, that its sailors and airmen had become as highly proficient at protecting themselves as they were at looking out for the men on the beach.

Over the last six months, the Japanese suicide tactics had become a regular feature of life on an American warship in the Central Pacific, and while the latest attacks were not to be underestimated in their potential for destruction and mayhem, they were nothing to make the sailors feel any less sorry for the guys they all knew were getting the crummiest deal in this operation—the poor army and marine dogfaces having to slog, slash and shoot their way through the honeycombed Japanese defenses ashore. Never forgetting to feel thankful for their own relative comfort (if not safety), the aviators and sailors of the Fifth Fleet kept their well-oiled machinery of war and destruction humming. If the boys ashore did their jobs as well as the fleet was doing its own, it was looking as if this could all be wrapped up in another couple of weeks.

No doubt many American sailors in the vicinity of Okinawa were entertaining such reassuring thoughts and hopes as April 6 dawned. Perhaps some of the crew of the radar picket destroyer *Colhoun* did, too, even after an unusually busy predawn morning of near-miss conventional bombing attacks by Japanese raiders. Things had quickly returned to normal after the raids, and the *Colhoun* spent the rest of the forenoon watch performing her usual duties, steaming in a ten-kilometer-wide circle on Radar Picket Station 2 about seventy-five kilometers north-northeast of Okinawa to provide CAP vectoring and early warning info for the rest of the fleet.

Business picked up shortly after noon. Reports began coming in over the radio that Task Force 58, presently steaming about one hundred kilometers east of Okinawa, was coming under attack by large numbers of suiciders approaching from the northeast.[1] Although the reports merited concern, there was nothing *Colhoun* could do to help, given her location and modest allotment of CAP, which in any case would be but a drop in the bucket compared with the combined aerial might TF 58 would be able to put up in its own defense. The destroyer maintained General Quarters, but remained on station, noting radar contacts and sending regular reports to "Delegate Base."

Around 1530, someone else's problem suddenly became *Colhoun*'s as well. Her radarmen picked up new waves of attackers headed straight for her position from the northeast. Minutes later, calls for immediate assistance came in from the *Bush,* a destroyer patrolling Radar Picket Station 1 some twenty kilometers to the west. She was reporting a direct kamikaze hit amidships. While her crew fought fires and waited for the cavalry to arrive, more Japanese planes began swarming overhead— circling, but for some reason, holding back from attacking. With both her own and the rapidly approaching *Colhoun's* allotted CAPs caught up in dogfights too far away to help, there was nothing for the crew of the *Bush* to do but continue fighting fires and pray for a miracle.

When the *Colhoun* showed up some thirty minutes later, the *Bush* was smoking and dead in the water. But with the kamikazes now circling both ships, the *Colhoun* could do nothing but take evasive action and try to draw the attackers' attention away from the now utterly helpless *Bush*. Beginning at 1700, perhaps after ascertaining that no Hellcats or Corsairs were going to be coming to the rescue of their quarry, the suiciders began to attack again, this time concentrating their wrath on the as of yet unmolested *Colhoun*. The destroyer put up a brave fight, pounding away at her tormentors with every weapon on board, but facing such numbers and without the protection of air cover, it was a hopeless struggle. By nightfall, both the *Bush* and the *Colhoun* were at the bottom of the South China Sea and 129 American sailors were dead or missing, never to be seen again.[2]

Farther to the east and south, the suiciders' fury continued unabated against Task Force 58 and the main invasion fleet, even as wave after wave of the attackers were cut down with deadly efficiency by veteran American fighter pilots and withering AA fire. The picket destroyers on station and supply ships in the invasion fleet anchorages caught the brunt of the attacks. Before the last suicider was splashed, another 238 sailors were killed, in addition to the *Bush* and *Colhoun* losses, and four more ships were sent to the bottom—the destroyer minesweeper *Emmons,* LST-447 and two ammunition carriers that went up with cataclysmic explosions.[3] A further eleven ships had been badly damaged, with several requiring Stateside repairs that took them out of the fight for the duration of the war.

The Japanese threw 355 planes and their aircrews into the attacks.[4] In hard tactical terms, the combat results did not compensate for this exorbitant expenditure in lives and machinery. The psychological effect on their enemy, however, was another story. Although Ten-Gō had just fired the most fearsome bolt it would manage to bring to bear for the rest of the campaign, the shocked American survivors had no way of knowing that there was not more of the same in store for them, brewing out beyond the northeast horizon like a malevolent storm that would sweep down from Kyūshū to smash their ships and take their lives. For the sailors of the Fifth, the remainder of the Okinawa campaign would be a gut-wrenching day-to-day struggle with their own terrible memories of April 6, and every waking minute afterwards would be spent with eyes on the skies and ears pricked for the telltale *pom-pom-pom* of AA fire and the unforgettable scream of a Japanese plane in an incoming dive. Most men proved able to face their fears, but others did not—the Fifth Fleet suffered battle stress casualties at levels never seen before or since by American fighting men on land or at sea.[5]

By the end of the Okinawa campaign in late June, nearly five thousand Fifth Fleet sailors had been killed—with again as many wounded—mostly through *tokkō* attacks. A total of 34 warships and other vessels had been sunk, with an additional 368 damaged. Seven hundred sixty-three warplanes were lost, hundreds of these turned into twisted hunks of metal on flight decks shattered by kamikazes.[6] More than three thousand imperial army and navy *tokkō* pilots—some six hundred in sorties from Chiran alone—sacrificed their lives to wreak this devastation.

All in all, the invasion of Okinawa was the bloodiest episode in the entire history of the United States Navy. The suicide attacks that characterized this battle were deemed so potentially damaging to public morale that the War Department censored any mention of them in news reports or personal correspondence from Fifth Fleet sailors, lest people on the home front realize what hell their young men were facing so far away. Most of the American public would not hear about the carnage wreaked by Japanese suicide attacks at Okinawa until the final weeks before V-J Day.

Takujiro Ōnishi must have been pleased.

For the first two weeks of Operation Ten-Gō, the boys departing Chiran were only on stopovers before going on to make their final attack sorties from the island of Tokunoshima in the South China Sea, so the Nadeshiko Unit could take some comfort during their farewells in thinking that, technically, they were not sending the fliers off to their deaths. But after the Tokunoshima base was destroyed by the Americans, the Shinbu units had to start flying directly from Chiran for the two-and-a-half-hour flight required to reach targets off Okinawa.

The first of these direct attack sorties was scheduled for the afternoon of April 12.* The girls—fully aware that the pilots were now going to be flying straight into battle and, if all went as scheduled, straight into an American warship—knew that the day's send-off was going to be even more emotionally charged than usual. Shōko brought along an armful of blossom-laden boughs she had cut from the big cherry tree in her grand-father's backyard (the girls had already stripped bare the cherry tree in the neighborhood Shinto shrine by this point for other send-offs). The branches were passed out to the other Nadeshiko Unit girls lining the Chi-ran air base runway. It was a serendipitous development for the newspa-per cameramen on hand for the event. One snapshot in particular of the Nadeshiko Unit's blossom bough waving farewell to the Hayabusas beginning their takeoff runs that April afternoon has gone on to become one of the classic Japanese home-front photographs of the war and a ver-itable icon for the paradoxical beauty and banality of the tokkō program itself.

Journalists were a regular fixture in the Chiran landscape, as they in-evitably were in any tokkō venue (with the notable exceptions of top-secret Kaiten and Ōka facilities). They even had their own permanent sangakuheisha in the barracks compound.[7] Although the girls were not responsible for attending to the upkeep of these quarters and thus did not have daily contact with their occupants, the propaganda value of the Nadeshiko Unit did not go unnoticed by the newsmen. In early April, af-ter an emotionally brutal day of no less than four send-offs, Shōko and six other girls were interviewed by a reporter named Kawagoe. The piece—published several weeks after the interviews were conducted—is reproduced here in its entirety:

---

*This was one of the last tokkō sorties from Chiran launched in daylight. As the Hellcat and Corsair raids became increasingly intense, predawn became the only time safe enough to gas up the planes and get them in the air to reach Okinawa with enough light for the pilots to see their targets.

## Potted Flowers for a Spartan Room:
A DAY IN THE LIFE OF OUR DIVINE EAGLES
### By Special Correspondent Kawagoe

APRIL 19, 1945, CHIRAN AIR BASE.\* A pure dawn mist pierced by silvery morning sunrays floats over the moss and through the trees of a wooded hillock. Here, young Divine Eagles sleep on fluffy futons provided by the generosity of local citizens. The innocence of little boys still remains on the faces of the pilots, sprawling comfortably in their bedding, dreaming of who knows what. Looking at them, it is hard to believe that before noon they will be flying over seas of flame to strike at the heart of the enemy.

Little bouquets of rapeseed blossom and wild camellia brighten up corners of their spartan wood barracks. Placed in old bottles filled with water, it is clear that the flowers were arranged by unsophisticated but tender hands. They are the handiwork of third graders from Chiran Girls' School who have volunteered to work in these barracks. Hinomaru headbands and poems written in blood arrive at the barracks daily, sent by still other schoolgirls from as far away as Manchuria and Tohoku for the young Eagles to wear and carry into battle.

In most cases, these pilots are only a year or two older than the girl students who work in their barracks, and they always have kind words for them, like, "You girls remind us of our little sisters back home. We'll take care of the enemy so that you can become upstanding, fine Japanese mothers

---

\*In the actual article, the location is deleted and described as "a Base Somewhere in Japan" (*Marumaru-kichi*). This convention is ignored in my translation for purposes of clarity.

someday." This reporter sees and hears beautiful exchanges like this on a daily basis here in these simple barracks, and it is clear that the pure hearts of the girls have had an ennobling and strengthening influence on the hearts of these young men.

The girls wash laundry and mend socks with feelings of warm affection for the young Eagles, remembering all of the others they have seen off on attack sorties in the past. Let us hear from their own lips some of the thoughts and feelings these girls have experienced performing their duties here:

SHŌKO MAEDA: "I remember Corporal Fuke, who before he left said that his only concern before he sortied was for the well-being of his younger sister. She is supposedly our age, and the corporal spoke at length of fond memories of their childhood together and of his hopes that she will grow up to be a fine Japanese woman. I know I speak for all of the other girls as well in saying how lucky we are to be Japanese girls who have such fine young men to look after us—who are so compassionate and concerned for our well-being even in the last moments before their sorties."

HIDEKO TSUJI: "I told Corporal Sasaki that I wanted to write to his family so I could describe for them the scene of his final sortie. When I handed him a piece of paper and pen and asked him to write his family's address, he wrote down 'A Nice Shady Tomb on the corner of Hades Avenue and Styx Street.' Then he explained to me that he was an only child and his mother and father were already dead. Although I was mortified at my gaffe, he wasn't the type to take offense easily. Rather, he was one of the most cheerful pilots in the barracks. I remember when his sortie kept getting delayed, he would always say, 'Well, looks like another day I've missed my chance to die. . . . I've lived another day too long.' I think he really regretted it, though, even though he tried to make light of his situation for our sake."

SHŌKO HIRATA: "Second Lieutenant Miyazaki asked us what we would do if the enemy invaded. When we all answered that we will try to kill at least one enemy each before we die, the lieutenant said, 'Don't be in such a hurry to die,' and told us stories about brave samurai wives in days of old."

YOKO MORI: "He told us to always have pride as Japanese women, and to let him worry about taking care of the enemy."

SHŌKO MAEDA: "Just before he left he gave us all of his personal belongings. I was given his fountain pen, and I promised to write to his sister and tell her about her brother's sortie. There were four send-offs today—so many we ran out of cherry boughs to give to the pilots. We stripped the trees at Chiran Shrine bare."

YONEKO SADA: "The air base people told us to climb up on the airplanes and put cherry boughs into the cockpits, but I didn't feel it was right to step up on the airplanes and defile these hallowed weapons with a woman's touch, so I declined the honor."*

FUKUKO IWAWAKI: "Watching the airplanes take off I couldn't help but feel caught up in the moment, and I was sure that the gods were with the

---

*This, apparently, is Miss Sada's own interpretation of the old Shinto taboo against female physical contact with hallowed ground or sacred weaponry. The most well known surviving legacy in modern-day Japan of this nearly extinct belief is the taboo against female contact with any of the apparatus involved in sumo wrestling, including setting foot in the ring. This causes protocol problems every year at the trophy presentation ceremony after the Osaka tourney, as the current governor of the prefecture is a woman. Despite initial protest not only on her part but also from women's rights groups and other liberals around the country, the governor caved to the forces of tradition just before her moment of truth, and has delegated the ceremonial duties to a male subordinate ever since.

pilots in the cockpits, holding on to the control sticks, lifting the planes into the air. The other girls said they had the same feeling watching the take-offs. One of the pilots told us that he would only stop being nervous once he heard the booming of the enemy's antiaircraft fire. We said to him that if the enemy was bound to come anyway, then he might as well take us along with him in the plane on his sortie. But he told us to stay alive, no matter what happens, because we have to become the Japanese mothers of the future—we have to pro-tect the country, too, in our own way."

YASU IWAWAKI: "I'll never forget how we used to all sing nursery rhymes like "The Old Woodcutter" together. It was so much fun. No one ever talked about death. I remember one of the pilots—whose mother was dead—looked so happy and proud on the day of his sortie when he said, 'I'm going to bring an enemy aircraft carrier with me to heaven as a souvenir for my mother.'"

SHŌKO MAEDA: "Before their sorties, Corporal Fuke wrote, 'Heaven can wait, I'm off to do some demon-killing,' and Corporal Iwama wrote, 'All that lives is born to die, and cherry blossoms will always blow away in the wind, every last one.' I gave them a picture of my cousin, who was killed in the Third Battle of the Solomons, and told them to take it with them into battle. They promised to do so, and told me not to worry, because they would be sure to get some enemy for my dear cousin, too." (*Kagoshima Nippō* [Kagoshima Daily], April 19, 1945.)

Obviously, the media treatment of the Nadeshiko Unit story com-pletely negated the girls' original orders not to tell their families about the nature of their work at the air base. With the big splash in the pa-pers, the cat was out of the bag. Many of the girls' now clued-in mothers were furious that the authorities had been callous enough to put their daughters through the emotional clothes wringer of such duty and to expose them to the constant danger posed by American raids on the airfield. But even these furious mothers were wise enough to vent their anger quietly or in the privacy of their own homes, and none of them were bold, headstrong, or concerned enough to request that their daughters be withdrawn from the Nadeshiko Unit.

As proprietress of the sole army-certified restaurant in town, Tome Torihama had known all along what the girls were doing at the base. For one thing, her daughter Reiko—who was the same inveterate chatterbox at fourteen that she is at seventy-two—ignored the army's gag order and told her mother everything the first night she came home from a workday of barracks duties. Tome was also able to glean a lot of information by piecing together overheard snippets of conversation from her uniformed customers, and knew that Chiran's mothers had every right to be concerned about their daughters' emotional and physical safety.

Tome worried, too. Every evening at dusk, she would stand by the window of the Tomiya Shokudō and listen for the truck that brought the Nadeshiko Unit members back to their homes after work (they had to wait until cover of nightfall to avoid getting strafed). Grimy and exhausted after yet another day at the base, the girls would sit in back of the flatbed and sing patriotic songs at the top of their lungs (but never, ever "Umi Yukaba"). Only when Tome heard the girls' singing and the sound of the army truck changing gears as it came up the main street could she feel safe about her daughter again—at least for the night—before the whole process started again the following morning.

During early and mid-April 1945, there were two interrelated developments in the Okinawa campaign raging five hundred kilometers south of Chiran that would conspire to end the Nadeshiko Unit's air base duties far earlier than the girls had originally expected. One of these factors was the very effectiveness of the *tokkō* sorties themselves. As losses in personnel and material mounted daily, American command put the highest priority on trying to knock out as much capacity at the mainland *tokkō* bases as possible before the Japanese planes could take to the air. Obviously, Chiran was high on the target list.

The second development was the Americans' rapid capture of Yontan and Kadena airfields on Okinawa. When USAAF B-25 Mitchell, P-51 Mustang, and P-38 Lightning squadrons were flown in from the Philippines to begin operating from these bases, it meant that TF 58's Hellcats and Corsairs could concentrate on fleet CAP for inbound *tokkō* interception and on tactical air support for the soldiers and marines on the ground, relegating more of their secondarily important mission load of interdiction and harassment raids on Kyūshū *tokkō* bases to the army tactical air units, who were more than up to the task. Superbly trained and experienced in ground attack from the long Philippine campaign, eager for payback against the "Jap suiciders" mauling fellow American servicemen at Okinawa, and plenty fired up at having the long-dreamed-of opportunity to strafe and bomb the Japanese "where they lived," they took to their new combat role with gusto.

During one mid-April raid on Chiran, a considerable number of bombs were dropped on the airfield. After the attack—with the drone of the American engines and choking, cordite-stinking smoke still lingering in the air—a vehicle was heard screeching to a stop at the bottom of the *sangakuheisha* compound knoll. There were shouted orders for two girl volunteers, and before they knew what was happening, Shōko and Reiko were being led to a staff car with a big hole ripped through the windshield and roof. A visibly shaken officer—who turned out to be none other than the base commander himself, Major Musashi Hashiguchi—grumbled for the girls to get in.

The car pulled to a stop at the southern end of the airfield. The girls were ordered out of the car and given five minutes to count the number of bomb craters on the runway. Of course, it was impossible for the girls to cover nearly fifteen hundred meters in only five minutes—especially trying to negotiate rubble-strewn ground in wooden geta—but they gave it their best shot, and counted as best they could, ever mindful of the staff car *putt-putt*ing at a crawl behind them. The faint sound of American engines flying away was another matter of concern, as it was always possible that the planes would suddenly double back to give the airfield one more good drilling in the hopes of catching personnel and vehicles out in the open. It was a trick the Americans had used before.

Breathless from smoke, nerves, and fatigue, the girls finally reached the north end of the runway. Shōko had spotted eighteen craters, while

Reiko reported seeing only seventeen. The officer was angry about the discrepancy in the count and threatened the girls with making them go back and do it again. Luckily, he did not back up this threat, but neither was he finished with the girls quite yet. Before rolling up his window and telling the driver to move on, he ordered them to go back to the compound and organize a work detail to start repairing the runway damage. The Nadeshiko Unit spent the rest of the day with shovels in their hands filling in bomb craters.

On April 18, Reiko, Shōko, and the other girls were hanging freshly washed socks and *fundoshi* on the clotheslines at the *sangakuheisha* compound. There had been no flight line send-off on this day, so spirits were more chipper than usual, and the girls chatted and laughed with each other and a few of the barracks residents as they worked. The sun was bright, the sky blue, and the birds were singing in the pine boughs. Vigilance was the last thing on anyone's mind, but even on the off chance that there was an air raid this morning, the sirens would give everyone plenty of warning. They always had in the past. Besides that, the *sangakuheisha* were well camouflaged, and the compound was apparently invisible from the air—even with clotheslines full of off-white underwear flapping in the breeze—as it had yet to be hit by the Americans.

Suddenly, the barracks compound's midmorning rhapsody was rent asunder by the distinctive roar of American engines overhead and crisscrossing chains of machine-gun bullets stitching the pine-needle forest floor. There were hoarse masculine shouts for everyone to take cover, barely audible over the din of aircraft, weapons fire, and shrill female screaming. The girls tripped and fell down in their ungainly wooden sandals as they scrambled to jump into sunken barracks entranceways and slit trenches with the pilots and other army personnel.

While everyone around her ran for cover, the ever-introspective Shōko watched in a stunned daze as an evil-looking, twin-boomed, shiny aluminum-skinned plane banked high over the treetops before leveling out and heading straight for her. Immobilized by deer-in-headlights paralysis, she seemed to watch from somewhere outside of her body as parallel trails of dirt puffs drilled the ground and raced toward her. Something—a friend's scream, perhaps—snapped her out of it and she jumped out of the way at the last second as the bullets cracked the air around her and the plane buzzed over with an angry snarl.

Now huddling in a slit trench with some of the other girls, Shōko was being alternately hugged and berated by her shelter mates when the sight of the sparkling white collars on her friends' middy blouses snapped her back to reality for the first time in twenty or thirty very long seconds.

"Our collars!" she shouted out. "They can see our collars! Tuck them in!"

The girls hurriedly did as Shōko said while trying to stay as small and low as possible. Whether or not the color of their uniforms was a factor in their being spotted from the air can never be known with certainty, but it seems probable that another general lapse in vigilance had some part in their predicament. As the girls huddled together in their trench, someone pointed out the dried-out leaves and branches on the roofs of the *sangakuheisha*. The girls had forgotten to change the camouflage covering on the barracks, and the foliage had dried out quicker than anyone had expected it to in the fine weather they had been enjoying of late. Instead of masking the compound, the bright yellow, desiccated foliage—contrasted against the deep green of the rest of the forest—must have been as conspicuous as a pattern of landing lights at night.

As the girls rued their camouflage carelessness, the twin-engine planes continued to rake the compound with machine-gun fire while others started dropping bombs on the air base runway. The Americans seemed neither anxious to leave anytime soon, nor particularly perturbed by the paltry AA fire from the base. And as usual, there was no Japanese opposition in the air to try to stop them.

"The Americans flew so low you could see their pink faces and blue eyes and those big, square, white-framed goggles they wore," Reiko recalls. "We hated to admit it, but we admired their cockiness, flying in so low like that. I'm still not sure if they were either very brave or just thought so little of us that there was nothing to be afraid of."

Apparently, Japanese masculinity did not share the same objective admiration for this impudent display of American cheek. One of the support troops ran out from a trench spitting mad, cursing and trying to throw rocks at the planes before a comrade scrambled out to pull him back. A spray of machine gun fire for good measure riddled the spot they had been standing in an eyeblink before.

This was not the first time the girls had been strafed; nor would it be the last. It was, however, the last time they would undergo the experience at Chiran air base. In fact, it was also the last time they would set foot on the base for the rest of the war. Major Hashiguchi was forced to admit that the morning's air raid—and with a barracks full of media people witnessing the whole thing, at that—had been too close for comfort. While the imagery of stalwart little *Yamato nadeshiko* serving tea and giving flowers to brave *tokkō* pilots was about as good as it got in terms of propaganda material, the country did not need to hear about fourteen-year-old girls dodging bullets on a Japanese military installation with no Japanese planes in the air trying to protect them, and it certainly did not need to hear about one of these girls stopping some of those bullets. It was not beyond the pale of imagination that one of the sappy hacks in the media barracks would write up something embarrassing in the event of a Nadeshiko Unit casualty that would somehow slip through the censorship cracks and make the papers. This was not going to happen on Major Hashiguchi's watch.

The historical record is not clear on the role of parental pressure in this matter, but the very next day, Major Hashiguchi made a rare personal appearance at the Nadeshiko Unit's morning formation. He personally thanked the girls for their services to date, then in the next breath told them that they did not have to bother coming anymore. For the next two months, until a combat nurse training program was started up for local girls in the neighboring town of Kawanabe, the Nadeshiko Unit was collectively unemployed.

But Chiran's involvement with the *tokkō* activities on base did not end there. The local Defense Women's Association, endeavoring to pick up the slack left by the cancellation of the Nadeshiko Unit work program, was eager to show the authorities that the town was still willing to help with the war effort. While most of the league's members were housewives, and thus too busy caring for their own families to wait hand and foot on the residents of the *sangakuheisha* compound, they were genuinely eager to help out in other areas. Tome Torihama was instrumental in guiding their efforts, and personally organized official send-off detachments and unofficial support facilities for *tokkō* family members visiting Chiran.

No one who knew Tome could have been very surprised that she rose to the forefront in such activities. Concern for the well-being of others came naturally to her. These qualities were in her blood, and selfless service was the dominant theme of every facet of her life, both profes-sional and personal. The Chiran air base authorities had chosen wisely in deciding to designate the Tomiya Shokudō as the only army-approved rest-and-relaxation center in town, and Tome made good use of her establishment's exemption as such from food and alcohol rationing to make sure there was always plenty on hand for the boys to eat and drink. When the cupboard began to run low and regular supply lines petered out, she would scour the countryside for every morsel or drop of sake or *shōchu* potato liquor she could get.[8] After all, she often re-marked, how could you skimp on a meal for a young man that might be his last?

From the earliest days of Chiran's special attack sorties until her death at the age of ninety in 1992, Tome was known by the pilots them-selves, townspeople, veterans, journalists, and eventually even national statesmen as *tokkō no haha* or "mother of the *tokkō* boys" for the love and care she gave to the lonely, homesick pilots. Tome became a legend in her own lifetime, and has been afforded something close to saint-hood now that she is gone. In the last years of her life, the author, right-wing pundit, and current Tokyo governor Shintarō Ishihara famously remarked that Tome was "the closest person to a living Buddha I have ever met."[9]

The anecdote on which the film *Hotaru* ("Firefly") is loosely based is probably the most famous legend involving Tome and the Tomiya Shokudō. Reiko-san, now the only surviving witness to the episode, in-sists that it is true. The story concerns an enlisted pilot named Saburō Miyakawa of the 104th Shinbu Unit who was in Chiran awaiting *tokkō* sortie orders as the Okinawan campaign was winding to a close. During his inclement weather–extended stay in Chiran, Miyakawa formed an especially close bond with Tome and her daughters, and his patronage of their establishment was frequent and enthusiastic. But as is the fate of all good things, the relationship had to come to an end—clearing skies and sortie orders for the morning of June 6 brought the curtain down on the sergeant's rustic idyll with his surrogate family away from home.

On the evening of June 5, Miyakawa visited the Tomiya Shokudō for what would be—literally and figuratively—his last supper. The day also happened to be his twentieth birthday. After his meal, Miyakawa took a short stroll with Tome, her daughters, and a squadmate named Takimoto by the river that ran past the inn. The night was starless, and blackout regulations had the entire town under an inky pall. The only light visible was from a small swarm of fireflies meandering in the cool air over the riverbank. Somebody remarked at how pretty they were. After a short silence, Miyakawa cleared his throat.

"*Obachan*," he started, using the diminutive, familiar term a young man uses when addressing an older woman for whom he feels something akin to a son's affection toward a mother. "I don't want to leave with any regrets, but I have to say this. After I'm dead, I really want to come back and see you again. . . . Is that okay?"

"Of course," Tome answered. "Come back anytime you want."

Just then, one of the fireflies broke from the swarm and flew over to hover over Miyakawa's head.

"That's it," the sergeant said. "That's me. I'm going to come back as that firefly tomorrow night. . . . Two of us will come back. Right, Takimoto?"

"Uhh . . . right," Takimoto answered.

"And don't let anyone chase those fireflies off," Miyakawa continued. "Because it will be us. Promise you'll sing 'Dōki no Sakura' for us."

"We will," Tome said.

"It's nine o'clock now," Miyakawa said, looking at his glowing watch dial. "We'll be back here this time tomorrow night. Make sure to leave the front door open for us."

The weather the next day was cloudy in the morning, turning to light rain by evening. Around seven that night, there was a knock on the front door of the blacked-out Tomiya Shokudō. The door slid open. It was a long-faced, soaking-wet Takimoto. He had been forced to turn back with engine trouble on the way to Okinawa. Sergeant Miyakawa's engine, however, had apparently functioned perfectly, as had every other engine in the 104th Shinbu Unit's planes. Takimoto was now orphaned, waiting for assignment to another unit, and trying to convince himself that people at the *sangakuheisha* were not looking at him askance. He was visibly miserable with his situation.

For the next few hours, Tome, Reiko, and Takimoto sat in the blacked-out restaurant listening to the radio and drinking tea. When the nine-o'clock news broadcast started, Reiko remembered Miyakawa's promise to return. No sooner had she opened the door only a few centimeters than a big firefly came buzzing into the room, almost as if it had been waiting outside to be let in. It made a few circuits of the room, lighting up the darkened space with urgent phosphorescent flashes before stopping on a crossbeam in the middle of the ceiling, where it began a steady rhythm of flashing.

The humans in the room stared at the insect in disbelief for a few moments before Tome blurted what everyone else was already thinking.

"It's Sabu-chan!"*

"Let's sing," Takimoto said, slowly rising to his feet.

The threesome stood together and began singing "Dōki no Sakura." It was not long before they were all holding one another by the shoulders as big, hot tears rolled down their cheeks. When the song was finished, the firefly flashed once more, then flew back out the open door and into the night. It never returned.[10]

Sergeant Takimoto was not the only *tokkō* pilot to sortie from Chiran who had to turn around and limp back to base with engine trouble. Through May and June, as the Okinawa campaign reached its crescendo, the number of planes sent forth from Kyūshū in subsequent Kikusui waves increased exponentially. So, too, did the number of *tokkō* pilots aborting missions due to reported mechanical problems; engine trouble, faulty instrumentation, and landing gear failing to retract were the most common complaints. Usually, inspection of the aircraft in question confirmed the malfunctions to be genuine, but instances of "imagined" problems or even pilot-induced vandalism/sabotage were also increasing. For Chiran air base HQ and the local Kempeitai detachment, this was a very disturbing trend that would have to be dealt with before it spread through the ranks and—perhaps even more distressingly—had adverse effects on the careers of certain professional military officers when and if rumors began to go around that there was a potential cowards' mutiny simmering in southern Kagoshima.

To the credit of the *tokkō* corps (though a tragic credit that is), this trickle of passive resistance to self-immolation orders never became a flood. But even a trickle of poor discipline or nonconformity was beyond

---

*A diminutive familiar abbreviation of Miyakawa's first name, Saburō.

the level of acceptability for the Imperial Japanese Army. Pilots suspected of any untoward motivation behind their decisions to turn back to base during sorties were duly made examples of by the Chiran administration. Beatings, public humiliation, and ostracism were the usual penalties for most first-time offenders, who were nonetheless given another chance to redeem themselves through subsequent sortie reassignment. For pilots considered the most hopeless and pathetic cases, however, waited the most dreaded punishment of all—orders for a solo, unescorted *tokkō* flight. A pilot given such an order was being doomed to almost certain interception by American CAP before ever getting anywhere near a target. Flying without escort, his lonely, meaningless death would go unwitnessed, uncredited, and unrecorded. It would mean nothing less than a consignment to oblivion not only in body but in soul and honor as well.

The Chiran Sojourn of Second Lieutenant Wataru Kawasaki of the 51st Shinbu is exemplary of what could happen when a *tokkō* pilot began to have doubts about his mission. On the morning of May 2, the nine Hayabusas of the 51st Shinbu Unit left Akeno air base in Mie Prefecture bound for Chiran, where they were scheduled to do a one-night layover before their sortie for Okinawa at dawn the next day.[11] Led by their commander, Second Lieutenant Haruo Araki (IMA '44), the formation was flying in the vicinity of Bofu in Yamaguchi Prefecture when Araki's plane suffered total engine failure and was forced to ditch in the Inland Sea. The rest of the 51st flew on to Chiran, where air ops decided that it would be best to wait for their commander to arrive in a new plane so that the unit could sortie together. However, it took considerably longer for Araki to get a replacement aircraft than anyone at first expected. Hours of waiting soon turned to days, and days soon began pushing a week.

During their virtually unprecedented eight-day layover at Chiran, the pilots of the 51st became regulars at the Tomiya Shokudō. One famous anecdote with its origins in this patronage is the story of Second Lieutenant Fumihiro Mitsuyama, who on the night of May 10 revealed to the astonishment of the Torihamas and his squadmates alike that his real name was Tak Kyong Hyong, and that he was an ethnic Korean.[12] He then proceeded to emphasize his point by regaling his gape-mouthed audience with an impromptu solo recital of Korean folk songs. This is yet another Tomiya Shokudō vignette that has entered the pantheon of modern-day Japanese legend by being worked into the semifictional plot-line of *Hotaru*.

For Wataru Kawasaki, the most crucial development during this Chi-ran interlude was considerably more personal. At age thirty, the recently married Kawasaki was not only the granddaddy of the 51st Shinbu, he was in fact one of the oldest pilots ever assigned to *tokkō*. A teaching professional with nearly eight years of classroom experience after gradu-ating from Nihon University's teachers college, he had an outlook on life that was considerably different from that of his high-teen and low-twenty-something fellow pilots, and worlds apart from his IMA grad unit com-mander. It had been obvious from the earliest days after the formation of the 51st that he was its least gung-ho member.

What finally—and fatally—cemented his mutually recognized status as the black sheep of the unit was the unannounced appearance of his wife, Tsuneko, at the Tomiya Shokudō on the afternoon of May 8.[13] With Tome's thoughtful assistance, Tsuneko Kawasaki was able to find lodging at a local inn, where she made an open-ended booking for a room, intending to stay until her husband's sortie. However, she may have been just as surprised as Lieutenant Kawasaki's squadmates were when her husband exercised his choice of billets privileges as a com-missioned officer and opted to spend his nights at the inn with his wife instead of at the *sangakuheisha* compound with his comrades. The sleeping arrangements raised eyebrows both inside and outside of the base gates.

After three nights of what must have been a surreal emotional mélange of newlywed bliss and wrenching grief, the couple's moment of truth ar-rived in the wee hours of May 11, when the pilots of the 51st headed to-ward the flight line through a gauntlet of Chiran ground staff, pilots' family members, a white-aproned official send-off detachment from the Defense Women's Association headed by Tome Torihama, and, most conspicuously, a loudly weeping Tsuneko Kawasaki.[14] The subsequent send-off was one of the most cathartic anyone at the base could remem-ber witnessing, climaxing with Mrs. Kawasaki's fainting on the flight line as her husband's plane took off. Tome caught her before she could hit the ground, and escorted her back to town.

In no emotional state to endure a grueling day of train rides and interminable waiting, Mrs. Kawasaki decided to stay one more day to compose herself and gather the strength she would need for her return journey. As things turned out, she could have gone ahead and booked the room for the rest of the month, because that was how long she would end up staying in it. Her husband showed up at her room that evening with a hangdog look, mumbling something about engine trouble. The scene would be repeated twice more before the lieutenant—apparently no longer able to bear the stress of the abuse he was suffering at the base every day, his own family's rejection of his new bride, and, perhaps most critically, the shame of being unable to face death on a *tokkō* mission—crashed his Hayabusa into a railroad embankment a stone's throw from his family's Kagoshima home during a "test flight" his superiors at the base had insisted he make before being sent out on his unprecedented fourth sortie attempt.

Although Wataru Kawasaki's case was notorious, it was not isolated. Army Ministry memoranda at the time pointed out the dangers of demoralization and loss of willingness to die posed by the ready availability of worldly pleasures for *tokkō* pilots in the final days before their sorties.[15] And as instances of aborted *tokkō* sorties from the local air base due to purported aircraft malfunctions increased, so did the tenacity and frequency of insidious rumors beginning to make the rounds in Chiran claiming to explain this rash of *tokkō* aircraft "malfunctions" as a matter of youthful indiscretions and overactive hormones. The head of the local Kempeitai detachment shared these suspicions, and was eager to find out whether or not a sudden reaffirmation of the physical joys of living on the part of some of the *tokkō* boys might be responsible for all these "engine failures" and "landing gear troubles" that planes out of Chiran were having of late. He was well abreast of reports of rampant and improper fraternization—singing, game playing and the like—between the pilots and the Nadeshiko Unit when the girls were helping around the *sangakuheisha*. And, of course, he was fully aware of the constant stream of *tokkō* pilots back and forth from Tomiya Shokudō every night, and that the owner's daughter, Reiko Torihama, had been one of the Nadeshiko Unit volunteers. In fact, she and another girl had been harrassed by the Kempeitai before over suspicions of excessive fraternization with the *tokkō* pilots.[16] Who knew what was going on at the Tomiya Shokudō, other than pilots being fed past nine P.M. in violation of army regulations?

Harassing teenage schoolgirls was bad enough, but when the Kempeitai arrested Tome Torihama to get to the bottom of things once and for all, they crossed a line they should not have; busting Tome in 1945 Chiran was about as appreciated an act as mugging Rosa Parks in 1994 Detroit. When Reiko ran back to the Tomiya Shokudō and threw open the front door to announce to a roomful of *tokkō* pilots what had happened to her mother, the young fliers immediately formed a posse and swaggered down to the Kempeitai HQ. Tome was successfully rescued, but not before suffering a few haymakers to the jaw at the hands of her secret police tormentors and getting her face stomped into the floor by their knee-high riding boots. The scars on her head were a lifelong reminder of that night's ordeal, but they were also a source of great personal pride. In her twilight years, she referred to them as her "badge of honor."[17]

Tome's beating at the hands of the military police was a bad beginning for a summer that only got worse as a slew of pestilence and privations was visited upon the town. The fall of Okinawa in late June eliminated the relevance of *tokkō* sorties from Chiran, with the last being flown on July 19.[18] Even so, the air raids did not let up, and periodic drops of American propaganda leaflets started rumors that an invasion was scheduled for the area. Reiko-san still has one of the pamphlets, which was dropped in early August over the nursing school in Kawanabe that she was attending with most of the other Nadeshiko Unit girls. Bearing the enigmatic slogan "An Emotionally Moving Handshake" (*kandō suru akushu*), it shows an American soldier and a Russian counterpart as looming, grinning colossi, shaking hands from opposite sides of the globe directly over an insignificantly small Japan.* On the back of the sheet is a verbose but rather amateurishly written surrender plea and a promise of fair treatment after the occupation. An explosively ominous coda to the innocuous pamphlets was added a few days later, when a daylight raid by about thirty B-29s destroyed houses and killed residents on the outskirts of Chiran on August 12.[19] Yet again, the air base failed to put up a single interceptor to try to stop the Americans.

---

*The symbolism seems to hint at the intriguing possibility that at this stage of the war—mid-August 1945—the Americans were psychologically preparing the Japanese people for the joint Soviet-American occupation scenario.

*How confident these Americans are,* Reiko-san recalls thinking at the time. *The fighting is not even over but they are already making plans for what to do after they win. . . .* While she had to admit that the Americans probably had every reason to be confident, she could neither come to terms with the notion that Japan was going to lose nor give up on the desperate hope that Japan would somehow win in the end. She continued to believe that a miracle would save the day. Reiko and her classmates had been taught since toddler age to believe in the invincibility of Japan, and the myth died hard.

"Our teachers told us that the *kami-kaze* would blow, just like in olden times," Fusako Mori says. "It would flip over the enemies' ships and sweep them away."

By mid-August,* living in Chiran without losing one's sanity required the patience of Job. Concurrent with the invasion panic gripping its residents, an epidemic of dysentery hit the town during rainy season in late June and early July, then lingered throughout the rest of the summer. Originating on the base, the sickness soon laid low so many army personnel that the base infirmary could not handle the volume of patients anymore and its doctors had to requisition floor space at the local elementary school to use as a makeshift hospital ward. The situation was exacerbated by the army doctors' refusal to diagnose the disease as dysentery—perhaps out of shame that it had originated on their watch at the base—instead insisting on calling it "intestinal catarrh."[20] Less-than-vigorous hygiene standards spread contamination through soiled blankets and the hands of local volunteer nurses hand-spooning gruel and water to the afflicted. As the rainy season in Chiran is also rice-planting time, the traditional use of untreated human waste as paddy fertilizer no doubt accelerated the spread of the disease amongst the townspeople.

At noon on August 15, when the voluntary nurse corps trainees at Kawanabe were formed up into platoons in front of the administration office to listen to "a special radio broadcast by the emperor," many of the girls were either in the early or recovering stages of the disease and could barely stand. But sick or not, they realized that what they were about to hear was of the greatest importance. Most of the girls—as

---

*Residents of the area—and most of the Japanese population—still had no knowledge of the atomic bombings by this time, and would not until several years after the war.

well as most of the other millions of Japanese formed up in front of radios around the empire at this very moment—expected to hear exhortations from His Majesty to fight on to the end.

At the strike of twelve, a radio was placed in the window of the administration office and turned up to full volume while the girls stood at as rigid a position of attention as they could manage. The emperor's high, warbling voice was barely audible through the terrible static of the broadcast, and the ancient formal court Japanese he used made the message even more cryptic. Somehow, though, almost by a chain-reaction osmosis of whispers and exchanged glances, the gist of the message spread through the formation. As the reality of what they were hearing sank in, another chain reaction swept through the company and the girls began crying. Some did so with dignity, heads lowered and pigtails bobbing as they quietly wept and wiped their eyes, but other girls fell prostrate on the ground, sobbing loudly and pounding the dust with their fists.

After the long spell of wailing in the dust subsided to sniffles, the girls were marched back to their barracks by the widely despised Miss Ueno, their teacher and chaperone from Chiran Girls' High School during the nurse training course. Before being dismissed, the girls were told to prepare their luggage for their return home. They were still sniffling and packing their bags by their bunk beds a few minutes later when Miss Ueno poked her head in the doorway.

"Listen carefully," she said in her characteristic crowlike squawk. "I want you to go home in pairs, and stay off the main roads, because the Americans might be landing paratroopers at Chiran Airfield any minute now. If you meet any Americans on your way home, make sure you kill yourselves by biting your tongues off before the soldiers have a chance to rape and murder you."

As Miss Ueno slammed the door and stomped off to go about her business, the barracks went berserk. What had been quiet sniffling a moment before was now hysterical, loud screaming. Many of the girls hugged each other, shivering in fear. Others, like Reiko, began pounding and kicking the walls and bunks, lashing out at anything but each other in their panic and rage. Some windowpanes were broken in the pandemonium.

When they had gathered enough wits among themselves to halfway function again, Reiko and other friends from Chiran began their long walk home, using old farmers' footpaths through the mountains in order to avoid the main roads. The girls arrived to find the town's residents making panicked preparations to follow their primordial peasant instincts and literally head for the hills.

Reiko's family was no different, and with a couple of other neighbors, they loaded up a pushcart with provisions and blankets and went up into the mountains bordering the northeast edge of town to hide out in a farmer's shed. The party of twenty or so townspeople spent interminably long days in their mountain hideaway keeping their eyes peeled on the horizon for vehicle movement from the south while the menfolk, including Reiko's father, Shigekazu, made occasional foraging forays into the ghost town by nightfall. Along with whatever meager foodstuffs they could scrounge, the men brought back with them the latest scuttlebutt from the die-hard holdouts still in Chiran proper, and each whopper was more outrageous than the next: "American paratroopers have occupied the airfield," "The mayor has committed suicide," "The emperor has committed hara-kiri." Rumor- and fearmongering ran rife without anyone having laid so much as an eye on any Americans. In fact, no one had even seen or heard any planes overhead. Eventually, terrified anticipation downgraded to bored waiting, and after a week of eating nuts and berries in the hills and scaring one another half out of their wits, the families finally decided it was safe to go home.

Despite the privations and pain of the war, there had been great disappointment and sadness for the townspeople when the surrender was broadcast. If anyone had experienced a sense of relief over the news, any expression of this emotion was either withheld out of respect for the recent dead or lost in the immediate post broadcast pandemonium. As the bad drunk of the days after August 15 subsided into the hangover of a defeated morning-after Japan, the residents of Chiran came down off the mountains.

With some semblance of a community functioning in town again, new waves of rumors started making the rounds. The more pessimistic told of coming famine and pestilence, or even genocidal fogs of poison gas dropped from the skies. Not everyone bought into this doom-and-gloom, but few doubted that at the very least the townspeople would have to endure witch hunts at the hands of Americans occupiers looking for wartime authority figures and, most likely, civilian collaborators with the *tokkō* program. Of course, if this last concern turned out to be legiti-mate, then nobody had more reason than the Torihama family to fear retribution from Yanks bent on revenge. Reiko and others became con-vinced that Tome would be executed for all she had done for the boy pilots from the air base during the war. There were some sincere and thought-ful suggestions by friends and neighbors that Tome make a run for it and come back when everything had blown over, but she ignored them, de-termined to hold her ground and take whatever she had coming. In the meantime, she planned to do whatever she could to get back some kind of a life, and she suggested that everyone else get about doing the same.

# twenty-two

## A PEACEFUL VILLAGE

As showstopping an entrance as it would have been, the Americans never got around to parachuting into Chiran. Rumors about what was in store for the town, however, continued unabated for months. These reached a peak in late November when prefectural authorities advised the township that a special unit of American marines—veterans of Saipan and Okinawa and probably to-the-bone Jap haters—were coming to dismantle the army air base facilities in a few weeks. The people of Chiran had worshiped the *tokkō* pilots as young gods, and extended every possible courtesy and cooperation to their efforts and those of the army air corps authorities. Thus, the thinking went, it was entirely reasonable to expect that the Americans, having suffered considerably under the attacks, would be coming to Chiran with revenge and mayhem as second- and third-agenda items during their cleanup mission.

In the final days before the American arrival, the rumor mill went into overdrive—and the worst offenders were to be found in the town hall, from whence an official advisory was issued suggesting that all the nubile young women in the village cut their hair to look like boys and do everything short of irreparable disfigurement to make themselves as physically unattractive as possible. As many households prepared baggage for yet another evacuation, the majority of the town's young women and girls chose to follow the advisory, chopping their hair in gender-bending bobs and dirtying their clothes and faces with charcoal dust—anything to

avert the eyes (and thus, it was hoped, the lust) of the feared Americans.*
Reiko, taking measures one step further, hid in the attic of the Tomiya
Shokudō for two weeks until her mother assured her that it was safe to
return to civilization.

The town got its first look at their fearsome American occupiers on a
foggy morning in December 1945, when a squad-sized detachment of
marines and technicians commanded by First Lieutenant Michael A.
Bilandic—future half-term mayor of Chicago (1977–79)—arrived in
Chiran in a small convoy of jeeps. During their six-week stay, the marines
disproved every ugly rumor the wartime authorities had spread about
Americans, and they formed close friendships with many of the townspeople, especially with the local children. The Nadeshiko girls have fond
memories of this time, and still remember some of their favorite marines
by name. At the top of everyone's list as the town favorite was the kindly,
fatherly Sergeant Harry Parshall, who always had pockets full of chocolate and hard candies and was never averse to going along with a joke or
trying to teach the kids happy-sounding but incomprehensible nursery
rhymes in English. Another favorite was the blond, blue-eyed "Jacket-
san," who played jacks and hopscotch with the girls and cried when his
unit shipped out in January. There was only one really scary soldier in
the detachment, and that was a battle-fatigued Georgia introvert named
"Hoskins," who had the unsettling habit of firing his .45 into the air—and
on one memorable occasion, into the ceiling of the Tomiya Shokudō—
during his frequent and mean sake benders. But even he was not completely immune to the charms of the town, and was never disqualified
from the mothering care and attentions of Tome Torihama, drunk or sober.

Some of the Nadeshiko girls still have dreams about their wartime experiences, but all of them have memories, and these can broadside them
out of the blue from time to time. The other day, Shōko-san saw some
blue-eyed grass flowering in a corner of her garden, and it whisked her

---

*Both during and immediately after the war, rumors of uncontrollable American sexual avarice
terrified the Japanese populace (perhaps fueled in part by the exploits of their own China campaign veterans?). One of the odder rumors was that American males were driven to paroxysms
of lust by the sight of bare female feet, prompting a desperate op-ed plea in the September 9,
1945, issue of the *Asahi Shimbun* for the immediate distribution of socks to the nation's
women before the bulk of the Occupation troops arrived.

right back to April 1946, when she, Reiko, and some other girls from the village made an unauthorized visit to the old *sangakuheisha* and saw that the grounds were covered in the white blossoms of this wildflower. Neither she nor the other girls will ever forget that first return to the barracks compound. They saw a tree where a pilot had carved his name the morning of his final flight. Another tree still carried the stubs of branches a lieutenant pilot had chopped with his *katana* one day during some downtime, after one of the girls had asked him if the swords the officer pilots carried were real.

Reiko and others continued this annual April *sangakuheisha* ritual for years afterward, bringing flowers to put in the corner of the concrete pit that is all that remains of the barracks, sitting on the ledge singing martial songs from the war like "Dōki no Sakura" and "Gōchin, Gōchin."[1]

"The faces of all of the pilots are still clear in my memory," Reiko-san says. "I can still see them, smiling as they said good-bye to us, patting us on the shoulder and telling us not to cry.

"These stories aren't just for Japanese people," Reiko-san continues. "They belong to the world. Nothing like [*tokkō*] can ever be allowed to happen again. We saw it. We know what we're talking about. There is nothing that can possibly be gained from wars except to kill people."

The other Nadeshiko girls sitting around Shōko Nagasaki's coffee table nod vigorously and in unison. But Reiko-san is not finished saying her piece. Perhaps she will never be finished.

"It was such a waste for those boys to have to die, with their whole lives ahead of them," she says. "It's just inconceivable. What kind of men could give orders like that? If those brave boys had been allowed to live instead, just imagine how much better off Japan would be now."

On the train ride home, Reiko's hypothetical questions linger in my mind. No one will ever be able to answer them, I think, but the world—and most important, the Japanese themselves—must never stop asking them.

# PART SIX

# BRIDE DOLL

# twenty-three

# THE WORLD TURNED UPSIDE DOWN

I t is a balmy morning in March 2002, and Yasukuni's cherries are in unseasonably early full bloom. I have arrived at the shrine about twenty minutes early for today's interview, so I decide to duck into a building here I have not visited yet—a low, long, L-angled wooden structure that seems to function as a spiritual frontier post between the outside world and the elevated boardwalk leading to the holy of holies in the main shrine's inner sanctum. The interior of the hall is all nicotine-browned bare wood and big, heavy roof beams—the cafeteria lodge of an Adirondack vacation resort for chain-smokers. Along the back wall, there is the ubiquitous souvenir concession stand, where various Yasukuni-themed bean cakes, *sembei* crackers and trinkets are sold. An impromptu A/V center has been set up in the middle of the room, consisting of about five rows of folding chairs arranged before a large-screen TV. This morning, the chairs are spottily occupied by an anonymous group of older visitors watching a video of various wartime documentary clips of kamikaze crashes. A masculine narration over the grainy combat footage poses the rhetorical question of whether or not today's Japanese young people understand the meaning of the sacrifices of their forefathers.

The spiritual epicenter of this space is a section of the north wall of the room, which is covered with a bank of shoebox-sized glass cases, each containing exquisitely detailed little *hanayome ningyo* dolls in kimonos, like hundreds of ghost Barbies, or female homunculi in cryogenic freeze.

Each case also contains a playing-card-sized wooden plaque on which are written the name, rank, and date of death of a Japanese serviceman killed in battle. I stop a young female attendant in red-and-white robes and ask her about the dolls. She explains that they are supposed to be brides for the souls of heroes enshrined at Yasukuni who died as bachelors.

"This is the season when they all come back, isn't it?" I ask.

The acolyte blinks once or twice, mystified.

"The cherry trees outside," I say, pointing toward the entrance. "All of the spirits of the servicemen are back now."

"*So—desu ne* [Yes, I suppose that's right]," she replies, indulging me with the briefest of noncommittal smiles before fluttering away in a busy, whisking bustle of robe cloth.

I head back outside to enjoy the cherry trees some more. Their pink and white blossom-laden boughs form towering archways of ethereal strawberry ice cream over the main promenade and other walkways of the shrine. I walk around for a while, snapping shots of flowers, old men and white pigeons before parking myself on a bench in the main rest area.

A few minutes later, an elegant woman rounds the corner at the far end of the cherry tree–lined path bordering the red benches and ash-trays. The woman's posture is ramrod straight, and her stride is purpose-ful but feminine as she walks toward me. From here, she looks to be in her mid- to late-fifties. She is wearing rose-tinted glasses and is dressed in a camel-hair coat. An Hermès scarf about her neck is tied off with ca-sual élan.

I blink a few times in mild disbelief as the woman gets closer because I now realize that she is not some middle-aged stranger, after all. She is Shigeko Araki, my interview subject. And although from ten or twenty paces she may look like a woman in her fifties, she is in reality almost eighty.

After greetings and de rigueur comments about the cherries, we enter the Yasukuni library, where the curator, Shinsuke Daitō, greets us in the main reading room. I begin to make introductions, but soon find this is not necessary. Anyone who has anything to do with *tokkō* research in Japan knows Araki-san, and Daitō-san is no exception. Always the gentle-man, he escorts us to a quiet spot in the library offices where we can conduct our interview, then takes his leave in his usual unobtrusive manner.

Sitting across from Araki-san, I am again struck by how physically attractive she is for a woman her age. A lifetime of traditional dance study and a healthy dollop of pride have given her the lithesome grace and presence of a lioness. But then again, perhaps she is too finely sculpted and physically delicate for scorching savanna imagery to be appropriate. A better metaphor would be something avian.

The Japanese have been likening individuals to different types of animals for purposes of physical description or mental cataloging in both folklore and daily life since time immemorial. This practice may have roots in Japan's animist/shamanistic spiritual heritage, or it may simply have started out for the more practical reason of being handy in a society where almost everyone is born with black hair and brown eyes. Whatever the case, I have unconsciously picked up on the practice during my stay here, and while I watch Araki-san's mannerisms and facial expressions as we go through our opening small talk routine, my Japanicized metaphor banks kick in with bird-of-prey imagery. Instead of a lioness, I see a female peregrine falcon, sharp-angled and exquisitely feathered, poised yet a bit wary, simultaneously delicate and formidable.

There is as much of the huntress in Araki-san's attitude as there is in her appearance. She has the pride and simmering charisma that only a mature woman who has been fawned upon by men for most of her life can possess. She is good, knows it, and knows I know it, and she is not beyond using that knowledge tactically. In a situation like this, where most Japanese women—regardless of age—would be fidgety and uncomfortable talking one-on-one with a male stranger (especially a gaijin), she is calmly collected, looking me straight in the eye as she asks questions about my personal and family background, sizing me up, no doubt, for the right slot in the intricate and all-encompassing mental processing mechanism of social hierarchies and protocols that Japanese of her generation carry in their heads from cradle to grave to gauge their own and others' relative positions in the Big Picture. Whatever decision she reaches about me in the next few moments will determine where I fit in this mental catalog, and thus determine not only what she chooses to tell me today, but even how she will say it. The very vocabulary, inflections, and grammatical forms she uses when addressing me will soon tell me whether or not she thinks I am worthy of her time, and whether or not I will be welcome to contact her again. I keep this in mind because I like her and want very much for her to approve of me, so I am careful to watch my manners and try to use respectful verb endings.

Apparently, I have passed muster, as my subject gradually begins to slip colloquialisms and familiar inflections into her speech. The formal Araki-san transforms into the winsome Shigeko-san, and the voice recorder is running.


Tokyo is a bustling, vibrant metropolis of 3 million people on the morning of September 1, 1923. Modern office buildings and mammoth department stores dominate the city's business and retail districts, and the downtown skyline is slashed at abrupt angles by towering cranes and scaffolding at the construction sites of even bigger buildings on their way up. Streetcars run everywhere under a riot of telephone poles and aboveground power lines, abundant flags and banners and colorful advertising balloons. Aircraft are becoming a common sight in Tokyo skies—at least, common enough not to stop traffic or have people leaning out of windows anymore every time one flies overhead. License-built Model Ts clog the roadways at rush hour. Plans for subway lines that will soon honeycomb the earth under the city's streets are in their final stages, and land development along these proposed lines will sprout suburbs to house millions of workers for new offices and factories.

Tokyo likes to play as hard as it works, and boasts what is probably the most exciting and cosmopolitan nightlife east of Berlin. The city's better-heeled male residents seek nocturnal diversion in the carnal pleasure grottos of Yoshiwara or the astringent chic of Nihonbashi teahouses,[1] but also, increasingly, under the neon buzz of newer entertainment districts like Ginza and Asakusa, where café patrons dance the foxtrot and Charleston with bob-haired flapper waitresses to jazz music blared from Edison phonographs.[2] In Chiyoda, just a stone's throw from the Imperial Palace, gleamingly pomaded guests in tuxedos and Erté evening gowns arrive nightly by Rolls Royce and Duesenberg for swanky soirees at a new hotel recently built by Frank Lloyd Wright. In neighborhoods around the city's great universities, students in straw boaters and plus fours practice French inhales on imported cigarettes while discussing Kant and Marx and the painterly merits of Picasso's Blue Period.

Tokyo's pleasures are a reflection of the freewheeling nature of the times, an era when campaigns for labor rights and universal suffrage are blasting holes in the last ramparts of old class distinctions stratified for centuries. Media freedom fosters unprecedented public political dialogue among an urban middle-class constituency enjoying the closest thing to true representative democracy in East Asia. These social and political experiments flourish under the reign of a mostly hands-off monarch night-and-day different from Emperor Meiji, his charismatic and autocratic father.[3] His Majesty the Emperor Taishō has been virtually hidden from public view for almost his entire reign, and there are whispered rumors of poor health and congenital mental infirmity on his part, but no one pries and few really care. Moreover, the people have nothing but admiration and high hopes for the emperor's very visible son, Hirohito, the sober, bookwormish crown prince patiently waiting his turn to ascend the Chrysanthemum Throne. Very few Japanese citizens outside of Diet or imperial household circles pay much attention to—or are even aware of—the snarling pit bull of militaristic fanaticism lurking in the young prince's shadow, despising all these treasonous new freedoms and perverse Western ways, licking its chops and waiting for the opening that a changing of the political guard will provide with Taishō's death and the crown prince's succession.

From the point of view of the man in the streets, all is right with His Majesty's domain. With the exception of the military hardliners and civilian ultranationalists on the right, and of a vociferous but closely monitored socialist intellectual clique on the left, the emperor's loyal subjects seem to approve for the most part of the direction the nation is taking and they voice few complaints about its governance publicly. Japan is at peace and her economy is growing, despite a mild post–World War I recession. The trains are running on time, the employment rate is high, infant mortality is plummeting, and the standard of living of the middle-class household is improving by leaps and bounds.

While the proletariat of most other industrialized nations around the world seethe in post–World War I socialist upheaval, the Japanese urban working class and disenfranchised regional peasantry still lack the political savvy to know that they are being exploited by the very capitalist social order they have made possible with their own sweat and sacrifice. They are more intent on making their own lives a little more comfortable than on challenging the system itself, and there is little trouble from them.

And to help make sure it stays this way, for the last four years the Home Ministry has been carrying out a very successful populist social education campaign to imbue in the working classes the notion that tireless, uncomplaining toil, selfless sacrifice, and the homespun wisdom of "knowing one's place" are innate and sterling attributes of the Japanese race. Meshing beautifully with a recent groundswell nativist agrarian movement in Japanese literature, philosophy, and social sciences that will help form a crystallization point for populist fascism over the next decade, the notion that the framework for the nation's social harmony and economic strength was etched into the Japanese racial memory in some misty, distant rice-paddy Camelot past appeals across the entire social spectrum of a citizenry whose collective identity as a unified nation is still barely two generations old.*

There is no precedent for popular revolution in the Japanese political experience, and despite the occasional headline-grabbing misbehavior of left-wing "activists" of late, few Japanese in 1923 pay serious attention to these highbrow troublemakers and consider the possibility of any bona-fide social upheaval remote. There is no reason for anyone to think that Japan's political institutions, like the capital's awe-inspiring edifices, are anything but rock-steady and secure.

As 11:57 A.M. becomes 11:58 A.M. on September 1, 1923, Aki Kaneko—the woman who will become Shigeko's mother nine weeks from now—is sweating in the lingering Tokyo summer blast-furnace heat, lugging a baby-heavy tummy around as she prepares lunch for her family. Like a million other housewives in a million other Tokyo homes at this moment, she is boiling rice over an open flame in the woodburning *kamado* kitchen hearth. Her daughter is helping to keep the fire fed and

---

*The Kokuchūkai (National Pillar Society)—a lay Nichiren Buddhist political organization—was one of the leading social and cultural proponents of this movement. Its membership included famed children's author, folklorist and nativist Kenji Miyazawa, and influential Nichiren Buddhist activist Chigaku Tanaka, one of the earliest proponents of *hakkō ichiu* doctrine as a justification for Japanese imperialist expansion on the Asian continent (Oguma [1996] pp. 150–151). Tanaka's teachings enjoyed a wide following among *Kōdōha* "Imperialist Way" faction army officers, and were used in part to justify a failed February 1936 coup attempt.

stoked, while her son, too young to be anything but underfoot at meal-times, is playing with pressed tin toy soldiers on the tatami in the next room.

While she cooks, Aki is having a conversation with her husband, Kiku-tarō, through the open door of his storefront workshop. The couple is discussing their unborn baby's future and wondering how they are going to support another mouth to feed on an ivory carver's income already stretched thin by the cost of maintaining a household and storefront in downtown Tokyo. Kikutarō's unmarried younger sister, Fumi, has re-cently stated her desire to adopt the baby in the event that a girl is born. The custom of *kuchiberashi* (literally "reducing the number of mouths to feed") is a perfectly acceptable instrument of family fiscal policy among Japanese commoners since time immemorial, and the sharing or parcel-ing out of offspring to childless siblings—even in-laws*—has been prac-ticed among all classes of Japanese society for just as long. There will be no shame at all involved on the family's part in acceding to Fumi's wishes, and moreover, the move makes sound economic sense. Fumi—in her early thirties—is famous, beautiful, and wealthy, and she will be able to pro-vide a comfortable life for the child.

Kikutarō is trying to explain the merits of this family-planning option to his wife when the Pacific and Eurasian continental plates collide with 8.0 Richter force somewhere under the Kanto region of Central Japan.

The Kanekos and their children come to their senses dazed but mirac-ulously alive as the dust is still settling. Extricating themselves from the heap of smashed timbers and roof tiles that was their home a moment before, they emerge into a dun gray wasteland of wreckage that stretches to the horizon in all directions. Plumes of fire spew from shattered gas pipes. Sparks leap from tangled snakes of fallen power lines hissing and popping in pools forming around broken water mains. Flames are al-ready beginning to lick at the piles of rubble, and they will soon merge to form sweeping tides of ten-, twenty-, thirty-meter-high walls of fire that fan across the ruins of the metropolis, devouring everything in their path in the most destructive urban conflagration the world will see until the man-made firestorms of World War II.

---

*Toshio Yoshitake's adoption is described in Part Two.

Nearly doubled over from the pain in her womb, Aki helps her husband and children gather up whatever can be salvaged from the wreckage of their home. There isn't much time. The fires are closing in. Carrying what they can on their backs, the Kanekos head southeast in the general direction of the family homestead in Hamachō, Nihonbashi, slowly picking their way over and around kilometer after kilometer of smoldering ruins and bodies. Kikutarō leads the way going on dead reckoning alone, because the very streets themselves have been obliterated, buried under structural wreckage and blackened lumps of organic matter only occasionally recognizable as having once been human. As the little family pokes its way across a twisted landscape out of Hieronymus Bosch's worst nightmare, the superstitious Aki instinctively pulls her kimono tighter to shield her fetus from the horrors she cannot avoid looking at herself.

Navigating the detritus of the devastated city is as physically exhausting as it is emotionally taxing, and even more so after the children get too tired and have to be piggybacked. Now laden with both kit and kinder, Aki and Kikutarō are fading fast. Breaths come short and painful in the rancid, smoky air. When they reach Asakusa, roughly halfway to their final destination, they stop for a rest. One place is just as rubble-strewn and smoky as the next, so this is as good a spot as any for a rest. Maybe there will even be some water to be found.

But when they stop to put down their bags, they realize the ground is crunchy underfoot with charred human remains. When the first waves of fires swept through here an hour or so ago, there was a panicked rush of people running to jump into the Sumida River to escape the flames. Thousands upon thousands of people all tried to squeeze through the same narrow streets to get to the riverbank, and then were caught when another advancing wall of fire cut off their escape route. They suffocated or burned to death where they stood, sardine-crammed between rows of wooden houses that went up like matchsticks. Now municipal authorities, soldiers, and hastily organized volunteer groups of ordinary citizens with the stomach to handle the horror work at huge makeshift cremation pits throughout the area, dousing mountainous heaps of tangled corpses with kerosene and setting them alight while monks from neighborhood temples stand nearby chanting sutras.

Smoke-choking and shivering with exhaustion and dread, the Kanekos gather every bit of strength they have left and keep moving. A few hours later, their journey through hell ends with a small miracle when they finally reach Nihonbashi late in the afternoon. Somehow, through providence and the vagaries of geology and wind direction, Kikutarō's old neighborhood has escaped the worst of the seismic shock and fires, and aside from some broken window glass, smoke damage and frazzled nerves, the Hamachō homestead is safe and sound.

A few kilometers away in an emergency command post set up in the relatively safe confines of the Imperial Palace grounds, Crown Prince Hirohito is getting his first taste of real-time military leadership under pressure as he supervises the martial law that has been declared for the disaster area.[4] Reports are beginning to come in of panic-causing rumors spread by right-wing Kokuryūkai* thugs that Korean residents and socialists are lighting fires and poisoning wells. By morning, over two thousand Koreans in the city will be lynched, burned, or beaten to death by enraged vigilante mobs while soldiers and police stand by watching,[5] and police death squads will line up and shoot a number of prominent leftist political activists on the pretext of preserving the peace.[6] Fires will rage throughout the night as the city continues its descent into hell and madness, and when the flames are finally extinguished, 70 percent of the city's structures will be piles of burned rubble, and some 110,000 of its citizens will be dead or missing.

The next morning, when the young crown prince steps out of his headquarters with a team of advisers and bodyguards to inspect the smoldering embers and carnage that are all that is left of Tokyo, he

---

*The name of this eminently scary ultranationalist political and criminal organization is only occasionally correctly translated as the "Amur River Society," but is more often mistakenly and overdramatically translated as "Black Dragon Society," an error probably stemming from some semi-Japanese-literate Western journalist's misinterpretation of the kanji rendering of the name of a Manchurian river as instead being an Oriental poeticism describing an ominous mythological beast (although the metaphor, in this case, is appropriate). Formed in 1901 by Mitsuru Tōyama and Ryōhei Uchida, the virulently xenophobic Kokuryūkai had the political aim of furthering Japanese imperialistic influence in Asia with the immediate aim of putting Manchuria under Japanese rule, a goal that was effectively achieved by 1931.

knows without being told that this is the worst catastrophe the capital has experienced in all the previous 350 years of its existence. But what he cannot possibly know—cannot even imagine in his worst nightmares—is that this will not be the last time he is destined to see his city in ruins.

"Things were such a mess, my mother couldn't even register my birth at the Koishikawa Municipal Office for nearly three months," Shigeko tells me. "But then, of course, she had more pressing problems than paperwork to worry about."

Thankful for the survival of loved ones while so many other families had suffered through unimaginable grief, the matriarch of the Kaneko homestead had been able to bury her hatchet for her despised daughter-in-law when Kikutarō and his family moved into the Hamachō house. But this would prove to be only a temporary truce, and it was not long before everyone was reminded why Kikutarō and Aki had chosen not to raise their family here in the first place. Grandmother Kaneko had never approved of Aki, an older woman and Russo-Japanese War widow who came into the marriage with a grade-school-aged son.* By the time of Shigeko's birth, all the old bad blood between Kikutarō's bride and his mother had resurfaced with a vengeance and the women were at each other's throats again, making everyone in the house miserable with their incessant bickering. It was soon obvious to all that this domestic arrangement was not going to work out, and the Kanekos—minus Shigeko—couldn't get home to Koishikawa soon enough when reconstruction on their home was finished.

Shigeko's new home with Aunt Fumi and Grandmother Kaneko was right in the middle of the Nihonbashi *karyūkai* ("flowery willow world") demimonde, a Tokyo community not much changed since its golden age was celebrated in Edo era woodblock prints, song, and poetry. Part art gallery, part deer park for the romantic escapades of the capital's elite, the neighborhood was prohibitively expensive, but there was never any concern on Fumi's part about supporting a household there, and Shigeko

*This son was in his late teens and already out of the home by 1923.

never knew hunger or physical want of any sort. When Shigeko's adoption papers were signed, the chic and elegant Fumi was an established Nihonbashi star whose photograph was featured in a picture postcard set that was a popular souvenir of Tokyo. One of the most celebrated beauties in the capital, Fumi was also a respected teacher of traditional *nagauta* singing, flower arrangement, tea ceremony, and Japanese dance. She counted among her entourage of patrons and admirers only the richest and most powerful movers and shakers in Japan's political and military elites—men who were prepared to pay handsomely to indulge their exquisite tastes.

By the late 1920s, Fumi had saved enough money from her years in the *karyūkai* to reinvent herself as a well-heeled restaurateur in the district, running a classy little place on the first floor of the Hamachō homestead. With her fame and reputation secure, she was free to pick and chose her own patrons from among the numerous suitors for her attention, and Fumi never settled for less than Cordon Bleu all the way. Her major sponsor during the early and mid-1930s was Lieutenant General Chojirō Onodera, paymaster of the army and protégé of legendary right-wing kingmaker and Kokuryūkai cofounder Mitsuru Tōyama. On his prearranged visit days, General Onodera would pull up in front of the restaurant in his big black limo, three-star pennants aflutter on the hood, and post armed guards at the door while he spent a few hours inside. Sometimes, he brought distinguished guests for working lunches, during which matters of service and state were discussed—and just as often angrily shouted—over tea or sake.

Onodera's official entertainment expense account was more than adequate to float his Hamachō patronage. Although the general—a male-chauvinist control freak typical of his generation—evidently felt that this patronage also gave him the right to claim the legendary Fumi as his own, the object of his attentions never agreed to anything beyond a business arrangement. Considering her age and status, Fumi was under no obligation to submit to that kind of relationship, and moreover, it was insulting for the general to expect one. She was running a business—not living in a gilded cage as someone's personal property. Of course, she was always sure to express her gratitude for the general's magnanimous generosity, but if he wanted to draw any conclusions about their relationship beyond those parameters, he did so at his own risk.

On Onodera's off-days, there were always other big shots around the Hamachō restaurant, using the privacy afforded by Fumi's place to brainstorm and plot in secure secrecy. Many of these bigwigs took a grandfatherly shine to her precocious daughter as well, and by the time Shigeko entered elementary school, she had been bounced on the knee of a serving prime minister, another future holder of that office, the founder of the greatest paramilitary criminal organization in history, several future Class A war criminals,* and more handlebar-mustachioed army generals than she could count on two hands.

---

*This cast of characters is, respectively: Gi'ichi Tanaka (prime minister 1927–1929), Kuni'aki Koiso (prime minister 1944–1945), Mitsuru Tōyama (cofounder of the Kokuryūkai), Iwane Matsui (commander of the IJA China Expeditionary Force that committed the Nanking Massacre in December 1937), and Sadao Araki (future army minister and spiritual leader of the Kōdōha or "Imperial Way Faction," a loose association of mostly junior and field-grade officers dedicated to the elimination of party influence from Japanese politics and restoring the emperor as an absolute ruler with the army as his main organ of policy). See Humphreys (1995) for detailed analysis of prewar IJA factionalism.

# twenty-four

## THE FLOWERY WILLOW WORLD

Shigeko's was obviously not a "normal" childhood in any sense of the word, even by Hamachō standards. As a child, she was often subtly aware of housewife gossipers whispering to each other with their hands to their mouths and staring holes in her back when she walked by, but anyone who has ever met Shigeko knows that she is not the type to lose much sleep over what other people say about her. She is made of tougher stuff than most Japanese women, and has always found that laughter is the best countermeasure when faced with unpleasantness. Growing up in Nihonbashi, she learned that such psychological armor came with the territory.

"Most of my childhood memories involve laughing," Shigeko says. "I just remember laughing all the time. Everything was a big joke to me. People from the *karyūkai* are usually like that. Our philosophy is that you'll make yourself sick if you take things too seriously. Whether something is good or bad, it'll be gone tomorrow, and then it won't matter anymore. That kind of thinking is in our blood."

Shigeko even laughed off the first of the many serious body blows life would deal her over the next half century. The experience came during the long and luxuriantly lazy summer after she graduated from elementary school, on a night when she was hanging out on the block with friends. As was the custom with *shitamachi*\* Tokyo folk in those pre-air-conditioned days, many residents would find temporary escape from the heat at night by sitting outside on wooden benches they placed in front of their houses, much like the American inner city tradition of "hanging out on the stoop." Less than eager to sleep in their hotbox homes, families put off the inevitable for as long as possible, often until the wee hours of the morning. The men played mah-jongg and drank, housewives gossiped, and the children played way past their bedtime. If they were going to be losing sleep anyway, they might as well be comfortable doing so.

It was on just such a night that thirteen-year-old Shigeko Kaneko heard something that would change her worldview and her relationship with her mother and grandmother forever.

"My mother told me something about you," Shigeko's best friend whispered around a lemonade straw, lanterns on the Hamachō shopfronts reflecting a conspiratorial gleam in her eyes. "And I want to know if it's true. She said that your mother isn't really your mother, and that your real father isn't dead like you've always been told. He's really your uncle from Koishikawa."

Oh, how Shigeko and her friend laughed. They laughed and laughed for what felt like hours, and Shigeko was still chuckling to herself when she went home and asked Fumi and Grandmother Kaneko if the story was true. Oddly, unlike Shigeko and her friend, they didn't find the story funny at all, and the angry, desperate faces they made as they denied the story bothered Shigeko so much that she couldn't sleep that night. Tossing and turning in her futon, she began to make mental connections. She thought about how her uncle Kikutarō always brought her special presents, and seemed to care so much about what she doing, just drinking up any boring little story or tidbit of information she told about herself. She thought about her aunt Aki, who was virtually banished from the Hamachō house, and all the vicious, hateful things her mother and grandmother would say about her, making those same scary faces they had made denying the adoption story a few hours before. Of course, the story was ridiculous. But it was one of those things that sounds crazy

---

\*Traditional inner-city neighborhoods of tight, winding streets and low wooden houses that are centrally located but nevertheless somewhat off the beaten path from more modern commercial districts.

when you first hear it, then gets stuck in your head and starts making sense when the pieces start to fall together.

By sunrise, Shigeko knew what to do, and she quietly packed a suitcase in the early morning light.

She did not call home for days, and then only after she had been accepted as a *sumikomi** live-in apprentice at a *buyō* (Japanese traditional dance) school on the other side of Nihonbashi. Shigeko had a great time at the school, enjoying a boot-camp trainee's camaraderie with her fellow apprentices. And although she seems to recall this experience as being another case of almost constant laughter, the regimen was severe, and the sensei, a personage in the district almost as famous as Fumi, was a slave driver in a good mood and positively diabolical if vexed, freely using a supple bamboo cane on the girls' bare ankles and calves if she felt they were not up to snuff. Work was virtually nonstop from the crack of dawn until late at night, with the girls polishing stage floorboards, doing laundry, sweeping, preparing the teacher's kimonos, washing dishes, making rice, etc. The only break in the drudgery would come at meals, and more important, during the evening classes, when a few girls who happened to be in the sensei's favor at the time would be allowed to watch the paying students' lessons. Late at night, after all the chores had been squared away, it was time for the girls' formal training en masse, and the sensei would transform into the Rockette stage manager from hell, the air sizzling with shrilly shrieked criticisms, the ever-whistling bamboo switch, and the inevitable puppy yelps of pain when the girls got thwacked.

Shigeko displayed natural talent in this demanding traditional art. But she was also realistic about her situation, and realized fairly early on in the game that she was not the kind of willowy-limbed, white-porcelain-doll trophy type—a Fumi type, in other words—that snagged the big time patrons. Shigeko, like the other girls, had heard all the stories about what happened to the also-rans who tried to go it on their own, and she was well aware that without a sponsor with the wherewithal to grease the right theatrical palms and buy all the staggeringly expensive costumes

*The institution of *sumikomi* ("live-in") apprenticeship is common to all traditional Japanese artistic and craft disciplines, and involves an arrangement under which the *deshi* apprentice receives free food, board, and instruction from the sensei master in return for performing menial chores such as cooking, cleaning, preparing materials for the sensei, etc.

required for a shot at a first-class career, a dancer trying to break into the business alone was handed a one-way ticket to the hot springs resort circuit, swatting off combed-over drunks at retirement parties while loan sharks lurked in the wings waiting for her to default on her kimono payments. And woe unto the girl who did that, for the gangsters who flitted through the shadows of the capital's halls of power—and walked wide-shouldered in the narrow alleys of Nihonbashi—would not think twice about tossing her into the meat grinder of Yoshiwara, never to be seen in one piece again.

So maybe she was not going to grow up to rival Fumi after all. And she knew that she did not have the stomach to tightrope-walk over a shaky career with debt and damnation waiting for her to stumble. But there was still an alternative honorable future scenario for her if she insisted on pursuing her art—she could become a teacher. The kimonos and accoutrements required for this career would be almost as expensive as those of a headliner, so again money was an obstacle. Perhaps Fumi could help with this.

Shigeko's approaching Fumi with this idea about six months into her apprenticeship provided the opportunity for a rapprochement between the estranged stepmother and daughter. Fumi finally came around and confessed to the family background charade, and promised financial assistance for Shigeko's future in the *karyūkai* as a *buyō* teacher. Residents of the "flowery willow world" did not pay much attention to book learning, as a general rule, not really needing to be any more literate than they had to be to read a menu or write up a receipt for services rendered. Fumi was certainly no exception, but she was savvy enough to know a good investment when she saw one, and wise enough to know that it would behoove her to show a little more consideration for the education of the person who would hopefully be taking care of her in her dotage someday. Now in her early forties, Fumi realized that the chances of finding a husband—at least, that is, one who would be capable of sustaining her in the style to which she had become accustomed—were woefully slim. It was time to pass on her wisdom to Shigeko—her future caretaker—starting with a basic course in Nihonbashi survival skills.

In between her dance studies, Shigeko passed her adolescence learning the ropes from Fumi and her grandmother, who introduced the teenager to the *karyūkai* code of pride, pleasure and freedom. It was a way of life that dictated that you never put the interests of a man over those of your "sisters," that you stayed free and light so you could move quickly and get what you could while you could, and last but certainly not least, that you looked damned good and had one hell of a good time while you were getting it. As an old hand in this culture, Fumi was supposed to have long since mastered these tenets, but at the age of forty-four and at the height of her powers after three decades of juggling male egos with detached, often disingenuous ease, she met a man who made her forget just about everything she had ever learned.

One night in late 1935, soon after her rapprochement with Shigeko, Fumi was invited to a party at the Nakazu restaurant of her best friend, O-Koi, a bright star in the Nihonbashi night sky who enjoyed the stupendously generous patronage of none other than Mitsuru Tōyama himself. Tonight Tōyama was the host, and as usual for one of the old man's parties, the whole place was rented out for the evening. Presiding over the festivities in the place of honor at the head table of the tatami room, Tōyama was a bespectacled octogenarian grandfather with a snowy storybook beard that reached to the middle of his chest. He was dressed in his trademark black formal kimono. Hulking bodyguards sat along the wall behind him within arm's reach.

The guest list was the standard mixture of Kokuryūkai oddballs— walking stereotypes out of a Japanese version of *Casablanca*: shifty-eyed slicksters in shiny double-breasted suits using tortoiseshell cigarette holders; expressionless, Brylcreemed torpedoes who never took off their sunglasses and kept one hand in their coat pockets; ramrod-backed army generals whose mouths moved like hinged nutcracker jaws behind preposterous Kaiser Wilhelm mustaches. Interspersed strategically amongst these honorable guests, a bevy of Nihonbashi professionals in stunning kimonos kept the mood stoked with happy off-color banter, copious male ego-stroking, and a never-ending flow of sake.

Fumi's partner for the evening was introduced as Gorō Araki, an IMA graduate and Tōyama protégé obviously in good standing with the old man, judging by his place in the seating arrangement. Hearing some details about Araki's background explained the relationship: After an interesting ten-year career in China as a mercenary and the bodyguard detachment commander of Manchurian warlord Zhang Zuolin,* Araki had come back to Japan and made a fortune off of manufacturing carpentry nails, of all things. Now he was a generous Kokuryūkai benefactor. Fumi thought making nails sounded like a funny way to get rich, and that the samurai descendant Gorō did not look at all like someone you would expect to be in the hardware business.† Rather, with his shaved head, big chin, jutting lower lip and weighty taciturnity, he seemed more like . . . well, more like the kind of men you always saw in Tōyama-sensei's inner circle, once you got past the elliptically orbiting buffer layers of thugs and ranters. He was sharp and cocksure, with a dangerous testosterone whiff of the rake about him—exactly the type for whom Fumi had a serious weakness. She was attracted to him immediately, and the sentiment was evidently mutual. By the end of the evening, the two were head over heels.

Fumi disappeared for several days after the party. At one point, Grandmother Kaneko and Shigeko even contemplated marching down to the corner police box and filling out a missing persons report on her. When she finally came home, floating on air and with nary an explanation for her absence, it was obvious to all that late spring had arrived for Fumi Kaneko.

Gorō Araki was thirty-eight, balding, penniless, and burning with an idea for a new type of carpentry nail when he returned to Japan in 1932. He could feel it in his bones—the nail idea was going to make him rich. Being

---

*Zhang was assassinated in 1928, when Kwantung Army officers bombed a railway overpass on the South Manchurian Railway near Mukden, destroying the warlord's private train. Gorō was with the bodyguard detachment at Mukden Station, ostensibly awaiting his employer's return from a summit meeting in Beijing.

†The Arakis were originally *ashigaru* samurai from the Nagasaki region. *Ashigaru* was the lowest rank of warrior recognized as samurai in the traditional four-tiered Japanese caste system. The title, directly translated as "light foot soldier," refers to this rank's original battlefield use as dismounted men-at-arms, which was probably a deployment of necessity given the prohibitive cost of maintaining a warhorse. An equivalent Western feudal rank would be a (sometimes barely) gentrified yeoman. *Ashigaru* households had often originally been given this status as a reward for outstanding service—usually but not exclusively military—to the local *daimyo* lord. The status became hereditary after its initial awarding. This process resulted in a gradual increase in the size of the samurai caste over the centuries, especially when battlefield deaths were effectively eliminated as demographically significant factors during the long Pax Edo.

the inventive and energetic go-getter that he was, he saw poverty as no obstacle, and he landed on his feet as usual, making rounds to the Tokyo Patent Office within days of his arrival, running around town scrounging up old contacts—aboveboard or not. A lot of very important people in the city owed him favors from his Manchurian days, and Gorō called in every single one of them he could think of to get together some start-up cash. In the meantime, he supported himself with odd jobs, borrowed money, and found a ramshackle old *machi kōjo* studio* where he could set up a small workshop to fine tune his design and manufacture samples.

The design he was working on was for a cross-sectionally triangular nail that would twist itself into wood as it was hammered. The concept was simple, logical, and—most fortunately for Gorō—original. A quick demonstration with a couple of short pieces of two-by-four was usually all a potential investor needed to be sold on the idea. By 1933, Gorō's factory was up and running. A year later, every house carpenter in Japan was using the nails, and Gorō was rolling.

Late in 1934, Gorō felt secure enough to support his adopted son, Haruo,† who at the age of ten was approaching the all-important entrance examination years that would in large part determine his path and status as an adult in Japanese society. Leaving operations at the nail factory in the hands of subordinates for a week, Gorō made a quick trip to Beijing to fetch Haruo from the uncaring hands of his estranged wife, Kiyoto, who was all too happy to wish the boy good riddance. She had her own life in the Chinese capital, comfortably set up as a self-proclaimed authority on haute Japanese culture for the expat community there, and had better things to do with her time than to look after a separated husband's adopted nephew. The only tears shed for Haruo's departure were by the wrinkled old Chinese amahs and wet-nurse hangers-on who had raised the child since he was a toddler.

Safely back in Tokyo, Gorō and Haruo now had the closest thing to a real family either had ever had, and establishing a relationship was unsure

---

*A kind of "mom and pop factory" in a residential district where piecework is done for larger companies.
†Haruo was actually his nephew—Gorō had adopted him as his son when his own marriage proved unable to produce children.

going for both of them. A live-in maid took care of the hands-on functions of running the house, but the emotional bonding that makes a house a household was slow in coming, if it can be said to have ever really come at all.

"Watching father and son together, you got the impression that Gorō was not really sure how to treat the boy," Shigeko recalls. "So I guess he just fell back on what was natural for him. He treated him like a soldier."

Likewise, the adjustment was difficult for Haruo as well. Making the transition from pampered Beijing luxury to Gorō's simulated IJA boot-camp regimen must have been a rude awakening for the gentle and introverted boy. Gorō laid out a detailed "chip off the old block" life plan for Haruo with no consideration whatsoever for the boy's promising artistic and literary talents (which had attained a prodigious flowering during his long years in Beijing) or for his temperament, which was the antithesis of Gorō's charismatic narcissism and merciless competitiveness. Nevertheless, there was never the slightest hint of rebellion on Haruo's part against Gorō. The boy made it his purpose in life from then on to do everything he could to make his guardian proud of him, and he never looked back.

The first step in Gorō's master plan for Haruo's climb to success was for the boy to win acceptance to Seijō Gakuen Junior High School,* a Tokyo prep school catering to children of the capital's elite. After completing a course of studies geared toward helping students pass rigorous college entrance examinations, its graduates usually went on to attend the top schools in the country, universities like Tokyo, Kyoto, Waseda, or Keiō. A considerable number of boys also opted for the service academies. Either track—civilian or military—virtually guaranteed a lifetime of power and status, and the network of friends and personal connections that a Seijō graduate formed during his time at the school would serve him well at every stage of a career that inevitably led to the halls of Japanese political, military, or financial power.

The next step called for Haruo to attend the IMA. Gorō would not let his son end up hustling around the fringes of power with the

---

*Junior high school was a six-year program under the prewar Japanese education system. Compulsory education extended only to the completion of elementary school. (This is explained in more detail in a Part One footnote on page 50.)

Kokuryūkai, rich one day, living hand-to-mouth and dodging creditors the next. Haruo was going to stay the straight and skinny, burn up the course and shoot into the highest stratum of the nation's military-industrial complex to accomplish all the things Gorō should have done with his life but did not. It was too late for Gorō to ever hope to bask in his own glory, but there was still plenty of time to ensure that he would someday bask in Haruo's.

The year 1935 saw a great deal of changes for the two-member family of Gorō and Haruo Araki. After a rigorous and expensive preparatory course of study with private tutors, Haruo passed the entrance exam to Seijō Gakuen, matriculating in the spring of that year. He was doing well in his studies, his art and literary talents had taken a favorable turn toward model-warplane building and fantasies of military glory, and he was also turning out to be a fine athlete—his sprouting, lanky height helping him to make a valuable contribution to the Seijō basketball team. Gorō couldn't have been more pleased with his nephew's development, nor with the progress of his business venture. The nail factory was chugging along nicely, and as icing on that financial cake, licensed production by big manufacturers was bringing in royalties hand over fist. Gorō was not just doing well—he was flush.

He was not, however, completely free and clear of obligations. The Kwantung Army and Manchurian *rōnin** connections he had called upon to help set up his business worked both ways. Now that Gorō was liquid, it was payback time, and he was beginning to attract hangers-on and moochers like a shark attracts scrap feeders. His house was always busy with various shady visitors and shakedown artists—characters in long capes on the lam from the cops or hit men from other gangs; scar-faced scowlers who wore leather trench coats year round and always walked away from their meetings with attaché cases full of Gorō's cash. Like it or not, Gorō had no choice but to pay up and shut up, because all of this activity was tied in with his most important obligation, i.e., his connection to *rōnin* patron saint Mitsuru Tōyama. The men who came around for handouts were, like Gorō himself, tied up somehow with

---

*Literally "masterless samurai"—in the twentieth century, a euphemism for "mercenary."

Tōyama's power and influence, and thus they could not be refused. The godfather's beneficence, after all, was responsible for much of Gorō's business success, and while Gorō may have been worthy of a few unsavory titles, he was not an ingrate.

In late 1935, Tōyama invited Gorō to a fund-raiser at a high-class restaurant in Nakazu, Tokyo. During the party, he was seated next to a beautiful and slightly older woman, a wealthy and famous Nihonbashi restaurateur named Fumi Kaneko. By the end of the evening, he was so taken with her that his head spun (the sake, of course, may have been accomplice to this condition). They left the party together, and during an incendiary romantic interlude of several days, they managed to squeeze in enough time to discuss several salient points regarding their relationship: firstly, they were madly, hopelessly in love; secondly, it would be best for everyone concerned if Gorō and his son moved in to the Hamachō house; and last but not least, Lieutenant General Chojirō Onodera's patronage had to come to an end.

# twenty-five

# WAR CLOUDS

In February 1939, Fumi sold the Hamachō house and restaurant and went fifty-fifty with Gorō on a new house in Takadano-baba, a quiet Tokyo residential district far from Nihonbashi. As Takadanobaba real estate was much cheaper than Nihonbashi land, the sale of the Hamachō property left them with a sizable profit—in modern-era American terms, probably something along the lines of several hundred thousand dollars. The couple promptly donated half of this windfall to the government. This was not a tax payment, but an actual out-and-out cash donation to a "patriotic" fund-raising drive being conducted by the Army Ministry at the time. Given the strong pragmatic streak in each of their characters, Gorō and Fumi's gesture would seem baffling if it were not for a series of seemingly unconnected developments that unfolded in the immediate wake of this generous endowment: the endless parade of grifters and shakedown artists that had marched through Gorō's doorway for years stopped as suddenly as if a switch had been thrown. Moreover, there was no more of the low-key Kempeitai harassment that had hounded Gorō since his return to Japan from Manchuria. At last, Gorō was out from under the cloud of government suspicion that had followed him since the Zhang Zuolin assassination in 1928.

For Fumi, the move from Hamachō was much more than a simple change of address—it was a farewell to the *karyūkai* that had been her home and performing stage since birth. Giving up the restaurant meant giving up her last toehold in the life and all the decades she had invested in creating her persona as a stellar fixture in the Nihonbashi scene. But now in her mid-forties, Fumi was beginning to find it harder and harder to wake up every morning—well, sometimes afternoon now—after her nightly routine at the restaurant. And as painful as it was for her to admit, all she had to do was to stand in front of a mirror to see that there had been exterior changes as well. While she was too busy having fun to notice, someone or something had sneaked up on her to put lines on her brow and a reed in her laugh, and the willowy teenage beauty and toast of the town was suddenly just another good-looking but hustle-wearied middle-aged woman working the capital's kicks and power game to keep her kimono collection up to date and the creditors at bay. There were hundreds of such women in Tokyo.

Although her prodigious alcohol consumption would hardly be slowed by her retirement, Fumi would never dance or pour a drink for another paying customer again. It was time to put all of that behind her and get on with her new life. Time to molt. Thirty years in the limelight were over, but she could learn to live with that. She had money and relative security, she was in love, and she had pulled off what was generally considered an impossible dream for an old Nihonbashi girl—a free and clear break from her past.

By early 1941, Gorō and Fumi had been under the same roof for over five years, with Shigeko tossed into the complicated arrangement as a full-time member of this common law "family" since the end of her *buyō* apprenticeship two years earlier. Haruo, however, was now out of the house, having been accepted at the IMA in fulfillment of the last major phase of Gorō's master plan for the course of his life. Gorō could not have been happier about this, and was walking on air for weeks after the acceptance letter came through.

Gorō had other reasons to believe that things were looking up. He was still doing well with his hardware enterprise, and he was fully aware of the opportunity implied in the war clouds that were beginning to gather on the eastern horizon. He could not help but be excited by the prospects of wild profits for a businessman savvy and bold enough to grab up his share of the lucrative military and naval contracts in the works. After hearing from friends in the Navy Ministry grapevine that there was going to be a need for extensive naval dry-dock and other anchorage facilities in the Borneo/Lingga roads area in the Southwest Pacific "before the year was out," Gorō planned a trip to the region to scout out potential investment opportunities. One look at a map was enough to know that, with its proximity to oil and other strategic material-rich British and Dutch colonial holdings in Singapore and Indonesia, the area was sure to be a major naval thoroughfare once the shooting started. If Gorō played his cards right, he could make a fortune, but his financial portfolio—impressive as it was—was still not enough to provide the kind of pump-priming scratch such major heavy industrial investments would require.

Gorō's solution to his wherewithal conundrum was to take up with a spectacularly wealthy Tokyo widow who accompanied him to Singapore in the spring of 1941. Fumi would see Gorō only sporadically through the war years, but whenever he darkened their Tokyo doorway, she let him in, no questions asked. She had long since accepted that in taking up with Gorō, she bought into the whole package—warts and all. And if she ever temporarily forgot that, she never forgot who was paying the bills and keeping a roof over her head now.

While Gorō the businessman was excited about the profits to be made in coming months and years, Gorō the old mercenary knew even before the war started that it bordered on the suicidal in terms of Japan's chances for success (or lack thereof). Shigeko-san remembers vividly the excited conversation around the Takadanobaba dinner table on December 14, 1941, during one of Gorō's infrequent visits back to Japan from Singapore. Tokyo was still abuzz from the electrifying radio and newspaper reports of the Pearl Harbor raid a week earlier, and no one was more excited than Haruo, who was at the house for his weekly Sunday-evening visit after a quick subway hop from the IMA campus. Fumi and Shigeko tittered with praise and approval as he spoke about how he was itching to run off and get in a few licks against the Yankees and Brits while he still could, seeing as how Japan's victory could not be much longer in coming.

"You don't actually think we're going to win, do you?" Gorō said.

The pronouncement started a brief three-on-one argument that Gorō swatted down with facts and common sense his opponents did not want to believe, but were nevertheless unable to refute. The rest of the evening passed in a gloomy pall until Haruo left to make it back to the IMA for lights-out.

Exactly five months later, on the afternoon of April 14, 1942, dun-brown twin-engine American bombers skimming the rooftops of down-town Tokyo emphasized Gorō's prophecies with the resounding thuds of five-hundred-pound high explosive bombs. A few days later, a cable arrived from Singapore—Gorō wanted Fumi and Shigeko out of town ASAP, and he told them to put the Takadanobaba house up for sale immediately, charging a reasonable price so it would go fast. Fumi found a new place in the fishing and tangerine-farming village of Kōzu, a stingy strip of pebbly soil and sand dune pinched between mountains and the Pacific Ocean about thirty kilometers southwest of the capital.

For lifelong big-city girls like Fumi and Shigeko, evacuation to a burg like Kōzu was a sentence to purgatory, and they hated it immediately. While the low cost of living in the area meant that Gorō's cash went a lot farther than it did in downtown Tokyo, there was nothing to spend it on here. And although the women's status as members of a VIP household (Gorō had moved his nail factory and metallurgy lab to Kōzu several years earlier, and was a respected businessman in the area) meant they never had to wait in line at the village marketplace, they were never made to feel at home. The locals were as roughhewn and unwelcoming as the landscape from which their tightly knit community sprang.

While the move to Kōzu put a serious cramp on socializing opportunities for Fumi and Shigeko, the town's nearby location to the IMA's new Zama campus meant that the weekly tradition of Haruo's Sunday evening dinner visits would be preserved, and no one was happier about this than the young cadet himself. But it was not for Fumi's homemade cooking that Haruo counted the hours between visits home—it was for Fumi's daughter.

Haruo had been madly in love with Shigeko since Gorō moved in with Fumi in 1935. Fumi—who after all had never given much motherly attention even to her own daughter—was of course too caught up in Gorō and her own scene to pay much mind to Haruo, who had to look elsewhere for doting female attention. In his case, he turned to Shigeko. Given Haruo's upbringing in a mental and physical landscape dominated by the void left by his largely absentee father, perhaps it was only natural that he latched on to Shigeko like he did. During the six years the foursome spent under the same roof, he had followed her around like a lovesick puppy.

Shigeko—six months her admirer's senior—never minded the attention, and in addition to getting an ego boost out of the adoration, she found Haruo cute, in a boyish kind of way. She remembers him as being tall, lanky, and long-necked even as a twelve-year-old. Although highly intelligent, he was also very naïve, with a nonconfrontational, introspective personality. Always intensely focused on his own projects—usually studying or building balsa and paper airplane models—he never joked and rarely smiled or laughed. Often, his gullibility proved too tempting for Shigeko's playful (and occasionally mean) sense of humor to pass up.

Soon after Gorō and his stepson moved into Fumi's house, Haruo wrote a gushing love letter to Shigeko and slipped it under her bedroom door. That night at dinner—much to Haruo's disbelief and horror—Shigeko pulled the letter out of her kimono sleeve and began waving it around with a big, triumphant grin on her face before proceeding to read its contents. After only a few lines of Shigeko's recitation, Gorō turned beet red and bolted upright. Reaching over the table, he grabbed Haruo by the collar and pulled him into the adjoining living room, slamming the sliding door shut behind them. Shigeko and Fumi heard a shrieked command of "Spread your legs!" followed by the sound of punches and slapped flesh as Gorō launched into a long lecture about young men who wanted to go to the IMA, and how they did not fritter away their time and energies daydreaming about women.

"If you like the girl, tell her like a man and do something about it," Gorō shouted between smacks. "Do you think I've gone through all of this trouble to get you into good schools so you can sit around writing love letters like a sissy? Is that what you are?! Is that the kind of boy I have raised?!"

After ten minutes or so, the living room door flew open, and Shigeko found herself looking down Gorō's stabbing index finger.

"And don't think you're getting off easy," Goro shouted. "If Haruo doesn't get into the Academy, I'm holding *you* responsible, too."

As she heard Haruo getting thrashed that night, Shigeko's maternal instincts kicked into overdrive—no doubt fueled by a guilty conscience—and she swore to herself that she would take care of the boy. From then on, although she was never really able to reciprocate his romantic sentiments, she was more inclined to let him indulge these feelings, and she responded to his affection if not with equivalent ardor then at least with a comforting and protective tenderness. In return, Haruo's love for her only grew as the years passed. From his mid-teens, he often broached the subject of marriage. Shigeko at first took this as some sort of joke, but the pledges of undying affection and gushing love letters continued even after Haruo's acceptance to the IMA, and she gradually realized he was serious. One day during his graduation leave in 1944, Haruo proposed to Shigeko while the couple strolled by the Kōzu seaside. But this time, instead of laughing off the subject as she always did, she accepted.

"He was going off to war," Shigeko-san tells me. "Under the circumstances, I thought sending him off happy and fulfilled was the least I could do. I felt sorry for him."

While Fumi was less than enthusiastic about her daughter's plans, Gorō was delighted, and immediately set things in motion after steamrolling his partner's objections. Bringing about the marriage, however, was not simply a matter of giving parental consent and hauling the young couple down to City Hall to fill out the paperwork. There were social complications involved, but these had nothing to do with the mercurial familial arrangement in the Kōzu household, which actually raised few eyebrows under the mores of the era. Rather, the problem was with Shigeko, and the Army Ministry regulation that said regular army commissioned officers could not marry women with less than three years of junior high school or equivalent education.

In Shigeko's case, a three-year apprenticeship as a Nihonbashi dancing girl was not going to clear the army's spousal qualification criteria. Moreover, she had barely cracked a book of any kind in years and had little or no math or science background, so any plan of action involving an entrance examination was doomed from the start. Of course, even in the outside chance that Shigeko could pass an entrance exam, the idea of a twenty-year-old enrolling in junior high for a three-year-stint with pre-pubescent classmates was preposterous. But Gorō—ever the hustling inventor—was dogged in his pursuit of pragmatic alternatives. After some inquiries and spadework, he found a Ministry of Education–accredited sewing academy* near Kōzu that was willing—for a price—to slip Shigeko into the next senior class so that she could graduate in March 1945. Gorō sealed the deal with a handshake and an elegant grandfather clock for the school auditorium. Shigeko—at least on paper—was going to be a qualified seamstress.

Shigeko was by heart and trade a dancer, and knew and cared about as much for sewing as she did for integral calculus. But these motivational concerns became moot when the entire student body was mobilized along with most of the other young women in the Kōzu area for war volunteer work in a nearby naval-provisions plant in the fall of 1944. Shigeko got her seamstress license on schedule the following March while being unable to as much as darn a sock, but she had never bought into the pretense that these credentials were the goal of her "education" in the first place. She had a diploma and was thus now qualified to marry Haruo. Mission accomplished. While waiting for Haruo's next visit home, Shigeko worked seven days a week with her classmates and neighbors compressing and canning potato starch and rice for the navy.

Haruo, in the meantime, had undergone a topsy-turvy first year as a commissioned officer. Although he had originally branched aviation while at IMA, his biological mother—whom he had neither seen nor heard from for the better part of two decades—suddenly reappeared in his life during his second year at the academy and pulled strings to get him branched armor, a posting she evidently felt offered her son a more reassuring life expectancy than an assignment as a fighter pilot.† Heartbroken, Haruo nevertheless pushed on with his tank training, and was looking at a post–Armor Officer's Basic Course assignment to Manchuria when the army announced a last-minute call to class of '44 IMA grads for aviation branch volunteers. Haruo jumped at this chance to alter his destiny, and this go-around, the timing left no opening for his mother to pull any more strings behind his back. He was going to be a pilot, and that was that.

Haruo was accepted into a special IMA grad–only Tokubetsu Sōjū Minarai Shikan (Tokusō) course in the fall of 1944, but by the time he had gotten his wings, virtually the only assignments left for newly trained army

---

*This was good enough to satisfy army spousal secondary education requirements.
†Haruo's biological mother—Gorō's older brother's wife—was a four-star general's daughter.

pilots were to *tokkō* units. In a bitter twist of irony, his mother's inter-ference in his career—resulting in the delay of his flight training—had virtually guaranteed such an assignment. If Haruo had been branched as originally scheduled, he could have at least had an outside chance of being assigned to a regular unit, or even ending up on the same flight in-structor early career track that saved the life of his IMA classmate Iwao Fukagawa.


Kōzu was rainy and windy on the night of Tuesday, April 9, 1945. Gorō—now home permanently to mind the nail factory after losing all of his Southeast Asia properties to the shifting fortunes of war—was eating a late supper with Fumi and Shigeko in the tatami-floored living room when the low, mournful moan of Kōzu's air raid siren floated up from town. No aircraft engines could be heard, but blackout rules were black-out rules, so the lights were turned off and the curtains drawn. The meal was finished in a meditative silence by the light of a single candle. Gorō drank *shōchu* and smoked cigarettes in the flickering shadows while Fumi and Shigeko cleared the dishes.

Around ten o'clock, the threesome heard the crunch of heavy, tired footfalls outside on the gravel walkway leading to the house. Shigeko as-sumed it was the old man who volunteered as the local air warden mak-ing his usual blackout rounds. A moment later, there was a knock at the entrance, followed by the rattling sound of the wood and glass door be-ing slid open. Then there was a male voice—but instead of the old air warden giving his customary "All clear," it was a young man's voice say-ing *"Tadaima."* ("I'm home.")

Haruo was back for the first time in many months, and the visit was ut-terly unexpected. But happy though the family members may have been, expressions of emotion were restrained, as is the Japanese custom in such occasions. There were no bear hugs and kissed cheeks, and if the women felt compelled to weep, this was kept to polite sniffles and a kimono sleeve dab or two to the eyes. Gorō may have allowed himself a slap on his son's shoulder before sending him upstairs to change out of his wet uni-form and into a nice dry *yukata* robe from the wardrobe closet.

When Haruo finished washing up and changing, he joined the rest of the family in the living room. Gorō growled for Fumi to break out the last of the good sake. After the "welcome home" toast and a pregnant pause, Haruo filled the family in on the particulars of his recent activities, speaking slowly and methodically in his soft, low voice. His monologue ended with the news that he had been given command of a *tokkō* Shinbu unit.

The mood around the table took an understandable nosedive after this revelation. Conversation tapered off to a sporadic sprinkling of short utterance/response couplets, falling into long silences when everyone ran out of things to say. Again, there was no excessive expression of emotion. Given the unspoken understanding that Haruo had no choice but to follow his orders, the family could do nothing but accept his fate stoically. Tears or laments or anger at this point would have been in bad taste.

During one of the longer lulls of uncomfortable silence, Haruo excused himself, then tugged Shigeko's sleeve for her to follow him out of the room.

"Haruo told me that, given his *tokkō* assignment, he wasn't going to hold me to my marriage promise any longer," Shigeko-san recalls of their conversation in the pitch-black hallway that night. "But I said I wasn't having any of that, and that a promise is a promise."

Haruo made a show of standing his ground, but his resistance was halfhearted, and he folded after a brief, whispered argument in the shadows. The couple returned to the living room and announced their intentions to Gorō and Fumi.

"*Sonna baka na!*" ("That's out of the question!") Fumi cried when the youngsters finished their pitch. She bolted from the room with muffled sobs and a slammed door.

Gorō, however, nodded slowly, with weighty solemnity, and not without a hint of satisfied fatherly pride flickering around the corners of his mouth. He ordered Fumi to come back at once, and to bring a pair of lacquerware saucers. They were going to hold a wedding ceremony right here and now.

The town air raid siren started up again as the sake was poured, providing an eerie accompaniment to Gorō's recitation of the ancient *Takasagoya*—a *nagauta* traditionally performed a cappella at Japanese weddings by fathers sending daughters off into marriage. Gorō held his notes long and loud, but his voice began to break with emotion in the last stanzas, and by the time he finished, all four people in the room were sobbing aloud. It was the first time Shigeko had seen either of the men cry.

The newlyweds drained their saucer cups, apologized to their respective parents for a lifetime of worries and troubles their upbringing had caused, then without further ado, retired for the evening to Shigeko's bedroom.

The household was up at dawn the next day to make sure Haruo had everything ready for his trip. Although everyone tried to keep up the appearance of normalcy, the mood around the breakfast table was tense. Toward the end of the meal, Haruo—already dressed in his khakis—tried to lighten things up.

"We can't fly if the weather is bad," he said. "I'll be back whenever it rains."

Everyone else nodded behind their raised teacups, avoiding eye contact, perhaps harboring some slim hope that this was true while doing their best to pretend it was.

After the meal, Haruo excused himself and walked out into the spacious backyard alone. As Fumi and Shigeko cleared the table, Gorō stood at the kitchen window, watching his son pace back and forth, occasionally stopping to touch a flower or stare off into the hills behind the house.

"He's saying good-bye to the place," Gorō muttered. "He knows he's not coming back."

Haruo continued his garden meditation for nearly an hour before coming back into the house and announcing his imminent departure. He shouldered his gear and made his final farewells to Gorō and Fumi while Shigeko polished his shoes in the foyer.

"Can I walk you to the station?" Shigeko asked, looking up from her chore.

"*Ah,*" Haruo replied, addressing his wife with the bluntest possible affirmative in the Japanese lexicon—an utterance just this side of a grunt. If anyone doubted the legitimacy of the previous night's nuptials, no one hearing the tone of voice Haruo used toward his new bride would doubt it this morning. He was now a traditional Japanese husband, through and through.

"It was the first word he said to me all morning," Shigeko remembers. "And one of the last. He made me walk three steps behind him all the way to the station. Just like a samurai wife in old days. He had nothing to say while we walked, either. A few times I thought I saw him getting ready to say something, but he never did. There were things I wanted to say, too, but couldn't. The timing just didn't feel right, and I was afraid of saying something I would regret. . . . Now, of course, I regret having not said anything."

When they reached the station, Haruo showed his high priority military orders to the clerk at the ticket window, paid for his fare, then hid the ticket with his hand so Shigeko could not read the destination. Shigeko asked anyway, but Haruo refused to divulge any information about where he was going.

"It's none of your business," Haruo replied when pressed.

Just as he had flatly refused any histrionics upon his welcome home the night before, he was not about to indulge in any this morning for his farewell. An eastbound train pulled into the station with a long whistle, and Haruo stalked off toward the ticket gate with his back to Shigeko.

"Sayonara," he said over his shoulder. "Now go home."

Haruo got on the train and took a seat by the window. He kept his gaze fixed straight ahead as the train hissed to life again and clacked away in the direction of Tokyo.

# twenty-six

## VISITORS

For the next two months, the Arakis kept their ears open for heavy footfalls on the gravel walkway, and stayed up until the last train pulled out of Kōzu Station every night. Even then, they left the gate and front door to the house open on the off chance that Haruo might come in at some wee hour of the morning. In line with Haruo's promise to come home when bad weather prevented flying, rain always brought on the most desperate expectations, with a single drop of precipitation never failing to send Fumi and Shigeko scrambling to scrape together every morsel they could to put a decent welcome home meal on the table. But come rain or shine, night or day, there was no sign of Haruo. Not even a letter or postcard.

In addition to fretting over the unknown fate of her young husband, Shigeko had a new major complication in her life. She missed her June period, which should have come the first week of the month. She had always been, in her own words, "as regular as clockwork," and missing a cycle—or even being late—had never happened to her before. Another clue to the nature of her condition was that the steaming rice and starch smells at work were beginning to sour her stomach every morning, and that had never happened before, either.

*But was that possible,* Shigeko thought, *in one night?*

Fumi was of little or no help in the way of constructive family-planning consultation, having no experience herself in such matters. But the friendly middle-aged woman who ran the sewing academy dormitory had a prodigious brood of kids, and she was easy to approach for advice. After hearing a tactfully handled explanation of the details, the headmistress recommended seeing a doctor at once, suggesting a trip posthaste to Odawara, the nearest town big enough to boast of an obstetrician. Fumi went along for the ride the next day, and the two returned to the Kōzu house/nail factory that afternoon with the news that Shigeko was pregnant.

Gorō was beside himself with joy, and he made no secret of his desire that the baby would be a male child, for such an eventuality would mean that the Araki line would go on. Shigeko had not seen Gorō this happy since Haruo's acceptance letter from the IMA arrived four years earlier. The happiness was infectious, and even Fumi—who had always been less than thrilled about her daughter's "marriage"—could not help but be caught up in the emotion of the moment. Gorō was on cloud nine, and Fumi was happy about seeing him like this, regardless of how she truly felt about the scheduled household-member addition. In the meantime, no one thought to ask Shigeko what she thought about it all, although much doting attention was devoted to her daily physical condition. The future of the house of Araki, after all, was now riding on her narrow but sturdy shoulders.

One particularly salient point of unpleasantness during this otherwise upbeat season was the frustrating inability of anyone in the house to contact Haruo with the happy news. Any inquiry into his whereabouts brought on a maddening bureaucratic runaround—or just a slammed receiver on the other end of the phone line—from every army official they contacted. Even Gorō's IMA credentials were not enough to cut through all the red tape. But despite the situation, no one in the house suspected—or at least voiced their suspicions—that there may have been reasons other than security concerns behind the army's taciturnity. Alternative explanations, although more than merely plausible, were also utterly unthinkable.

One steamy afternoon in mid-June, a slightly worse-for-wear, bushyhaired civilian in his late thirties visited the Kōzu house. He introduced himself as Toshirō Takagi—a Nichiei cameraman by trade. He had just come back to the Tokyo area from a town in Kyūshū named Chiran. In case the family had not read about it in the papers, it was a big *tokkō* base. Takagi had met Haruo there, and Haruo had given him some items to bring back to the house.

"Here they are," Takagi said, pulling a parcel wrapped in *furōshiki* batik-dyed cloth from his shoulder bag.

Gorō had come into the house from the factory out back when he heard the visitor arrive, and now peered over Fumi's and Shigeko's shoulders as the women accepted the parcel with deep bows of respectful gratitude.

"*Waza waza tōi tokoro kara . . .*" Fumi said, expressing her sincere—if mildly perturbed—thanks to Takagi for making the effort of journeying so long and from so far away to hand deliver the parcel. "Won't you stay for tea?"

"Please don't go to the trouble," Takagi said, graciously refusing the offer, as Japanese protocol demanded. "I'm just here to deliver the package, and if possible, to light an incense stick for your son."

Gorō, Fumi, and Shigeko froze to the spot, ashen-faced. Sixty years later, Shigeko-san would recall of that moment that she experienced a sensation of falling—as if a fathomless chasm had suddenly appeared under her feet to send her plummeting through cold, black space.

Taken aback by the abrupt emotional temperature drop in the foyer, Takagi looked up from the entranceway with a puzzled expression for a moment before a flash of horrified realization crossed his face.

"Oh, no," he said. "What have I done . . . ? You haven't been told yet, have you? The army hasn't contacted you. Please forgive me. . . ."

After a few moments of confusion, heartbreaking confirmations, and overall excruciating discomfort for all concerned, Takagi was welcomed into the house to a place of honor in the living room, where he proceeded to tell the family about Chiran, the 51st Shinbu and Haruo's last hours on earth. Haruo's *furōshiki*-bound package was unwrapped with loving care and its contents were passed around and examined: There was a small box containing clippings of Haruo's hair and fingernails, and another containing the epaulets and collar tabs from his dress uniform. These items were to be used in lieu of his body for funerary purposes. The parcel also contained Haruo's *isho** warrior's farewell in flowery, formal language. This was addressed to Gorō.

---

*This word, in Japanese, can also mean "last will and testament." For examples of those translated into English, see Japan Memorial Society for the Students Killed in the War (2000). See also Yasukuni Shrine (1995) for less well known but equally exemplary letters, in addition to informative photographs of *hanayome ningyo* and other *tokkō* pilots' personal effects.

Takagi told everyone that he actually had several more letter-delivery stops to make in Kōzu and other northern Kanagawa Prefecture towns today. Many of the *tokkō* pilots at Chiran had given over their *isho* for him to hand-deliver instead of trusting the letters to army mail. As Takagi explained, it was a way to slip in more personal and frank sentiment that might otherwise fall victim to an army censor's black fat-tipped pen. The higher-ups preferred the pilots' letters to stick to hackneyed writing styles, and tended to savage—or even demand total rewrites—of anything that strayed from the narrow selection of approved formats.

Almost as an afterthought, Takagi handed Shigeko a note on simple stationery with her name written on the outside fold. She slipped the note into her kimono lapel and began planning an escape from the parlor to read it. She knew she would not be able to do so without breaking down and sobbing, for it was all she could do to keep her composure as things were. Gorō had told Shigeko often in recent months that, as an army wife, she was now forbidden to cry in front of other people. "If you have to cry, save it for when you're home alone, out of sight," he always said. Luckily, Takagi proved to be a thirsty guest, so this gave Shigeko a chance to excuse herself and run back to the kitchen for a crying jag on the pretext of putting more water on to boil for another pot of tea. It was a tactic she would employ several times before the visit was over.

Once in the privacy of the kitchen, Shigeko opened the note. One thing she noticed immediately was that here Haruo addressed her simply as "Shigeko," and not as "Shigeko-dono," the highly formal honorific he had always used when addressing her directly. Coming from an extremely formal Japanese gentleman like Haruo, the dropped honorific implied a deep emotional intimacy it would have been entirely out of character for him to ever express to his bride—at least verbally—in person. Shigeko was profoundly moved by the gesture, and hot tears rolled down her cheeks as she read the rest of the note:

> *Shigeko,*
>
> *It has been a month since that night we spent together. Tomorrow morning, I will cross the River Sanzu [Japanese Buddhist equivalent of River Styx into Hades—author] and take as many Yankees with me as I can. I am sorry for any trouble I have ever*

*given you. Please forgive my selfishness. It breaks my heart to
think of the long life you will live that I won't be able to share
with you. Be strong and virtuous for me. Please take care of Father when I'm gone.*

*Haruo*

Shigeko tucked the note away again, dried her tears with her sleeve, and
brought a tray with more tea and rice crackers out to the guest.

Toward the end of what turned out to be a rather lengthy visit, Takagi
pulled a manila envelope from his bag containing at least a roll's worth
of posed publicity shots he had taken of the 51st Shinbu members on
the afternoon of May 10, just after Haruo arrived at Chiran and scant
hours from the unit's combat sortie to Okinawa the next morning. Takagi
said that reports of the action, as in the case of so many *tokkō* missions,
were spotty, but at least one plane from Haruo's flight was confirmed to
have hit an American destroyer. The family could take some comfort in
believing that it was Haruo's plane that had gotten through the fighters
and antiaircraft fire to barrel in for the strike. And in any case, whether
or not Haruo's mission had been successful, the family had every reason
to be proud of him, knowing that he had gone out as a hero.

After Takagi left, Shigeko went back to her room for the rest of the
night to sob into her pillow and mourn in private. Gorō and Fumi also retired to their own separate rooms to grieve. Grief was private—almost
something to be ashamed of (as it still is, in Japanese social mores)—and
the agony of loss was a hell that had to be endured alone. Shigeko has
never forgotten the door-rattling moans and anguished invocations of
Haruo's name that emanated from the thin walls of Gorō's room into the
wee hours before the old soldier finally cried and drank himself to sleep.

It was a long, abominable night for everyone in the house.

With Haruo's death now confirmed, Shigeko's status as the soon-to-be
bearer of his sole offspring received obsessive attention in the Kōzu
household. Having just lost a son, Gorō was going to do everything he
could to prevent another tragedy in the family, and he was intensely concerned about Shigeko's physical safety. Accordingly, he was vehemently

opposed to her expressed desire to continue working at the naval cannery, even though she had assured him that there was nothing to worry about, and that she would quit as soon as she felt even the slightest bit put out by her developing condition.

When pleading her case, Shigeko was especially careful not to mention anything about the target-of-opportunity attack by American fighters on the plant several weeks earlier, when Hellcats—apparently using up remaining ammunition on their way home after the morning's missions in the Tokyo area—strafed the cannery for a few minutes, started some minor fires, and even shot at some girls unlucky enough to have been caught out in the open riding their bicycles to work when the first planes buzzed over. Fortunately, the girls had been swift enough to ditch their bikes and take cover as soon as the first rounds began kicking up dust, so no one was hurt, but it had been close. If Gorō had heard about it, he would have hit the roof, and that would have been the end of Shigeko's contribution to the war effort.

In late June, Kōzu proper was hit by an intense early-morning Hellcat raid. The carrier borne fighters had been pesky for several weeks now, shooting up anything with a decent-sized smokestack, or taking potshots at the occasional vehicle driven by someone stupid enough to be out on the road in the daytime. But this raid was the first time Kōzu itself seemed to have been the primary target. Gorō surmised that the Americans had run out of more worthwhile targets farther up toward the capital and had sunk everything there was to be sunk in the nearby Yokohama navy yards, so they were ranging farther out into the rural areas to destroy basic infrastructure. This morning, their apparent target was Kōzu's fishing fleet, as they concentrated their fury on the town waterfront. But the planes did not limit themselves to the trawlers and scows afloat in the harbor—they also shot up other prominent structures in town, including the Araki home. While no one in the house was hurt, the Arakis' outhouse—fortunately unoccupied at the time—was not so lucky. It was blown away in a hail of .50-caliber bullets from a glossy dark blue plane that came shrieking in low enough to decapitate some of the trees in the garden and whip the morning's laundry off the clotheslines as it passed over.

For Gorō, the outhouse strafing was the last straw. Shigeko was going to be evacuated to a safer place whether she agreed to it or not. He made financial arrangements with an old couple who worked a sweet potato plot high up on the southwestern slopes of Mount Fuji to let her stay with them until further notice.

On the day of Shigeko's evacuation, Gorō and Shigeko rode the train from Kōzu, changing at Numazu for a local branch line that would take them well up into Fuji's foothills to Gotenba. The rest of the trip up to Fuji's fifth station would have to be negotiated on foot. Shigeko carried what she could manage in a roped bundle on her back, while Gorō pushed a wheelbarrow piled high with food provisions, blankets, and other supplies.

The twosome was disappointed at the end of their sweaty hike. Shigeko's "shelter" turned out to be nothing more than a floppy old tatami mat or two tossed on the hay-strewn dirt floor of a horse stable. But Gorō was in a position neither to bargain nor to complain—at least not very vociferously. By June 1945, it was most definitely a sellers' market for shelter space anywhere within fifty kilometers of Tokyo. The farmer had heard nothing about putting the girl up in the house proper, and was hearing nothing about it now. Gorō was told he could take the accommodations as-is, or look elsewhere, so he had no choice but to hold his nose and shell out his war scrip. Shigeko would be spending her days and nights buttoned up in the barn with a flea-bitten old plowhorse.

Gorō helped Shigeko unpack her supplies, then paused when he reached the last item—a small brocade sack—almost as if he were deciding what to do with it. After a long moment of contemplation, he handed it over to Shigeko and told her to open it. She did so, and pulled a thirty-centimeter-long army officer's lacquer-sheathed short sword out of the pouch.

"That's for the off chance that the Americans catch you and try to have their way with you," Gorō said, now long-faced and somber. "I don't think they'll bother coming this far up the mountain, and there's nothing of any military value up here, so you don't have to worry too much about it. But still, you should be prepared.

"Of course, you're not a man, and I don't expect you to be able to shove it into your belly like one," Gorō continued. "I want you to listen very, very carefully to me. This is how pregnant noblewomen in olden times would do themselves in when their castles were being overrun by the enemy."

Gorō pulled a grease pencil from his shirt pocket and drew a small black circle on Shigeko's kimono, directly over the left side of her womb.

"If you ever find yourself in a situation where . . . well, where you expect the worst is about to happen . . . put the tip of the dagger right here," Gorō said, pointing at the circle he had just drawn. "Hold it in place and run into the door of the horse stall. You must make sure you keep the dagger exactly on that spot, so it will kill you and the baby as quickly as possible. I think it will be easier if you close your eyes while you do it, so you won't flinch and lose your nerve at the last second. Do you understand?"

Shigeko nodded. Gorō paused for a moment, stern-eyed, his lower lip jutting out the way it always did when he was deep in troubled thought.

"You know, if it were you alone up here," he said, looking down at the hay-strewn dirt to avoid Shigeko's gaze, "I would say just shut your eyes, turn your face to the wall, endure whatever you have to, and try to stay alive. But it's not just you. You're also carrying Haruo's child. . . . And the honor of the Araki family. It would be unfitting for you to be sullied by the Americans. And anyway, Haruo would be happier if you and the baby joined him as soon as possible. Think of how lonely he must be right now. If you keep that in mind, I'm sure you'll be able to do what you have to do when the time comes."

Gorō left Shigeko with that reassuring thought and a promise to return two weeks later with another wheelbarrow's worth of supplies. Until that time, Shigeko was to keep the stable door and windows shut at all times, day or night, even if the heat inside became intolerable. And any venture outside to bathe or attend to other bodily functions was to be kept as short and close by as possible. Evil and chaos would soon be on the loose. The times called for lying low and maintaining vigilance.

Shigeko awakened after a long first night of miserable off-and-on sleep to find her feet, legs, and arms literally covered with stinging, blood-sucking fleas. She would never forget the *fffttt, fffffttt* sound it made as she brushed them off her exposed skin with her hands. It was a morning ritual to which she would have to become accustomed.

After that first harrowing "debugging" experience, she made a quick, fog-shrouded dawn foray out into her new environs, trying not to stray too far from the dilapidated stable she now called home. One pleasant find resulting from her exploration was a nearby stream fed by melting snow runoff from Mount Fuji. It made for frigid bathing but excellent drinking, and during that long, hot summer, Shigeko would often find herself unable to resist violating Gorō's curfew restrictions in order to indulge herself in the relative luxuries of this clear, cold water source.

Another point of interest and possible future use discovered during the morning reconnaissance was a cliff with a straight-down hundred-meter drop a few minutes' walk from the stable. It was almost an answer to Shigeko's prayers of the awful night before, during which she had spent long hours contemplating Gorō's suicide instructions and how and if she would be able to comply with them. She had come to the conclusion that—officer's wife or not—she just did not have the intestinal fortitude to use a blade on her own body, especially knowing now that there was a child in her womb. That was just not going to happen, no matter how threatened she felt.

Nor did she think that she would have it in her to rush her attackers with the blade, hoping for a quick death from gunshot. The cliff discovery, however, posed a considerably less gruesome solution than either of the other choices. If worse came to worst and Shigeko heard murder and mayhem coming up the footpath from the farming hamlet below, she could be out of the shack at a flat out run, over the cliff, and dead on the boulders below within a minute. There was a sense of morbid relief in knowing that she now had this option. This knowledge would provide a stingy modicum of comfort during what would prove to be a seemingly interminable summer of solitude, grinding boredom, lingering grief and depression over Haruo's death, and the incessant physical torment of fleas, heat, and hunger.

On August 15, Shigeko—now showing noticeably under her dusty *monpe* workclothes—was walking down the road past her landlords' fallow potato field on her way back to the stable after an afternoon of scrounging for food in the surrounding countryside. On this particular day, she was returning empty-handed and not feeling particularly chipper about her own or the world's condition. Gorō had not calculated for the increase in Shigeko's appetite as her fetus grew, and the last wheelbarrow shipment had run out sooner than expected, forcing Shigeko to forage to supplement her dwindling supplies.

Rounding a bend in the road, she came upon a sight she had not seen since her arrival in Gotenba—her landlords actually doing some work in their field. Today, they were digging with shovels, but upon closer inspection, the activity turned out to have nothing to do with agriculture. The old farmer and his equally curmudgeonly wife were excavating strongboxes and sealed jars.

"*Ojisan,*"* Shigeko called out. "What are you doing?"

"Never mind what we're doing," the farmer snapped. "Haven't you heard the news?"

"What news?"

"The war is over. The emperor announced it on the radio at noon."

"You mean we've won?" Shigeko asked, electrified with a sudden surge of elation.

The old couple stopped digging for a moment and looked at her, then at each other. In a different context, they might have started laughing, but this was evidently not a time for mirth.

"No," the farmer said, openly exasperated. "Japan lost."

Shigeko remembers her knees giving out slightly as she absorbed the impact and import of this information. A sudden barrage of angry thoughts and panicked disbelief buzzed through her brain like shards of broken window glass: Why had the divine wind not blown? Had the gods turned their backs on Japan? How could the Americans have won when the *tokkō* had made such magnificent sacrifices? All of those thousands of young men dead . . . Haruo . . . As the reality sank in, she experienced a falling sensation not unlike what she had felt when told of Haruo's death two months earlier. But the old farmer's gravelly voice snapped her back to the here and now.

"My wife and I are leaving tonight," he said. "Heading deeper inland, to stay with relatives. Too close to the coast here. The Americans are bound to pass through. . . . If I were you, I wouldn't try venturing out of the stable anymore like you've been doing recently. No telling what might happen. . . . And keep those windows shut."

---

*Japanese for "uncle," but also used by youngsters as a term of respect when addressing older males (generally mid-thirties and up). Similar in usage to French *père*. Sometimes considered pejorative/politically incorrect in modern usage, as it involves a subjective judgment of relative age difference on the part of the user toward the addressee.

For the next two weeks, Shigeko followed the farmer's advice to the letter, even after the last of her food ran out. But just as she was beginning to wonder when she would begin succumbing to hunger, a breathless Gorō arrived at the barn with an empty wheelbarrow on the evening of September 1. He told Shigeko that the Americans were beginning to roll through the Tokyo area, and that there were no reports of atrocities. Using rusty but still serviceable mercenary's pidgin left over from his Manchurian adventurer days, he had even talked to an advance party jeepload of Americans who had passed through Kōzu the previous day. They were uncouth and a bit cocky, he thought, but he also sensed that they were basically decent men—not the rape/pillage/burn type he was all too familiar with from his own soldiering days on the continent. There was nothing to worry about. All of those panicky warnings on the radio and in the papers had been nonsense. Things were beginning to settle down. It was safe to go home, and that was where he planned to take Shigeko now.

Gorō packed Shigeko's baggage and bedrolls, and Shigeko took a seat on top of the pile with her geta-shod feet hanging over the front edge of the wheelbarrow. It was hardly the most dignified mode of transportation for an officer's widow, but it was functional. Without further ado, Gorō pushed his daughter-in-law down the mountain to Gotenba Station to return to what was left of their lives.


Shigeko gave birth to a baby boy on Christmas Day, 1945. They named him Yūkyū ("Eternal"), in honor of his father's *tokkō* unit, the 51st Shinbu Yūkyūtai. The birth was a beacon of hope in a dark season, and over the next year, the Kōzu household was transformed into an entirely Yūkyū-centric universe. Gorō and Fumi became doting grandparents no one could have ever imagined them becoming in their freewheeling days as Tokyo boulevardiers. Shigeko vowed and strove to raise a son of whom the spirit of her dead husband could be proud. Although the child had been born undersize and premature, everyone was certain that the Araki blood in his veins would make him grow up to be a strong young man like his father someday.

Hopes were high for one happy year, but the falling leaves of late autumn portended another dark season in store for the family. One cold morning in December 1946, Yūkyū stopped breathing while being nursed. The cause of death was never determined. His ashes were buried with his father's fingernail cuttings and collar insignia in the Araki family grave.

After Yūkyū's death, Shigeko ran away from everything and everyone in Kōzu, heading back to the big city to try to get her dancing career back on track. But she could not land a wealthy sponsor, and the long arm of Gorō ended up reeling her back into orbit around his household. Under the sticky tangle of traditional Japanese familial obligations, Shigeko—as Haruo's widow—was now duty-bound to take care of Gorō for the rest of his natural life, regardless of the status of his relationship with Fumi.

Gorō and Fumi drifted apart after the war, although as is with all great loves, the flame of their own never quite died out completely. Gorō was a frequent if irregular resident in the rectory of the Rankanji in Asakusa, Tokyo, the Buddhist temple where Fumi lived out the last two decades of her life as the temple abbotess. Fumi died in 1964 at the age of seventy-three—for most of her adult life, she had ignored the advice of nearly every doctor she had ever seen to cut down on her drinking. Shigeko-san will always think that this was her final undoing.

Gorō lived to seventy-nine, hard-drinking and being cared for by different Tokyo women of wealth and taste to the last of his days. He died at the Rankanji in 1972 shortly after tape-recording his memoirs in a series of interviews with biographer Seigo Hayashi. People who knew him say that he never stopped grieving for Haruo and Yūkyū.

Shigeko ended up marrying another IMA man, Tadaharu Eguchi, in 1949, and raising two sons in a comfortable Tokyo home while her husband learned the ropes of the metallurgy business from Gorō. During the 1950s, the father- and son-in-law team developed a heat-resistant alloy for railway car bogie springs and, for several fat decades, sold their product under an exclusive contract to the Japan National Railways System. Eguchi took over the family company when the old man began to slow down, and it was still going strong when Eguchi himself died of a stroke in 1979. Bad investments and a failure to diversify, however, meant that the virtually single-client company would not survive the double punch of the privatization of Japan National Railways in 1987 and the crash of the bubble economy a few years later.

And yet the Arakis continue to survive—and thrive—in Tokyo. Shigeko-san's sons have successful careers, and her grandchildren have all graduated from top universities. There is yet plenty to live for.

Although twice-widowed Shigeko-san has been alone now for a quarter of a century, she refuses to let the body blows life has given her over the years get her down. She continued her *buyō* dancing well into her seventies, and now keeps herself occupied with other hobbies, a busy social life, and frequent *tokkō* memorial activities. She cried herself out over Haruo and Yūkyū long enough to put all of her attendant ghosts to rest. One important gesture toward this closure was burying Yūkyū's *ihai* name tablet near the ruins of the old pilots' barracks at Chiran with Reiko Akabane in 1974. Another was in 1976, when the Chiran Tokkō Heiwa Kaikan (Chiran Peace Museum for Kamikaze Pilots) museum opened.

"The moment I walked into the hall and saw that huge mosaic of the *ten'nyo* angels cradling the dead *tokkō* pilot in their arms and lifting him to heaven,* I just sobbed like a baby," Shigeko says, recalling her first visit to the Chiran shrine. "That was the moment I knew everything was all right with Haruo. I know he's happy—wherever he is—and that he is watching me and looking after me.

"Of course, I know my second husband is watching, too," she adds with a conspiratorial smirk. "Sometimes I worry about how I'm going to handle the introductions when we all finally meet."

I ask Shigeko if she hopes Haruo's plane was the one that hit the American destroyer on May 11, 1945. Ever the quick tactician, Shigeko gives me a brief sidewise glance here, as if she is a bit wary that I may be laying a trap with the question. Then she tells me that nobody knows whose plane from the 51st Shinbu Yūkyūtai hit the American ship that day, but that yes, she hopes it was Haruo's. This is not, she is careful to stress, because it would mean Haruo could get some licks in against the Americans—as he had always vowed to do—but because hitting a ship was what he was trying to do at the moment he drew his last breath. It was, literally, his death wish. Shigeko-san says it is nice to think that Haruo might rest easier having accomplished his mission, so whom would it hurt to believe that is the way it was?

Although Shigeko still mourns her dead, she does not dwell on them

---

*This mural can be seen online at:
http://www.town.chiran.kagoshima.jp/touristinfo/heiwakaikan/sub03.html.

enough to make her miserable. She grieved long enough like that, and long enough turned out to be a lot of years.

"Life is too short to spend being sad," Shigeko says. "Some people have never recovered from the war. Losing loved ones ruined the rest of their own lives. I don't know how they've gone all this time like that. As for me, I want to be happy in the time I have left. And I know that's the way Haruo would have wanted it for me."

# PART SEVEN

# DOCTOR HIROSHIMA

# twenty-seven

# SETAGAYA KAN'NON

The weather on the afternoon of June 18, 2002, is typical for Tokyo's rainy season—clammy, gray, and wet. Despite the rain, hundreds of thousands of Tokyoites—mostly young people—are gathering in front of huge outdoor LED screens in parks and main thoroughfares throughout the city to watch the Japanese national team play Turkey in the semiquarterfinals of the World Cup soccer tournament. Millions of others are about to watch the event on TVs in homes, classrooms, or offices. But at a small Buddhist temple in the quiet Setagaya Ward neighborhood of Geba, a group of twenty or so people is gathering to participate in a decidedly more low-key affair.

Located on the west end of Setagaya, Geba is a charming community of narrow, twisting, tree-lined streets, parks, low-rise luxury apartment buildings, and impressive private homes—a verdant oasis in the midst of the hyperactive concrete sprawl of the metropolis. Not surprisingly for such desirable residential turf, the cost of living in the area does not come cheap. Even with the precipitous post–bubble economy drop in real estate values in this and other Tokyo districts, it is daunting to imagine the fiscal astringency necessary for a middle-class family to make ends meet here, and a passing perusal of BMWs and Jaguars in driveways indicates that unless retirees and people in company-sponsored dormitories count, the breed is rare in these parts. From all appearances, residence in the area is effectively closed to all but an eclectic mélange of wealthy professionals and old folks lucky enough to have staked a piece of ground here before land prices went into the stratosphere in the 1970s.

Another neighborhood "resident" that timed its pre-real-estate-boom arrival well is the venue for today's congregation. Setagaya Kan'non is a Buddhist temple established with a modest investment in 1951 that now sits on real estate worth about ten million dollars. The half-acre temple compound consists of a substantial and very ornately carved wooden archway, a few modestly sized one-room wooden chapels, a rectory for Abbot Kenshō Ōta and family, a community house, and a mini pagoda. Outside of the community house and rectory, the compound's structures are built in a highly decorative, Chinese-influenced Kyoto style, and judging from the breathtaking craftsmanship and heavy elemental weathering of the buildings, a reasonable guess would date their construction to shogunate days. But as we have noted in our earlier explorations of the Yasukuni facilities, exposure to the humid, polluted Tokyo climate makes natural building materials appear very old, very quickly. This mechanism has painted Setagaya Kan'non's masonry with damp moss and soot streaks and bleached its woodwork to give the temple an antiquated dignity belying its mere fifty-odd years of existence.

In addition to all the tastefully weathered stonework, there is also an abundance of decorative statuary here—roaring mythical beasts, stone snow lanterns, and presiding over the temple's well-stocked carp pond with the languid poise of an Angkor Wat love goddess, a bronze statue of Kan'non-sama, the hermaphrodite Buddhist deity of mercy. The statue is a popular draw to the temple during entrance exam season, for it is said that test-taking hopefuls who pray before it can get into the school of their choice, even if their aim is a bit higher than their academic ability merits. The pond itself is also a perennial favorite, especially for the local children who come to feed or pester its captive creatures, secure in the common knowledge that nothing short of outright fish rustling will rouse a protest from the ever-convivial Abbot Ōta and his mild-mannered son.

On the eighteenth of each month, Setagaya Kan'non has for the last half century also been the destination of a very different variety of regular visitor: those who attend the monthly memorial services held in the temple's Tokkō Chapel, a one-room tatami-floored structure built around a raised wooden platform on the northern edge of the compound. Built in 1952 (the year the American occupation ended), the chapel owes its existence in large part to the efforts of the late Lieutenant General Michio Sugawara (IMA '10).

Despite Sugawara's selfless largesse, assessments of his legacy have not been exclusively favorable over the years. Beyond his postwar role as benefactor to Setagaya Kan'non, the general carved a larger slice of history for himself as the commander of the 6th Air Army and one of the chief architects of the Okinawa Ten-Gō *tokkō* campaign. The nature of this final command alone would have been enough to shadow his legacy with a certain measure of controversy, but it was the simple fact of his own survival that ended up causing him the most grief. While many of his general officer and flag-rank *tokkō* commander peers committed suicide at the end of the war, Sugawara refused to make such a gesture, thereby earning the lasting enmity of many veterans and war bereaved. He endured sporadic verbal assaults, published character assassinations,* and other forms of harassment for the last four decades of his long life.

Even in death, Sugawara's penance continues, attended to on this mortal plane by his children. Since the general's passing in 1983 at the age of ninety-five, his sons Michiyoshi Fukabori (INA '45)[†] and Michihiro Sugawara (IMA '48)[‡] have maintained the family tradition of tireless service to the Tokkō Zaidan organization their father helped to form and attendance at monthly services at the temple he helped build.

After a soggy stroll from the nearby ramen shop where I have eaten my late lunch, I arrive at Setagaya Kan'non and join a small queue of people climbing the short flight of wooden stairs to the Tokkō Chapel. At the top of the stairs, we remove our shoes before entering the close, incense-smoky confines of the chapel, where the abbot is straightening out folding chairs and seating cushions on the tatami. Sure enough, Michiyoshi Fukabori is here, and I exchange head nods and greetings

---

*In an American or European milieu, Sugawara would no doubt have been involved in libel litigation for much of the remainder of his life. But in this, the land of fifty-year-long lawsuit cases, all but the very rich or the very foolish avoid civil cases like the plague.

†Surname differs because he married into a family without a male heir, and assumed their surname.

‡Obviously, there was no IMA graduating class of '48—the war having ended during the summer of Sugawara's plebe year.

with him, as well as with Shigeko Araki, Iwao Fukagawa, and other people I have met during the course of my research. After waiting on another
short line to sign the guestbook, I take a seat next to Shigeko-san, my
usual memorial service neighbor.

At two o'clock, Abbot Ōta rings a chime, and the congregation approaches a brocade-draped altar in pairs to sprinkle finely chipped san-
dalwood into an incense burner pot. When this is done, copies of prayer
text are passed around, and with a long, climbing first syllable, the abbot
begins chanting the customary *tokkō* sutra. The congregation catches up
a syllable or two later, singing the praises of the brave pilots and their
sacrifices against daunting odds in combating Western colonialism, and
thanking them for the peace and prosperity of modern day Japan. Most
people here do not need the cheat sheets, having said the prayer hundreds or even thousands of times in their lives, but I cannot count myself
among this in-group. I try to keep up with the archaic language used in
the text—crossing my fingers in the part where it bad-mouths the West,
of course—but even with Shigeko-san frequently reaching over to point
out what verse I should be on, I just get lost again a few lines later.

Eventually I give up, and pass the rest of the service as I always do,
people watching and looking around at all the old bric-a-brac in the
room: a painted statuette of an impossibly beautiful *tokkō* pilot in a glass
case, like a male version of a *hanayome ningyo*; some journeyman artist's
oil paintings of flaming aerial combat; hand-brushed quotations of great
men and solemn blood oaths in bold grass-hand; age-yellowed photos of
glorious dead along the walls. To the left of the altar, there is a blowup of
one of Toshirō Takagi's famous Chiran shots. In the picture, a long-
necked Haruo Araki with a Mona Lisa smile and the countenance of a
confident young Plains Indian chief is going over flight maps with his pilots before their sortie. On the other side of the room, a bull-necked Takijirō Ōnishi—looking ever the irritable electrician—glowers down at me
with an unwelcoming stare from a dark alcove.

With the end of services, everyone gathers in the congregation house
on the south side of the compound. The comfortably homey tatami-
floored wooden structure is usually used for religious lectures or various
club meetings, as well as for accommodating mourners when funerals or
memorial services are held at the temple. There is a sizable kitchen facility in the building staffed by middle-aged and elderly neighborhood

women and overseen by Abbot Ōta's wife, and it can put together a decent spread for up to about one hundred people. But today there will be no need for any big productions—just packets of snack food and a few bottles of beer for a light-drinking group of twenty.

When everyone is seated, Abbot Ōta calls for a toast, after which the gathering spends the next hour or so discussing research projects, current activities of other memorial groups, verbal obituaries for recently deceased comrades and friends, personal news, and political developments in Tokyo. It is this last subject that inevitably brings on the heaviest exchanges, with right-leaning opinions generally lengthier and noisier than more tolerant views.

Recent Chinese cheek and North Korean high jinks have been the biggest topics of late, with discussion characterized by collective laments over constitutional restraints on formal rearmament and openly expressed disgust with the limp-wristedness of Japanese diplomacy and bureaucracy. Today we are discussing a recent incident in which Chinese police violated the territoriality of the Japanese consulate in Shenyang to arrest a group of asylum seekers while the consulate staff stood by without lifting a hand. Someone remarks that the Americans would never stand for the Chinese walking all over them like that.

Suddenly, all eyes in the room are on me, but I field the inquiry with universal body language for "no comment"—a shrug and sideways tip of my head. I always feel uncomfortable when Japanese compare their country unfavorably with America in my presence—especially when other Japanese are within earshot. Nothing healthy and constructive can come out of it, and in any case, Americans have no need to swagger in this part of the world. Our footprints here are deep enough, and the Japanese—certainly the generation of the people in this room—are perfectly aware of what we are capable of in a confrontation.

The topic is bounced around the table a bit longer, ending with the general consensus that something like the consulate incident never would have happened in the old days, and that nobody respects Japan anymore.

In the lull that follows, I cannot help but think that some American responsibility has just been implied. But perhaps I am being paranoid. Nevertheless, I am relieved when conversation resumes and nibble on a new nut.

The afternoon's meeting ends on a peaceful note, with promises, as always, to meet again in a month. As the rest of the gathering disperses to go home, I remain behind on the tatami floor of the meeting hall, chatting with today's interview subject, Dr. Fumitake Hiroshima.

Although his name sounds more like a James Bond nemesis, Dr. Hiroshima is in actuality nothing more menacing than a kindly old Seta-gaya veterinarian, and his fireplug build and cheerful bear-cub personality would be more at home in the cartoons of Hanna-Barbera than the pages of an Ian Fleming novel. He looks and sounds every bit of what he is—a man who has devoted his life to making others happy.

At our first meeting six months ago, I can remember the personal warmth I immediately sensed from the doctor—the kind that makes you think, *I hope nothing bad ever happens to this person*. It did not take too long, however, to catch on to the sadness playing foil to the smile in his eyes. As we spoke and the doctor's story unfolded, I learned that despite a naturally happy disposition and a career that could have been screen-written for a Robin Williams vehicle, this was a man who has also suffered some enormous losses in his day. But this knowledge did not make me feel sorry for him—it only increased my feelings of affinity for this gentle human being. After all, how could you not help but like a man who does volunteer work in his spare time driving a petting-zoo-on-wheels for kindergartners?

During the past half year I have been let in on the rough outline of the doctor's wartime experiences, but until now I have not pushed for too much detail. Today, however, I plan to be frank. I inform the doctor of my intentions, and he gives his consent. Best to get it all down while he still can, he says. His brother deserves the truth to be told.

As the doctor and I settle down to begin our interview, he arranges some notes on the tabletop. Then he reaches into his jacket pocket and takes out something he never leaves home without—a laminated photo of his brother Tadao in the nineteenth summer of his life. Resplendent in his naval aviator flight suit and Rising Sun *hachimaki*, Tadao is the very image of a proud and resolute warrior in the picture, and minus sixty years of wear and tear, he has the same rawboned, salt-of-the-earth, Kyūshū-countryboy face as his younger brother. For all their resemblance, the siblings could almost be identical twins.

The doctor inevitably shows this picture whenever he meets someone new at Setagaya Kan'non. But the doctor and I are not meeting for the first time; he knows I have seen the photo before, and he is not taking it out now for my sake at all. Rather, its display is a form of what I am tempted to call, for lack of a better term, photographic transubstantiation. Anyone who has ever been to a Japanese wake has seen this concept at work when a photo of the deceased (serene facial expressions are favored) is positioned to look down at the mourners from on high, as if placed there to thank personally each person who approaches the casket to light an incense punk. Photos of the deceased are also often seen carried by family or trusted former employees to be paraded at building openings or ship christenings or other such commemorative events when the principals behind the original projects have not lived long enough to see the fruit of their labor. Readers may recall Sydney Olympics 100 kg judo champion Kōsei Inoue cradling his mother's photo on the medal podium. Similar displays are sometimes even seen at the conclusion of murder trials, when family members of the victim will carry a large framed photo of the deceased into the courtroom to hear the judge's verdict read.* In all of these cases, the deceased, through traces of phantasmal essence captured in the displayed photo,† is considered to be present and accounted for to participate in the proceedings.

Likewise, when the doctor places his brother's photo on the tabletop to face me, the meaning of the gesture is clear: Tadao will be joining our conversation today. Perhaps, I cannot help wondering, he is also here to look out for his kid brother Fumitake, just as he always did when they were boys.

Fumitake Hiroshima was born in 1927 in Tsuyazaki, Fukuoka Prefecture, a small village on the Sea of Japan coastline of northwestern Kyūshū. He was the sixth of six children of Mankichi Hiroshima, a prosperous landowner and local government official. When not tending to

---

*There is no provision for trial by jury of peers in the Japanese legal system, although there have been proposals of late for its institution.

†Until the end of the nineteenth century, many Japanese, especially in rural areas, attributed supernatural powers to photographs, believing—similar to American Plains Indians of the era—that a person's spirit could be trapped when their picture was taken. The custom described here may have its roots in some legacy of this folk belief.

his duties at the local municipal office, Mankichi raised rice and livestock with his wife, Haruō, to supplement his income from the salt beds he operated on the beach behind his house. Previous generations of Hiroshimas had been prosperous salt makers in the region since the late Edo period before adding agriculture to the family business; the salt beds they built are still there.

"You can see them from the air," Dr. Hiroshima says proudly. "Whenever I fly into Fukuoka I can always look down and see exactly where I grew up."

The doctor's earliest memories are of that beach, because the locale was the backdrop of most of his childhood bonding with Tadao.

"I think we spent more time on the beach than we did in the house," the doctor says.

While all of the Hiroshima siblings enjoyed good relationships with one another, their wide age spread meant that the oldest children in the house—sisters Shizuko and Tamae—were already fielding suitors by the time Fumitake was beginning to walk and talk. Likewise, oldest sons Junkō and Keijirō were approaching puberty and not inclined to bother much with a toddler. They were fond and protective of their little brother, but the age gap precluded close bonding.

Third son Tadao, however, was only a year and a half older than Fumitake, and the rest of the family regarded and raised the boys almost as twins. Perhaps as a result of this egalitarian treatment, the two were as much best friends as they were brothers, and absolutely inseparable when growing up. Well into their teens, they were still playing, studying, and bathing together. They even shared the same futon blanket at night.

The bond was just as tight away from home, and the boys always looked out for each other. For Fumitake, being only one grade behind Tadao at school meant that a devoted and fearless protector was never farther than a shout for help away. Although Tadao disliked aggression, he had a rock-solid sense of justice and always came running when his kid brother was in trouble. As a result, school bullies and local toughs learned to leave Fumitake alone when looking for punching bags.

While the brothers bore an almost clonelike physical resemblance to each other, they were temperamentally quite distinct, with Fumitake's caring and gregarious personality the polar opposite of his older brother's bookish and rather dispassionate introspection. Dr. Hiroshima notes that

Tadao was born in the Year of the Cow, according to the Chinese zodiac, and had a stolid, patient personality to match. He had no rough edges to be accommodated, and—unless prompted to action by extreme circumstances—was utterly nonconfrontational. But this did not mean that he was averse to play-wrestling with his brother in front of the living room radio when sumo matches were broadcast, acting out moves and throws as the announcer narrated the ring action.

Sumo pantomiming aside, the two rarely fought in earnest, but when they did, things could get nasty. Fumitake was an especially sore loser and grudge holder, and often did mean things in the wake of fights that he later regretted. Some of those acts still cause regret seventy years later.

"I remember ripping Tadao's favorite picture of himself after one of our fights," Dr. Hiroshima says. "It was a picture of him riding a hobby-horse during a visit to our rich uncle in Osaka. We were able to paste the photo back together, and Tadao soon forgot all about the incident, but I never did."

Personality differences were also manifested in the boys' choices of organized sports at school. Where Fumitake enjoyed the close, sweaty, and aggressive exertions of kendo, the reserved Tadao—when not burying his face in some highbrow novel—played tennis. The sport was a rarity in rural Japan at the time, and seen as an activity only for cosmopolitan rich kids. But then, Tadao was an exceptional child in many ways, with intellectual abilities far beyond most of his peers. At the age of twelve, when he entered junior high, only about one out of ten male classmates—and an infinitesimally small number of girls—followed him. With the move, he also became the first person in family history to pursue education beyond the elementary school level. More precedent was set the next year when Fumitake followed in his brother's footsteps, making the Hiroshimas the first family in Tsuyazaki ever to send more than one child to junior high.

The Hiroshimas' academic accomplishments were not their only "firsts" in their little farming community. The family was also the first in Tsuyazaki to have a radio—a gift from the aforementioned rich Osaka uncle—and it was not long before neighbors began paying visits to the Hiroshimas' living room, at first merely to gawk at the new gadget; later, they began gathering weekly to listen to popular radio dramas like *Naniwabushi,* a thrilling chop-'em-up about *yakuza* and masterless samurai battles in a harbor town in old Edo. Most of the rest of the time, however, the living room—and thus control of the radio—was the exclusive domain of Tadao and Fumitake, who used the space as a study area.

On the morning of Monday, December 8, 1941, the boys were studying for midterm exams in the living room with the radio on when the regularly scheduled program was interrupted by a special news report. Books and pens were put down and ears pricked up as an urgent-sounding announcer launched into an impassioned account of a daring dawn raid on the American naval installation at Pearl Harbor. According to the report, most of the American Pacific Fleet was either sunk or in flames. Fumitake and Tadao looked at each other wide-eyed before they started jumping up and down and shouting for anyone else within earshot to join them in the living room for the big news. As soon as the short broadcast ended, the boys ran excitedly to school, where a holiday mood prevailed. If the news was to be believed—and of course it was, coming from Imperial GHQ itself—the war against the Americans was now as good as won. It was a proud day to be Japanese.

The small farming community had even more reason to be proud several weeks later, when the names of the midget sub crews from the Pearl Harbor raid appeared in the papers. Not only were two of the crewmen from Kyūshū, but one of them—Ensign Shigemi Furuno—was a local boy, hailing from the next village down the coast from Tsuyazaki. The next day, the entire student body of the local junior high school marched several kilometers to pay their respects in front of the Furuno family home en masse.

In the Hiroshima household, no one was more electrified by all of these dramatic developments than Tadao, who had already been talking for several years now about a possible career in naval aviation. A large part of Tadao's motivation was due to the influence of his older brother Keijirō, who had entered the navy as an apprentice sailor in 1934 at the age of fourteen. An early candidate for the Yokaren program, he ended up being turned down for admission at the last minute, even though he had passed his initial test battery. Now in his seventh year of uniformed service as an aircraft engine maintenance specialist, he had long since gotten over the disappointment of not making the Yokaren cut. Tadao, however, had not, and now that the nation was at war, he vowed to make sure someone in the family realized his older brother's dreams of flying. A family discussion on the subject resulted in approval of Tadao's wishes. His teachers at school were also very encouraging of these future plans, and felt that with his robust physical constitution and exceptional academic aptitude, he would be an excellent candidate for Yokaren training. However, they also suggested that it would be best for Tadao's military career to be put on hold until he finished his fourth year of junior high so that he could qualify for the elite Kō Shū Yokaren course instead of going in now to the Otsu Shū course with younger boys, most of whom had completed only elementary school education.* Tadao begrudgingly accepted the wisdom of this argument, which meant that for the next year or so, he was forced to limit his contributions to the war effort to patriotic essay homework assignments and watching war movies with Fumitake after school at the local cinema.

Of the many films the brothers watched together, by far the most impressive and exciting was *Hawai/Mare/Oki Kaisen* ("Naval Battles of Hawaii and the Malay Straits"), a Navy Ministry public affairs office–financed Toho Studios production released in December 1942 to commemorate the first anniversary of the events it depicted, namely, the Pearl Harbor raid and the sinking of the British *Repulse* and *Prince of Wales* by land-based torpedo bombers.[1] Featuring major stars Denjirō Ōkōchi and Setsuko Hara, among other notables of Japanese cinema, the film electrified audiences throughout the nation with its superb special effects, which were supervised by SFX wizard Eiji Tsuburaya (later of *Godzilla* fame—he is the progenitor of the "monsters stomp Tokyo" pop-culture archetype).[†]

During his long year of waiting, Tadao studied for the competitive battery of tests he would be taking in February 1943. Special textbooks for Yokaren exam preparation were readily available in bookstores, and Tadao bought every one of them he could. In March 1943, his efforts paid off with an acceptance letter from the Navy Ministry. A month later

---

*Age restrictions for Kō Shū were lowered after Tadao's group, which is what allowed Tokurō Takei and Akinori Asano to enter the Kō-13 cycle at fourteen.

†Tsuburaya's techniques were so impressive, it is said that when American occupation authorities viewed the film for the first time after the war, they thought the aerial combat sequences were genuine documentary footage (http://www001.upp.so-net.ne.jp/okapi/tokusatu.htm).

Tadao left home for the new Yokaren campus at Kagoshima as a member of Cycle Kō-12.

In the lonely months following Tadao's departure for Yokaren, Fumitake also began talking about entering the military. The dominant sentiment behind this thinking was sincere and patriotic in nature, but there were also aspects in keeping with a lifetime pattern of both emulation of, and competition with, his brother. His parents, however, were less than enthusiastic about the idea, their own patriotic sentiments notwithstanding. New developments on the home front had as much to do with their consternation as did concern for their son's personal safety. The Hiroshima's eldest son, Junkō, had married in February 1943, then gotten drafted by the army a mere five months later. Somewhat long in the tooth for a draftee, at the age of twenty-eight, Junkō was an unlikely candidate for induction at a point in the war when the armed services had not yet reached barrel-scraping desperation to fill their ranks. As an eldest son and newlywed, an appeal to the draft board for deferment—or at least for local civil defense assignment—would have had a good chance of reaching a sympathetic ear. But Junkō raised no such appeal, and he was duly sent to Manchuria after his basic training, leaving behind his new bride in the now eerily quiet Hiroshima household. With Keijirō a career navy man, Tadao off at Yokaren, and the calamity of Junkō's induction, Fumitake was the only Hiroshima son safe and sound at home, and his parents had a strong desire to keep him there. But they would not be able to keep their son out of harm's way forever. The draft age had been dropped from twenty to nineteen earlier in the year, and rumors were that it would drop again in 1944.

In the meantime, Fumitake spent his time on the sidelines going about his normal—if now considerably quieter—routine as a junior high school student. This all changed when junior high classes throughout the country were halted "for the duration" by official decree in March 1944 to free up labor for war industries and civil defense projects. In the case of Tsuyazaki Junior High School, its students were at first organized into work units digging reinforced bunkers and camouflaged revetments for aircraft at military air bases in the Fukuoka area. Later, the students were parceled out to local war industry plants. Fumitake and several of his friends were assigned to a factory making aircraft parts in the suburbs of Fukuoka City. The boys were pushed through a crash course in machinist's skills, then put to work on day/night swing shifts tooling and assembling molybdenum wing root* frames for the Tōkai Type 11, a late-war anti–sub patrol design that was a near-copy of the German Ju-88. Fumitake and other local boys commuted to the plant from their homes, but student workers mobilized from communities farther away were forced to live in crowded, uncomfortable dormitories near the factories.

Like so many other Japanese boys of his wartime generation, Fumitake considered working in a factory a rather drab contribution to the war effort compared with being a professional soldier—preferably an officer—and he dreamed of securing an appointment to one of the service academies before going on to a stellar military or naval career. Letters and news from Tadao about his own progress in naval aviation only fanned the flames of Fumitake's motivation, and as the grind of late 1944 wound into early 1945, he spent most his rare downtime from the aircraft plant looking into application processes for the IMA and INA. He smiled to himself thinking of what a laugh it would be if he could pull rank as an officer on Tadao someday. Sweet revenge for all those lost sumo bouts in front of the living room radio!

Fumitake's lifestyle at the time, however, was in no way conducive to the dedicated study necessary to pass the service academy tests. He had hardly cracked a book in the year since schools were shut down, and he had little time to prepare for his exams. But try he did, and despite giving it his best, he failed to get into either of the academies.

Although his family was well off by Tsuyazaki standards, the tuition required to send him to a decent private university was beyond their means. Despondent, Fumitake sought advice from an old junior high teacher who suggested a rather unconventional but perfectly legitimate path to an officer's commission: veterinary school. What was more, Tsuyazaki Junior High had a few *suisen nyūgaku* (admission based on school recommendation) slots each year for the vet program at Miyazaki University, a campus of the national university system in eastern Kyūshū. The teacher felt that Fumitake was more than qualified.

---

*Attachment point between an aircraft's wings and fuselage.

Suddenly, Fumitake had hope again. Even with the school recommendation, there would still be the hurdle of a competitive entrance exam—which had only a 10 percent passing rate—but he had grown up tending to the family's farm animals, and he had also enjoyed and excelled at biology in junior high. He got in as much studying as he could, sat for the exam, and in March 1945, he was informed of his acceptance into the program.

By the spring of 1945, students in academic majors considered nonessential for national defense—i.e., pretty much everything except for medicine (including veterinary), agriculture, and hard sciences—had long since been drafted or mobilized, and Miyazaki University was a virtual ghost campus when Fumitake arrived in April to begin his studies. But even before the new semester started, he and the other few remaining students were put to work digging slit trenches around the university buildings and dormitories. No one really believed the earthworks would be needed, though, until Corsairs roared over campus one day in early May.

The raid came utterly without warning, even with an IJA air base directly adjoining the university, and nary a Japanese plane rose to confront the marauders. Fumitake and his classmates huddled in the slit trenches as the American planes buzzed in low, dropping bombs and machine-gunning everything in sight. Bullets crisscrossed the grass and asphalt, stitching building walls, taking out windows. After a terrifying ten minutes of strafing and bombardment, the all-clear was finally given. Fumitake had just gotten up out of his foxhole and started to head back to the dormitory when one last American fighter screamed in to drop a bomb that landed directly on top of the foxhole he had just vacated. Fortunately for Fumitake and the other students in his group, it was a dud.

Faculty and students spent the rest of the day assessing damage and cleaning up debris. Outside of some flying glass cuts, ringing ears, and jangled nerves, no one was injured. The facilities had taken a pounding, however, with the most regrettable casualty being the campus food storehouse, where fresh vegetables and several weeks' worth of rice were ruined by the aerosolized contents of a napalm canister that had punched a hole through the roof of the building and burst on impact but failed to ignite. Everything stank so badly of the jellied gasoline compound that not a morsel could be salvaged. Even the campus livestock would not touch it.

Sporadic American strafing continued throughout the first semester, and Fumitake was relieved when summer vacation came along at the end of July. He was eager to get home, to take a break from homework and air raids for a while. But most important, he wanted to see if there was any news of Tadao. The last word he had received from his favorite brother was this note on the back of an official navy postcard:

Fumitake,
I've returned from my assignment safe and sound.
I'm doing fine, as always, so please don't worry about me.
We must strive to fulfill the duties we have sworn to perform.
Please take care of yourself.
Tadao
July (date censored) 1945, Hyakurihara Air Base, Ibaraki Prefecture

The message was unusual in its cryptic brevity, for Tadao typically wrote fairly lengthy and descriptive letters and cards. Also, the mention of "returning" from an assignment did not make sense to Fumitake, because as far as he knew, Tadao was where he had been for the last eleven months—in Ibaraki Prefecture, north of Tokyo, assigned to the 51st Squadron of the elite 601st KKT as a Suisei dive-bomber pilot. The mystery was solved when Fumitake went back to Tsuyazaki and his parents told him about their last meeting with Tadao.

Two months earlier, a postcard from Tadao with a Kajiki, Kagoshima Prefecture, postmark had arrived at the house. Mr. and Mrs. Hiroshima had not seen their son for over a year by this point, and were all too aware from the newspapers of the battle then raging in Okinawa just a couple of hundred kilometers south of Kagoshima. If Tadao was on temporary duty there, they had thought, it could mean only that he was about to ship out. A visit to Ibaraki over the past year had been impossible because of the sheer distance and tight restrictions on civilian rail travel, but a trip to Kagoshima—although still a considerable journey under wartime conditions—was within the realm of reason. With a little luck, the stationmaster could be persuaded to sell them some tickets.

After all, there was no telling whether this was going to be the last time they would ever get to see their son alive again.

The Hiroshimas packed light, said a quick prayer at the family *kami-dana*, and headed for Tsuyazaki Station. Fortunately, the stationmaster was a reasonable and kindhearted man, and he made sure they got tickets for a southbound train. They reached Kajiki the next morning, and soon found their way to the local air base, only to have the gate sentries explain that no visits with base personnel were allowed. But the Hiroshimas were not going to be turned away so easily. They explained their situation, describing the long journey they had just made to see their son. Inquiries were made, and after a short wait, Tadao appeared, resplendent in flight suit, white flying scarf, and Hinomaru *hachimaki*. His proud father pulled his old Brownie box camera out and took a picture of him on the spot.*

Once Tadao had cleared a few hours of impromptu leave with his superiors, he proceeded to show his parents around the nearby town. But more impressive for the Hiroshimas than the scenic charms of Kajiki was the way the townspeople they passed in the streets were bowing to their son. These were not head nods, but the ninety-degree-angle bows from the hip that Japanese reserve only for those situations or persons deserving of the utmost respect. Curious as to why civilians would be displaying such weighty regard for a nineteen-year-old petty officer second class, Mr. Hiroshima asked his son to explain. Tadao hesitated for a moment, then told his parents that the townspeople were aware of the meaning of his headband. He and the rest of the Suisei pilots in the 51st Squadron had just been assigned to *tokkō*.

The Hiroshimas—like everyone else in Japan by this point—knew all too well what the word *tokkō* meant.

While Fumitake was shocked to hear of his brother's situation in Kagoshima, he was able to take some comfort in the fact that Tadao had since written from his home base of Hyakurihara to report the end of this temporary "assignment." When the surrender was announced on

---

*It is a laminated copy of this picture that Dr. Hiroshima carries in his jacket pocket to this day.

August 15, he hoped and prayed and waited along with everyone else in the family that seeing Tadao and his other brothers home from the war safe and sound would be only a matter of weeks. But as the long, hot summer began to cool down and the days became shorter, only Keijirō had thus far darkened the Hiroshimas' doorway.

With Junkō ostensibly still in Manchuria or northern China, it was reasonable to assume that his repatriation could take months. But as other neighborhood boys in uniform began trickling—then flooding—back home through the early autumn of 1945, Tadao's absence became increasingly ominous and harder to explain without thinking the unthinkable. Fumitake, however, was having none of that, and he refused to contemplate any scenario that did not involve Tadao's making it back alive. When fall semester at Miyazaki started up at the end of September, Fumitake was still waiting for his brother, and it was only with great reluctance that he eventually caved to his family's demands that he return to school to resume his studies.

One day in late October, Mankichi Hiroshima visited Fukuoka City on official prefectural business. Boarding a streetcar from the train station, he noticed a young man in a thrown-together getup of mixed civilian mufti and old navy-issue items—a typical "uniform of defeat" look for the millions of ex-servicemen now wandering the country in search of livelihood and some semblance of pride. Both commodities were in dismally short supply for Japanese males in the autumn of 1945.

Mr. Hiroshima gave his down-at-the-heels, straphanging neighbor a casual look-over, noting with interest that the young man was wearing the distinctive tan leather slip-on ankle boots of a naval aviator.[2] The wearer's name and unit were written in black along the top edges of the boots, as per navy custom, and Mr. Hiroshima was just about to look away when he realized with a jolt that the unit assignment on the boots read 51ST SQUADRON. With his heart in his throat, he tapped the young man on the shoulder and introduced himself as Tadao Hiroshima's father.

After a quick exchange of desperate queries and crushing confirmations, the young man bowed and offered his condolences. Mr. Hiroshima got off at the next stop, got on a streetcar headed in the opposite direction, and went home to let his family know that their worst fears had been realized. Tadao was gone.

"My father's black hair turned snow white almost overnight," Dr. Hiroshima tells me. "My mother was never the same after hearing the news. It knocked all the joy of living out of her, and she never got it back."

The following November, a letter arrived at the Hiroshima home from the former commander of the 601st KKT, Captain Toshikazu Sugiyama, informing the family of Tadao's death and expressing the captain's sincerest condolences. The letter also gave the Hiroshimas the first hard information they had come across about Tadao's final weeks—and most important, his final hours.

As it was explained to them, the functional loss of Okinawa in mid-June 1945 had caused a considerable slowing in *tokkō* activity for most of the rest of the war. During the long summer lull, many units that had been deployed to Kyūshū to participate in the Okinawa campaign were sent back to their regular bases to reequip, replace personnel, and otherwise prepare to defend other possible American invasion points. The 601st KKT was included among these redeployed units, returning to Hyakurihara to help guard the northern approaches to the capital and await a new mission it seemed possible might never come during the long weeks of inactivity that followed.

But activity in home waters picked up in the last week of July when a flotilla of American battleships and cruisers—with carrier support—began an intense shelling campaign against industrial plants along the Pacific coast of central Hōnshū, slowly working their way north from Hamamatsu in Shizuoka Prefecture.[3] By the beginning of the second week of August the enemy force—Task Group 38.3 under Rear Admiral Sherman—had reached far enough north to come within range of Hyakurihara's *tokkō* planes, and on the morning of August 9, the 601st was given standby orders by new Third Air Fleet CO Rear Admiral Sadayoshi Yamada. Sortie orders were issued at 1400 hours for attacks against the main element of the force, which had been spotted east of Kinkazan Island in Miyagi Prefecture. Tadao—riding alone in his two-seater*—took off in the third wave of three Suiseis at 1425 hours,

---

*The other Suiseis that sortied this day all carried full two-man crew complements, with the rear-seater manning a rearward-firing defensive machine gun. Why Tadao alone was made to fly solo has never been explained.

but soon had to turn back with engine trouble. The malfunction was quickly repaired, and Tadao was sent back out with a stragglers' attack group of three planes at 1640 hours.

According to the official 601st KKT combat report of the day's action, Tadao's three-plane flight was whittled down to a force of one by engine trouble and damage from enemy fighters. The malfunctioning planes eventually made successful emergency landings at nearby airfields, leaving Tadao's plane to soldier on alone and unescorted through the CAP and AA toward Task Force 38.3. The 601st recon elements tracking the action from a distance report that his plane "appeared to hit a cruiser at approximately 1815 hours."[4] But U.S. Navy records state that the only *tokkō* damage of the day (it also happened to be the last of the war) occurred at 1456 hours (local time), when a single attacker of indeterminate type hit the destroyer USS *Borie,* causing the loss of forty-eight killed or missing and sixty-six wounded.[5]

As is the case with so many *tokkō* pilots, there is no way of determining with 100 percent certainty what happened to Tadao, or whether or not his mission was successful. But similar to Shigeko Araki's sentiments about her husband Haruo's final flight, Dr. Hiroshima wants to believe that Tadao's plane got through. It was the mission his brother died trying to accomplish, and what his parents spent the remainder of their lives believing he had been able to do.

Like most upstanding young Japanese men of his generation, Tadao grew up with the phrase *oya kōkō* never far from his lips. This was the Confucian concept of loyalty to one's parents and the virtue of making them proud through one's deeds and manner. Dr. Hiroshima has always wanted to believe that Tadao performed his duties as a *tokkō* pilot more out of this sentiment—that is, of wanting to protect his homeland and bring honor to the family name—than out of any "Long live the emperor" mentality. The doctor is extremely proud of having had a brother like this—a young man who had the courage to die for the things and people he loved.

"Tadao was my hero," the doctor says. "And he always will be."

I ask the doctor if the perspective of decades and distance has made him bitter about his brother's death, or cynical about the government policies and strategies that caused it, especially given the fact that his brother was killed only six days before the end of the war.

"No," the doctor answers. "Those were the times we lived in, and we were educated to be patriotic. Tadao had no choice but to do his duty. I don't think young people in this country can understand that kind of thinking now."

Several days after Captain Sugiyama's letter was delivered, official notification of Tadao's death finally arrived from the Navy Ministry, expressing the emperor's and nation's undying gratitude for the family's sacrifices, and informing them of Tadao's posthumous three-rank promotion to ensign.* Although there was scant comfort for Tadao's parents in this final gesture from His Majesty's government, Fumitake was very proud of his brother's becoming an officer.

The following summer, an official memorial service was held in the auditorium of the local elementary school to honor Tadao and six other boys from Tsuyazaki who had died in the chaotic final weeks of the war. The ceremony was attended by most of the townsfolk, and after an eminently forgettable speech by the mayor, a big show was made of handing out the customary white-draped ossuary boxes to the bereaved families. Cradling their tragic treasure, the Hiroshimas returned home to open the box and find that there was nothing in it but Tadao's name penned in businesslike brush-written kanji on a slip of paper.

Adding to the Hiroshima family's grief was the continued mystery of Junkō's whereabouts. Now going on a year since war's end, they had yet to hear any news at all from him, although reports of as many as half a million Japanese servicemen being captured in Manchuria and now held in Siberian gulags by their Soviet captors provided the most likely scenario of his fate.

One day in the spring of 1947, a cable from Junkō arrived telling them that he had just landed at Maizuru Port on the Sea of Japan coast of Kyoto Prefecture. Released by the Soviets because poor health precluded his usefulness in forced labor, he had come home on a POW repatriation boat and was now preparing to board a train for home.

Hearing the news, Fumitake rushed back to Tsuyazaki for the homecoming, but he did not make it in time to greet his brother at the train station with the rest of the family. As the scene at the depot was later

---

*The Japanese Navy and Army Ministries were still functioning in administrative matters and repatriation efforts at this point in the Occupation.

described to him, when the weakened, skeleton-thin Junkō stepped down from his freedom train, he seemed to register a measure of mild shock at his father's white hair. Then, after the expected emotional greetings with the other family members present, he asked about Tadao, anxious but hopeful: *He was never posted overseas, right? Certainly he must be home by now?* Everyone's tears of happiness were quickly tinged with sorrow as Mankichi Hiroshima let his son in on sad news the rest of the family had already known for almost two years. What should have been a day of thanks and elation became something far less than happy.

Junkō's bittersweet return closed the last chapter of the Hiroshimas' war. As they went about rebuilding their lives, Fumitake returned to his studies at Miyazaki University, getting his degree in 1948 before heading up to Tokyo to finish up his doctorate requirements. His first job in the big city was as a research assistant at the veterinary medicine department of Tokyo University, where he was in charge of the school's famed horse stables. Subsequent experience in private-sector veterinary medicine led the doctor to start his own practice in Setagaya Ward, Tokyo, in 1955. He has been a beloved fixture of the neighborhood ever since.

# twenty-eight

## PILGRIMAGE TO CHIRAN

It is Saturday, October 25, 2002, and I am sitting in the coach section of a Japan Air Lines 767 on final approach to Kagoshima Airport. If all has proceeded according to plan, Dr. Hiroshima should be at the arrivals gate with a rented car. He came down to Kagoshima yesterday for the same reason he comes here every October—the annual reunion of his Miyazaki University veterinary department graduating class. But this year he has an extra stop or two included on his usual itinerary. The previous August, during a meeting at Yasukuni to photocopy Tadao's scrapbook in the shrine archives, the doctor broached the idea of my accompanying him for a tour of Kagoshima sometime in the fall. "You cannot write a book about *tokkō* without seeing Kagoshima . . . especially Chiran," he said.

Japan Air Lines puts me on the ground on time, and a smiling Dr. Hiroshima is right on schedule, too. It seems an auspicious beginning to our pilgrimage, and the weather is balmy and beautiful, matching my partner's high-spirited eagerness. He does not get behind the wheel in wide-open country as much as he would like to, he says, and he is really looking forward to today's jaunt down the scenic mountain roadway to Chiran. It will be a nice, challenging drive.

The remark ties a quick, tight knot of nerves in my stomach, but this begins to unwind once we are on the open road and the doctor displays his rigorously careful driving and in-sistence on keeping the car a good twenty or thirty kilometers an hour below the speed limit gets us honked at a few times on the way, but given all of the hairpin turns and blind shoulders in the road, I am all in favor of his driving policy of erring on the side of caution. Besides, being able to relax a bit lets me enjoy the scenery.

After an imposing eyeful of Sakurajima, the jagged brown semiactive volcano that dominates the upper reaches of Kagoshima Bay, we get on the Ibusuki Skyline, a forlorn little turnpike of crumbly two-lane macadam that traverses a starkly beautiful landscape of lush foliage and rust—a Chinese-scroll watercolor of bamboo-covered limestone cliffs graffittied over with brutal brown slashes of abandoned industrial plant. Dark green, steeply sloped mountains push up the horizon and crowd the sky in every direction, but up close, the man-made scenery is strictly Gdánsk-on-the-Yangtze—dead factories, forgotten stone quarries, red-brown skeletal remains of gantries and cranes, roadside restaurants with collapsed roofs and weeds pushing through broken bay windows.

Strewn along the highway at irregular intervals are kitschy artifacts from happier days of a bygone era, when outsiders apparently showed more interest in this place. We drive by boarded-over roadside stands; a faded fiberglass Takamori Saigō sitting atop a storehouse, scowling at the passing traffic; flaking metal signboards for long-bankrupt tourist attractions. In one of these, half-obscured by tall undergrowth, you can just make out a swinging couple of nondescript ethnicity looking like Speed Racer and his girlfriend in matching Botany 500 sportswear on a date at Expo '70. They gaze off toward a minimalist rendering of a smoking Sakurajima wearing expressions that are somewhere between religious ecstasy and lower back pain.

During the hour's drive down the Satsuma Peninsula, we have passed maybe a dozen cars, at the most—and the Ibusuki Skyline is supposedly one of the area's major arteries. None of those fabled Japanese traffic snarls to worry about here. As we approach our destination, we finally run into a little congestion when we stop at an intersection for a convoy of buses full of bright-eyed high schoolers to pass. A couple of them smile and wave at me from the windows. We pull in behind the kiddie caravan and trail it straight into Chiran.

The Tomiya Inn is on the town's meticulously pruned main drag, functionally joined at the hip with its next-door neighbor, the reconstructed Tomiya Shokudō. The latter establishment is no longer a cafeteria for airmen, but rather, a small museum and *tokkō* memorabilia gift/book shop. Unfortunately, we have little time to browse. We are running late for the next item on our itinerary—an appointment with Mayor Kampei Shimoide and Director of Social Welfare Shige'aki Yamamoto. These gentlemen have been kind enough to make time in their busy schedules to give us a tour of the town's largest collection of *tokkō* exhibits at the unexpectedly upbeat Chiran Peace Museum for Kamikaze Pilots.

On this particular Saturday afternoon, the atmosphere around the Peace Museum seems more bustling medieval fair than thoughtful war memorial. A drum corps is playing for a ball game nearby, heard but unseen, and the museum grounds and its parking lot are flanked with merchants' booths where reasonably priced souvenirs are sold. Hinomaru *hachimaki* go for five hundred yen (about $4 U.S.), *tokkō*-themed T-shirts for about a thousand. Key holders or Chinese Zippo knockoffs embossed with various models of Japanese navy and army aircraft are available for a little more. On an impulse, I plunk down fifteen hundred for a Shidenkai tie clip.

Other stalls sell hot snack food or that most popular of Japanese road trip souvenirs—boxed confectionary. References to last year's hit film *Hotaru* are in abundance, as is imagery of anime-esque, cherubic *tokkō* pilots as cute as any Hello Kitty character. A noodle restaurant doing brisk business near the entrance to the museum is named Hayabusa Ramen.

I ask Yamamoto-san what he thinks of the tourist-industry commercialization of the facilities here. He replies that it is good for Chiran's economy. A more elegant and irrefutable answer I cannot imagine, and my mind goes back to the Setagaya Kan'non prayer, in which the faithful profess their belief that modern Japan has the sacrifices of the *tokkō* pilots to thank for its peace and prosperity. Dr. Hiroshima and I have just driven through an hour's worth of near-Appalachian desolation, and this is the first place we have seen that is not rusted shut and overgrown with weeds. The presence of an oasis like this in the midst of a moonscape of thirty-year-long economic strangulation seems to border on the miraculous. Has some spiritual life force been imparted to this ground, I wonder—bled and wept into the soil—or are all the tourist buses just the result of smart marketing and nostalgia? Moot question. The mecca exists. It has been built, and they are coming.

Mayor Shimoide leaves our party after we pay our respects at the museum memorial shrine* and ring its bronze Peace Bell, but Yamamoto-san stays to take us through the main exhibits. One of the more impressive of these is a three-quarter-scale mock-up of the musty, catacomblike interior of a *sangakuheisha* barracks, its dark wooden walls lined with helmets, canteens, and crashed aircraft artifacts, thin bedding laid out on the sleeping shelves as if in expectation of a truckload of phantom *tokkō* pilots. The space is claustrophobic and every bit as somber as the Nadeshiko girls described it to me. After taking a few snapshots, I am late for the door.

Yamamoto-san leads us into the high-ceilinged front lobby of the museum proper, a well-lit, clean space dominated by a thirteen-square-meter ceramic mural on the wall facing the entrance. The 1975 work, by local artist Katsuyoshi Nakaya, is entitled *Chinkon no Mitsugi* ("Heaven-sent Requiem"). It depicts a slumped *tokkō* pilot in an almost Christ-like crucifixion pose being extricated from his flaming Hayabusa in midair by six stunningly beautiful *ten'nyo* angels. Magically suspended against a marmalade sky, the deities show enticing flashes of golden midriff and supple thigh through their filmy white garments, their tender cradling of the pilot in this cheesecake pietà toeing a provocatively fuzzy line between mother's caress and lover's embrace. Keeping the eroticism of the main composition from going into overdrive, a blossom-laden cherry branch—obviously suggesting the famous send-off gifts of the Nadeshiko Unit—is shown tumbling from the cockpit, blown back in the propwash of the doomed fighter plane.

This, of course, is the artwork that Shigeko Araki talked about in our interview, claiming that it put to rest forever her concerns for her first husband's posthumous fate. Watching the reactions of other visitors as they enter the museum foyer and see the work, it seems that most are extremely moved, a few even to tears. While I would hesitate to agree with Shigeko-san's assessment of the work as "wonderful," or in the opposite direction, with Ian Buruma's verdict of "ghastly,"[1] the mural is certainly dramatic—in all semantic permutations of the word—and no one can deny the comfort to be found in the thought that, for a young man in

---

*This is not a Shinto shrine, but an annex facility of Setagaya Kan'non. It was dedicated in 1955.

his physical prime, there could be worse afterlife scenarios than being embraced by gorgeous angels for all eternity.

After the fantasy of *Heaven-sent Requiem,* the museum's main exhibition hall is a hard cheek slap of reality—four long walls lined with photographs of young men who burned themselves up for their country. To me, at least, their sepia-toned stares seem to ask, *What did my death achieve?* As a father of sons—and even just as a human being—I find it impossible to stand here without experiencing a confluent rush of grief for the loss of all this youth and potential, and a slow-boiling rage for the obstinate, middle-aged brutes who willed its destruction.

I look around at my fellow visitors for signs of kindred spirits, but most of the people here seem to walk through the exhibit with expressions akin to religious awe—as if to even dare to think that the deaths of these boys were a tragic waste of life might bring a bolt from the blue down upon their heads. There is no anger. They are in the presence of young war gods, not the slaughtered innocent. This is the Alamo for Texans, Kosovo for Slavs, the Tomb of Ali for Shi'ites. Although not as stridently posed as at Yasukuni, there is an agenda at work here—a somber celebration of Japaneseness. The party line holds fast.

Yamamoto-san leads us through the rest of the exhibits. There are several aircraft on display here: a beautifully restored Hayate; a glossy refurbishment of a Hien in-line engine fighter; a three-quarter-scale airworthy Hayabusa; and most poignantly, the barnacle- and seawater-eroded wreckage of a Zero salvaged from nearby waters in 1980.[2] Of course, there are also the prerequisite purple-prosed *isho* farewell letters. But after reading hundreds of these over the last year, I have become oddly inured to their highly stylized sentiment, and I find that there is far more raw emotional impact in the displays of everyday personal items—cigarette holders, sweaters, notebooks, razor blades, postcards, even toys. It is these common, recognizable objects that humanize and render most painfully immediate the loss being honored and mourned here.

When we finish with the museum, Yamamoto-san is kind enough to take the wheel of our rental car and drive us around to some of the more notable spots in the environs of the old air base. Our first stop is the ruins of the original *sangakuheisha* compound. At the bottom of the hill, sweet potatoes are growing in the basin of an old half-sunken airplane revetment. We climb the dirt-and-log stairs up to the compound proper. Someone has placed a bouquet of fresh wildflowers on top of the simple stone monument that sits here amidst the crumbling concrete foundations of the barracks. This, of course, is the exact spot where Haruo Araki spent his last night—where Reiko, Shōko, and the other Nadeshiko girls once played Jacob's ladder and sang nursery rhymes with teenage *tokkō* pilots. Six decades later, the same gently rustling boughs of pine the girls described to me still form a cool green roof over the space.

Our last stop is the grounds of the old air base itself—now a giant expanse of flowers and more sweet-potato patches. Yamamoto-san explains that we are standing on the exact site of the Chiran Air Base flight ops building. He indicates the direction of takeoff when southerly winds prevailed, pointing toward the ultramarine, steeply sloping silhouette of Mount Kaimon-dake on the southeastern horizon. The mountain—sometimes called "the Satsuma Fuji-san" for its close resemblance to its larger Honshū cousin—is the second half of the pair of imposing and still-rumbling volcanoes that dominate lower Kagoshima Prefecture. It is said that pilots flying out of Chiran on their final missions would salute the mountain as they flew past it, knowing that it was the last of their homeland that they would ever set eyes upon. For those given a life extension by engine failures—whether real or feigned—the mountain was a landmark to follow back to base after lonely, cheerless journeys home over the East China Sea.

At the end of our tour, we thank Yamamoto-san for his kindness and return to the Tomiya Inn, where the doctor and I enjoy a leisurely dinner before calling it a night and retiring to our separate rooms. The combination of a Kirin beer nightcap and Arnold Schwarzenegger dubbed in Japanese proves to have amazingly sleep-inducing qualities, and I am soon out like a light. But my sleep is not peaceful for long, and I am awakened about three in the morning by the telltale sounds of old-man insomnia emanating from Dr. Hiroshima's room—coughs and luggage fussing heard loud and clear through the thin walls, backed with a murmuring ambience of radio talk shows and folk-song programs. It is nothing intolerable, though, and after a while I am able to drift off again.

The next sleep interruption, however, is not so easy to ignore. It is a siren at deafening volume, echoing through the streets and off of the surrounding mountains. As a longtime resident of this archipelago, I immediately react with, *Oh, Jesus! Earthquake!* But this unwelcome predawn adrenaline rush is soon replaced by annoyed resignation when a stomach-turningly chipper female voice launches into an announcement reminding town residents to vote in the upcoming elections. A long program of announcements follows, including what sounds like—as far as my sleep-deprived, early-morning Japanese ability can ascertain— agricultural reports. I have a sudden image of one wall of my room turning into a Big Brother TV screen—*Sheftall! 6079 Sheftall, M. G.! Yes, you! Bend lower . . . anyone under forty-five is perfectly capable of touching his toes!**

Like almost all of the Japanese countryside, the entire township is wired for sound, and the powers-that-be in this burg—in their paternal and caring wisdom—have determined that no one within earshot of their loudspeaker system has any business sleeping past dawn, Sunday or not. Surely if anyone in town was sound asleep a moment ago, they are wide-awake now.

I check my watch. It is six A.M.

This cannot be happening.

But it is, and all metaphysical questions aside, the reality is that there will be no more sleep for me this morning. I smoke Cuban cigarillos and read Reiko Akabane's wartime memoirs by dawn's early light until it is time for breakfast.

Before our meal, the doctor and I go downstairs to light incense punks at the small Tome Torihama shrine off the lobby. We are joined by another inn guest, Isshin Yoshida, a Buddhist monk who wears blue denim karate clothes and looks like a bald Leonard Nimoy. He informs us that he is currently on a tour of major Buddhist war memorials around the country. After his travels, he plans to leave his present cushy post at a temple in Aichi Prefecture and establish a small outpost memorial shrine in the sparsely populated Bōnin Islands, as close to Iwo Jima as he can get. Obviously intrigued with this ascetic seeker and moved by his pious earnestness, the ever-extroverted Dr. Hiroshima outlines the rest of our itinerary, then invites the monk to come along with us to Kagoshima.

---

*With apologies to George Orwell.

After breakfast, we set out on the last leg of our pilgrimage—a modern-day Chaucerian traveling party of veterinarian, Buddhist monk, and long-nosed Japanologist headed north along the western shore of Kagoshima Bay in a white Nissan compact. Maybe it is still a little early in the morning for gab, or perhaps it is just that Brother Yoshida's augustly introspective presence in the car has a contemplative effect, but the normally effervescent Dr. Hiroshima is uncharacteristically low-key, and there is only sporadic conversation for most of the drive.

Things pick up on the approach to Kagoshima when we make a turn in the road and the sudden looming presence of big brown Sakurajima brings on a flurry of comments about the scenery. Man-made features of the landscape are certainly an improvement over the sad vistas of yesterday's pork-barrel skyway, but still, this is no French Riviera. Large areas of the city look like transplanted sections of seventies Miami Beach, replete with palm-lined boulevards and pastel-themed condos facing the shoreline strip.

We leave the car in front of one of these high-rises, and walk into a narrow park sandwiched between the strip and the water. Dr. Hiroshima leads us to the famous "Kisama to Ore" memorial for Kagoshima campus Yokaren graduates killed in the war. "Kisama to Ore" ("You and I") refers to the refrain from the song "Dōki no Sakura," which celebrated the comradeship of two naval aviators who are parted in death. There are several versions of the song with alternate verses, but the three best-known verses are carved on a granite block next to the monument:

> *You and I, blossoms of the same cherry tree*
> *That bloomed in the naval academy's garden*
> *Blossoms know they must blow in the wind someday*
> *Blossoms in the wind, fallen for their country*
>
> *You and I, blossoms of the same cherry tree*
> *That bloomed in the flight school garden*
> *I wanted us to fall together, just as we had sworn to do*
> *Oh, why did you have to die, and fall before me?*
>
> *You and I, blossoms of the same cherry tree*
> *Though we fall far away from one another*

*We will bloom again together in Yasukuni Shrine*
*Spring will find us again, blossoms of the same cherry tree*[3]

The dominant motif of the cenotaph is a pair of upright granite slabs, squared off on their outer edges but irregularly shaped along their inner edges in the nature-imitative fashion of traditional Japanese memorial stonework. On closer inspection, it is evident that the five- or six-meter-tall slabs are actually two uneven halves of a larger, fractured whole, and when I realize this the symbolism clicks into place: abrupt discontinuity, buds severed before they could fully flower.

On the front of one of the slab halves, there is a bronze bas-relief of a slumped, lifeless pilot, although unlike the protagonist of Chiran Peace Museum's ceramic mural, this fallen airman is in an unassisted free ascent heavenward. The other, smaller slab features seven gold circles arranged vertically. A sign at the base of the memorial explains that these represent the famous seven-buttoned tunic fronts of the Yokaren dress uniform.

The slabs stand upon a stone altar flanked with snow lanterns and laden with fresh bouquets of colorful tropical flora native to the region. In front of the stone altar there is a brass plaque with a long list of names. The doctor points to Tadao's. We pray in silence before taking some snapshots in front of the monument.

Walking back to our car, the doctor points to an unremarkable white concrete municipal building nearby.

"That's where the Kagoshima Yokaren barracks used to be," he says, then points to a copse of tall old pine trees next to the building. "And that was where we met Tadao when we came down to visit from Fukuoka. Right under those very same trees. Of course, they're a lot bigger now than the first time I saw them."

The doctor gives the site one last, lingering look before we head back to the car. There is yet one more stop on today's itinerary, and we will take the Tarumizu car ferry across Kagoshima Bay to get there. We leave the car in the bowels of the ferry and climb up to the fantail deck, braving a chilly breeze off the water to enjoy the view. Brother Yoshida soon begs leave on account of the cold sea air, seeking refuge within the warmth of the enclosed passenger deck.

I stay behind on the fantail bench of the ferry with a pensive Dr. Hiroshima. Though the sky has become overcast, the scenery is still awe-inspiring, especially when the ferry passes closest to Sakurajima. The volcano is even more spectacular than it was this morning, and seen in this much eye-filling detail, its brooding brown bulk exudes an aura of immeasurable mass and coiled, pent-up potential energy. The thin plume of yellow, sulfuric smoke puffing from its craggy summit suggests a lit fuse—like the whole thing is ready to blow and take most of Kagoshima Bay with it in a gigantic mushroom cloud of steam and pulverized basalt.

I comment on the strength and beauty of the mountain, but the doctor's reaction is subdued. The mountain is too raw and savage to be called beautiful, he says. This being a matter of taste, I opt not to defend my position. I change the topic by asking the doctor if he knows that the geography of the bay bears a close resemblance to Pearl Harbor, and that the IJN used the area to practice for the raid. He answers that he does, but he lets the thread of conversation taper off without further comment. He is staring at something in the distance. I follow his line of sight and get a sudden fifth-wheel sensation, mentally kicking myself for not joining Brother Yoshida a few minutes earlier. Maybe the monk really had not been cold after all, but had just been sensitive enough to pick up on Dr. Hiroshima's need to be alone where I had not.

Mumbling something about going inside to buy more film at the snack bar, I leave the doctor gazing at a nondescript concrete building and a copse of old pine trees by the shore sinking away into the wake of the Tarumizu ferry.

# PART EIGHT

# TORPEDOMEN IN TWILIGHT

## twenty-nine

# KUDAN KAIKAN

A five-minute walk down Kudan Slope from the east gate of Yasukuni Shrine, there is a six-story brick-and-stone building incongruously tucked between glass cliffs of typical downtown Tokyo office space. Originally named Gunjin Kaikan (Professional Soldier Hall), the architecturally eclectic structure was built in 1934 as a swanky entertainment facility and hotel for members of the National Association of Army Officers. While the building's history is long, its brightest moment in the spotlight of notoriety came while the mortar between its bricks was still drying, when it was used as the command center for martial-law authorities suppressing an attempted military coup d'état in the capital.

In what would later be remembered as the "2-2-6 Incident," death squads of young ultranationalist army officers made a whirlwind series of daring predawn raids around Tokyo on the snowy morning of February 26, 1936. After butchering a who's-who list of civilian and military bureaucrats and cabinet ministers in their beds, they holed up in prearranged defensive positions at the nearby Imperial Military Academy campus in Ichigaya.* As a stunned nation watched, the rebels then presented their manifesto for the establishment of an absolute monarchy free of civilian "corruption." Meanwhile, the Imperial Household Guard

---

*The building they used was later the site of the postwar Tokyo Tribunals and, on November 25, 1970, the dramatic suicide of novelist and right-wing activist Yukio Mishima.

and other troops loyal to the authorities moved swiftly to quarantine the mutineers as a flotilla of battleships under Admiral Isoroku Yamamoto sailed up from Yokosuka to train their guns on the IMA campus from Tokyo Bay.

Although the mutiny was put down quickly and relatively bloodlessly (not counting the initial round of assassinations, of course), its repercussions were lasting and disastrous. The coup attempt's exposure of civilian authority weakness and the precedent it established for military intervention in Japanese politics—by armed force in the streets of Tokyo if necessary—effectively put a gun to the heads of the last policy makers who could have had any chance to rein in army adventurism on the Asian continent and avoid the devastating clash with the West that was sure to follow. With critics of radical militarism now cowed into submission for the duration, the nation's march toward total war advanced at the quick step.

While many in politics and the media openly praised the rebels' "patriotic" motives during and after the event, the punishment for the coup's ringleaders was swift and severe: Those who did not fall on their own swords were summarily executed by firing squad.

Somewhere between their arrests and their untimely ends, many of the mutineers were no doubt interrogated—perhaps even tortured— within the brick walls of Gunjin Kaikan, and, visually, the structure certainly seems a fitting venue for the ghosts of wild-eyed young xenophobes in khaki and jackboots. The building's design employs Asian and industrial motifs that combine to create less of an identifiably nativist Japanese feeling than something that could be described as Tibetan Art Deco—a cross between a Tudor manor, a Central Park West doorman building, and Grauman's Chinese Theater. Its upper floors are capped with a handsome green oxidized-copper roof, accented with wrought-iron moon windows, and ringed with a limestone frieze of geometrically stylized boutonnieres. On lower floors, tall windows offer glimpses from the street of chandeliers hanging over what could have once been a grand ballroom. At street level, a covered driveway flanked with rows of brown-tiled columns borders a parking lot on the northern side of the building. Overlooked by a terra-cotta-colored Florentine watchtower, the driveway— which once hopped with sleek black limousines and Kempeitai staff cars—is now host mainly to guided-tour busloads of elderly visitors from the provinces.

Since the building's postwar "rehabilitation" it has been known as Kudan Kaikan, now a very modestly priced hotel with fairly extensive conference and wedding-reception facilities conveniently located in midtown Tokyo. Kudan Kaikan is not, however, your run-of-the-mill Tokyo hotel. This is evident not only from its bargain-basement room rates and eccentric architecture, but also from the large war map of East Asia and the Pacific on permanent display in the front lobby. The map, showing the distribution, in thousands, of Japanese military and civilian casualties in World War II, is flanked with photos of far-flung memorial cenotaphs in various forbidding landscapes from the Solomons to the Aleutians. Suggested reading available in the lobby gift shop is displayed in a nearby glass case, the selections including the usual array of veterans' memoirs, Chicken Little warnings about the impending fall of Japanese civilization, and the ubiquitous ultranationalist comic books of baby-boom right-winger Yoshinori Kobayashi.

Given the reading material advertised, a visitor could be forgiven for suspecting that the lobby wall map is here for the benefit of Japanese strategic planners trying to make sure they do things right next time, but it is more likely here as a somber if not particularly subtle reminder of Kudan Kaikan's main raisons d'être. Primarily, this is a lodging facility for Yasukuni pilgrims. It is also a symbolically and logistically well situated base of operations for the building's owners, the Nippon Izoku Kai (National Association of War Bereaved), perennial Yasukuni champions, and one of the most powerful conservative lobbying groups in Japanese politics. Kudan Kaikan is also, for similarly symbolic and logistical reasons, my preferred base of operations when on business in Tokyo.

On the steamy morning of June 19, 2002, I am sitting in a quiet corner of the hotel lobby waiting for the day's interview subjects to arrive. The concierge has been kind enough to grant me use of the lobby for my interview, and I have staked out a nice big table for the task at hand. I have time to kill, which I spend thumbing through the day's newspapers and people watching. The lobby is surprisingly empty for a large Tokyo hotel on a workday morning, and in half an hour I have seen only a dozen or so people enter the building, mostly wholesome-looking teenagers with harsh flattop Johnny Unitas buzz cuts. Their mashed noses and cauliflower ears leave little doubt that the boys are connected with the judo tournament being held a stone's throw across the Imperial Moat from here at Budōkan, which some readers may remember as the Tokyo venue of the Beatles' '66 Japan tour, and KISS and Cheap Trick glory a decade later.

A few minutes before ten A.M., I look over the top of my newspaper just in time to catch the profile of a serenely elegant, bronze-complexioned elderly gentleman with ramrod-straight posture entering the lobby. I soon recognize him as one of my interview subjects, Toshiharu Konada (INA '43). But Konada-san does not notice me at first, and before I have a chance to say anything, he walks right by me to approach an old man with a shock of white pompadour sitting on the far side of the room. The men exchange curt but formal bows. I watch their somewhat stiff interaction for a few seconds before realizing that the second man is my other subject, Harumi Kawasaki, who has been sitting here all of this time without my realizing it. Feeling slightly embarrassed at my faux pas, I greet my guests and thank them by apologizing—as required by Japanese etiquette—for the time and effort I have caused them to expend in coming to see me this morning.

As we sit down and regard each other across the table, I sense immediately that this morning's session is going to be different from the others I have conducted for my project. The two-on-one arrangement has a formal, almost job-interview feeling to it that I find inhibiting and not conducive to the kind of deeply personal interaction that I have sought in other sessions. Perhaps this is intentional on my subjects' part. Not knowing me from Adam, frankly, it is certainly their prerogative if they wish to keep things businesslike. I wonder, however, if there is not also a mutually censorial, policing function at work here between the two old men. I know from experience that opportunities for candid responses from Japanese war veterans are severely hampered by the presence of other veterans within earshot. Both politics and peer pressure in such situations ensure that remarks and conjecture never stray far from the party line, with critical comments about *tokkō* philosophy, Japanese war aims, and/or Japanese nationalism most definitely taboo.

While I am not holding out much hope for any personal bombshells of the kind Toshio Yoshitake, Shigeko Araki, and some of my other interview subjects have laid at my plate, I have every reason to believe that Toshiharu Konada and Harumi Kawasaki also have important stories to tell, for both men spent nearly a year of their young adulthood some six decades ago as members of the most elite and secretive *tokkō* unit of them all—the Kaiten human torpedo corps.

# thirty

# TOSHIHARU KONADA

Toshiharu Konada's ancestral home is the old fiefdom of Asano (of Forty-seven Rōnin fame\*) in what is modern-day Hiroshima Prefecture. Although his forebears were not samurai themselves, they were about as close as farmers could get to membership in the power elite, commissioned by the local samurai clan as sword-bearing hereditary village chiefs in the farming community they called home throughout the Edo period and up until the end of the nineteenth century.

The household thrived for the first three decades of the Meiji era under the broad new range of social and economic freedoms they could enjoy as a result of the emperor's beneficence (or political acumen, whichever the case). But ironically, the civic responsibilities that came along with Meiji's privilege package proved, in a sense, to be the undoing of the family's pastoral bliss. True, social reforms abolished the centuries-old four-tiered social caste system, made all Japanese ostensibly equal before the law, and gave the Konadas and millions of other commoners the

---

\*The Forty-seven Rōnin were a band of samurai whose lord, Asaro, was forced to commit ritual suicide to atone for the capital crime of drawing a sword in the Shōgun's palace during a quarrel with a certain Lord Kira. The rōnin exacted revenge by killing Kira after a year of lying low and plotting their attack. After the 1707 incident, all forty-seven rōnin were also obliged to kill themselves. The tale has been considered exemplary of bushidō values, and was used as such in the moral education of Japanese schoolboys from the late Edo period until the end of World War II.

surnames their descendants use to this day. But the reforms also meant that with the abolition of the formal warrior caste, millions of young men across the land were now liable for compulsory military service. Konada-san's grandfather was one of them, and his conscription into the army during the Sino-Japanese War of 1894–95 sent his family's agricultural fortunes into a tailspin. After his discharge, he was forced to sell off the farm to cover debts that had accrued during his absence. With family ties to the soil they had tilled for centuries now irrevocably severed, the Konadas migrated to the port city of Kure, Hiroshima Prefecture, where they eventually opened a dry-goods shop.

Konada-san's father, Toshio, was born in 1899, shortly after the family homestead move. Intellectually gifted, young Toshio showed no inclination whatsoever of wanting to pursue a mercantile career. In early adolescence, he made known his desire to attend college someday, but family finances precluded the private higher-education route that was still the exclusive domain of the nation's wealthier classes at the time. This did not, however, mean that his future was locked into a path of dry-goods sales. In 1917, Toshio Konada took an alternative route up and away from the fabric rolls and finger-worn abacus of the family store by sitting for and passing the rigorous entrance exams for the naval academy at Etajima.

Toshiharu Konada was born in 1924 at the sprawling naval base complex at Kure in Hiroshima Prefecture, where his father was stationed after his Etajima graduation. Although Kure was near the ancestral home, his father's frequent transfers meant that Toshiharu spent little time in the area while he was growing up. By the time he reached sixth grade, the introspective, serious youngster had already endured five changes in locale and elementary school. The experience left its mark on the boy's character, and he learned at an early age that dedicating himself to intellectual pursuits and his studies could be a source of stability in his life that his physical environment could not always provide. Although always quick at making new friends after yet another big move, he was just as happy—if not happier—to be curled up on the tatami at home with thick "grown-up" books on subjects like astronomy, geography, world history, and biology.

Toshiharu's scholastic efforts and natural intellectual gifts meant that many promising future paths were open for him as he approached the beginning of young adulthood, but the career in medical research he wanted to pursue was not one of them. Born into a more peaceful era, a gifted student like Toshiharu could very well have been able to realize this goal, but for a navy brat in 1930s Japan, the dream would have to remain just that. With war raging in China and conflict with the West looming in the near future, these were not times for self-centered pursuits. A more honorable and patriotic alternative career path would be to follow in his father's footsteps and take the Etajima admissions tests.

Toshiharu sat for the first round of entrance exams at the Etajima campus in August 1940, and was informed of his passing score on November 3, then a national holiday in honor of Emperor Meiji's birthday.* The Konadas were overjoyed at the news and proud that their son had made the 10 percent cutoff for the academic testing phase, but Toshiharu was not yet a shoo-in. He still had to get through Etajima's exacting physical and medical tests in the last week of November, a final stage in the application that would wash out yet another 50 percent of admissions hopefuls.

After getting his clean bill of health from the navy doctors, Toshiharu stayed in temporary dorm facilities in the Etajima officers' club with the other successful candidates. On December 1, the group marched through the academy gates as members of the new INA Class of 1943. Toshiharu had worked long and hard to get this far, but his hard work was only beginning.

Japanese naval academy midshipmen followed a challenging scholastic regimen similar to that of the military academy, concentrating on core-curriculum subjects for the first eighteen months of their three-year course of studies, then more specialized naval subjects during the second half of their Etajima careers. In addition to having to cope with a daunting academic course load, the middies were also constantly drilled in kendo, judo, and other martial arts to strengthen fighting spirit and build character. Although Konada-san recalls living conditions at the academy as being "relatively comfortable," they were not by

---

*Still a holiday today, although it is now referred to as "Culture Day." Hirohito's (Emperor Shōwa) birthday on April 29 was and still is a national holiday—now called "Green Day." The Emperor Taishō, for some reason, has not been so honored after his death, perhaps because his birthday of October 31 falls so close to his father's.

any measure luxurious. Midshipmen lived forty to a room, with supervised activity filling every day from reveille to lights-out. As Konada-san describes it, "We had nary a minute of privacy in three years." Although physical hazing had been officially banned some years before, the senior midshipmen still kept a stern eye on the underclassmen, and screwups could expect to be dealt with accordingly.

Despite its privations, midshipman life was nothing like the spartan and dehumanizing routine of straitjacketed conformity endured by cadet peers in the IMA. The Japanese navy had long prided itself on its strongly British-influenced culture—especially among the commissioned ranks—and Etajima put almost as much emphasis on developing the "gentleman" in their charges as it did on the "officer" aspects of their education in preparing them for careers as naval professionals. Instruction in English and other foreign languages, etiquette, and even Western table manners was still required for Etajima midshipmen long after Japan's xenophobic ideological turn in the late 1930s, when the Army Ministry had banned such subjects from the IMA curriculum as decadent foreign influences.*

Etajima graduates were traditionally expected to be cosmopolitan, genteel, well-rounded officers capable of serving in any capacity the nation required of them, including overseas diplomatic assignments as junior naval attachés. But as the class of 1943 entered its final year of instruction, postings for cocktail party patrol at peaceful embassies were few and far between for new ensigns, even in the extreme unlikelihood that any of them desired such an assignment while their brothers were fighting and dying. As graduation neared, most of the midshipmen were painfully aware that Japan was losing the war, and that as academy men, they would be called upon to set the example for the enormous sacrifices that would be required of the nation to deny victory to the Americans.

"Even though we may have known that we couldn't win the war," Konada-san recalls, expressing a notion I have heard from many other Japanese veterans, "there was no way that we could accept losing it."

For Konada and the overwhelming majority of his classmates, something had to be done to turn around the nation's fortunes and save the

---

*In fact, English instruction continued at the academy even after the outbreak of the war, and was stopped only by direct intervention of the Navy Ministry out of political considerations.

slipping war effort, and air power was seen as having the best chance of accomplishing this. Accordingly, the overwhelmingly popular postgraduation service branch destination was aviation, preferably carrier-borne fighters in a hot combat zone. As the navy's elite, Etajima graduates were traditionally awarded their first choice of branch assignments, but in this case, competition for flight training was so intense that in the end only 50 percent of applicants got slots. Much to his chagrin, Konada was not among this select group. The Navy Ministry had decided that his fine analytical mind could be put to best use in the fire computer and control room of a warship.

After a two-month training ship shakedown cruise with other INA classmates bound for surface units, Officer Candidate Konada was assigned as a gunnery officer on the thirteen-thousand-ton heavy cruiser *Ashigara*,[1] joining her crew at the Lingga Roads anchorage in November 1943. A frustratingly quiet nine months of sea duty followed. While seemingly every other ship in the navy was fighting with its back to the wall for the nation's very survival, the *Ashigara* plied the tranquil East Indies and Japanese home waters in uneventful patrol duty interspersed with interminable refits and upgrades at various Southeast Asian and Japanese ports.

The last straw for Konada's patience regarding his current assignment came when the *Ashigara* sat out the Battle of the Philippine Sea, the largest naval engagement of the war by that point (Leyte Gulf was still four months away). As reports from the disaster off Saipan came in mere hours after the battle, Konada realized that serving Japan to the best of his abilities meant serving her somewhere other than the plotting table of the *Ashigara*'s FC & C room. Although it was not normally in his temperament to bother superiors with personal matters, he had no other choice in his present situation but to send a request up the chain of command for transfer to other duties. He was rewarded for his troubles with orders to report no later than August 15, 1944, to submarine school at Ōtake, Hiroshima Prefecture.

# thirty-one

# HARUMI KAWASAKI

Although I use the term with reservations in attempting to describe my first impression of an eighty-year-old Japanese man, Harumi Kawasaki strikes me as streetwise. Not in a hustling sense, but more like someone who knows all the tricks and angles and can fend off an opponent's attempt to play them with a dexterous if somewhat world-weary ease. He also exudes a healthy sense of the ridiculous, letting on that he is clued in on the cosmic joke with a slightly iconoclastic—almost impish—energy in his personality and manner of speech that is a neat counterpoint to Konada-san's staid and august aura. It is immediately apparent that Kawasaki-san will be neither bamboozled nor steamrolled by a persistent interviewer. Nor will he be misquoted—I realize that I am in the presence of a master tactician when, with a sly grin that reminds me of Spanky about to give a hotfoot to a truant officer in some *Little Rascals* episode, he pulls a tape recorder from his shoulder bag and places it on the table between us at the start of our interview.

Kawasaki-san was born in 1924 as the third of what would soon be five children of a Kōbe, Hyōgo Prefecture, family. Changes in the home situation resulted in the children being put in the care of their paternal grandfather in Yamaguchi Prefecture while they were still small. The new arrangement worked about as well as could be expected for a multigenerational extended family household in Depression-era rural Japan, but it was painfully evident even to these small children that their grandfather—who was also helping to take care of their uncle's family—was stretched thin by the arrangement both physically and financially.

In explaining why he struck out on his own at the age of twelve, Kawasaki-san mentions *kuchiberashi*—as so many other of my interview subjects have—a phrase referring to the once acceptable practice of easing the financial burden on a family by reducing the number of mouths it had to feed. In most cases, this meant biological parents giving away "superfluous" children (i.e., any other than firstborn sons) for adoption, almost always to relatives or acquaintances. In the case of more desperate or unscrupulous families, another version of *kuchiberashi* saw children sold off to traveling dealers who trawled the impoverished countryside to keep the assembly lines of the nation's factories—and the pleasure quarters of its cities—well stocked with vigorous young bodies.

In twelve-year-old Harumi's case, however, his own *kuchiberashi* experience was self-imposed—the noblest type, of course, from the Confucian standpoint of filial piety. Recognizing the burden of his continued presence in his grandfather's home, he left as soon as it was legally permissible and never looked back.

Kawasaki-san is understandably reluctant to go into a lot of detail about a Dickensian adolescence spent in menial labor and harsh living conditions, but he does tell me that he made allowances of time and money to pursue an education on his own over the next six or seven years of his life, even as he had to scrape by to survive. The investment initially paid off when he came across a Yokaren recruiting notice on a bulletin board at a night school he was attending for his junior high school equivalency diploma.

By the late fall of 1943, Harumi had already been eligible for the draft for several months since the lowering of the minimum conscription age to nineteen earlier that summer. As he figured his prospects, there was little doubt that he would be wearing someone's uniform sooner or later—either army or navy—but if he had a choice in the matter, he would prefer not to do it in brown khaki with a rifle on his shoulder and eating dust all day. The cockpit of an airplane seemed a much more dignified—not to mention more comfortable—way to go to war. Without further ado, he applied for a Yokaren slot, passed his exams, and entered His Majesty's navy as an enlisted flight cadet with the Kō-13 class in December 1943.*

Kawasaki underwent his Yokaren training at the new Nara campus, which was located in the middle of a densely populated civilian residential district.† The Nara Yokaren operated out of massive religious retreat facilities appropriated by the navy from Tenrikyō, an evangelical Shinto cult that astutely put more emphasis on ceremony and the tithing of its followers than it did on the fuzzy monotheistic gospel it espoused. Founded in the early nineteenth century, Tenrikyō had since grown into one of Japan's most successful "new religions," a status acquired in large part through the cult's wholehearted political cooperation with the Japanese state since late Meiji times.[1] The clout the cult had amassed over the years was clearly evident in the sheer scope of its Nara lodging facilities, originally built to accommodate thousands of worshipers at a time when mass pilgrimages would descend on Nara from around the country or even from Japanese expatriate communities in Brazil and Peru. After the facilities' appropriation by the navy, they were easily able to accommodate the twelve thousand–odd cadets on the Nara Yokaren roster.

The Tenri compound itself comprised fifty or so two-story long wooden dormitories, each capable of lodging 250 people. The layout of the factorylike structures was uniform: At both ends of the second floor, there were communal day areas for gatherings, feedback on training, relaxation, etc. The rest of the interior space on both floors was taken up by tatami-floored rooms on either side of a long corridor that ran from one end of the building to the other.

Living conditions were cramped, but perhaps more in a psychological than a physical sense. To facilitate the snooping eyes of inspecting NCOs patrolling the corridors at night, the sliding paper shoji doors had been removed from all rooms, so there was no privacy whatsoever. Seven or eight boys slept to each eight-tatami-sized room, right on the floor mats. In the winter, when the interior of the unheated, drafty buildings differed little from the temperature outside, the boys would sleep in two

---

*This was the same class as Tokurō Takei and Akinori Asano, the former Ōka pilots.
†This area is now part of Tenri City, Nara Prefecture.

groups of four under their piled up government-issue blankets, lined up like spoons in a pantry drawer to share body warmth.

For most of the nine months they spent in the Nara compound, Kawasaki and his classmates went through their Yokaren course with dreams of glorious aerial combat lightening all of the privation and slog they knew they had to endure on their way to winning naval aviator's wings. But things did not quite work out as they had expected. Less than one month from graduation for the Nara Kō-13 class, the cadets were told that due to the dwindling number of aircraft now available for training, and a nationwide surplus of new Yokaren gradutes, it was unlikely that more than a handful of them would ever see flight school.

Given no time to absorb the bombshell of having just been told that all of their blood, sweat, and tears of the previous nine months were basically for naught, the cadets were then told that volunteers for a "special weapons project" were needed. Kawasaki wrote his name down when the paper slips were handed out, and after graduation on September 1, 1944, he and a group of about 650 other boys were marched to Nara Station and put on an official navy train. Nothing was said about the westbound train's destination, but when they passed Kobe without stopping, rumors began circulating through the passenger cars that they were all headed for submarine school at Kure.

When the group arrived at Kure, the boys were ordered to get off the train and form up on the platform. Here, 250 cadets were called out of ranks—including Kawasaki—and told to stay put on the platform while the remaining four hundred new petty officers were marched off to another platform for a train to Ōtake. Kawasaki learned after the war that this latter group was trained at the enlisted submariner's school there as Kairyū two-man and Kōryū five-man midget sub crewmen.

In the meantime, Kawasaki and his group were marched from Kure Station to temporary barracks in the Kure naval complex, where they were told that they would soon be shipping out to an installation with the mysterious designation of "Q-base." No one was told where Q-base was, or given any details about its function.

## thirty-two

# REARRANGING THE FIRMAMENT

I n the years following the First World War, Japanese naval strategists began planning in earnest for the possibility—if not probability—of an all-out naval clash with the United States, by then Japan's premier strategic rival in the Western Pacific. Chillingly prescient war-game simulations included scenarios for fleet-sized "decisive engagements" in the waters off Midway or Saipan, as well as surprise attacks on Pearl Harbor, all decades before the pasteboard gaming models and dice throws became burning ships and casualties.

The salient problem facing the IJN's war planners was the superior strategic strength of their hypothetical (if likely) foe. America's overwhelming industrial capacity, coupled with naval arms-limitations treaties that favored American interests at Japan's expense, meant that at least for the foreseeable future, no matter how the war-gaming dice rolled, the fact of that superiority was inescapable. The IJN always conceded this disadvantage in their simulations, and formulated strategic and tactical doctrine accordingly.

The keystone of IJN doctrine was the concept of whittling down piecemeal a U.S. fleet barreling westward across the Pacific through a long-range running-attrition campaign of hit-and-run engagements, then taking on the weakened American force in a final toe-to-toe winner-take-all brawl to be fought on more favorable terms closer to Japanese home waters. The Japanese had understandably fond memories of a similar engagement in 1905, when Czar Nicholas II's journey-wearied and storm-battered Baltic Fleet was trounced at Tsushima, effectively ending the Russo-Japanese War.

The best minds in the IJN agreed that in order to win a similarly decisive victory against the U.S. Pacific Fleet, the prerequisite attrition campaign would require superior surface- and submarine-launched torpedo tactics.[1] During the interwar years, the IJN put maximum effort into developing and/or otherwise acquiring the new weapons technology necessary to support their new tactical portfolio, paying special attention to large-diameter ship-launched torpedoes with unprecedented range and one-hit/one-kill stopping power. Following the classic Japanese technological learning curve, the navy copied and adopted what it could from the West—in this case, the innovations of industry-leading Italian naval-munitions firm Whitehead of Fiume[2]—then tweaked and improved on the design to meet its own specific needs. By 1933, IJN technicians were putting the finishing touches on what would be the finest ship-launched torpedo in the world until the end of World War II: the Type 93 "Long Lance."*

Although Japan was already embroiled in open warfare on the Asian continent by the time the Type 93 was ready for deployment, the lack of significant naval engagements against their Chinese foe meant that the Japanese were unable to demonstrate their new ship killer to the world for the next eight years. But with the opening salvos of the Pacific war, Allied naval forces got more demonstration of the capabilities of the Japanese torpedo than they needed. The Long Lance wreaked havoc on American, Dutch, British, and Australian warships in the early stages of the conflict, most notably at the Battle of the Java Sea, Savo and the other drubbings the IJN handed the Allies in a series of infamous battles in and around the Guadalcanal "Slot" in late 1942 and early 1943.

Changes in Japan's war fortunes and in the nature of Pacific naval combat, however, meant that the Long Lance's reign of terror was—at least from the Allied perspective—mercifully brief. Even as munitions manufacturers worked around the clock to keep up production of the

---

*The Japanese never actually called the Type 93 the "Long Lance"; the poetic tag was coined by Morison, and is now standard usage among World War II historians and naval buffs. See Kohata (2003) for a Japanese account of the torpedo's development.

peerless torpedo, the warships necessary to deploy it were becoming an increasingly endangered species as Japan's war rapidly deteriorated into a grim defensive struggle. Moreover, the midwar paradigm shift in Pacific-theater naval tactics brought about by the coming-of-age of carrier-based airpower also greatly diminished the weapon's relevance. Most naval combat was now conducted without surface forces seeing any more of their opponent than green blips on a radar screen—if even that much—and the ship killers of choice had become bombs and torpedoes dropped from aircraft. Even for the Americans—with near-complete air supremacy everywhere they went—the main contribution of their battleships, cruisers, and destroyers had been relegated to the roles of beachhead prep and fire support for amphibious operations, antisubmarine warfare, and as floating flak towers to protect the now all-important carriers. The days when the outcomes of naval engagements were determined by battlewagon salvos and torpedo spreads launched by squadrons of swift destroyers were all but over.

With Japan's war prospects heading south at flank speed, the IJN was becoming increasingly desperate and frustrated by a logistical situation in which it had vast warehouses full of technologically superlative but now tactically redundant torpedoes. As is so often true in the decision-making processes of large organizations, the most innovative thinking regarding the conundrum came from the lower ranks. In late 1943, two junior officers stationed at Ōtsushima, a top-secret island sub pen in Japan's Inland Sea, were discussing possibilities for the Type 93 when they hit on a revolutionary idea: The effectiveness of the torpedo could be increased exponentially if it was given a larger warhead, modified to accommodate a human pilot, and capable of being launched in stealth, underwater, from a submarine mother ship.

Lieutenant Hiroshi Kuroki and Ensign Sekio Nishina had just conceived Japan's first dedicated *tokkō* weapon.

Both officers had sound engineering backgrounds, Kuroki a graduate of the prestigious Naval Engineering College at Maizuru,[3] Nishina a class of '42 Etajima man.[4] Working the nuts-and-bolts problems of their concept in their free time—often at the expense of sleep—they had drawings and numbers good enough to write up in a formal proposal to send up the chain of command by December 1943. On the twenty-eighth of that month, the paperwork reached the Ministry of the Navy.[5]

Tokyo's response to the manned-torpedo proposal was a firm but nonetheless appreciative "No." The admirals admired the fighting spirit and patriotism of the young sub officers and praised the ingenuity of their engineering work, but neither the service nor the general public was deemed ready to accept the concept of organized *taiatari* tactics—at least not yet. The officers were thanked for their efforts and told to continue having these good thoughts, but to consider the matter of human torpedoes closed.

But Kuroki and Nishina were not to be deterred. According to IJN legend, the young submariners wrote up a second appeal—this time inked in their own blood. Neither the display's militant determination nor the possible morale damage of rejecting such an obviously sincere request was lost on the brass hats in Tokyo. This time, whether out of appreciative sentimentality, political considerations, pragmatic assessments of a deteriorating tactical situation, or some combination of these three trains of thought, the Navy Ministry gave the nod to the human torpedo project with the cosmetic codicil that provisions for pilot survival would at least be considered.* On February 28, 1944, memoranda were issued for R & D to begin at Kure Arsenal for a project to be given the metaphysically intriguing name of Kaiten.

Kaiten—which can be inelegantly but adequately translated as "heavens rearranger" or "fate reverser"—was a mildly blasphemous metaphor from a strict Buddhist standpoint, implying as it did the notion that something wrought by mere mortals could alter divinely preordained destiny. From a morale standpoint, however, the naming was brilliant, expressing both in its dash and desperation the hope that the new superweapon was going to reverse the nation's star-crossed war fortunes by rearranging with boldness and high explosive the very firmament itself if necessary. Fate would be cheated. Japan's bad luck stopped here.

---

*Proposals such as jettisonable crew pods were studied, then quickly dropped from the design as impractical. See Warner (1982) and O'Neill (1999).

## thirty-three

# METAL IMPLEMENT NUMBER SIX

The day before the scheduled September 5 start of their instruction at submarine school in Ōtake, Ensign Toshiharu Konada and six other INA '43 classmates were told that there had been a sudden change in their orders, and that effective immediately, they were all assigned to a unit called Dai'ichi Tokubetsu Kichitai ("Special Base Unit One"). No further explanation was given about what "Special Base Unit One" was or even where it was located. The assignment change was in the form of an order, not a request for volunteers, and as INA graduates, Konada and his classmates were not in a position to ask questions for clarification—just to get their gear together and prepare to ship out immediately.

The next morning, Konada and his group found themselves on a fast motor launch headed for Kurahashijima, an island in Kure Bay. The passengers spent the thirty-minute trip in relative silence, no doubt mulling over possible scenarios for whatever it was that awaited them at their destination. Watching the rocky shore of Kurahashijima get larger on the horizon, Konada recalled a snippet of conversation between officers he had heard while still aboard the *Ashigara* some weeks before, when the cruiser was passing this very spot. One of the officers had said something about a top-secret and incredibly powerful "nation-saving weapon" being developed on the island, then confessed to knowing nothing more than that it was code-named *Maruroku Kanamono* ("Metal Fixture Number Six"). "Top secret" and "incredibly powerful"

407

were certainly promising descriptions for a superweapon, but what about "Metal Fixture Number Six"? Could something that sounded like a column entry in a quartermaster's manifest of plumbing supplies really save the country?

After the launch moored at the island base, Konada and the others were escorted to the officers' billets. There, the group met up with an INA '43 classmate who had finished the sub course at Kure some months earlier, and was now stationed here on Kurahashijima. While the old friends were catching up on what they had been doing over the past year, someone mentioned the assignment to Special Base Unit One, assuming that the base and Kurahashijima were one and the same entity.

"This is Special Base Unit One," the Kurahashijima officer said, his expression suddenly serious. "But you fellows are going to the annex base at Ōtsushima. And you know what they're doing out there, right? . . . They're getting *taiatari* weapons ready . . . the human torpedoes."

Sixty years later, Konada-san describes the combination of surprise, pride, and elation he felt when he first heard the phrase *human torpedo*.

"Of course, such a weapon seemed desperate and drastic to me, but I could accept that, because it was already apparent by this point in the war that nothing less than drastic measures were going to save Japan," he says. "I was not afraid, as I knew that the very survival of the Japanese race itself was at stake. My own life seemed unimportant compared with a duty of that magnitude. If, by giving up my life, I could fulfill my duty and help save the country, that act would make me happier than anything I could accomplish living. Everyone else in my group felt the same way, too. . . . We were so excited by what we had just heard that we spent all of that night talking about it."

The Kurahashijima sojourn was a short one. The next morning, the group boarded an oceangoing tugboat for Ōtsushima, an island off the coast of Yamaguchi Prefecture about seventy kilometers to the west. After threading the innumerable islets and myriad channels of the Inland Sea, the tugboat arrived at its destination to enter a cliff-ringed, beachless lagoon with no level shoreline to speak of beyond a stone quay and concrete piers crammed with gear and wooden sheds. The rest of the base was arrayed up and down the densely foliated rock face, like a habitat for maritime cliff dwellers. From the looks of it, a stiff breeze could send the whole place crashing into the sea.

On the cramped and busy waterfront, sailors in summer khaki work-clothes operated cranes and assembled machinery right on the docks. Others manhandled hand trolleys carrying what appeared to be swollen Type 93 torpedoes, one of which was being lowered down into the water at the end of a chain from a swing-armed gantry.

Special Base Unit One's Ōtsushima annex had inherited a base per-fectly suited to their mission, with infrastructure designed specifically for torpedo work already in place from the days when the facility had been used in the development of the Type 93 in the 1930s. Gantries and cranes lined the quay, torpedo and sub pens were built right out over the water, and the surrounding cliffsides were honeycombed with new deep storage tunnels that were virtually impregnable to shelling or bombard-ment. A James Bond fan twenty or thirty years later would recognize the milieu immediately—it was Blofeld's island lair being built with 1940s technology.

Konada's group was met by an orderly at the quay, and led up a wind-ing footpath carved into the cliff face that led to the top of the promon-tory, where the large clapboard HQ building was located. After signing in on the duty roster and offering formal greetings to the base CO, leg-endary sub captain Lieutenant Commander Mitsuma Itakura, the en-signs were escorted to their new communal home in the island's officers' billets, which were located on a level outcropping about halfway back down the cliff-face path to the waterfront. The slapped-together plywood-and-corrugated-tin accommodations were crude but adequate. They had Western-style beds, and the tatami flooring in the sleeping quarters was a nice touch of hygienic, homey comfort much appreciated after the steel decks of the *Ashigara*, which had been microbial breeding grounds for the itchy miseries of athlete's foot and impetigo.

The trip-weary ensigns had barely put their seabags down and begun field-testing their new bunks when an out-of-breath orderly flew through the front door of the billets.

*"Shitsurei shimasu!"* the clerk yelled between gasps, using the stock Japanese apology for intruding on a superior's territory. "Lieutenant Higuchi and Lieutenant Kuroki have been in an accident. All personnel are to report to the quay immediately to form search parties."

There was a rush for the door as everyone followed the haggard orderly down to the waterfront at a full run. When the ensigns reached the quay, they were sent out into the training area of the lagoon with every other able body on the island in launches, patrol boats, rowboats, rafts, and anything else that could float. "We're looking for the *Maruroku* prototype . . . looks like a big black torpedo," they were told, and they followed this standing order as long as daylight allowed. As afternoon became evening, flashlights were distributed so the search could continue through the night.

"We even tried using a trawler to dredge the bottom of the lagoon, but that didn't work, either," Konada-san says. "Then around dawn, someone spotted bubbles and the divers went down to look."

A salvage boat arrived at the scene, and tow cables were sent down with the divers to raise what had been found. Konada watched as whining salvage cranes brought a long black craft to the surface. A hatch in its manhole-sized conning tower was opened with an insistent hiss of escaping bad air, revealing two slumped bodies in the crew compartment.

"It was then that I finally had the honor of meeting Lieutenant Kuroki," Konada-san says in utmost sincerity, using the formal *keigo* language the Japanese reserve for occasions of deepest solemnity. *"Meet"?!* I think. *Surely Konada-san must be speaking figuratively or sarcastically.* I pause for a moment, studying his bronze statue face for some trace of irony. But I find none, and the qualifying follow-up remark I wait for does not come. In my peripheral vision, I sense Kawasaki-san checking out my reaction. When I return his glance he replies by closing his eyes, raising his eyebrows, and giving the slightest, barely perceptible shrug.

In a clear if somewhat monotone basso profundo, Konada-san retrieves the conversational ball and continues with his account of September 6, 1944, telling me that after the salvaged craft was brought back to the base, an inspection of its interior shed some light on the circumstances of the accident. While Kuroki and Higuchi slowly asphyxiated in a craft hopeless mired in muck at the bottom of the lagoon, they kept copious instrumentation notes as well as detailed physiological descriptions of the effects of the ordeal on their own bodies and mental capacities. Their last log entries—written in a shaky, obviously oxygen-starved hand—were recorded some fourteen hours after their first. In the agony of their final moments, they had even managed to scrawl farewell notes to their mothers.

The officers' deaths were mourned, but even though they had not died in the kind of glorious combat mission they had worked so long and hard for, everyone on the island agreed that their deaths had been honorable. There was not a man on Ōtsushima who did not share the sentiment that the accident and its consequences were more than anything a proud affirmation of the young officers' bravery and dedication, for the notes Kuroki and Higuchi had kept in the last hours of their lives provided invaluable data on the capabilities and limitations of Japan's new superweapon. The officers were duly enshrined both in the Shinto altars and in the collective memory of Special Base Unit One, becoming something akin to patron saints for the human torpedo corps for the rest of the war.

From Konada's perspective, the incident provided exemplary role models in the deceased persons of Kuroki and Higuchi, but it also whispered sobering intimations of the hazards his new duties were going to entail. Training on Metal Fixture Number Six, he thought, was going to be just as dangerous as being a test pilot on experimental aircraft. Perhaps his new job would be even more dangerous, for at least a test pilot had a chance to bail out in the event of catastrophe. A submariner trapped fathoms beneath the surface in a floundering craft had no such option.

Once the commotion in the wake of the accident subsided, Konada and his classmates were taken to a sub hangar for their belated orientation briefing. A senior officer began his presentation with a rundown of the general concept and construction of something he called Kaiten. The weapon had been developed, he explained, by bisecting a Type 93 torpedo, connecting the sixty-centimeter-wide halves with a one-meter-wide one-man crew compartment, then widening the front half of the weapon with a one meter wide "sleeve" to compensate for the width of the crew compartment and to carry additional fuel and oxygen tanks. The most crucial function of the forward area, of course, was that it would also house the weapon's whopping 1,550 kg warhead. With more than three times the explosive charge of a standard Type 93, the ensigns were told, the Kaiten would be able to break the back of anything afloat with a single hit.

In addition to overwhelming destructive power, the Kaiten's stealth, maneuverability, speed, and range were also going to be crucial elements in its performance portfolio once the weapon went operational. Inheriting the Type 93's gasoline/pressurized-liquid-oxygen propulsion system meant that the Kaiten—like its technological parent—would be wakeless (i.e., no telltale bubble trail as it ran underwater) and relatively quiet. Piggybacked on the top deck of a mother sub and connected to the same by releasable bolts and a tubular access hatchway, the weapon would be ferried to the objective and released far enough away to escape early detection yet close enough to keep targets within operational range. At a submerged cruising speed of twelve knots, this range was about eighty kilometers. At flank speed of thirty knots, the Kaiten could turn on a dime as new targets presented themselves, and run circles around pursuers while still providing a range of over twenty kilometers. Most of the Kaiten's navigation would be done by stopwatch and compass reckoning, with a periscope provided for quick pop-ups to assess the surface situation and to allow the pilot to steer the Kaiten into the target on the final attack run.

At the end of the briefing, the officer gave an order, the doors of a storage shed opened, and a fifteen-meter-long black Kaiten was rolled out on dollies by a team of sailors. Konada and his classmates were floored by what they saw, and let out gasps of admiration when they were allowed to examine the machine up close.

"I thought, This is it! This is the weapon that will save Japan!" Konada-san recalls of the experience.

In the book *Gyokusaisen To Tokubetsukōgekitai* ("Gyokusai [No Surrender] Warfare and Special Attack Units") Konada-san describes his thoughts and feelings that day sixty years ago:

> [The Kaiten] was the first bright light on the horizon for Japan that any of us had seen in a long time. . . . In my mind's eye, I envisaged a hundred Kaitens sneaking into the enemy's anchorage, laying waste his entire fleet. . . . Even before the war started, Japanese newspapers carried articles about how the Americans boasted that, if hostilities ever began, they would burn our cities of wood and paper to cinders. We knew that this was a foe we could not afford to let anywhere near our

homeland. . . . American ostracism of and prejudice toward Japanese were truly awful in the prewar era. When they fought, their attitude toward us was just the same as their attitude toward Indians that you can see in any Western shoot-'em-up: wholesale butchery. . . . The only option left to us to prevent the invasion of our homeland by this enemy was to transform ourselves into human bombs. At the time, this was the reasoned, objective thought of almost all young Japanese men. We saw this as the most effective use of the sacrifice of our individual lives. Given the war situation at the time, this was a completely logical conclusion. . . . "One life for one enemy ship"—it did not get any more effective than that. . . . Self-preservation is a primal instinct of any living organism . . . but anyone who qualifies as a human being is capable of sacrificing himself to save the lives of others or to protect loved ones in danger. It is just the same as jumping into a river to save a drowning child. That is human nature.[1]

For the next two months, simultaneously burdened and inspired by such thoughts, Konada and his classmates trained under the personal guidance of Kaiten coinventor Sekio Nishina, dedicating all of their energies and waking moments to learning everything they could about the craft and mastering its operation. Their focus, frugal lifestyle, self-sacrificial mindset, and unwavering faith in the justice of their cause almost had more in common with a monastic order than a military organization.

From a metaphysical standpoint, the comparison is not too much of an exaggeration, for the capabilities and possibilities of the Kaiten gave every indication that the weapon was going to live up to the theological affectation of its name after all. Putting this much power into the hands of a single human being was akin to a process of semideification, a matter bordering on the supernatural. The symbolic and psychological implications of this were never lost on the Kaiten program's chain of command.

# thirty-four

## ENTER THE KAITEN

Roughly concurrent with Ensign Toshiharu Konada's near-religious experience at Ōtsushima during his initial encounter with the Kaiten, Petty Officer Third Class Harumi Kawasaki and his Nara classmates were getting their own orientation briefing seventy kilometers to the east at "Q-base" on the island of Kurahashijima. The basics of the message were the same—Japan's war situation was desperate enough by now to merit human torpedoes of enormous destructive capability, and the navy needed men to pilot them.

There were several fundamental differences, however, between the Special Base Unit One and Q-base briefings. First of all, the Q-base version for the enlisted men did not go into as much strategic and philosophical profundity as the lecture Special Base Unit One's ensigns received. Also, the Q-base talk was given in the format of a call for volunteers—the new petty officers were told that they could duck out of the duty if they felt that, for whatever reason, they would not be able to carry it out when the time to do so came. Lastly, there was a considerable difference in the two groups' collective reactions to their respective briefings. While none of Kawasaki's classmates had raised their hands to say "I quit" when the opportunity presented itself, neither were many of them exactly bubbling over with enthusiasm. Unlike their commissioned Kaiten counterparts at Ōtsushima, the Nara Yokaren boys at Kurahashijima did not float back to their barracks on a heady wave of *dulce et decorum* self-sacrificial beatitude after breaking ranks. In fact, as

Kawasaki-san recalls, there was a considerable volume of bitching and moaning of the "I didn't go through nine months of Yokaren for this crap" variety that night, not to superiors, of course—perish the thought—but amongst themselves. During the ensuing weeks, while the Nara group trained at Kurahashijima and waited for assignment to operational Kaiten units,* the more persistent self-preservationists in the group were able to finagle medical discharges from the program or assignments to different duties. The vast majority of the boys, however, stayed the course, and after their assignment to Kaiten units, their training as pilots began in earnest.

The steepest learning curve in Kaiten training was required for mastery of the machine's quirky handling characteristics and complex onboard systems, which it was said a pilot "needed six hands and eyes" to keep under control.[1] Also, no one clambering down the hatch of a Kaiten for the first time ever got the impression that the weapon had been built with crew comfort as a crucial design consideration. The vessel's interior was a claustrophobe's worst nightmare—dark, dank, cramped, with the bulkheads and deck almost completely obscured in a Gordian knot of knobs, dripping pipes, valves, and pressurized canisters. It was so cramped, in fact, that the pilot could not even extend both of his legs. Because of the positioning of a large stabilizing gyro, the pilot would have to sit with his left knee jammed up against his chest.

While explaining this arrangement, Kawasaki-san does something I could not imagine Konada-san doing in a million years. He pushes his chair away from the table, and right here in the lobby of Kudan Kaikan, demonstrates the cramped sitting posture and hand gestures of a busy pilot at the controls of a Kaiten. With his left knee to his chest, his right foot working phantom rudder pedals, and both hands going through a flurry of knob-turning, handle-pumping and lever-pulling motions, the effect is of a man operating a steam-operating flying machine—a contraption, perhaps, out of a Jules Verne story.

---

*One hundred new petty officers from the Tsuchi'ura Yokaren Kō-13 class had rotated into Ōtsushima to begin Kaiten training only days before the Nara Kō-13 group was scheduled to arrive. It soon became apparent that the Ōtsushima facilities were too small to accommodate both groups of Yokaren graduates, so in a case of first come, first served, the Nara group had to wait for other assignments while the Tsuchi'ura group proceeded with Kaiten training. The snafu likely saved Kawasaki-san's life.

While Konada-san gives a slow-motion *huh-huh-huh* chuckle at his partner's pantomimed interpretation of Kaiten piloting, I comment that the arrangement inside the vessel looks to have been pretty uncomfortable.

"It wasn't so bad, really," Kawasaki-san says. "[In combat] pilots were in their Kaitens for four or five hours. And by the point where [the Nara Kō-13 group's] missions would have become necessary, the targets would have been so close to our coastline that we wouldn't have had to sit in the Kaitens very long [as the Kaitens would have been launched straight from Ōtsushima and later bases]."

Surely there must have been *some* discomfort involved, I insist. Noise? Some bad smells, perhaps?

Konada-san recalls that the dominant smells inside the Kaiten were strong odors of rust, lubricant oil, and bilgewater. The latter bouquets were a given in any submersible vehicle, but rust problems were especially intense on the Kaiten on account of the pure compressed liquid oxygen used as an oxidant for its propulsion system. The tanks containing this oxygen leaked constantly whether the Kaiten was in operation or in storage, and as a result, rust ate away at the steel components inside the vessel at an unnaturally voracious rate, making for major maintenance headaches in addition to giving the interior of the vessel its distinctive odor.

Not surprisingly for a vehicle in which the passenger/pilot shared space inside a hollow metal tube with a 550-horsepower internal-combustion engine, noise came with the territory. Konada-san and Kawasaki-san recall the experience of riding in a Kaiten as being loud, but not painfully so. The sound was not the throb or hum of a normal gasoline-powered engine, but more like a steam locomotive—a gaseous *shoo-shoo-shoo-shoo* as the pistons pumped and drove the propeller shaft around. As throttle was applied, the sound rose in pitch and frequency to a hypnotic whir.

"After a while," Konada-san says, "the sound became almost soothing."

The reward for enduring the cramped space and noise of the Kaiten was a thoroughly enjoyable piloting experience—that is, as long as the vessel did not fall prey to its disquieting and fairly frequent habit of suddenly zooming away into the depths out of control, its pilot never seen alive again. Although it was cumbersome at low throttle, it picked up a graceful agility at high speed. With higher-velocity water flow over the

control surfaces, the craft became so responsive that pitching and yawing through three-dimensional underwater space was more akin to flying
a high-performance aircraft than to steering a naval vessel. Another feature that helped in no small way to make the Kaiten pilot's life easier
was an autopilot mechanism that could be used to set speed, depth, and
heading for a lengthy, stealthy incursion into the objective area, then
manually overridden by the pilot during the final attack run, when only
the finesse of a human hand could provide a reasonable chance of putting the warhead on a target.

In addition to speed, another factor in the Kaiten's responsiveness was
its pneumatically assisted rudder and diving controls. This power was provided by a compressed air canister that leaked during operation, causing
the Kaiten's cabin pressure to gradually build up during the course of a
run. When the conning tower hatch was unlocked at the end of a training
mission, it hissed like a gigantic bottle of Coca-Cola being opened.

Training runs at Ōtsushima were time-consuming enterprises involving considerable personnel and resources. At the beginning of a run, a
pilot—armed with his orders, a map with heading notations, and a full
canteen—would board the Kaiten in one of the torpedo sheds on base.
After this, the Kaiten would be towed down to the quay, lowered into the
water by crane, then towed out to the training range by a motor launch
that would double as an escort boat once the actual run began. The
range itself was similar in concept to a very large-scale version of the old
20,000 Leagues Under the Sea ride at Disney World, involving the negotiation of obstacles and the simulated engagement of targets* arranged
along a set course in relatively shallow water.

Since Kuroki and Higuchi's mishap, the tops of the training Kaitens
were painted white for visibility. This scheme served two functions, one
being to assist search efforts in the event of another accidental sinking,
the other being to allow the escort boat to track the Kaiten visually during its training runs. Small signaling charges were thrown into the water
to warn the pilot if the Kaiten was headed for hazards like shoals or coming too close to the targets. Collisions with underwater obstacles or the
target barges were the leading cause of training deaths in the Kaiten
program, so the escort's job was vital.

---

*In Ōtsushima's case, these were barges at anchor—not giant squids.

Every night at around 1800 hours, after evening mess, there were debriefs and feedback sessions between instructors and trainees to discuss results and observations from the day's training runs. In a typical session, trainees would stand in turn in front of a blackboard to give detailed self-evaluation reports of their runs, complete with figures and diagrams. This was followed by a fire-hose-like stream of aggressive questioning from the cadre, and woe unto the trainee who could not answer each and every item satisfactorily. Punishment for an unsatisfactory presentation was a thoroughly humiliating hazing in front of the group, and even more painfully, a precipitous drop down the training-order roster. In rare cases of clearly hopeless incompetence, a pilot could suffer the ultimate humiliation of being dropped from the roster altogether and permanently relegated to maintenance duties.

After the debrief sessions—which rarely ended before midnight and sometimes lasted until one or two in the morning—the trainees would stagger to their bunks emotionally and physically exhausted. And they would need every minute of sleep they could manage, for another day of more of the same would start with reveille a few hours later at 0500.


While life as a human torpedo was certainly no day at the beach, it was not without its share of comforts and amenities. Similar to its treatment of Ōka personnel, the Navy Ministry thought that nothing was too good for the Kaiten boys in terms of rations. Sailors and officers with a taste for the bottle could drink their fill of high-grade sake during their rare spells of downtime; Kinshi, Homare and Cherry cigarettes were always plentiful; and the larders in the mess hall were almost always full. When not, there was always good fishing to be had in the sea around Ōtsushima. One of the benefits of being stationed on a top-secret island base surrounded by waters off-limits to civilian fishermen was that bountiful catches were virtually guaranteed.

The enlisted men soon learned to fish with the dynamite left behind by naval engineers who had built the base. A lit stick or two tossed into the lagoon was usually sufficient to stun and float enough fish to feed a platoon. Signaling rounds could also be used. These had an explosive charge roughly equivalent to an M-80, and were activated by peeling back a piece of electrical tape over one end and tossing the round into the water. Though results were not as spectacular as those obtained from TNT trawling, they were good enough to snare a quick snack of small fish. Sardines speared on twigs and cooked over a little driftwood fire made for surprisingly good eating and a nice way to pass the time on boring sentry duty.

Due to security issues, Ōtsushima was closed to all nonessential personnel—even, with the exception of special occasions, to the ubiquitous PR and Nichiei reporter types one normally found on most army or navy *tokkō* bases. For the first few months after the Kaiten unit's activation, its personnel could leave the island only for special cases such as treatment for serious injuries or illnesses that could not be handled by the base's very modest infirmary, for family emergencies, or in the case of the higher-ranking officers, for official navy business. Things gradually loosened up after the base was running smoothly, and short leaves were available, but Konada and most of the other commissioned pilots were far too busy to take advantage of this privilege. Instead, they were dependent on what minor provisions for entertainment command had deemed fit for the isolated base. Most often, this involved not much more than availing themselves of one of the *shōgi* chessboards at the officers' liaison room for an hour or two between training, duty officer stints, and debriefing sessions.

Options for organized athletics were extremely limited, as there was not enough flat space on the island to accommodate sports such as rugby, soccer, or baseball. However, there was just enough space on the waterfront for *bōtaoshi* ("pole toppling"), a sport in which one team would attempt to knock over a caberlike pole defended by an opposing team. The sport—possibly of British Royal Navy origin and a time-honored tradition at Etajima since the academy's inception—was encouraged by base command as it was thought to foster close-knit teamwork, leadership, and aggressiveness. The best tactic for the attackers was to have a first line run up to the defenders, then crouch down to form human steps so others behind them could get height advantage and leverage when grabbing on to the pole to knock it over. No holds were barred, and kicking, punching, and gouging were allowed, so not surprisingly, injuries such as busted noses and broken teeth were frequent.

Provisions for recreation were more generous at Hikari Naval Arsenal in Yamaguchi Prefecture, site of the second major Kaiten installation and the base where Harumi Kawasaki spent six of the last eight months of the war. Facilities were available for baseball and basketball, as well as a small martial arts hall for the usual kendo and judo. As security procedures loosened up and settled into a routine, there were occasional visits to the bases by road-show troupes of professional performers. On occasion, when such high-caliber entertainment was not available, some of the more theatrically gifted personnel on base were not averse to sharing their talents with their comrades. At Hikari, a group of motivated thespians even organized a drama contest replete with costumed productions and a jug-band orchestra.

But despite the best efforts of professional and amateur alike, anyone involved in the Kaiten program who is still alive today would have to agree that the most impressive dramatic productions they saw during their time in the service were the send-off ceremonies.

## thirty-five

# A PILLAR OF SMOKE BY DAY

On September 20, 1944, American forces took possession of Ulithi, the world's fourth-largest lagoon. Ringed by palm-dotted coral reefs and sandbars, this relatively shallow body of water was spacious enough to accommodate thousands of ships at a time. Its location about one-third of the way between Guam and Leyte Gulf also made it ideally situated as a staging area and supply point for the Philippine invasion campaign about to commence.

From the American perspective, the only eventful things about the "invasion" of the atoll were the accidental death of an Ulithian princess after a beach prep Hellcat strafing[1] and the infinitely happier discovery that the local womenfolk went about topless. Happier still was the fact that the landings went completely unopposed. The previous nonnative occupants of this ring of skinny sandbars—a Japanese observation station and naval seaplane unit—were already several weeks gone when the first GI boot hit the coral.

Within days of taking the real estate, the Americans had a working installation up and running, and within the span of the next few weeks, while the attention of the rest of a world at war was focused elsewhere, Navy Seabees and stevedores transformed this forgotten backwater in the Southwest Pacific into the busiest temporary military harbor in history. By late October, Ulithi was so thick with fleet carriers, cruisers, destroyers, and merchantmen ferrying to and from the new Leyte Gulf beachheads that an observer in an overhead plane would have to be forgiven for thinking he was looking down at some gray metropolis mysteriously plunked down in the middle of a turquoise lagoon.

Whether the residents of this floating city knew it or not, they were being observed in just this manner on a fairly regular basis. IJN planners—no doubt ruing their decision to give up Ulithi without a fight when they ordered its abandonment three months earlier—were by now fully aware of the lagoon's sudden and crucial importance, and were kept posted of comings and goings at the new anchorage by sub patrols and high-altitude photo-recon flyovers out of the IJN base at Truk. Everyone at Combined Fleet HQ agreed that Ulithi made a most tempting target, and with the still-top-secret Kaiten now coming online, they had what they thought was just the right weapon to juke the anchorage's now formidable defenses, send some serious tonnage to the bottom of the lagoon, and just as important, strike a blow against American morale with another psychological shock to follow up on the Shikishima flight *tokkō* successes at Leyte on October 25. By the first week of November, three submarines—*I-36*, *I-37*, and *I-47*—had been modified to carry Kaitens, and detailed attack plans were ready for the mission.

On the morning of November 7, 1944, Vice Admiral Shigeyoshi Miwa, commander of the Sixth Fleet,* arrived at Ōtsushima with an entourage of adjutants, aides-de-camp, a small brass band, and a few closely escorted navy PR types in tow. That afternoon, under snapping pennants and flags, the admiral addressed the assembled base personnel. Lined up front and center were Sekio Nishina and the eleven other Kaiten pilots of the newly formed and named Kikusui Unit. These were the men—all commissioned officers—who would be the first to ride the Kaiten into battle. After the speech, the band struck up a medley of martial tunes as the admiral handed out short swords† and white headbands to the twelve pilots standing tall in the new human-torpedo uniforms—smart khaki zip-up coveralls with a green-on-black embroidered shoulder patch featuring Masashige Kusunoki's Kikusui floating chrysanthemum emblem.

Newly promoted and Kaiten-qualified Lieutenant (JG) Toshiharu

---

*The IJN's unified sub command.

†These swords, as noted in Part Three, were from the same mass-produced batch handed out several weeks later to the Ōka pilots at Kōnoike.

Konada was in attendance as a spectator at the short-sword ceremony that afternoon, and also at the high-spirited and emotionally charged send-off party held for the pilots later that evening at the officers' liaison room, the crude but adequately spacious structure that also served as the base officers' club. Songs were sung and short, informal speeches were made throughout the party, as guests and guests of honor alike supped on sumptuous fare and drank liberal amounts of sake.

Naval etiquette dictated that subordinates could not leave a party before their commanding officer did, so the admiral—conscious that the boys needed their sleep for the big day tomorrow—stood up to leave at a decent hour. The evening ended with a series of banzai cheers for the soon-to-be-departed, and the men filtered back to the billets in pairs or small groups, with some of the more sentimental individuals in tears.

On the morn, under a cold and partly cloudy sky, the base personnel formed up in two long parallel lines leading from the HQ building down to the water, where three IJN submarines—*I-36*, *I-37*, and *I-47*—were moored at the quay, their crews lined up along the handrails at a rigid position of attention. Bolted to the deck of each sub were four glossy, coal black Kaitens with white Kikusui emblems painted on their conning towers. Trampoline-sized Hinomaru flags painted on canvas sheets were lashed to the conning towers of the mother subs, and Rising Sun battle jacks, almost as large, flew from the periscope masts.

On a signal, Nishina and the other Kikusui pilots—resplendent in gleaming white headbands and crisp uniforms—emerged from the HQ building and filed down to the water through the lines of officers and sailors amidst a rolling chorus of cheers as the banners waved and Admiral Miwa's little band thumped a patriotic march. Nishina, at the head of the file, carried a white ossuary box containing the sacred reliquary of Kuroki's ashes. Behind him, another man carried the mortal dust of Lieutenant Higuchi. The dead officers would be making the sortie with their comrades.

When the pilots reached the quay, they stopped for deep bows and a quick prayer at the base Shinto shrine, then split up into three groups of four men each to board their respective subs. Once aboard, they clambered atop their Kaitens to brandish their *katana* swords over their heads as the subs cast off and pulled away into the lagoon, the Ōtsushima personnel now thronging the water's edge, crying and shouting themselves hoarse as the subs faded away into the morning mist, their top-secret destination known only to their captains.

After carrying her volatile cargo of diesel oil and aviation gas from the United States across most of the Pacific Ocean, the 25,000-ton USS *Mississinewa* (AO-59)—a fleet oiler supporting Rear Admiral Frederick Sherman's Task Group 38.3—spent the afternoon of November 19, 1944, at Ulithi Berth 131 shifting aviation-grade gasoline from two of her huge storage tanks to tanks on the other side of the ship. This balancing operation was being undertaken to right the noticeable list the ship had taken after pumping operations earlier in the day.

Handling fuel in this kind of volume was by nature an extremely hazardous procedure, and the danger did not go away after the pumps were done with their work. Drained of their contents, the tanks were actually at a higher risk of explosion empty than they were full. Thoroughly saturated with aerated fuel fumes, the interior of a recently emptied tank was not unlike a fueled cylinder head in a car engine just before it is ignited by a spark plug. In order to prevent the kind of cataclysm that could result if an errant spark somehow found its way into such a volatile environment, Navy SOP called for "purging" the tanks with seawater immediately after unloading operations. This was done without fail while at sea, and usually—but not always—done while at port.

As the sailors on *Mississinewa*'s pump detail were unloading the last of the day's order and preparing to purge tanks, the rest of the crew was assembling in the raised cargo deck aft of the bridge to watch a movie someone had been able to wangle while ashore. The film was called *Black Parachute*,[2] a B-grade spy thriller about a brave OSS agent, played by Larry Parks, fighting to liberate Eastern Europe from the yoke of Nazi tyranny. Ostensibly, the title referred to the hero's method of entry behind enemy lines—a night drop to take care of the evil German general played by John Carradine (who *else* could it have in a 1940s B-film?) and liberate the country before sweeping resistance fighter Jeanne Bates off her feet in the last reel. *Citizen Kane* it was not, but it would nevertheless be a welcome break from the monotony of pumping gas and sitting at anchor at Ulithi.

What happened next is something of a mystery—but among *Mississinewa*'s survivors still with us today, there are two basic theories. The more popular version holds that the ship's skipper, Captain Philip G. Beck, may have been appreciative of the outstanding job the pump men had done this afternoon and aware that they were getting edgy about missing the movie. Thinking there could be little harm in letting them go early to join their shipmates for the film, he decided to forgo the usual tank purge after the fuel-pumping operation. After all, it was not like the *Mississinewa*—or any other oiler in the fleet, for that matter—had never missed a tank purge or two while at anchor. The captain had every right to expect that the ship would be perfectly safe and sound here at Ulithi, with antisubmarine nets guarding the entrances to the lagoon and combat air patrols from Sherman's carriers overhead twenty-four hours a day. And as long as nobody on board did something stupid like tossing a lit cigarette where they shouldn't, there was no reason to think anything untoward would happen.

The second version holds that the captain was not the sort of commander who would give much of a damn about his men missing a movie, and that there must have been some other reason—perhaps mere expediency—to explain the decision not to purge.

In either case, what is known with certainty is that after the pumping operations, Captain Beck belayed the SOP purge order for the empty tanks, and the pump men were now free to go aft to watch their movie.[3]

Some twelve hours later, Ulithi lagoon was waking up to the business of another workday in fits and starts. Here and there packet boats and patrol craft plied the powder-blue water between mammoth warships and freighters hulking in the morning mist. Galleys on the ships had been up and running for several hours now, going through the major production of preparing breakfasts for hundreds (or in the case of the big warships, thousands) of men, but elsewhere, most of those sailors lucky enough not to be on watch still slumbered peacefully.

At Ulithi Berth 131, the *Mississinewa* was quietly riding at anchor, bathed on one side in pale orange light from the eastern horizon. Most of her complement of 278 sailors and twenty officers were still asleep, perhaps a few of them dreaming about sweeping Jeanne Bates off her feet, probably more than a few of them dreaming about home, and certainly all of them blissfully unaware that at this very moment, they were being stalked.

The ship still carried hundreds of thousands of gallons of aviation fuel in her forward tanks, and this is where one of *I-47*'s Kaitens hit at 0545,* instantly killing fifteen crewmen asleep on the cargo deck over the tanks, killing dozens more amidships, and ripping a twenty-five-meter-long hole in the ship's hull. A split-second later, the fumes in the *Mississinewa*'s empty centerline tank ignited in an even larger explosion, cracking the ship's keel and blowing yet another gaping hole in the hull. A series of secondary explosions now rocked the vessel as flaming fuel oil raced across her decks, cooking off the ammo for her antiaircraft batteries in the searing heat.

Amidships, the carnage was indescribable. As the anchorage was jolted into frenzied activity, the sirens of ships going to general quarters yelped and whooped across the waters of the lagoon, drowning out the screams of men being burned alive aboard the *Mississinewa* or in the flaming oil slicks now ringing the ship. Above the conflagration, a column of impenetrable black smoke rose kilometers high straight up into the blue sky like some Old Testament fire-and-brimstone display.

While the inferno raged, it was increasingly obvious that the *Mississinewa* could not be saved. Captain Beck, naked after stripping off his burning pajamas, gave the order to abandon ship, and everyone who still could either jumped or was thrown overboard. As destroyers charged about searching for mystery intruders and depth-charging the entrance of the lagoon, other boats raced in from around the anchorage to rescue the *Mississinewa*'s survivors. At one point, even an old Kingfisher seaplane got into the action, throwing towlines to men in the water and using its prop blast to clear the area of burning oil slicks.[4] Miraculously, 218 of the ship's crew and seventeen of her officers were rescued. Sixty sailors and three officers were not so fortunate.[5]

Neither was the *Mississinewa*. At 0830, after two and a half hours of brave but fruitless salvage efforts, the ship rolled and sank, coming to rest where she trickled diesel oil until 2003† and still lies peacefully to

---

*It is not known if this craft was piloted by Sekio Nishina or not, although IJN lore has traditionally credited the Kaiten coinventor with the deed.

†Her leak was finally taken care of by a special U.S. Navy salvage team that pumped out the remainder of the *Mississinewa*'s oil in February 2003 (Mike Mair, personal correspondence).

this day—under twenty-three fathoms of water on the sandy bottom of Ulithi lagoon.

Before being chased into a crash dive by the sight of American destroyers approaching at flank speed, submarine *I-47* had spent most of the early morning hours of November 20 at periscope depth so that her skipper, Lieutenant Commander Zenji Orita, could watch for distant fireballs from the direction of Ulithi after launching his sub's four Kaiten. Orita logged entries for two large explosions in quick succession at 0545, then recorded numerous smaller explosions throughout the morning. These observations were duly reported at the big Kikusui debrief held at Kure on November 24.[6]

Also present at the Kure debrief was the commander of *I-36*, Lieutenant Commander Iwao Teramoto, who confirmed Orita's log entries with his own observations of explosions in the Ulithi anchorage. No doubt much to Teramoto's chagrin, however, he also had to report the disappointing fact that three of *I-36*'s four Kaiten had lodged in their deck braces or proved otherwise inoperable, preventing their use in the mission. In the end, only one of his Kaitens had been able to join in the attack.

Notably absent from the Kure proceedings was anyone from *I-37*, which had followed a slightly different mission profile that called for its Kaiten to be deployed against American shipping in the Kossol Passage to the northwest of Ulithi. Neither hide nor hair had been seen of the sub since sallying forth from Ōtsushima, and it was not until many years after the war that a team of Japanese researchers (including Konada-san) were able to conclude from Department of Defense records that the *I-37* had been sunk on station at its mission objective by American destroyers on November 19, 1944. It never had a chance to loose its Kaitens, and went down with all hands.

During discussions following Orita's and Teramoto's reports, the sub skippers made the tactical suggestion that the Kaiten could probably be employed more effectively on the high seas, where the formidable antisub measures available to the enemy in a harbor- or anchorage-type situation could not be brought to bear. The brass in attendance were hearing none of this, however, and remained convinced of the merit of their original concept of the Kaiten as a weapon to be deployed against shipping at anchor. Orita and Teramoto were thanked for their input, and their observations of November 20 were freely interpreted by command as an indication that the brave pilots of the illustrious Kikusui Unit had sunk three aircraft carriers and two battleships at Ulithi.[7] So it was written, so it was done, and glowing reports of the mission and of the new super-weapon's capabilities were delivered in a Tokyo audience with His Majesty on December 12.[8] The general public would have to wait a while longer for the good news.

Understandably high up on the Kaiten program's need-to-know food chain—higher even than His Majesty—Konada and the other pilots back at Ōtsushima were let in on the confidential contents of the Kikusui after-action report soon after it was written. Despite literary interpretations to the contrary in various books about the Kaiten, Konada-san does not remember the Kikusui news as being greeted with any particular enthusiasm or rejoicing at Ōtsushima. For one thing, a report of successful deployment of the Kaiten also meant, by necessity, that friends and comrades were dead. Decorum alone in such a situation demanded a respectful response to such news, no matter what combat successes might have been brought about by these sacrifices. Second of all, as far as the pilots were concerned, there was no reason to register surprise at a report of three carriers and two battleships being sent to the bottom. Rather, considering the fact that twelve Kaitens and their brave pilots were sent out on the sortie, the report numbers seemed a little on the low side. Konada himself felt such supreme confidence in the Kaiten that he expected to bring down nothing less than a fleet carrier when his own moment of truth came.

For Konada, waiting for that moment of truth was an existence of time passed in a gray zone somewhere between life and death. This was an experience common to all *tokkō* personnel and generally measured in days or weeks for aircraft pilots, but in the case of the Ōtsushima Kaiten pilots, this period of psychological limbo had to be endured for eight or nine months or more. Life was lived on borrowed time with death lurking just close enough to deny a pilot the closure of knowing if any given sunset watched from the beach, a game of chess enjoyed with a friend, or even just a nice meal in the mess hall would be one's last. It was an existence every Kaiten pilot learned to deal with in his own way. Some drank, others slept whenever they could, still others—like Konada—poured everything they had into every minute detail of their duties. Anything to keep their minds off the infernal waiting, which had to be endured with the unbearable knowledge that friends and loved ones were dying—under the Americans' guns at sea and under their bombs in the burning cities. As the war ground on, many came to believe that comrades given attack orders were deserving not only of respect, but of envy.

Konada would go on to spend eleven months in this purgatory. The vagaries of attack roster selection meant that he was the only INA graduate pilot in the original Ōtsushima group not to sortie from the island. Fate intervened in May 1945—at the most furious stage of the Okinawa combat that had claimed so many Etajima buddies—when Konada was posted to the new Kaiten base on Hachijōjima Island, a rough volcanic outcropping in the Pacific Ocean three hundred kilometers south of Tokyo.

IJN planners had ordered Kaitens to Hachijōjima after deeming that the island's strategic location in the middle of sea-lane approaches to the Japanese capital made it a likely next target for the American juggernaut after Okinawa's inevitable loss. Of course, historical hindsight shows that further American incursions into Japanese territory were unnecessary after Okinawa—but such developments were not anticipated by the Kaiten men of Hachijōjima, who were on constant standby for attack orders that could come at any time virtually from the moment they set foot on the island. As the Americans tightened their noose on the home islands, this death-shadowed expectation only grew in intensity, peaking but not necessarily subsiding completely on August 15.

Like every other Japanese of his generation still with us, Konada-san has vivid memories of that day—few of them happy. Following orders posted earlier in the morning, all of the Hachijōjima personnel formed up in front of the HQ building a few minutes before twelve noon for "an important announcement from the emperor." When the radio was turned on, the static was very bad. Konada-san suspected then—and has since always believed—that someone was trying to jam the signal.* Only bits

---

*Given the timing, the most plausible motive for deliberate electronic interference with the emperor's message lies with Japanese militarists who wanted the war to continue.

and snippets were received, and what did make it through was so garbled in transmission that no one could make heads or tails of it. At the end of the broadcast, the radio was switched off and the base CO, blinking rapidly and literally scratching his head, turned to his men. He had decided to look on the bright side, he said, and interpret the message as yet another fight-to-the-finish speech from Tokyo. The assembly was dismissed and all personnel were ordered to return to their posts and remain on standby.

Lieutenant Konada, however, had doubts about the accuracy of the CO's interpretation of the imperial broadcast. After the formation broke ranks, he decided to visit the enlisted men running the radio relay station on top of the island's main mountain to see if they had had any better luck with their antenna's reception. Konada soon ascertained that they had not, although they had been able to pick up a transcript of the message sent out over military frequencies in naval code a few minutes after the voice broadcast. The courtly medieval Japanese text the emperor's scribes had prepared for the broadcast was a devil to try to muddle through in plain *katakana* phonetic transcription, but the gist of the message was clear enough—Bear the unbearable, endure the unendurable. The war was over, and His Majesty had just said so.

Konada returned to the main base to pass on his message from the mountaintop. The CO acknowledged the need to modify his earlier interpretation of the broadcast, but he saw no need to modify the standing orders for the base to remain on full alert. Until they got a better picture of what was happening in the outside world, they would have to assume that attack orders were imminent.

In the meanwhile, during breaks from his duties, Konada kept vigil in front of a radio he had set up in the hallway of the officers' billets, switching back and forth between Japanese military frequencies and American Japanese-language propaganda broadcasts beamed at the home islands from Saipan (think Tokyo Rose in reverse). Gradually, the picture began coming together, and it seemed that the HQ radiomen were correct in their interpretation of the emperor's broadcast. Konada felt that it was intrinsically wrong to take the American broadcasts at face value, but when he compared and contrasted this information with the bits and pieces he was gleaning from uncoded Japanese military traffic, the Americans appeared to be telling the truth when they reported that the war was over. Konada continued his radio monitoring over the next few days, interspersing this activity with frequent visits to the mountain radio shack to look at their decoded-messages log.

Out of all of the messages he read during this time, none was more disturbing than the news that the feared and hated Soviets had at last entered the war. Konada could only read with helpless rage reports from points north that the Russians were at this very moment pouring armored divisions into Manchuria and threatening Hokkaido after rolling up the Kuriles like a cheap carpet. Losing to the Americans was bad enough, but the thought of the Soviets running riot over the country with no way of stopping them was absolutely unbearable.

Hachijōjima's remote location in the middle of the ocean may have made it vulnerable to radio-frequency jamming by holdout fanatics in the IJN's chain of command, but this was not the case for naval bases in the home islands. Despite His Majesty's medieval vocabulary, the officers monitoring a shortwave radio at the 23rd Totsugeki Unit Kaiten base at Susaki, Kōchi Prefecture, knew as soon as the broadcast was over that they had just been told to lay down their arms. Japan had just surrendered.

After being told that the war was over and given orders to stand by for further instructions, Petty Officer Harumi Kawasaki spent the rest of the day as many of his fellow 23rd Totsugeki pilots did—staggering around the confines of the base as a sotted, sullen pistolero, with a sake bottle in one hand and a pilot's service revolver in the other, shooting at signs, windows, into the dunes, or simply straight up into the air. Too ashamed to share their tears with each other, the pilots wandered off singly to sob with grief, howl with rage or just stand stonily silent and numb with shock, staring blankly out at the summer sea and hoping that this was all a bad dream.

The next day, the pilots awoke to pounding hangovers and the grimmest morning-after imaginable as the bleak reality set in that yesterday had not been just a bad dream after all. Then, with everyone expecting that the day would see a repeat of more sake-drenched tantrums thrown on top of jangled nerves and bad adrenaline, a glimmer of hope appeared in the form of an oddly uplifting piece of scuttlebutt making its way around the base. The latest interpretations of His Majesty's broadcast were that maybe it had just been an order for a temporary cease-fire, and that the nation's armed forces were to remain on full alert to be ready to attack if attacked first and/or if American invasion landings seemed imminent.

The rumor breathed new life into the unit, and spirits rebounded even further when, later that morning, reports came in that an American fleet was approaching nearby Tosa Bay. This was enough to convince the Susaki commander that the rumor was true. Standby orders were issued, and the base kicked into high gear to prepare the Kaitens for attack missions.

In the nearby fishing village of Tei, where the 23rd Totsugeki had an annex base, a different type of *tokkō* weapon was being readied. The *Shin'yō* ("Ocean Shaker") was a ten-meter-long plywood motorboat carrying a 300 kg warhead in the bow. Usually powered by old automobile engines pressed into maritime service, the boats tended to be rather slow and extremely vulnerable to the batteries of 20 and 40 mm guns most American vessels carried for air defense. To give the Shin'yō pilot at least a slim chance of getting in close enough to his target to do damage, the boat was also armed with two forward-firing one-shot-only 12 cm rocket scatter guns that could be used to try to keep the American gunners' heads down during the attack run.[9]

Considering the numbers of boats built and pilots sacrificed during missions in the Philippines and Okinawa, the Shin'yō had a less than glowing performance record, but the pilots trained in the weapon's use were as motivated as the crewmen in any of the IJN's other *tokkō* programs. The Shin'yō pilots of the 23rd Totsugeki were no exception. In their haste and excitement after hearing the reports of approaching American ships earlier in the morning, the Tei personnel had been only too happy to interpret the subsequent standby notice from Susaki HQ as actual attack orders. By early evening, maintenance crews were practically falling over each other as they rushed to arm and gas up the unit's twenty-three boats, lined up nice and tight along the Tei beach cove.

In the midst of all this frenzied activity, an errant sailor spilled a sizable amount of gasoline on a boat that, for some reason, already had its engine running. There was a spark in the wrong place at the wrong time, and before anyone knew it, the boat was up in flames. No one needed a lengthy lecture about the dangers of combining fire with overflowing gas tanks and high explosives, and as the flames rose higher, there was a tangled khaki gaggle of asses and elbows as the maintenance crews and boat pilots scrambled for cover in the dunes behind the cove.

At one point, the flames seemed to subside. A couple of brave souls ventured back down to the boats to investigate. The all-clear was given, and with sweaty brows and a few nervous laughs, the rest of the sailors returned to work. A few minutes later, the still-smoldering boat and its warhead blew sky-high, touching off a domino run of explosions in either direction along the row of boats ringing the cove. It was all over in a matter of seconds.

Hearing the explosions and seeing the thick black smoke rising from the direction of the cove, radiomen from a nearby army unit got onto the national command grid and began screaming to high heaven and anyone else still listening that the Shin'yō boys of the 23rd Totsugeki were giving hell to an American invasion force in Tosa Bay. Air units were scrambled and naval elements began racing to the area before the error was realized and urgent bulletins denying the reports of combat in Shikoku were flashed to bases around the country. But while the combat may have been specious, the reports of mass destruction were not. The explosions had reduced the Shin'yō boats to piles of smoldering ash and twisted metal, and 111 sailors were dead.

After killing 6,310 Japanese and killing or maiming over 15,000 Allied servicemen, Japan's *tokkō* program had just claimed the last of its victims. But there was yet one more blood sacrifice to be made before an unprecedentedly horrific chapter in Japanese history could be finally closed.

## thirty-six

# GOING HOME

After hosting a small party for loyal staff members and trusted confidantes at his Tokyo home late into the night of August 15, 1945, Admiral Takijirō Ōnishi retired to his tatami-floored study to write letters until sometime in the wee hours of the following morning. One of the letters he wrote was an apologetic farewell to his wife. A second letter was addressed to "Heroic Souls of the Tokkō-tai." Despite its title, this seems more likely to have been written with the admiral's place in history in mind. In it, Ōnishi accepts personal responsibility for the sacrifice of the *tokkō* thousands. In closing, he exhorts the Japanese race to maintain its pride, even in defeat, and to do its utmost "in the best *tokkō* tradition" for the common good of the nation and world peace.

Finally, in beautiful calligraphy, the admiral wrote the following haiku:

> *Oh, how uplifting*
> *The moon shining so clearly*
> *Now that storms have passed.*[1]

After setting down his calligraphy brush, the admiral picked up a short sword, shoved the blade into the left side of his abdomen, and drew it as far across his torso as he could before pain paralyzed his hand. The wound was fatal, but unfortunately for Ōnishi, it did not sever any of the major arteries whose rupture would have mercifully hastened the inevitable.* When his house servant discovered him still very much alive and conscious around dawn, he was curled up in agony on the blood-soaked tatami of his study, holding his shredded guts in with his bare hands. Refusing medical assistance, the admiral stayed in this position for another twelve hours before finally succumbing to his wounds on the evening of August 16, 1945.

Media handling of the incident was respectful, treating the admiral's death as the passing of a modern-day hero in the best samurai tradition. Few Japanese at the time disagreed with the semantic implications when front-page headlines in the nation's major dailies referred to Ōnishi's decision to take his own life using the heroic term *jiketsu* ("self-determined final judgment") rather than the usual *jisatsu* (generic term for "suicide," which would be used under less honorable circumstances). The incident was one of the more sensational topics of nationwide discussion in the otherwise stunned and stupefied early aftermath of the surrender broadcast.

While the nation was abuzz with news of the Ōnishi incident mere hours after the fact, it would be several months before Konada, still stranded on Hachijōjima, would learn of the demise of the visionary firebrand he and so many other young naval officers had idolized during the war. But even if he had heard the news when everyone else did, he would have had little time to mourn the admiral, for he was busy attending to last rites of a more immediate nature—burying the Kaiten, and on an even more personal level, bidding sad farewell to his own identity as an officer in His Majesty's imperial navy.

In no particular hurry to go home and face an unknown future in which the only certainty was scarred pride, Konada stayed on at Hachijōjima for several months after the war to help oversee the work crews dismantling the Kaiten stockpiles and facilities on the island. Most of the heavy lifting had been done by early autumn, but Konada stayed on with the skeleton cadre remaining on Hachijōjima that would oversee the official handover of the base to Allied occupation forces.

---

*Some *tokkō* survivors hold that Ōnishi did this by design, to prolong his suffering and penance before his "sleep of a million years," as he described death in his second farewell letter.

The mission of the American inspection teams that arrived on October 30 was to ensure that the Kaitens and any equipment that could be used to deploy or maintain them were permanently denied to the Japanese. Konada, as one of the most experienced Kaiten men still left on the base, was put in charge of liaising with the Americans and coordinating the scrapping operations. Of utmost priority was the extremely hazardous task of disarming and separating the huge warheads from the bodies of the Kaitens. Disposing of the warheads themselves was an even touchier job, and at first no one on the base was quite sure what to do with them. Their immense explosive yield meant that simply detonating them in a ditch somewhere like dud artillery shells was out of the question, and attempting to cut them open and remove the unstable explosive charge inside was, for the same reason, an even less appealing option. It was finally decided that the best solution was to dump them at sea, and local fishermen familiar with the surrounding waters were hired for this task. Whether or not the fishermen were fully aware of the danger involved in this temporary work is not known, but their ability to find the dumping grounds at a later date could not have been better with GPS technology at their disposal; some five years later, when the value of scrap steel in Japan shot through the ceiling at the height of the Korean War, they went back to their explosive stash, raised the warheads from the seabeds, and sold them on the scrap market for a tidy profit.[2]

The Kaiten fuselages left over from the disarming operation were trucked by hand trolley into one of the deep storage tunnels dug into the cliffs of Hachijōjima. TNT was rigged among the machines and around the entrance of the tunnel. The subsequent blast buried the remnant of the Kaiten forever under thousands of tons of rock.

"I'll never forget that final explosion," says Konada-san. "That was when it really hit me that this was the end. It was all over."

The Kaiten would now live on only in the history books, and in the dreams and memories of men like Toshiharu Konada and Harumi Kawasaki. While the courage and dedication of the Kaiten pilots was never in question, the legacy of the weapon itself left much to be desired. From an operational standpoint, the Kaiten had performed no more impressively than the IJN's other flopped wonder weapon, the Ōka. With all of the herculean effort and sacrifice in human lives and matériel involved in the Kaiten program, only one Allied ship—the USS *Mississinewa*—

had been sunk, with another—the destroyer USS *Underhill*—damaged severely enough to require later scuttling.

In a dubious honor shared with its rocket-propelled cousin, the Kaiten had been responsible for more Japanese deaths than enemy fatalities. As opposed to less than two hundred American or other Allied casualties caused by Kaiten operations, over a thousand IJN personnel had lost their lives deploying the weapon. This tally included 810 crewmembers of subs sunk during Kaiten-ferrying missions, 148 sailors on transport ships carrying Kaitens to outlying bases, 118 killed in American air raids and other causes, and 89 Kaiten pilots killed in combat. A further 15 pilots were victims of training mishaps.*

It took several weeks for everything on Hachijōjima to be wrecked to the Americans' satisfaction, and it was not until November 22 that Konada finally left the island. It was his first time off the base in nearly five months, during which time there had been an ominous lack of correspondence from his family in Kure. Adding to this anxiety was his knowledge that Kure had been heavily bombed, and that nearby Hiroshima had been destroyed in the closing days of the war with a weapon of unimaginable destructive power, supposedly killing tens or even hundreds of thousands in an eyeblink. He had no way of knowing whether or not anyone in his family was among the victims without going to Kure to see for himself. But as a regular navy officer, he would not be free to do this until he had officially resigned his commission at the still-functioning Navy Ministry in Tokyo. His resignation was tendered and accepted by the navy on November 25, and when twenty-one-year-old Toshiharu Konada walked out of the ministry building to make his way to Tokyo Station through the rubble-strewn, refugee-thronged streets of an alien city under foreign occupation, he did so as a civilian. His war was over.

Konada arrived in Kure several days later to find that the worst of his fears about family and home had not come to pass. His own life, however, was a shambles, and it would be a long, hard road to pick up the pieces. But like six million other former comrades in arms, time, youth,

*Konada, personal correspondence. Two post-surrender-broadcast suicides at Ōtsushima usually included in Japanese counts are not included here.

and energy were commodities he possessed in abundance, and the world would not keep Toshiharu Konada—or Japan—down for long. In 1947, after a year of rejections from other universities on account of his Eta-jima credentials, he was able to matriculate to the elite Kyoto University, which had the top natural-science department in the country. Majoring in marine biology, he went on to a successful career in the maritime industry, retiring in 1990 as an executive with a large shipping concern.

Unlike so many other *tokkō* survivors, Konada-san has never been ashamed of his wartime experiences, nor of his participation in Japan's special attack corps. In 1962 he was instrumental in founding the first veterans' group to openly acknowledge its former *tokkō* affiliations—the National Kaiten Pilots' Association. He has served this organization with pride and distinction ever since. He now lives with his wife and eldest daughter in the greater Tokyo area, where he remains active in conservative politics and "correct" history-awareness programs for young people.

When Harumi Kawasaki's war ended, he literally had no place to go. For the previous two years, the navy had been the first real home he had had since early childhood, and for the past year, his fellow Kaiten pilots had been the closest thing to family he had perhaps ever experienced in his life. But the surrender meant that all of that was suddenly gone, and the demobilization activity dominating the Susaki base over the next few weeks provided nothing better than an opportunity to get three squares a day while watching it all die a slow, anticlimactic death. Still, that was better than having to face the displaced-persons stations and gruel lines back in the real world. Given the circumstances, it is not too difficult to understand why Kawasaki stayed in uniform as long as possible, which, from his perspective, could never be long enough. It seemed that he had no option now but to sit tight and wait to be told to leave.

Orders to heave-ho and vacate the premises came down on August 25. Rumors of rebellion on other bases came and went with regularity, so the authorities were taking no chances, especially with ex-*tokkō* types, who were deemed capable of stirring up serious trouble if kept together too long on the bases. When the departure date arrived, however, one of

Japan's biggest typhoons of the century was hot on its heels.* The demobilization ships scheduled to take the men home were forced to cancel their stops at Susaki on account of the storm. Finally, after days had passed with no sign of the naval vessels, base authorities were forced to hire commercial vessels to take the increasingly restless men home. Stops would be made at Osaka and northern Kyūshū. The men were free to disembark at either location.

Kawasaki, however, with no particular "home" to "go home" to, therefore had no reason to board the repatriation boat. With a small group of like-minded individuals, he petitioned the base commander for permission to set up a small logging company to work the heavily wooded local mountains. The idea was nixed, but Kawasaki's separation from the IJN was given a stay of several months when he was hired to help with personnel outprocessing and equipment dismantling operations at the base.

The temp work at Susaki continued until December, after which there could be no more reality avoidance. With the base now gone, the IJN no more, and no jobs to be had nearby, Kawasaki had no choice but to track down his older brother in Yamaguchi Prefecture and hope he would be allowed to hang his hat for a while until he could get his life together. He had made a rather uncomfortable visit to this married brother the previous July during his final presortie leave (before posting to Susaki, that is—not before an actual attack mission, which Kawasaki obviously never made), so he was not expecting much of a welcome this time, either.

Luckily for all concerned, the Yamaguchi sojourn was a short one. Kawasaki was able to get a slot on the crew of a repatriation ship making runs from Asia to Japan. The work lasted all the way to April 1947, after which Kawasaki experienced another brief period of drift before securing steadier work in a flour factory, where he would stay for twenty years and rise to union rep, all while attending night school for a bachelor's degree

---

*Ironically, had an American invasion fleet proved necessary, this storm may very well have turned out to be—at least in terms of its consequences for the invader—the mythical *kami kaze* for which the Japanese had prayed so long during the war. As things were, the typhoon did enormous damage to Third Fleet anchorages in Okinawa as well as to other American naval units in Japanese waters at the time.

in accounting. Leaving the flour company in 1967, he moved on to a successful second career as an accountant in the women's-wear industry. Only recently retired as of the writing of this book, he now lives with his wife and son in Tokyo, and keeps himself busy with various veterans' affairs, including membership in the National Kaiten Pilots' Association.

# EPILOGUE

For the last topic in our talk at Kudan Kaikan, I ask Konada-san and Kawasaki-san something I always ask *tokkō* veterans at the end of an interview—"How would you like to see the *tokkō* program remembered by future generations of Japanese?"

Kawasaki-san comments that his family has never shown any interest in his war stories, and he has never forced the issue at home. As almost any Japanese veteran will tell you, this is just the way things are now. The young people do not want to know, and the only people who seem to care are other vets.

Konada-san echoes these sentiments, adding that it is unfortunate that more is not known about the Kaiten by the general public, and that he would like the truth about this unique naval organization recorded and preserved for the sake of future generations. In the meantime, while he still can, Konada-san is doing what he can to help teach people about the Kaiten, and on a more general level, to raise historical awareness about the war and Japanese heritage as a whole. However, he maintains, there are powerful forces trying to block his way. He believes that the Japanese education system was "destroyed by postwar policy reforms," and that Nikkyōso—the national teachers' union that has lobbied for liberal education policies since the early 1950s—has done tremendous damage to the moral fabric of the nation, especially for younger generations.

"The Japanese were a strong and beautiful race before the war," Konada-san laments. "But we have become selfish and weak."

The three of us sit on that comment without response for a little longer than I feel comfortable doing, and I finally break the silence by thanking my subjects for their time.

After leaving Konada-san and Kawasaki-san at the subway stop, I head back to the hotel to pay my tab. Entering the lobby, I find a squad of chipper young crew-cut judo team members with matching gym bags and blazers formed up in loose ranks in front of the gift shop. They are being given a quick pep talk by someone I assume to be their coach—an equally chipper middle-aged man with cauliflower ears and the same harsh crew cut as his charges. "Coach" ends his speech with an emphatic *"Ganbare,"* and the boys break ranks with a manly jock grunt that tapers off into a long, drawn-out collective hiss, as if several bicycles have suddenly had their tires slashed simultaneously.

Regarding the boys as they file out of the hotel, chins up and chests out, I find it is not much of a stretch to imagine them in khaki flight suits, trotting down to a flight line of gassed-up Zeros with running engines. The imagery is poignant for me not because of any fatalistic or romantic intimations, but because it emphasizes the rarity of brave, motivated young Japanese men these days. East Asia may have been won on the judo mats and kendo floors of Budōkan in a not-so-distant gloried past of Japanese masculinity, but are future battles, I wonder, now being won on weblogs and the game consoles of Nintendo?

Whither the fabled Japanese fighting man? Extinct, or merely dormant? What if Japan were someday in danger again, caught in a situation where, for one reason or another, America was in no position to help—would the nation's young men be up to the challenge, ready to risk their lives in their country's defense?

"Probably not" is the answer most middle-aged and elderly Japanese give to this hypothetical question. Even more worryingly, it is also the answer I hear from most young people.

In talking with Japanese veterans about the reasons for such a situation coming to pass, most blame the general lack of fighting spirit and patriotism of the nation's younger generations on lingering shame and loss of confidence from the 1945 defeat. Many go further to explain the awful staying power of this multigenerational malaise on long-range educational policies imposed by the American occupation authorities after the war to "declaw" the Japanese race and ensure that it would never be politically, legally, or temperamentally capable of taking up arms again, leaving it eternally dependent on America for its protection.

I have had many lively conversations on this topic with Japanese over the years, with perhaps the most memorable of these being a talk I had in March 2002 with Hisao Horiyama, an IMA classmate of Iwao Fukagawa and Toshio Yoshitake and also a *tokkō* survivor (194th Shinbu). Horiyama-san is a recently retired business executive with over fifty years' experience in the chemical industry. He is also an accomplished *tokkō* researcher and has written an authoritative book on IJA *tokkō* operations titled *Tatebayashi no Sora* ("The Skies of Tatebayashi").[1]

While discussing history-education policy in Japanese schools, I shared an anecdote with Horiyama-san that I have heard many times from students during my years teaching college in Japan—the way Japanese history is currently taught in junior high and high schools, the semester or school year inevitably ends just before the curriculum must deal with post–Meiji era material. In other words, as far as the vast majority of Japanese young people are concerned, the entire past century of their nation's history is one big blank, and since this "controversial" period is also largely ignored in entrance exams, this stunning gap in their historical consciousness is left as is. The old Japanese proverb "When something stinks, put a lid on it" describes perfectly the institutional amnesia afflicting Japanese history education today. Even more disturbingly, the only people in this country who display any passion about addressing this problem are those who would distort the history books to their own political ends.*

"I think ignorance about our culture is going to destroy our country," Horiyama said, echoing something Konada-san would say to me three months later. "Excuse my frankness, but I think this is exactly what America intended to happen when GHQ enforced new education regulations during the occupation.

---

*The most salient of these efforts at present is the right-wing agenda to have Japan's conflict portrayed as an Asian war of liberation from Western colonialism. It has been my personal observation, however, that Asian neighbors feel about as much gratitude toward Japan for their postwar "liberation" as Hiroshima residents feel toward the atomic bomb for their postwar "urban renewal."

"The Japanese government and mass media have really been spineless since the defeat," he continued. "Making things worse, the government put all of its efforts into rebuilding the economy after the war, and did not pay enough attention to educating the nation's young about protecting their heritage. Today's young people are the second consecutive generation of Japanese who have little or no sense of their own nationality. I worry that they will grow up to be 'world citizens' instead of Japanese. How can a people with poor knowledge of their own culture be taken seriously by other cultures? They can't.

"Now, I'm all for this so-called globalization stuff if it's supposed to be all about bringing different peoples closer and fostering goodwill, but I think what America has done to Japan since the war is more along the lines of cultural invasion, destroying our heritage and trying to Westernize our societal values."

If there is any truth in Horiyama-san's suspicions, it lends credibility to the theory—shared by most Japanese veterans as well as the late Richard M. Nixon—that a hastily-acted-upon desire on the part of war-weary victors to sow salt in the spiritual fields of a formidable foe was operant in the formulation of many of GHQ's policies, including the outlining of educational policy and the framing of the modern Japanese constitution.* But still, I am more tempted to pin the larger share of blame for this weakening of the Japanese spirit on domestic rather than foreign pathogens: weakening paternal roles in the modern Japanese family; the vapid, effeminate infantilism proselytized by Japanese popular culture; the failure of the education system to promote creative thinking and ambition in the nation's young; a value system based on crass materialism for the last half century, now even further debased by more than a dozen years of seemingly terminal economic slump—all of these are factors contributing to the demise of Japanese pride and the once-vaunted and -feared Japanese fighting spirit.

So, will warriors ever spring again from the rocky soil of this once-bold land, now transformed by the wave of a wand and a sprinkling of

---

*During the early stages of the Cold War, when America belatedly realized that a strong ally was more of an asset in this part of the world than a vassal state requiring protection, then–Vice President Richard Nixon remarked that the "no-war clause" of the constitution imposed on Japan by GHQ after World War II had been "a mistake" (La Feber [1997], p. 298).

pixie dust into a kingdom of pink kitsch and nonconfrontational, cuddly feel-good? Understandably, there is a desperate need among the residents of these isles to believe that young men raised on Hello Kitty and Pokémon can defend the future of Japan. But most also find it necessary to bolster this hope with silent prayers that dear old Uncle Sam will always be nearby to keep the Bogeyman away.

Japan's last samurai—an ever-dwindling population of war veterans like Hisao Horiyama and Iwao Fukagawa—are heartbroken by the moral, social and political direction the nation has taken since the end of the war. Yet with few exceptions, they are hesitant to take a public stand in warning or protest over these developments. As veterans of Japan's only defeat, they feel unqualified—or rather, *dis*qualified—to serve as mentors and guides for the nation's soul. In a modern day variation on a bushidō creed that would have demanded their suicide in a more brutal era, they have shouldered the guilt of their lost war with contrition and humility, keeping their opinions about duty, honor and country amongst themselves, if expressed at all. Most do not even discuss such matters with their families. This is as true for this generation as eighty-year-old men as it was for them as twenty-somethings clearing postwar rubble, as thirty- and forty-somethings forming the backbone and muscle of a nascent Japan, Inc., and as fifty- and sixty-somethings running a country second only to America in global economic influence. Through the decades, their silence has been their penance.

Somewhere between August 15, 1945, and the coming of age of the first generation with no memory of the war, Japan tossed a spiritual baby out with the bathwater. Call it a primal strength, if you will, that once dwelled in the Japanese soul but is no longer there. Many people in this part of the world still haunted by the ghosts of remembered massacres—and even many Japanese themselves—think that the Japanese in their postwar incarnation as a peace-loving race are better off without this spiritual strength, and are somehow more civilized with a sense of collective purpose expurgated from their national character. But I am tempted to say that "civilized" in this sense only approaches Chief Dan George's definition of the term—it just means the Japanese have become easier to sneak up on.

In *The Image Factory*, a collection of essays on modern Japanese culture, Donald Richie writes that in defeat, Japan suffered "a trauma that might be compared to that of the . . . believer who suddenly finds himself an atheist . . . Japan lost its god, and the hole left by a vanished deity remains."[2] Considering this fate, I can begin to understand the inconsolable feelings of the old men like Horiyama-san and others I have talked to who say that they actually envy their comrades who died in *tokkō* attacks, going out in a blaze of glory for what they loved and believed in even as they knew their cause was doomed. While their sacrifice was tragic, entailing as it did the loss of everything these fine young men had and might have accomplished had they survived their war, it also meant that they did not have to live to see the destruction of their world as they knew it, and the consignment to irrelevance and humiliation in postwar Japan of their pride and nearly everything else they had fought for and cherished. They died as the last of a now-extinct breed of Japanese who never had to know their country with the stain of defeat on the pages of its history.

For the last half century, the Japanese have been extraordinarily successful at accumulating material affluence, and have done almost as well at erasing the war from the collective conscience of younger generations. Most Japanese under sixty have never experienced poverty and have little interest and even less knowledge about World War II beyond a vague idea that Japan lost and that, for some reason—perhaps just plain old Anglo-Saxon meanness—the Americans saw fit to vaporize a lot of innocent civilians in Hiroshima and Nagasaki when they already had the war in the bag. In a deft ideological sleight of hand, postwar generations of schoolchildren have been taught—when taught about the Pacific War at all, that is—that Japan's fundamental experience in the conflict was one of pitiable victimization, not of suffering the logical consequences of ill-advised action. This position is an issue where Japanese of all political stripes can find common ground, and as far as they are concerned, it is a tribal matter not open to negotiation with outsiders.

Japan's collective memory of the war, as with so many other issues in its history, has a tendency toward selective amnesia. Memory, then, is also the crux of any dialogue about the legacy of the kamikaze, and it raises many questions: How will *tokkō* be remembered by future Japanese generations? Is there an option that will not see the *tokkō* war dead ghoulishly shanghaied as unwitting Nippon Über Alles poster boys on one hand, or as pitiable characters in a Greek chorus of masochistic national self-denial on the other? Should *tokkō* even be remembered at all? Might the Japanese—as so many of them seem to think—be happier forgetting about this painful topic? Only the Japanese themselves are entitled to make the final choice, but that does not mean that the rest of us cannot express a preference, and I will exercise that right by quoting something Iwao Fukagawa said to me at the conclusion of our first interview in February 2002, after I had just posed my standard wrap-up question:

"As a former *tokkō* pilot, if you could leave behind a single, vital message to be passed on to future generations of Japanese, what would it be?"

Without a second's hesitation, Fukagawa-san transformed from kindly grandfather to grizzled old soldier.

"I'd say, 'Your forefathers crashed planes into ships for their country,'" he growled. "'Never forget that.'"

I think Fukagawa-san's remark is both a rallying cry and a warning to his countrymen. Japan's war wounds will heal only when the nation finds the moral courage to honor its dead and face up to its past with equal sincerity. It is my hope that this book has in some small way demonstrated that these tasks do not have to be contradictory. The sacrifices of Japan's wartime generation will have been for naught only if the Japanese—and the rest of the world—choose to forget them.

M. G. Sheftall
Shizuoka University
July 2005

# ACKNOWLEDGMENTS

First and foremost, I would like to thank, from the bottom my heart, the "witnesses to history" who gave hundreds of hours of their precious time to make the dream of *Blossoms in the Wind* a reality: Toshio Yoshitake, Tokurō Takei, Akinori Asano, Hideo Suzuki, Tokuji Naitō, Iwao Fukagawa, Reiko Akabane, Shōko Nagasaki, Kayoko Mori, Fusako Mori, Mutsuko Miyake, Yuri Kuwashiro, Shigeko Araki, Dr. Fumitake Hiroshima, Toshi-haru Konada, Harumi Kawasaki, and Hisao Horiyama. My gratitude toward these individuals also extends to their respective families, who put up with two and a half years of incessant phone calls, written queries, and, all too frequently, unannounced visits on my part.

I would also like to thank American veterans Evan "Holly" Crawforth of the USS *St. Lo*, Charles Stanford of the USS *Mannert L. Abele*, and Raymond "Hap" Halloran of B-29 V-Square 27 *Rover Boys Express* for their willingness to share memories of painful events, that I might do justice to their own bravery and to the brave actions of their shipmates and/or flying mates no longer with us to relate another side of the "kamikaze story."

If a journey of a thousand miles begins with one step, I think it just as often begins with one person—a guide or pathfinder. And if the research and fieldwork that went into the writing of this book can be likened to such a journey, then I must credit Mr. Tatsuji Imori for making sure I did not start off with bad directions. After making my acquaintance in the often murky ether of the Internet, and then wisely and carefully ascertaining that my credentials were in order and my intentions honorable, Imori-san introduced me to the good offices of the Tokkōtai Senbotsusha Irei Heiwa Kinen Kyōkai (Special Attack Forces Memorial Association). From that fateful introduction, "open sesame" was uttered, the gates opened, and precious treasure of theretofore privileged knowledge spilled forth.

Coming so soon in the wake of the September 11, 2001 attacks on the World Trade Center and the Pentagon, when talking heads on American TV screens were likening Al-Qaeda's civilian-targeting terrorism to the Pearl Harbor raid and kamikaze attacks of the Second World War (comparisons that deeply wounded not only thousands of Japanese war veterans and their families, but millions of citizens of a nation at the top of America's rapidly shrinking list of steadfast friends), the officers and members of the memorial association would have been entirely within their rights to refuse the probing of an American busybody into their affairs. But they did not. Instead, the association welcomed me completely and without any reservation, ushering me to a privileged vantage point from which I could observe not only the inner workings of their organization, but research the most intimate details of its members' personal lives as well. Special thanks in this regard is due to Sadaharu Mogami, Motomasa Kimura, and Hiroshi Kurihara of the memorial association's front office.

There are too many other memorial association members deserving of thanks to mention everyone here by name, so let me suffice by expressing my gratitude collectively (and I fear woefully inadequately). I will never forget the kindness, understanding, and cooperation that everyone in the association has given me from the beginning to end of this long, tiring, but ultimately rewarding project. You made this book possible.

No mention of the memorial association can be made in the context of personal gratitude without also expressing thanks to Abbot Kenshō Ōta of Setagaya Kan'non and his family for their kind hospitality during my regular intrusions at monthly memorial services at the temple. Allowing me to use the temple rectory as a frequent interview venue is also greatly appreciated.

I would also like to thank the administrations of Yasukuni Shrine and of the Kaikōsha for their cooperation and hospitality, allowing me access to their records and to use their facilities without charge, often as an interview venue, and, on more occasions than I would like to admit, without my making a prior appointment. Your patience and uncomplaining indulgence are greatly appreciated. *Hontō ni osewa ni narimashita.*

On the subject of institutional thanks, I must also extend my gratitude to the members of the Zero Fighter Pilots' Association, and to the Jinrai Memorial Association. To Asano-san, especially, thanks for always keeping me in the loop.

I would also like to thank the following individuals here in Japan for their help and assistance in this project: Murray Sayle of *The Atlantic Monthly,* who regaled me with his esoteric Japan knowledge and constructive criticism during long phone conversations in the early stages of my project and advised me to start out my narrative "with a bang"; Akira Hamano of the Wakase Association for providing me with material on IJA "special attack boats"; Mutsurō Soga for material on the Banda and Fugaku special attack bomber units; IJN fighter aces Kaname Harada and Isamu Miyazaki for sharing war stories with me—I will someday, with great pride, tell my grandchildren about how I once spent an unforgettable few hours talking and drinking with legends; Dr. Walter Edwards of Tenri University, for explaining the intricacies of Japanese anthropology and its influence on modern national identity; my colleagues at the Faculty of Informatics at Shizuoka University, for serving as a sounding board for countless hours' worth of my unconventional (and probably often insulting) ideas and theories about Japanese language, culture, and history, and for giving countless tips, pointers, and corrections on the finer points of same, with special thanks to Professors Masahiko Amemiya, Shōji Arakawa, Masamichi Asama, Takeo Isarida, Jun Nishihara, Yasunori Okada, Hiroyuki Tokuyama, Junki Yaegashi and Masatoshi Yano; Yamaguchi-san and Oike-san of our faculty's administrative staff, for showing me where to cross my Ts and dot my Is on all the paperwork I have had to file over the last three years; Mike Boyce for constructive comments and a young man's fresh perspective on an old story; and Asao Shirai, for a telephone directory–sized stack of *tokkō* reference material.

On the other side of the Big Pond, I would like to thank: Mike Mair, official historian of the USS *Mississinewa* Veterans' Association, who was kind enough to share with me his encyclopedic knowledge of the Kaiten raid at Ulithi, and to read and critique my section on the topic; my parents, George and Louise Sheftall, for love, guidance, and constructive criticism through a long haul; two dear and loyal old comrades in arms,

Lieutenant Colonel Bo Friesen and Marty Roach, for encouragement, proofreading, and still making me laugh my ass off on a regular basis after all these years (to wit, Bo, I'm still laughing about the *"Fly"* routine you did from the barracks window when I was walking tours on North Area); Colonel Ralph Wetterhahn USAF (Ret.), for expert advice—both as an aviator and a professional writer—and alerting me to vestiges of plebe English 101 still lurking in my prose; Abram Hall, for reminding me when I first came up with the idea for this book that we have a mutual friend in the publishing business, Stuyvesant High School classmate and fellow Frank McCourt disciple Doug Grad; the production staff at Penguin Group (USA) and NAL Caliber for doing a dynamite job of putting this book together; and last but not least, to Doug Grad himself, loyal fan of my artistic madness since the mid-1970s, as well as my long-suffering and infinitely patient editor at Penguin, in a baritone, syrupy Tupelo drawl, I give an extra special "Thanyuh . . . Thanyuhveruhmuch . . ."

In closing, I would like to give a very, very special thanks to my wife, Keiko, a true daughter of samurai, who dealt with all of my snit fits, freakouts, and meltdowns during this project with her usual beauty and grace under fire (while raising two toddlers, no less), and who helped me to believe in myself and push on when the end seemed nowhere in sight. I clocked way too much AWOL time parenting-wise while I was bent over the computer or off running around the Japanese archipelago working on this book. I hope that you and the boys can forgive me for that—for not always being there to change the diapers and dry the tears when you needed me. For providing the environment and inspiration I needed to realize my vision you have my eternal gratitude, and as always, the three of you have my undying love.

# NOTES

## 1. *St. Lo* Overture

1. Official Web site of the USS *St. Lo* (formerly *Midway*) CVE63/VC65: http://www.stlomidway6365.org
2. E. H. Crawforth, personal correspondence.
3. http://www.stlomidway6365.org
4. E. H. Crawforth, personal communication.

## 3. The Road to Mabalacat

1. Taylor (1954), p. 254.
2. See Oide (1984) for detailed descriptions of Ōnishi's human frailties regarding personal recreation.
3. See Peattie (2001) for details of Ōnishi's role in the development of Japanese naval air power.
4. See Jukes (2002) for an excellent analysis of the battle in the Tsushima Strait in 1905.
5. See Tillman (1979) and Hammel (1992) for American-perspective accounts of the "Marianas Turkey Shoot."
6. Buruma and Margalit (2004) give a cogent and very post-9/11 relevant explanation of this mind-set.
7. Dower (1986), Lafeber (1997).
8. See Agawa (1979) for a candid look at Ōnishi's true take on the

prewar strategic picture. Interestingly enough, he was initially opposed to the Pearl Harbor raid, correctly assessing the galvanizing effect it would have on American public opinion regarding the war effort.

9. Warner (1982), Maga (2002), and Mikano (1998).
10. Morimoto (1992), p. 23.

## 4. Ōnishi's Gamble

1. Morison (1985), Volume 12, p. 106.
2. Morison (1985) gives the figure of 322,265 tons for the month of October 1944, Volume 12, p. 405.
3. Inoguchi (1985), p. 5.
4. Morimoto (1992), p. 25.
5. See Turnbull (1996) and Friday (2004) for authoritative treatises on samurai tactical thought and Japanese fusilology.
6. Kofukuda (1985) outlines the technical and philosophical evolution of the Japanese fighter aircraft from early designs through the superlative Zero and finally late war types.
7. See Hoyt (1983), pp. 10–12. See also Masuyu (2000), pp. 280–281.

## 5. Poster Boy

1. See Bix (2000), p. 187.
2. See Reischauer (1970), Beaky (1990), and Bernman (2003) for a societal scale analysis of this process. Raina (2004) studies its effect on legendary samurai Takemori Saigo, on whose life the film *The Last Samurai* was loosely based. See also Shinoraura (1999) for a contemporary Japanese celebration of this "nation-building" populist social engineering.
3. This translation of the *Sen jin kun,* or Japanese Servicemen's Code of Conduct, is from Warner (1982), pp. 5–6.

## 6. Fed up with Losing and Ready to Die

1. Kaneko (2001), pp. 47–48.
2. Kaneko (2001), p. 62.
3. See Mori (1995), p. 494.
4. See "USS West Virginia (BB-48) Action Report: Leyte Gulf/Surigao Strait." http://ibildio.org/hyperwar/USN/ships/logs/BB/bb48-surigao.html
5. Mori (1995), pp. 501–505.
6. Oide (1984), p. 78.

## 7. An Old Man's Dream

1. See Chang (1997) for a rebuttal of this opinion.
2. These positions are clearly explained in bilingual displays at Yasukuni's museum, which is open to the public, and in its English Web site at http://www.yasukuni.or.jp/english/.

## 8. The Lights of Talisay

1. See Kawachiyama (1990) for details of this and other early IJA *tokkō* operations.

## 10. The Yokaren Candidate

1. See Hudson (1999), Edwards (2000), and http://www.pitt.edu/~annj/courses/notes/jomon_genes.html
2. For what I believe are the best recent interpretations of this mind-set, see Huntington (1996), Lewis (2003) and Buruma and Margalit (2004).
3. See Reischauer (1970) for an explanation of this process. See Suzuki (1959) for a detailed aesthetic analysis of the result.
4. Akabane, personal correspondence.
5. Takei, personal correspondence.
6. Lyrics by Yaso Saijō and Yūki Koseki, Columbia Records (Japan), 1943.
7. Ohnuki (2002), p. 162.

8. In Japanese, *seishinbō* and *battā*, respectively.
9. See Tagaya (2004) for details of Yoraken expansion.

## 11. I Wanted Wings

1. See Yuzawa (1995) and Nohara (2000) for performance details of the Shidenkai.
2. Takei, personal correspondence.
3. Kimata (2001), p. 88.
4. Kimata (2001), p. 89.
5. Naitō, personal correspondence.

## 12. Amenities

1. For more details on Kōnoike base life, see Kamisu Chō Kyōiku Iinkai (1995).
2. Kaigun Jinrai Butai Senyukai (1995).

## 13. Looking for a Few Good War Gods

1. See Smethurst (1974) for details on the establishment and function of the Army Reservist Association in Japanese society.
2. Fukagawa, personal correspondence.
3. Ibid.
4. This relationship—known in Japanese as *amae*—is best explained in Takeo Doi's *The Anatomy of Dependence* (1973).
5. Fukagawa, personal correspondence. Ruth Benedict also addresses this phenomenon in *The Chrysanthemum and the Sword* (1946), pp. 248–252, which is highly recommended for readers interested in understanding Japan and Japanese society.
6. This is a reconstruction based on Sukuzi-san's recollection of the conversation.
7. Nine CV fleet carriers and eight CVL light carriers, per Morison (1985), Volume 12, p. 90.
8. This is a reconstruction based on Sukuzi-san's recollection of the cablegram.

9. Takei, personal correspondence.
10. Naitō (1999), p. 98.
11. http://www.history.navy.mil/photos/sh-fornv/japan/japsh-s/shinano.htm
12. http://64.124.221.191/Shinano.htm
13. Naitō (1999), p. 106.
14. H. Halloran, personal correspondence.
15. www.haphalloran.com
16. Takaki and Sakaida (2001).
17. Kimata (2001), p. 99.
18. See Taylor (1954) for numerous examples of the admiral's vicious eloquence on this topic.
19. The Doolittle raid was an operation Mitscher had played a crucial role in as commander of the carrier *Hornet*. See Cohen (1983) for details and an excellent photographic record of the mission.

## 14. FLIGHT OF THE THUNDER GODS

1. Inoguchi (1958), p. 142; Hoyt (1983), p. 239.
2. Inoguchi (1958), p. 143.
3. Naitō (1999), p. 148.
4. Naitō (1999), p. 155.
5. Inoguchi (1958), p. 144.
6. Naitō (1999), p. 161.
7. Tillman (1979), p. 210.
8. C. W. Stanford, personal correspondence.
9. http://www.multied.com/navy/destroyer/MannertLAbeledd733.html
10. Stanford, personal correspondence.

## 15. ECHOES OF THUNDER

1. http://www.asahi-net.or.jp/~un3k-mn/ooka-history.htm

## 16. BRIGHT-EYED BOYS FROM THE PROVINCES

1. See Gellner (1983) and Hobsbawm (1990) for enlightening analyses of the petit bourgeois *nouveau regime* in a Western context.
2. Harries (1991), p. 168.

## 17. Fighter Jock

1. *57-ki Kōkūshi*, p. 49.
2. Fukagawa (1995); *57-ki Kōkūshi Bunka-hen*, pp. 71–72.
3. Fukagawa (1995), et al., pp. 71–72.
4. Fukagawa, personal correspondence.
5. *Mainichi Shimbun*, June 11, 1945. Reprinted courtesy of *Mainichi Shimburn*.

## 18. Belt of a Thousand Stitches

1. See Nagatsuka (1972), p. 41, for a more graphic description of the unwashed *senninbari* phenomenon.
2. For an interesting contrast of modern Japanese thought on the *tokkō* pilots' sacrifice, see Kudō (2001) and Fukabon (2001).

## 19. Band of Sisters

1. Tim Maga's *America Attacks Japan: The Invasion That Never Was* (2002) offers an interesting conjectural exploration of the nightmare scenario of the fight to the last man.
2. See Kōnishi (1999) and Edwards (2003) for analysis of this program.
3. Shōko Nagasaki, personal communication.
4. http://www.town.chiran.kagoshima.jp
5. Lisa Takeuchi Cullen, "Ascent of the Fireflies," *Time*, September 2, 2002.
6. See Chiran Kōjo Nadeshiko Kai (1979) for a collection of group members' wartime diary entries and reminiscences.
7. For details on the land acquisition process, see Takagi (1973).
8. See Lord (1957), Prange (1981), and O'Neill (1982) for details of the midget sub operations at Pearl.

## 21. Fireflies

1. Warner (1982), p. 188.
2. Morison (1985), Volume 14, p. 390.
3. Ibid.

4. Tilman (1979), p. 211.
5. See Burt (1995) for a harrowing personal account of the lifelong psychological consequences of surviving a *tokkō* attack.
6. http://www.globalsecurity.org/military/facility/okinawa-battle.htm
7. Shokō Nagasaki, personal correspondence.
8. Akabane (2001), p. 76.
9. From text of display at Tomiya Ryokan.
10. Dialogue reconstructed from Akabane (2001), pp. 160–166, and interview of May 31, 2002.
11. Shigeko Araki, personal communication.
12. http://www.tcr.org/tcr/essays/Eprize_kamikaze.pdf
13. Axell and Kase (2002), p. 55.
14. Takagi (1973), p. 119.
15. Axell and Kase (2002), p. 70.
16. Satō (1997), p. 20.
17. Satō (1997), p. 21.
18. Shino (2000), p. 186.
19. Takagi (1973), p. 202.
20. Takagi (1973), p. 200.

## 22. A Peaceful Village

1. See Kosaka (2001) for more about the former Nadeshiko Unit members' immediate postwar memorial activities in Chiran.

## 23. The World Turned Upside Down

1. See Longstreet (1970) and Pincus (1996) for studies of these respective Japanese subcultures.
2. See Silverberg (1998) for a sociological and gender analysis of this phenomenon.
3. Donald Keene's *Emperor of Japan: Meiji and His World 1852–1912* (2002) is the most authoritative English language biography of the emperor.
4. See Behr (1989), pp. 45–47, for an account of Hirohito's conduct in the aftermath of the earthquake.

5. Morris-Suzuki (1998), p. 105.
6. Bix (2000), p. 140.

## 27. Setagaya Kan'non

1. http://www.jmdb.ne.jp/1942/br001160.htm
2. See Nila (2002) for details of IJN aviators' kit.
3. Morison (1985), Volume 14, p. 332. This was the shelling that blew the roof off Tokurō Takei's junior high school.
4. Sugiyama (1962), p. 68.
5. Morison (1985), Volume 14, pp. 332–333.

## 28. Pilgrimage to Chiran

1. Buruma (1995), p. 227.
2. http://www.town.chiran.kagoshima.jp/touristinfo/heiwakaikan/
3. Lyrics by Yaso Saijo, music by Yoshiaki Ōmura.

## 30. Toshiharu Konada

1. *Ashigara* was a Takao-class heavy cruiser. For technical details on the Takao class, see Worth (2001).

## 31. Harumi Kawaski

1. See Gavon (1997) for details of Tenrikyō's transformation from pariah to stakeholder through its support of state militarism.

## 32. Rearranging the Firmament

1. http://www.combinedfleet.com/torps.htm
2. O'Neill (1999), p. 187.
3. See Ikari (1991) for an account of the admission process for—and life at—the college.
4. See Maeda (1989) and Yokota (1994) for biographical details on Kuroki and Nishina.
5. http://www.asahi-net.or.jp/~un3k-mn/kai-nenpyo.htm

## 33. METAL IMPLEMENT NUMBER SIX

1. Konada (1998) in *Gyokusaisen to Tokubetsukōgekitai*, pp. 104–105 (note: For the sake of clear translation, I have taken the liberty of editing the order in which some of these sentences appear in the text).

## 34. ENTER THE KAITEN

1. http://motlc.wiesenthal.com/text/x21/xr2145.html

## 35. A PILLAR OF SMOKE BY DAY

1. http://community-2.webtv.net/ebb26/ULITHI/
2. Mike Mair, personal correspondence.
3. http://www.usni.org/navalhistory/articles03/nhlambert04.htm
4. http://www.usni.org/navalhistory/articles03/nhlambert04.htm
5. http://www.ussmississinewa.com
6. Warner (1982), p. 131.
7. O'Neill (1999), p. 200.
8. Warner (1982), p. 131.
9. See Wakashio Kai (1992–2001) for personal accounts and technical information about the army's nearly identical suicide motorboat program.

## 36. GOING HOME

1. Oide (1984), p. 237. In an attempt to keep as closely as possible to the meaning of the original Japanese while maintaining plausible English syntax, I took the liberty of switching the line order in my translation while preserving the correct 5-7-5 haiku syllabic scheme.
2. Kawasaki, personal correspondence.

## EPILOGUE

1. See Horiyama (2002).
2. Richie (2003), p. 120.

# BIBLIOGRAPHY AND SUGGESTED READING

### WORKS IN ENGLISH LANGUAGE OR ENGLISH TRANSLATIONS OF JAPANESE WORKS

Agawa, Hiroyuki (translated by John Bester). *The Reluctant Admiral: Yamamoto and the Imperial Navy*. Tokyo, New York, San Francisco: Kodansha International Ltd., 1979.

Axell, Albert and Hideaki Kase. *Kamikaze: Japan's Suicide Gods*. Longman, 2002.

Beasley, W. G. *The Rise of Modern Japan*. Tokyo: Charles E. Tuttle, 1990.

Befu, Harumi. *Hegemony of Homogeneity: An Anthropological Analysis of* Nihonjinron. Melbourne: Trans Pacific Press, 2001.

Behr, Edward. *Hirohito: Behind the Myth*. New York: Vintage Books, 1989.

Benedict, Ruth. *The Chrysanthemum and the Sword: Patterns of Japanese Culture*. Boston: Houghton Mifflin Company, 1946.

Bix, Herbert. *Hirohito and the Making of Modern Japan*. New York: HarperCollins Publishers, Inc., 2000.

Bueschel, Richard M. *Nakajima Ki-84 a/b Hayate in Japanese Army Air Force Service*. Atglen, PA: Schiffer Military/Aviation History, 1997.

Buruma, Ian. *Inventing Japan*. New York: The Modern Library, 2003.

Buruma, Ian. *The Wages of Guilt: Memories of War in Germany and Japan*. London: Phoenix, 1995.

Buruma, Ian and Avishai Margalit. *Occidentalism: The West in the Eyes of Its Enemies*. New York: The Penguin Press, 2004.

Burt, Ron. *Kamikaze Nightmare*. Corpus Christi, TX: Alfie Publishing, 1995.

Chang, Iris. *The Rape of Nanking: The Forgotten Holocaust of World War II*. New York: Penguin Books, 1997.

Cohen, Stan. *Destination: Tokyo: A Pictorial History of Doolittle's Tokyo Raid, April 18, 1942*. Missoula, MT: Pictorial Histories Publishing Company, 1983.

Cullen, Lisa Takeuchi. "Ascent of the Fireflies" in *Time*, September 2, 2002, vol. 160, no. 6.

Davis, Burke. *Get Yamamoto*. London: Arthur Barker Limited, 1969.

Doi, Takeo (translated by John Bester). *The Anatomy of Dependence*. Tokyo, New York and London: Kodansha International, 1973.

Dower, John. *Embracing Defeat: Japan in the Wake of World War II*. New York: W.W. Norton & Company, 1999.

Dower, John. *War Without Mercy: Race & Power in the Pacific War*. New York: Pantheon Books, 1986.

Edwards, Walter. "Contested Access: The Imperial Tombs in the Postwar Period." *Journal of Japanese Studies* 26, no. 2 (2000): 371–392.

Edwards, Walter. "Forging Tradition for a Holy War: The Hakkō Ichiu Tower in Miyazaki and Japanese Wartime Ideology." *Journal of Japanese Studies* 29, no. 2 (2003): 289–324.

Friday, Karl F. *Samurai, Warfare and the State in Early Medieval Japan*. New York and London: Routledge, 2004.

Garon, Sheldon. *Molding Japanese Minds: The State in Everyday Life*. Princeton, NJ: Princeton University Press, 1997.

Gellner, Ernest. *Nations and Nationalism*. Ithaca, NY: Cornell University Press, 1983.

Hammel, Eric. *Aces Against Japan: The American Aces Speak, vol. I*. Pacifica, CA: Pacifica Press, 1992.

Harries, Meirion and Susie. *Soldiers of the Sun: The Rise and Fall of the Imperial Japanese Army*. New York: Random House, 1991.

Hashimoto, Mitsuru. "Chihō: Yanagita Kunio's 'Japan'" in *Mirror of Modernity: Invented Traditions of Modern Japan* (edited by Stephen Vlastos) 133–143. Berkeley, CA, Los Angeles and London: University of California Press, 1998.

Hobsbawm, E. J. *Nations and Nationalism since 1780: Programme, Myth, Reality*. Cambridge: Cambridge University Press, 1990.

Hoyt, Edwin P. *The Kamikazes: Suicide Squadrons of World War II*. Short Hills, NJ: Burford Books, 1983.

Hoyt, Edwin P. *The Last Kamikaze: The Story of Admiral Matome Ugaki*. Westport, CT: Praeger, 1993.

Hudson, Mark J. *Ruins of Identity: Ethnogenesis in the Japanese Islands*. Honolulu: University of Hawai'i Press, 1999.

Humphreys, Leonard A. *The Way of the Heavenly Sword: The Japanese Army in the 1920's*. Stanford, CA: Stanford University Press, 1995.

Huntington, Samuel P. *The Clash of Civilizations and the Remaking of World Order*. New York, London, Toronto, Sydney: Simon & Schuster, 1996.

Inoguchi, Rikihei and Tadashi Nakajima with Roger Pineau. *The Divine Wind: Japan's Kamikaze Force in World War II*. Annapolis, MD: Naval Institute Press, 1958.

Japan Memorial Society for the Students Killed in the War—Wadatsumi Society (translated by Midori Yamanouchi and Joseph L. Quinn, S. J.). *Listen to the Voices from the Sea*. Scranton, PA: The University of Scranton Press, 2000.

Jukes, Geoffrey. *The Russo-Japanese War 1904–1905*. Oxford, UK: Osprey Publishing, 2002.

Keene, Donald. *Emperor of Japan: Meiji and His World 1852–1912*. New York: Columbia University Press, 2002.

Kōnishi, Takamitsu (translated by Joko Iori). "Constructing Imperial Mythology: *Kojiki* and *Nihon Shoki*" in *Inventing the Classics: Modernity, National Identity, and Japanese Literature* (edited by Haruo Shirane and Tomi Suzuki), 51–71. Stanford, CA: Stanford University Press, 1999.

Lafeber, Walter. *The Clash: U.S.-Japanese Relations Throughout History*. New York, London: W.W. Norton and Company, 1997.

Lewis, Bernard. *The Crisis of Islam: Holy War and Unholy Terror*. New York: The Modern Library, 2003.

Longstreet, Stephen and Ethel. *Yoshiwara: The Pleasure Quarters of Old Tokyo*. Rutland, VT, and Tokyo: Charles E. Tuttle Company, 1970.

Lord, Walter. *Day of Infamy*. New York: Henry Holt & Company, 1957.

Lott, Arnold S. *Brave Ship, Brave Men*. Annapolis, MD: Naval Institute Press, 1964.

Maga, Tim. *America Attacks Japan: The Invasion That Never Was.* Lexington, KY: The University Press of Kentucky, 2002.

Morison, Samuel Eliot. *History of United States Naval Operations in World War II.* Champaign, IL: University of Illinois Press, 1985.

Morris-Suzuki, Tessa. *Re-inventing Japan: Time, Space, Nation.* Armonk, NY: M.E. Sharpe, 1998.

Nagatsuka, Ryuji (translated from the French by Nina Rootes). *I Was a Kamikaze.* New York: Macmillan Publishing Co., 1972.

Nathan, John. *Japan Unbound: A Volatile Nation's Quest for Pride and Purpose.* Boston and New York: Houghton Mifflin Company, 2004.

Nila, Gary. *Japanese Naval Aviation Uniforms and Equipment 1937–45.* Oxford, UK: Osprey Publishing, 2002.

Oguma, Eiji (translated by David Askew). *A Genealogy of "Japanese" Self-images.* Melbourne: Trans Pacific Press, 1996.

Ohnuki-Tierney, Emiko. *Kamikaze, Cherry Blossoms, and Nationalisms: The Militarization of Aesthetics in Japanese History.* Chicago: The University of Chicago Press, 2002.

O'Neill, Richard. *Suicide Squads: The Men and Machines of World War II Special Operations.* Guilford, CT: The Lyons Press, 1999.

Orr, James J. *The Victim as Hero: Ideologies of Peace and National Identity in Postwar Japan.* Honolulu: University of Hawai'i Press, 2001.

Peattie, Mark R. *Sunburst: The Rise of Japanese Naval Air Power, 1909–1941.* Annapolis, MD: Naval Institute Press, 2001.

Pincus, Leslie. *Authenticating Culture in Imperial Japan.* Berkeley and Los Angeles, CA: University of California Press, 1996.

Prange, Gordon W. *At Dawn We Slept: The Untold Story of Pearl Harbor.* New York: Penguin Books, 1981.

Ravina, Mark. *The Last Samurai: The Life and Battles of Saigō Takamori.* Hoboken, NJ: John Wiley & Sons, 2004.

Reischauer, Edwin. *Japan: The Story of a Nation.* New York: Alfred A. Knopf, Inc., 1970.

Richie, Donald. *The Image Factory: Fads and Fashions in Japan.* London: Reaktion Books, 2003.

Sakai, Saburo, with Martin Caidin and Fred Saito. *Samurai: The Rise and Fall of the Japanese Naval Air Force*. New York: ibooks, inc., 1997.

Sakaida, Henry. *Imperial Japanese Navy Aces 1937–45*. Oxford, UK: Osprey Publishing, 1998.

Sakaida, Henry. *Japanese Army Air Force Aces 1937–45*. Oxford, UK: Osprey Publishing, 1997.

Scheiner, Irving. "The Japanese Village: Imagined, Real, Contested" in *Mirror of Modernity: Invented Traditions of Modern Japan* (edited by Stephen Vlastos), 67–78. Berkeley, Los Angeles, and London: University of California Press, 1998.

Silverberg, Miriam. "The Café Waitress Serving Modern Japan" in *Mirror of Modernity: Invented Traditions of Modern Japan* (edited by Stephen Vlastos), 208–225. Berkeley, Los Angeles and London: University of California Press, 1998.

Smethurst, Richard J. *A Social Basis for Prewar Japanese Militarism: The Army and the Rural Community*. Berkeley, Los Angeles and London: University of California Press, 1974.

Suzuki, Daisetz T. *Zen and Japanese Culture*. Tokyo: Charles E. Tuttle Company, 1959.

Tagaya, Osamu. *Imperial Japanese Naval Aviator 1937–45*. Oxford, UK: Osprey Publishing, 2004.

Takaki, Koji and Henry Sakaida. *B-29 Hunters of the JAAF*. Oxford, UK: Osprey Publishing, 2001.

Taylor, Theodore. *The Magnificent Mitscher*. Annapolis, MD: Naval Institute Press, 1954.

Tillman, Barrett. *Hellcat: The F6F in World War II*. Annapolis, MD: Naval Institute Press, 1979.

Turnbull, Stephen. *Samurai Warfare*. London: Cassell, 1996.

Ugaki, Matome (translated by Masataka Chihaya). *Fading Victory: The Diary of Admiral Matome Ugaki 1941–1945*. Pittsburgh, PA: University of Pittsburgh Press, 1991.

Van Wolferen, Karel. *The Enigma of Japanese Power: People and Politics in a Stateless Nation*. London: Papermac, 1989.

Warner, Denis and Peggy Warner. *The Sacred Warriors: Japan's Suicide Legions*. New York: Avon Books, 1982.

Worth, Richard. *Fleets of World War II*. Cambridge, MA: Da Capo Press, 2001.

## Works in Japanese Language

Akabane, Reiko and Hiroshi Ishii. *Hotaru Kaeru*. Tokyo: Sososha, 2001.

*Asahi Shimbun*, September 9, 1945.

Chiran Kōjo Nadeshiko Kai (editor). *Gunsei: Chiran Tokkō Kichi Yori*. Kagoshima, Japan: Takagi Shobo Shuppan, 1979.

Fukabori, Michiyoshi. *Tokkō no Shinjitsu: Meirei to Kenshin to Izoku no Kokoro*. Tokyo: Hara Kōbo, 2001.

Fukabori, Michiyoshi, others. *Tokkō no Sōkatsu: Nemure, Nemure, Haha no Mune ni*. Tokyo: Hara Kōbo, 2003.

Fukagawa, Iwao. "Tokkō Haimei no Sono Toki, Sore Kara, Sono Ato" in *Rikushi 57-ki Kōkūshi: Bunka-hen* (Hideyuki Monma, editor). Tokyo: Private, noncommercial publication for Rikushi Dai 57-ki Dōkiseikai, 1995.

Hayashi, Seigo. *Ōdo no Ishibumi: Kantōgun ni Hamukau Nihonjin*. Tokyo: Kōfūsha Shoten, 1973.

Hiroshima, Mankichi (editor). *Chinkon: Kaigun Shōi Hiroshima Tadao*. Tokyo: Private, noncommercial publication, 1977.

Horiyama, Hisao. *Tatebayashi no Sora*. Tokyo: Private, noncommercial publication, 2002.

Ikari, Yoshirou. *Kaigun Kikan Gakkō Hachinin no Pairotto*. Tokyo: Kōjinsha, 1991.

*Kagoshima Nippō*, April 19, 1945.

Kaigun Hikō Senshū Yobigakusei Dai 14 Ki Kai (editor). *Kaigun Dai 14 Kikai Hōshū Satsuhan*. Tokyo: Private, noncommercial publication for Kaigun Hikō Senshū Yobigakusei Dai 14 Ki Kai, 2001.

Kaigun Jinrai Butai Senyūkai (editor). *Kaigun Jinrai Butai*. Tokyo: Private, noncommercial publication for Kaigun Jinrai Butai Senyūkai, 1997.

Kamisu Chō Kyōiku Iinkai (editor). *Bunkazai Kamisu*, vol. 19, 1995.

Kaneko, Toshio. *Kamikaze Tokkō no Kiroku*. Tokyo: Kōjinsha, 2001.

Kawachiyama, Yuzuru. *On'ai no Kizuna: Dachigatashi*. Tokyo: Kōjinsha, 1990.

Kimata, Jirō. *Ōka Tokkōtai: Shirarezaru Ningen Bakudan no Higeki*. Tokyo: Kōjinsha, 2001.

Kofukuda, Terufumi. *Zerosen Kaihatsu Monogatari: Nihon Kaigun Sentōki Zenkishu no Shōgai*. Tokyo: Kōjinsha, 1985.

Kohata, Akinobu. "Kaiten no Botai: Kyūsan Gyorai" in *Tokkō no Sōkatsu:*

*Nemure, Nemure, Haha no Mune ni* (Michiyoshi Fukabori, editor). Tokyo: Hara Kōbo, 2003.

Konada, Toshiharu. "Ningen Gyorai 'Kaiten' ga Nihon wo Sukū!: Jidai wo Koete Iroasenu 'Tokkō no Kokoro' ni Omō" in *Gyokusaisen to Tokubetsukōgekitai: Senki Shirīzu Vol. 39* (Yatsuka Shiino, editor). Tokyo: Shinjinbutsu Ōraisha, 1998.

Kōsaka, Jirō. *Tokkōtaiin no Inochi no Koe ga Kikoeru: Sensō, Jinsei, soshite Sokoku.* Tokyo: PHP Bunko, 2001.

Kudō, Yukie. *Tokkō no Rekuiemu.* Tokyo: Chūōkōronsha, 2001.

Maeda, Masahiro. *Kaiten Kikusui Tai no Yonnin: Kaigun Chūi Nishina Sekio no Shōgai.* Tokyo: Kōjinsha, 1989.

*Mainichi Shimbun,* June 11, 1945.

*Mainichi Shimbun,* October 28, 1944.

Masuya, Takeo (editor). *Kessen Tokkoutai no Kiroku.* Kawajiri, Japan: Tsubasa Kougyou Kabushiki Kaisha Shuppanbu, 2000.

Mikano, Daiji. "Daihon'ei no Sensō Shidōga Unda 'Gyokusai' no Haikei" in *Gyokusaisen to Tokubetsukōgekitai: Senki Shirīzu Vol. 39* (Yatsuka Shiino, editor), 22–27. Tokyo: Shinjinbutsu Ōraisha, 1998.

Mori, Shirou. *Shikishima Tai no Gonin.* Tokyo: Kōjinsha, 1995.

Morimoto, Tadao. *Tokko: Tōsotsu no Gedō to Ningen no Jōken.* Tokyo: Bungei Shunjū, 1992.

Naitō, Hatsuho. *Kyokugen no Tokkōki Ōka.* Tokyo: Chūōkōron Shinsha, 1999.

Nohara, Shigeru. *Kawanishi Kyokuchi Sentōki "Shidenkai": Earo Ditēru 26.* Tokyo: Dainippon Kaiga Co., Ltd., 2000.

Nohara, Shigeru and Ryuichi Mochizuki. *Nakajima Isshiki Sentōki "Hayabusa": Earo Ditēru 29.* Tokyo: Dainippon Kaiga Co., Ltd., 2000.

Ogawa, Takeshi. *Tokkō no Jisshō.* Tokyo: Chōeisha, 2001.

Oide, Hisashi. *Tokkō Chōkan: Ōnishi Takijirō.* Tokyo: Tokuma Shoten, 1984.

Saeki, Masa'aki, others. *Kyōfu no Ningen Bakudan: "Ōka" Hasshin Junbi Yoshi.* Tokyo: Kōjinsha, 1991.

Satō, Sanae. *Tokkō no Machi: Chiran.* Tokyo: Kōjinsha, 1997.

Shiino, Yatsuka (editor). *Gyokusaisen to Tokubetsukōgekitai: Senki Shirīzu Vol. 39.* Tokyo: Shinjinbutsu Ōraisha, 1998.

Shiino, Yatsuka (editor). *Kaigun Kōkūtai to Kamikaze: Senki Shirīzu Vol. 52.* Tokyo: Shinjinbutsu Ōraisha, 2000.

Shinozawa, Hideo. *Aikokushin no Tankyū*. Tokyo: Bungei Shunjū, 1999.

Sugiyama, Toshikazu. *Kaikyū*. Shizuoka, Japan: Private, noncommercial publication, 1962.

Takagi, Toshirō. *Tokkō Kichi Chiran*. Tokyo: Kadokawa Shoten, 1973.

Wakashio Kai (editor). *Wakashio Kai Kantō Shibu Kai Hō*, vols. 24–33. 1992–2001.

Watanabe, Yoshiyuki (editor). *Teikoku Kaigun Isshiki Rikkō: Sōhatsuki no Gainen wo Ryōga shita Chūgata Rikujō Kōgekiki no Shinjitsu/Rekishi Gunzō Taiheiyō Senshi Shirīzu Vol. 42.* Tokyo: Gakushū Kenkyūsha, 2003.

Yasukuni Shrine (editor). *Sange no Kokoro to Chinkon no Makoto (Furusato to Yasukuni* Series vol. 4). Tokyo: Tendensha, 1995.

Yokota, Hiroshi. *Aa, Kaiten Tokkōtai: Kaerazaru Seishun no Kiroku.* Tokyo: Kōjinsha, 1994.

Yoshitake, Toshio. *Nagai Hibi*. Tokyo: Private publication, 2001.

Yuzawa, Yutaka (editor). *Isshiki Rikkō Kōgekiki Sekai no Kessakki Shirīzu Vol. 59.* Tokyo: Bunrindō, 1996.

Yuzawa, Yutaka (editor). *Kyōfū, Shiden, Shidenkai: Sekai no Kessakki Shirīzu Vol. 53.* Tokyo: Bunrindō, 1995.

## WEB SITES

"Battle of Okinawa." http://www.globalsecurity.org/military/facility/okinawa-battle.htm

"Chiran Chinkon no Mitsugi." http://www.town.chiran.kagoshima.jp/touristinfo/heiwakaikan/sub03.html

"Chiran Tokkō Heiwa Kaikan." http://www.town.chiran.kagoshima.jp/touristinfo/heiwakaikan/sub03.html

"Chiran Town." http://www.town.chiran.kagoshima.jp

"First Patrol." http://www.cavalla.org/firstpat.html

"Hawai/Marē Oki Kaisen." http://www.jmdb.ne.jp/1942/br001160 .htm

"Japanese Torpedoes." http://www.combinedfleet.com/torps.htm

"Jinrai Butai Ōka." http://www.asahi-net.or.jp/~un3k-mn/ooka-history.htm

"Jomon Genes Using DNA, researchers probe the genetic origins of modern Japanese." http://www.pitt.edu/~annj/courses/notes/jomon_genes.html

"Kaiten Tokubetsu Kōgekitai Nenpyō." http://www.asahi-net.or.jp/
~un3k-mn/kai-nenpyo.htm

"Manner L. Abele DD 733." http://www.multied.com/navy/destroyer/
MannertLAbeledd733.html

"Naval Historical Center, Japanese Navy Ships—CV Shinano."
http://www.history.navy.mil/photos/sh-fornv/japan/japsh-s/shinano.htm

"Naval History Magazine: The Hunt for the Last Mystery Shipwreck,
by Chip Lambert, with Mike Mail." http://www.usni.org/navalhistory/
articles03/nhlambert04.htm

"Official Website of the USS St. Lo (formerly Midway) CVE63/VC65."
http://www.stlomidway6365.org/

"Raymond 'Hap' Halloran." http://www.haphalloran.com/ "USS
Darter." http://www.csp.navy.mil/ww2boats/darter.htm

"U.S.S. Mississinewa AO-59 Website." http://www.ussmississinewa
.com/

"USS West Virginia (BB-48) Action Report: Leyte Gulf/Surigao Strait."
http://www.ibiblio.org/hyperwar/USN/ships/logs/BB/bb48-Surigao.html

"Watashi no shumi no pe-ji: Tokusatsu Hen." http://www001.upp
.so-net.ne.jp/okapi/tokusatu.htm

"Who Became Kamikaze Pilots, and How Did They Feel Towards
Their Suicide Mission." by Mako Sasaki. http://ww.tcr.org/tcr/essays/
EPrize_kamikaze.pdf

"Yasukuni Shrine." http://www.yasukuni.or.jp/english/

# INDEX